W9-ASM-022

SOCIAL
WELFARE
IN AMERICA

SOCIAL WELFARE IN AMERICA

An Annotated Bibliography

Edited by
Walter I. Trattner
and
W. Andrew Achenbaum

GREENWOOD PRESS
Westport, Connecticut • London, England

Library of Congress Cataloging in Publication Data
Main entry under title:

Social welfare in America.

  Includes bibliographical references and indexes.
  Contents: The process and progress of social welfare /
Walter I. Trattner and W. Andrew Achenbaum — Caring for
the infant and child / Walter I. Trattner — The problems
of youth / Robert Mennel — [etc.]
  1. Public welfare—United States—Bibliography.
2. Charities—United States—Bibliography. 3. United
States—Social conditions—Bibliography. I. Trattner,
Walter I. II. Achenbaum, W. Andrew.
Z7164.C4S6 1983   016.361'973   83-10855
[HV91]
ISBN 0-313-23002-1 (lib. bdg.)

Library of Congress Catalog Card Number: 83-10855
ISBN: 0-313-23002-1

First published in 1983

Greenwood Press
A division of Congressional Information Service, Inc.
88 Post Road West, Westport, Connecticut 06881

Printed in the United States of America

10 9 8 7 6 5 4 3 2 1

FOR OUR MENTORS
AND TO OUR STUDENTS

CONTENTS

Chapter Three: ADDRESSING THE PROBLEMS OF YOUTH
Robert Mennel   **148**

NOTE ON THE CONTRIBUTORS

W. ANDREW ACHENBAUM is associate professor of history in the Applied History and Social Science Program at Carnegie-Mellon University and a consultant at the Institute of Gerontology in the University of Michigan, Ann Arbor. He has written several books and articles on the history of old age in America, including *Old Age in the New Land: The American Experience Since 1790* (Baltimore: Johns Hopkins University Press, 1978), and *Shades of Gray: Old Age, American Values and Federal Policies Since 1920* (Boston: Little, Brown, 1983). He currently is preparing a history of Social Security in America for the Twentieth Century Fund.

MICHEL DAHLIN is instructor of history at the University of Wisconsin-Milwaukee. She has authored and co-authored several articles on the history of old age in America and is editor of the *Conference Group in Women's History Newsletter.*

LILITH R. KUNKEL did her graduate work at the University of Wisconsin-Madison and has taught history at Southwest Texas State University and St. Lawrence University. Her research interests include the history of institutions for the aged, health and health care in American history, and women's history.

ROBERT MENNEL is professor of history at the University of New Hampshire. He is the author of *Thorns and Thistles: Juvenile Delinquents in the United States, 1825-1940* (Hanover, N.H.: University Press of New England, 1973) and numerous articles on child welfare. He currently is editing the correspondence between Felix Frankfurter and Oliver Wendell Holmes, Jr.

WALTER I. TRATTNER is professor of history at the University of Wisconsin-Milwaukee. A former president of the Social Welfare History

Group, he has authored numerous articles and three books, *Homer Folks: Pioneer in Social Welfare* (New York: Columbia University Press, 1968), *Crusade for the Children: A History of the National Child Labor Committee and Child Labor Reform in America* (Chicago: Quadrangle Books, 1970), and *From Poor Law to Welfare State: A History of Social Welfare in America* (2d ed., rev., New York: Free Press, 1979). Most recently, he edited *Social Welfare or Social Control? Some Historical Reflections on REGULATING THE POOR* (Knoxville: University of Tennessee Press, 1983).

ACKNOWLEDGMENTS

We would like to express our gratitude to the many kind people who helped us prepare this annotated bibliography. We particularly wish to thank our fellow contributors—Michel Dahlin, Lilith R. Kunkel, and Robert Mennel—for the care with which they executed their tasks and for meeting our deadlines. Jan Lewis deserves credit for originally suggesting that we compile such a bibliography. Our thanks also go to Greenwood Press, especially to Marilyn Brownstein, Acquisitions Editor, for encouraging us to go ahead with the project and for seeing it through to completion. We also are indebted to Alexander Keyssar for reading and commenting on Chapter Five. Ellen Parkes and Pamela Holcomb provided editorial assistance at Carnegie-Mellon University, and Marie Meyer patiently prepared the final draft of the manuscript on a word processor at the University of Wisconsin-Milwaukee (while just learning how to operate the machine, not an easy task); we are very grateful to each of them. Last but not least, we wish to thank Joan D. Trattner for providing the editors with a steady supply of delicious food and good humor as they spent three long days putting the citations into final order.

Introduction

THE STATE OF THE FIELD—AND THE SCOPE OF THIS WORK

Walter I. Trattner
University of Wisconsin-Milwaukee

There is a certain timeliness to the publication of this work that the editors did not see when, several years ago, they discussed the need for such a project and decided to proceed with it. As most readers know, after a sweeping electoral victory in the fall of 1980, the Reagan administration, with its neo-conservative philosophy of government, came into office intent on implementing its campaign promises to alter the direction of public affairs, particularly with regard to reducing the scope and costs of federal activities. Since that time it has consistently sought, with some success, to diminish the range of activities in the nation's capital, especially in the area of welfare. Indeed, it has cut back various federal and federally subsidized welfare programs and, under the label of the New Federalism, has attempted to reverse the long, steady drift towards greater federal involvement in the nation's social welfare system. Above all, the president and his business-oriented advisors have sought to restructure the balance between public welfare and private charity, not only at the federal but at the state and local levels as well—all this at a time when inflation, high taxes, low productivity, and near-record rates of unemployment have been increasing hardship daily. There is, then, a special urgency to the study and writing of American social welfare history, to a consideration of questions about poverty and dependency— and the victims of those distressing forces. Scholars and policymakers alike must discover, or uncover, what is real and what is mythical about the subject, what is workable and unworkable, what is right and what is wrong, what is just and what is unjust. This work, then, which not only lists and discusses what already has been written on the subject but suggests what research remains to be done in the area, should be of assistance in that important task.

There are, of course, numerous other reasons that justify the writing and publication of this work—those that motivated the editors before the current administration came into office. Rather than recite them, most of which readers no doubt already are familiar with, a few words from the pen of Will Durant, the late historian-philosopher, will suffice: "Science gives us knowledge," Durant wrote, "but only History and Philosophy can give us wisdom."

Historians of social welfare have been trying to provide their readers with wisdom for some time, although, perhaps it should be noted, not as long in America as elsewhere, especially in Great Britain. In fact, the study and writing of American social welfare history began in the late nineteenth and early twentieth centuries, thanks, in part, to the influence of commentators on the other side of the Atlantic—especially Charles Booth, Sir George Nicholls, E. M. Leonard, Beatrice and Sidney Webb, among others in England.[1] However, a number of important changes on this side of the ocean also influenced emergence of the new field, including the development of a child welfare movement, a growing emphasis on the social causes of poverty, the initiation of preventive measures, and the emergence of a profession of social work (out of the field of "charities and correction").

Most of the early American studies were narratives on the poor laws and their administration, accounts of certain agencies and the changes they were undergoing, or reform tracts of one kind or another written by sociologists, economists, social workers—primarily executives of public and private agencies—and social reformers rather than by historians. Written by participants or "makers" of social welfare history in order to justify their own activities, whether they were to improve the legal structure and administration of social welfare, to maintain the role of private agencies in an age of growing public responsibility, to further various social reforms they were advocating, or to explain the need for the new profession, these studies tended to present history as a policy social science whose chief function was to provide guidance and a rationale for current practice.[2] The writers' interest in the subject, in other words, was aroused and dictated largely by their own activities and their concerns with the problems of their day.[3]

These works were climaxed by some seventeen studies of state poor laws written between 1930 and 1943 at the University of Chicago's School of Social Service Administration, which, under the leadership of Edith Abbott and Sophonisba Breckinridge, was noted for its research and scholarship and for its concern with social policy and public administration. While many of those studies were and remain quite useful, especially David Schneider and Albert Deutsch's two-volume *History of Public Welfare in New York State* (1609-1940),[4] they nevertheless left much to be desired. As Raymond Mohl has pointed out in a perceptive review essay on "Mainstream Social Welfare History and Its Problems," they generally took a narrow and legal administrative approach to their subjects, a natural result of the limited range of sources on which they were based—primarily state legislation, court decisions, and the records of public and private welfare institutions and agencies. Furthermore, the authors rarely placed the developments they described into the broad social, intellectual, or somewhat surprisingly, even political, context in which they occurred. As Mohl put it:

Essentially, this genre of scholarship sought to endow social work with its own history and to strengthen the emerging sense of professionalism among welfare practitioners. But it was not especially good history. It was often self-congratulatory and self-serving. It was devoid of conceptualization. It failed to probe beneath the administrative and institutional framework of private charity and public welfare. And it did not say very much about the human and social experiences of the recipients of charity, public assistance, casework, counseling, or institutional care.[5]

While Mohl may have expected too much from these pioneer works, his comments nevertheless are well taken. In any event, the professional historian's serious interest in social welfare history really began with publication, in 1956, of Robert Bremner's pathbreaking work, *From the Depths: The Discovery of Poverty in the United States*—a fascinating study of America's awakening to poverty as a social problem.[6] Influenced, no doubt, by the growing interest in the history of ideas and the advent of the American Studies movement, with its concern for literary sources and mythic analysis, Bremner approached the subject with a new breadth of interest and imagination, including the use of literary and artistic materials, and showed how a field dominated by social workers and other "activists" could, with the attention of "uninvolved" scholars, be incorporated into the larger picture of American social and intellectual history. He thus went far beyond his predecessors in the field—and his work promised a new and more incisive approach to the subject.

Still, social welfare history did not immediately come of age. The 1950s, with their preoccupation with Communism, at home and abroad, and with material gain, including the widespread (and misguided) belief in mass prosperity, were not conducive to much scholarly concern with destitution and injustice.

The era of complacency, however, came to a quick and dramatic end. The civil rights movement and the mass migration of millions of poverty-stricken Americans from obscure rural areas to the nation's cities where they swelled the welfare rolls and became visible, the rediscovery of these "other Americans" by scholars and by virtually everyone else during the urban riots of the decade, the so-called War on Poverty and the welfare rights demonstrations—these and numerous other events led a growing number of historians and other social scientists to turn their attention to this important field of study, and the publication record demonstrated that surge of interest. Before long, a multitude of articles and monographs appeared on the creation and development of welfare institutions and agencies, both public and private—prisons, reform schools, juvenile courts, asylums, almshouses, orphanages, charity organizations, settlement houses, reform societies, etc.—and on public policies related to "welfare"—housing, social insurance, workmen's compensation, income redistribution, the rights of labor, medical care, and the like. Numerous biographies of social welfare leaders appeared as well, as did analyses of the professionalization of social work, accounts of tenement house and child labor reform, histories of the needy and their treatment at various times, and so on.[7]

Although these studies were written by professional historians, and in many ways were considerably better than the earlier works in the field, the promise, and hope, of a new social welfare history were not completely fulfilled by this spate of publications. While there were exceptions and their quality, of course, varied, as a whole these works were built on the framework of their predecessors. Hence, for the most part, they continued to be institutional and administrative studies in nature, focusing largely on the legislative history of one reform or another, the administration of this or that agency, or the life of some important social welfare leader. In other words, they continued to describe mainstream developments, to concentrate on the response to problems rather than on the problems themselves, and to elaborate (and extol) the achievements of public benefactors; they failed to provide fresh insights into such things as the "mechanics" of welfare agencies, local and regional variations, the effects, if any, of gender differences, the "welfarization" of society, and, above all, the recipients, as opposed to the providers of welfare.

Thus in a paper on "The State of Social Welfare History" delivered at the 1969 meeting of the Organization of American Historians, Robert Bremner urged social welfare historians to pay more attention to the viewpoint of the client and less to those who operate, administer, and finance social welfare activities. He also suggested that scholars of the subject write fewer chronologies of poor laws and produce, instead, "more realistic accounts of how social welfare programs actually worked in given times and places," more quantitative studies, more comparative studies (of different states and regions within America as well as among nations of the world), and more biographies, not so much of leaders in the field but collective accounts of those who have been the objects of social workers' concerns—the aged, orphans, widows, paupers, the unemployed, and so forth.[8]

Another obvious need in the field, one, however, that Bremner did not specify, was for a general survey, a broad interpretive history of social welfare from the colonial period to the modern era, one that placed developments in the field within the broader context of American social, political, and intellectual history. The first such work appeared in 1974, and two others followed within the next four years.[9] All three of these general surveys, however, whatever their differences, also tended to view social welfare history from legal, administrative, and institutional perspectives; they emphasized welfare legislation, the organizational structure and administrative history of public and private welfare agencies, the general outlines of welfare policies and programs, and the perceptions and activities of "reformers." In short, they concentrated on traditional themes and employed traditional outlooks; they, too, viewed social welfare history from the top down, from the point of view of agents and agencies of the privileged as they operated to provide assistance and services to the poor and others society defined and treated as deviant and delinquent.

Furthermore, they tended to be "progressive," both in intentions and in supposed results; that is, rather than emphasize, or even probe, cleavages, tensions, self-interest, and the like, they celebrated unity, harmony, and good will. They saw social welfare as meliorative in nature and as evidence of the expanding capacity of high-minded people (usually affluent white Protestants) and the state to come to the aid of needy citizens, however slowly and perhaps even at times grudgingly.

Meanwhile, a slew of other works on social welfare were being published which began calling into question those very ideas. Indeed, the literature on the subject was becoming dominated by those who asserted just the opposite—that the powerful classes (the political and economic elite) designed and used the nation's welfare institutions and organizations, public and private, not to help the needy but to serve their own interests—to direct and control the lives of the poor and unfortunate in order to prevent violence and to maintain the capitalist system. In fact, so pervasive did that notion become that David Rothman, one of the authors of a work on the subject, *Doing Good: The Limits of Benevolence*, published in 1979, suggested that the very idea of doing good had come under widespread and acute suspicion: "Whereas once historians and policy analysts were prone to label some movements reform, thereby assuming their humanitarian aspects," Rothman wrote, "they are presently far more comfortable with a designation of social control, thereby assuming their coercive quality. . . . The prevailing perspective looks first to how a measure may regulate the poor," not to how it might relieve or help them, he concluded.[10]

There were ample reasons for raising questions about the older, more traditional, and prevailing premises of American social history and policy. Basically, however, the challenge to humanitarianism, moralism, and liberalism as masks for intrusion, domination, and self-interest was a reflection of the unsettled mood, especially the widespread cynicism and alienation that characterized the tumultuous 1960s and early 1970s—the same forces, in part at least, that awakened scholars to the field of social welfare as an area of serious historical inquiry. The prevailing outlook, which minimized social ills and conflict and celebrated mainstream America and the belief that the nation's citizens, with few exceptions, had been treated fairly by an affluent, just, and peaceful society, one that had overcome its problems, resolved its tensions, and reconciled its divisions—"The Cult of the American Consensus," to use John Higham's words[11]—became very difficult, indeed almost impossible, to accept by many younger scholars coming to maturity when the civil rights movement, rediscovery of the "other America," and widespread urban rioting raised serious questions about that outlook. That was not all; all sorts of other occurrences, such as the women's liberation and counterculture movements, the fight for gay rights, the anti-Vietnam War movement, the various political and racial assassinations and assassination attempts, the student movement, the Watergate incident, and numerous others, forced historians and others to call into question the supposed benignity of the American experience and to face what to them was the myth of a democratic, egalitarian, affluent, and peaceful America, and the reality of a seemingly repressive, exploitive, poverty-stricken, and imperialist society.

It was not surprising, then, that the nation's social welfare institutions and programs, even the concept of benevolence itself, came under intense scrutiny and attack. Altruistic explanations were not very marketable in an age of turmoil and cynicism, one compounded by the obvious failure of the widely heralded "war on poverty" (dubbed by one scholar a "phony war of stalemate and standstill," a "sitzkrieg" rather than a blitzkrieg) and the persistence of so much hardship, destitution, and dependency in a society with the resources to eliminate them.

So, as popular groups and writers stressed the glaring weaknesses they perceived in other areas of American life, many historians of social welfare, starting with the assumption that American society was, among other things, structured institutionally to enhance and protect the political and economic elite, challenged the idealistic and moralistic interpretations of welfare programs and their implementation. Humanitarian and reformist rhetoric aside, progressive ideas and intentions did not shape social welfare policy, the critics argued. Rather, the system and the "reforms" it has undergone were designed by the state and the ruling class in order to manipulate and co-opt those at the bottom of society, and thereby perpetuate inequality; by buying off the poor, on occasion, with short-term and meaningless benefits, the elite have managed to inhibit the growth of class consciousness and conflict and thus preserve the existing social and economic systems.[12]

Whether or not this "new" social welfare history is any better or more accurate than the older progressive version remains to be seen. Only time will tell, also, whether or not it merely is a product of a passing age. In fact, signs indicate that the pendulum is beginning to swing the other way again, or at least that a new, more balanced approach is beginning to emerge.[13] What is clear, however, is that a definitive history of social welfare in America has not yet been written, for among other things, however much the sympathies of these social control historians rested with the needy rather than the well-to-do, and however much they emphasized self-interest and manipulation rather than benevolence and humanity, they, too, tended to view the subject from the top down. They focused, for the most part, on the providers or benefactors rather than on the recipients of aid, on the welfare institutions and agencies that did things for, or perhaps to, the poor rather than on the poor themselves—who they were and how they got that way, their culture and their lifestyles, their reactions to or feelings toward the system, their efforts to accommodate to or undermine that system, and so on.[14] Clearly then, as the last chapter of this work suggests, a great deal more work in the area remains to be done.

Meanwhile, this annotated bibliography is designed to supply interested persons with a ready source of reference to the literature on social welfare history, whatever its shortcomings and needs. It is by no means an exhaustive guide but rather a much more modest undertaking. At best, it includes only the major works in a limited number of areas of social welfare history; the field of "social welfare" is so broad and amorphous and the number of works dealing with all aspects of it so virtually limitless, that to do otherwise would be impossible.

What is "social welfare"? Most students of the subject agree that it concerns the material, social, and emotional well-being of individuals, families, and groups of people. That, however, is not very useful for our purposes, for so defined, agricultural programs, which provide financial help and other forms of assistance to farm families (not always needy ones, it should be added), might plausibly be considered part of the nation's welfare system. So, too, might educational institutions, labor unions, political machines, and religious bodies, among others, all of which also have helped the needy in past and present times. Indeed, almost all human endeavors in some way affect(ed) the material, social, and emotional well-being of people, as William Graham Sumner, the ardent social Darwinist, observed in his essay on "Sociology" (1881): "In truth," he wrote, "the human race has never done anything else but struggle with the problem of social welfare. That struggle constitutes history, or the life of the human race on earth." Adherence to this definition, then, would be impossible, or would require us to produce a veritable magnum opus, at the very least. It is essential, therefore, to arrive at a narrower, less amorphous definition for this more limited effort.

Unfortunately, the historical record does not resolve the issue or provide such a definition. Since the fourteenth century, "welfare" has been commonly used to indicate happiness or prosperity; for the past five centuries the term also has referred to "merrymaking," typically in a derogatory sense. Welfare's connotation as an object of organized care or provision dates from the early twentieth century, when older terms became imbued with unacceptable, inappropriate, or anachronistic associations. Comparatively new terms—such as "welfare policy" (1905), "welfare work" (1916), and "welfare state" (1939)—still must be defined carefully, since there is no agreement in the Anglo-American community about what issues are subsumed under their rubrics.

Precisely because "social welfare" has been broadly defined and has meant so many different things to different people at different times, it was necessary to establish a specific, or at least a reasonably manageable, definition of the term for this annotated bibliography, however arbitrary it might be. Thus by "social welfare" *we* mean

those responses, remedies, and preventive measures made by governments (at the local, state, and national levels) and by private individuals and institutions (ranging from the family network through voluntary associations to philanthropic or corporate bureaucracies) to help persons and families who are perceived to be in need.

This definition has certain virtues. It embraces the concerns and activities of those who once were engaged in "charities and correction" and were charged with the care of the "dependent, defective, and delinquent classes." Yet it is elastic enough to embrace the self-described and prescribed functions of contemporary do-gooders, social workers, government officials, and professional reformers. Utilizing this definition, moreover, has required us to pay close attention to the socio-economic context in which various elements in American society—insiders and outsiders, welfare actors and those acted upon—have defined those who were (or should be) included in the American welfare system. We have been sensitive to innovations and modifications in strategies, services, programs, and organizations devised to deal with "problems of poverty" Americans perceived in their midst.

Perhaps the bias in our definition of "social welfare" should be made a bit more explicit, since it set the bounds for the sorts of materials we included in this bibliography. We obviously have placed primary emphasis on the *organized* efforts of private citizens and public officials to promote the *material* well-being of those who society at large felt needed and deserved assistance, through both ameliorative and preventive means. Over time, these objectives have been accomplished primarily by providing relief and by improving the environment. The former has been done in two ways: (1) by giving categorical assistance or maintaining incomes at a politically and/or socially acceptable level, and (2) by attending to the noneconomic needs of "dependents" in ways deemed to be the responsibility of the community, however defined. The latter has been done through social and economic reform. Hence, we did not include references that stressed acts of kindness that neighbors might have engaged in toward those in straitened circumstances. We mainly cite books, articles, and dissertations that deal with formal exchanges of goods and services between society and the needy as well as between family members and kith and kin and with selected social and economic reforms.

Some readers no doubt will be dismayed by the paucity of references to activities undertaken by "modern" professionals, social workers and others, involving casework and group work. Similarly, welfare initiatives in the areas of recreation or housing and community developments for the most part have been omitted, as has the area of corrections, with the exception of juvenile justice. We also excluded works that described past and present efforts to enhance the physical, mental, or emotional health of the disabled and the handicapped, and, in general, of the ill as well. However, insofar as health-care matters were poverty-producing factors or have been reform issues or "current" policy questions, we have attempted to include the standard monographs and incisive references on those subjects, including Medicare and Medicaid, for example. Once again, then, our focus has been on continuities and changes in the problem of economic need as it affected people over the life cycle: we have sought to highlight developments in caring for or treating those in *financial distress* and in creating conditions that would prevent destitution and assuage dependency at various stages of life. Hopefully, what we have sacrificed in breadth, we have compensated for in depth.

Yet, even within those areas that are included in this bibliography, however deeply they are examined, coverage is by no means inclusive. The work merely contains general surveys, major monographs, scholarly articles, and dissertations written since 1945, as well as some documentaries and a number of older works—selected classics which are of importance as much because of what they reveal about the attitudes and characteristics of their times as because of their substance—that provide useful insights and data concerning social welfare, as defined, from the early 1600s to the early 1980s. It does not include manuscript collections and other unpublished works, with the exception of selected dissertations, as well as many pertinent, even major, public documents. As with any selection or group of works, there will be disagreement among knowledgeable people about the choice of items included—and no doubt some will be missing simply because of an oversight. However, the works listed represent the best efforts, and collective wisdom, of those who contributed to this volume.

The overarching theme, or framework, for this work is the life cycle approach. Such an approach was chosen for two reasons. First, it reflects a perennial theme girding American approaches to welfare—the well-being of children and adults in both formal and informal institutional arrangements and a concern with the stability of "family life," hence the problems of unemployment, poverty, deviance, etc., problems that plague people throughout their lives. And second, this approach enables the editors to underscore the connections they see between the older, more traditional welfare history and the newer social and family histories, badly needed avenues for future research; hopefully, the organization of our materials in this way will help facilitate such an orientation. Thus, an opening chapter on "The Process and Progress of Social Welfare" is followed by one on "Caring for the Infant and Child," which in turn is followed by ones on "Addressing the Problems of Youth" and "Relieving the Domestic Crises of Adulthood," and so on. (Within that "cradle-to-grave" framework, references have been organized topically and chronologically, as the table of contents suggests.) The work concludes with an Epilogue on "An Agenda for Future Research in American Social Welfare History," an essay that discusses more fully than this introduction the existing gaps in knowledge, and makes explicit some things to be done in the field of American social welfare history.

NOTES

1. See, for example, Charles Booth, *Life and Labour of the People of London* (17 vols., London: Macmillan, 1891-1903); Sir George Nicholls, *A History of the English Poor Law* (3 vols., London: King, 1898); E. M. Leonard, *The Early History of English Poor Relief* (Cambridge: Cambridge University Press, 1900); Sidney and Beatrice Webb, *English Poor Law Policy* (London: Longmans, Green, and Co., 1910); Dorothy Marshall, *The English Poor Law in the Eighteenth Century* (London: Routledge, 1926); and Sidney and Beatrice Webb, *English Local Government: English Poor Law History Part I, The Old Poor Law* (London: Longmans, Green, and Co., 1927).

2. Thus, for example, see the following: Jacob Riis, *How the Other Half Lives: Studies Among the Tenements of New York* (New York: Scribner's, 1890); Amos G. Warner, *American Charities: A Study in Philanthropy and Economics* (New York: Crowell, 1894); Homer Folks, *The Care of Destitute, Neglected, and Delinquent Children* (New York: Macmillan, 1902); Jeffrey R. Brackett, *Supervision and Education in Charity* (New York: Macmillan, 1903); Robert Hunter, *Poverty* (New York: Macmillan, 1904); Florence Kelley, *Some Ethical Gains Through Legislation* (New York: Macmillan, 1905); Joseph Lee, *Constructive and Preventive Philanthropy* (New York: Macmillan, 1906); Hastings Hart, *Treatment for Neglected Children* (New York: Russell Sage Foundation, 1910); Edward T. Devine, *The Spirit of Social Work* (New York: Macmillan, 1911); Edward N. Clopper, *Child Labor in City Streets* (New York: Macmillan, 1912); and Isaac Rubinow, *Social Insurance* (New York: Holt, 1913).

3. Another example of this would be the work of John R. Commons and the "Wisconsin school" of economists, whose interest in working conditions and labor unionism led them to collect and utilize a remarkable body of historical materials, many of which touched on "welfare."

4. David M. Schneider, *The History of Public Welfare in New York State, 1609-1866* (Chicago: University of Chicago Press, 1938); and David M. Schneider and Albert Deutsch, *The History of Public Welfare in New York State, 1867-1940* (Chicago: University of Chicago Press, 1941). For examples of some of the other such works, see Chapter One, 1.5 (Classic Case Studies).

5. Raymond Mohl, "Mainstream Social Welfare History and Its Problems," *Reviews in American History*, vol. 7, no. 4 (Dec. 1979), pp. 469-76.

6. Robert H. Bremner, *From the Depths: The Discovery of Poverty in the United States* (New York: New York University Press, 1956). That same year the Social

Welfare History Group was founded by a number of concerned social workers and historians.

7. Thus, for example, see, among many others: W. David Lewis, *From Newgate to Dannemora: The Rise of the Penitentiary in New York, 1796-1848* (Ithaca: Cornell University Press, 1965); Robert S. Pickett, *House of Refuge: Origins of Juvenile Reform in New York State, 1815-1857* (Syracuse: Syracuse University Press, 1969); James Leiby, *Charity and Correction in New Jersey: A History of State Welfare Institutions* (New Brunswick, N.J.: Rutgers University Press, 1967); Otto M. Nelson, "The Chicago Relief and Aid Society, 1850-1874," *Illinois State Historical Society Journal*, vol. 59, no. 1 (Spring 1966), pp. 48-66; Walter I. Trattner, "Louisa Lee Schuyler and the Founding of the [N.Y.] State Charities Aid Association," *New York State Historical Society Quarterly*, vol. 51, no. 3 (July 1967), pp. 233-48; Verl S. Lewis, "Stephen Humphreys Gurteen and the American Origins of Charity Organization," *Social Service Review*, vol. 40, no. 2 (June 1966), pp. 190-201; Allen F. Davis, *Spearheads for Reform: The Social Settlements and the Progressive Movement, 1890-1914* (New York: Oxford University Press, 1967); Clarke A. Chambers and Andrea Hinding, "Charity Workers, the Settlements, and the Poor," *Social Casework*, vol. 49, no. 2 (Feb. 1968), pp. 96-101; Miriam Langsam, *Children West: A History of the Placing Out of the New York Children's Aid Society* (Madison: State Historical Society, 1964); Roy Lubove, *The Progressives and the Slums: Tenement House Reform in New York, 1890-1917* (Pittsburgh: University of Pittsburgh Press, 1962); James T. Patterson, "Mary Dewson and the American Minimum Wage Movement," *Labor History*, vol. 5, no. 2 (Spring 1964), pp. 134-52; Irwin Yellowitz, "The Origins of Unemployment Reform in the United States," *Labor History*, vol. 9, no. 3 (Fall 1968), pp. 338-60; Samuel Mencher, *Poor Law to Poverty Program: Economic Security Policy in Britain and the United States* (Pittsburgh: University of Pittsburgh Press, 1967); Roy Lubove, *The Struggle for Social Security, 1900-1935* (Cambridge, Mass.: Harvard University Press, 1968); Hace Sorel Tishler, *Self-Reliance and Social Security, 1870-1917* (Port Washington, N. Y.: Kennikat Press, 1971); Louise C. Wade, *Graham Taylor: Pioneer for Social Justice* (Chicago: University of Chicago Press, 1964); Anne F. Scott, "Jane Addams and the City," *Virginia Quarterly Review*, vol. 43, no. 1 (Winter 1967), pp. 53-60; Dorothy M. Blumberg, *Florence Kelley: The Making of a Social Pioneer* (New York: Kelley, 1967); Walter I. Trattner, *Homer Folks: Pioneer in Social Welfare* (New York: Columbia University Press, 1968); Roy Lubove, *The Professional Altruist: The Emergence of Social Work as a Career, 1880-1930* (Cambridge, Mass.: Harvard University Press, 1963); Jeremy P. Felt, *Hostages of Fortune: Child Labor Reform in New York State* (Syracuse: Syracuse University Press, 1965); Walter I. Trattner, *Crusade for the Children: A History of the National Child Labor Committee and Child Labor Reform in America* (Chicago: Quadrangle, 1970); and Clarke A. Chambers, *Seedtime of Reform: American Social Service and Social Action 1918-1933* (Minneapolis: University of Minnesota Press, 1963).

8. Robert H. Bremner, "The State of Social Welfare History," in *The State of American History*, ed. Herbert J. Bass (Chicago: Quadrangle, 1970), p. 95.

9. Walter I. Trattner, *From Poor Law to Welfare State: A History of Social Welfare in America* (New York: The Free Press, 1974); June Axinn and Herman Levin, *Social Welfare: A History of the American Response to Need* (New York: Dodd, Mead and Co., 1975); and James Leiby, *A History of Social Welfare and Social Work in the United States* (New York: Columbia University Press, 1978).

10. Willard Gaylin, Ira Glasser, Steven Marcus, and David Rothman, *Doing Good: The Limits of Benevolence* (New York: Pantheon, 1978), p. 83.

11. John Higham, "The Cult of the American Consensus," *Commentary*, vol. 27 (February 1959), pp. 93-100.

12. Perhaps the clearest, most forcefully presented, and influential of these works stressing social welfare as a means of social control is, Frances F. Piven and Richard A. Cloward, *Regulating the Poor: The Functions of Public Welfare* (New York: Pantheon, 1971). A representative sample of other such works, in chronological order, is: Marvin Gettleman, "Charity and Social Classes in the United States, 1874-1900," *American Journal of Economics and Sociology*, vol. 22, no. 2 (April 1963) pp. 313-30, and no. 3 (July 1963), pp. 417-26; Clifford Griffin, *Their Brothers' Keeper: Moral Stewardship in the United States, 1800-1865* (New Brunswick, N.J.: Rutgers University Press, 1965); Anthony M. Platt, *Child Savers: The Invention of Delinquency* (Chicago: University of Chicago Press, 1965); Joseph Hawes, *Children in Urban Society: Juvenile Delinquency in Nineteenth Century America* (New York: Oxford University Press, 1971); Nathan Huggins, *Protestants Against Poverty: Boston's Charities, 1870-1900* (Westport, Conn.: Greenwood Press, 1971); Raymond Mohl, *Poverty in New York, 1783-1825* (New York: Oxford University Press, 1971); Raymond Mohl and Neil Betten, "Paternalism and Pluralism: Immigrants and Social Welfare in Gary Indiana, 1906-1940," *American Studies*, vol. 15, no. 1 (Spring 1974), pp. 5-30; Marvin Gettleman, "Philanthropy as a Social Control in Late Nineteenth Century America: Some Hypotheses and Data on the Rise of Social Work," *Societas*, vol. 5, no. 1 (Winter 1975), pp. 49-50; Allan S. Horlick, *Country Boys and Merchant Princes: The Social Control of Young Men in New York* (Lewisburg, Pa.: Bucknell University Press, 1975); Steven Schlossman, *Love and the American Deliquent: The Theory and Practice of "Progressive" Juvenile Justice, 1825-1920* (Chicago: University of Chicago Press, 1977); Paul Boyer, *Urban Masses and Moral Order in America, 1820-1920* (Cambridge, Mass.: Harvard University Press, 1978); and William Graebner, *A History of Retirement: The Meaning and Function of an American Institution, 1885-1978* (New Haven: Yale University Press, 1980).

13. See James T. Patterson, *America's Struggle Against Poverty, 1900-1980* (Cambridge, Mass.: Harvard University Press, 1981); David A. Rochefort, "Progressive and Social Control Perspectives on Social Welfare," *Social Service Review*, vol. 55, no. 4 (Dec. 1981), pp. 568-92; and Walter I. Trattner, *Social Welfare or Social Control? Some Historical Reflections on REGULATING THE POOR* (Knoxville: University of Tennessee Press, 1983).

14. The same thing might be said of Patterson's *America's Struggle Against Poverty*. For all of its virtues, particularly its balanced approach to the subject, the book mainly deals with reformers' attitudes toward poverty and measures to deal

with it. As Patterson himself states in the preface to the work, no "historian has yet published a broad demographic history of the poor, a social history of poor people, or a synthetic study of the changing causes of poverty in the United States."

A NOTE ON THE PRINCIPLES ADOPTED IN COMPILING AND ORGANIZING THE BIBLIOGRAPHY

As noted in the Introduction, any bibliography of this size and scope must perforce be somewhat arbitrary. It also must unintentionally exclude some citations worthy of inclusion. For our sins of omission, we apologize. With regard to our acts of commission, however, we took a great many steps to reduce the likelihood of being capricious and erratic. Furthermore, insofar as the work is designed primarily for three kinds of people with potentially disparate needs—graduate students interested in American social welfare history, undergraduates writing term papers and essays in the field, and instructors and scholars concerned about the subject for one reason or another but who probably have done little prior research in any of the particular subfields covered here—we sought to maximize the chances that the user would be able to locate, through this bibliography, sources he or she might find useful. Thus, as we reviewed the entries and reworked the chapters, we adhered to the following principles:

1. To list an author's book in preference to an article on the same subject, and an article or essay in preference to a dissertation. We did so because we thought that books were more readily accessible than articles and dissertations and were more likely to express the author's most mature points of view on the subject. In those cases in which we included articles as well as as subsequent monographs (or prior dissertations), we did so because we felt that the pieces in question conveyed either a different perspective or covered a larger scope than the latest publication.

2. To fully index every citation in both the author and topical indexes. Works produced by more than one author appear under such authors' names in the Author Index. Works that sensibly might have been placed in any one of several categories are indexed (by number) under all plausible categories in the Subject Index. Hence, the number of the citation referring to John Cumbler's essay, "The Politics of Charity: Gender and Class in Late Nineteenth Century Charity Policy," appears in the topical index under the cate-

gories of politics, class, postbellum, and welfare policy, and so on, as well as under Cumbler's name in the Author Index.

3. To make no effort to eliminate duplicate entries. While books, articles, and dissertations cited in Chapter One represent, in the editors' opinions, the "core" materials of American social welfare historiography as of the early 1980s, many of these works are also cited in subsequent chapters. Indeed, if several contributors independently included the same articles, we felt our assessment of the piece's worth had been justified. There is, however, no redundancy within Chapter One; there, each entry was placed within the category in which it seemed to fit most logically.

4. To use a consistent, but not perfectly uniform, organizational framework throughout the bibliography. As indicated by the table of contents, Chapters Two through Six concentrate on major issues and problems characteristic of successive stages of life. In structure, they follow the format adopted in Chapter One. Each chapter begins with the truly seminal works that deal with the subject at hand. (Auto)biographies, documentaries, and classic case studies follow. Then come units that list, respectively, works treating specific periods of American history and highlighting key geographical, gender, racial, ethnic, and class variations. The materials cited in section 4 vary from chapter to chapter; nonetheless, it is in this unit that the distinctive age-specific or life-cycle case studies will most likely be found. Each chapter concludes with works that put the American experience into comparative perspective.

5. To divide each chapter's general or synthetic works into *thematic* (1.1) and *temporal* (1.2) categories. Citations in 1.1 tend to raise issues and discuss themes of central importance to anyone interested in the topics covered in that chapter. Citations in 1.2 were placed there, for the most part, because they were of special significance for their treatment of more limited subjects or developments, but their chronological boundaries extended beyond the more narrowly prescribed ones for the "period pieces" in section 2.

6. To place autobiographies and biographies—as well as articles about individuals—into a separate category in each chapter (1.3). Included in this group are works by and about central figures in American social welfare history. Users of the volume should not ignore the citations in this section; many of the entries deal not only with a selected person but with his or her reactions to various policy matters and responses to the needs of specific groups. There are citations in sections 2 to 5 that also shed light on important individuals; such citations, however, deal primarily with the issues rather than the personalities of the individuals involved.

7. To place major primary materials written prior to 1956 as well as the proceedings of public policy conferences held before that date in a category called Documentaries (1.4). Obviously, commission reports and official statements about developments that occurred after 1956, such as the War

on Poverty, do not appear in this section; they have been placed in the time-specific period pieces in section 2—and have been kept to a minimum.

8. To include many well known historical analyses published prior to 1956 in the category called Classic Case Studies (1.5). By and large, these studies deal with events in a specific locale over a relatively long period of time.

9. To include those works that treat topics in a clearly defined, and for the most part, fairly brief period of American history, in the category called Period Pieces (2). The rationale we employed in choosing end-dates for each period need not be spelled out here; the boundaries make sense in terms of American social welfare history and should not perplex or disturb readers.

10. To place in section 3, Salient Variations, those items that highlight the extent to which the concerns of social welfare historians mesh with the practitioners of the so-called new social history.

11. To permit, even encourage, variation from chapter to chapter in material placed in section 4 (Age-Specific and Life-Cycle Studies). Thus, in Chapter One we included recent books and articles that illustrated the historical literature on age and aging and on changes in family life cycles over time. The materials that authors included in the fourth section of their individual chapters depended on the age-specific problems and institutional responses pertinent to their area of responsibility. For instance, Achenbaum included references to old-age homes and asylums and to public and private retirement programs in section 4 of his chapter on "Coping With the Difficulties of Old Age." Dahlin listed many citations that dealt with federal manpower policies and programs in section 4 of her chapter on "Dealing With the Economic Woes of Adulthood." These topics do not overlap and there is no duplication in the citations. However, since the chronological distinctions between childhood and youth cannot be precisely drawn, and some services and institutions served both, there is an overlap in the topics covered in section 4 by Trattner and Mennel in Chapters Two and Three respectively, and some of the same sources are listed by each.

12. To include in section 5 in each chapter only works of a comparative nature that include discussion of the United States. We recognize that in so doing we have omitted numerous important, and useful, works, even for students of American social welfare history. But for the sake of manageability we were forced to omit works that deal exclusively with European (or other foreign) developments.

We hope that the reader finds this explanatory note, and the entire bibliography, useful. For works published after this bibliography was prepared, readers should consult indexes in their reference libraries and current periodicals.

SOCIAL
WELFARE
IN AMERICA

Chapter One

THE PROCESS AND PROGRESS OF SOCIAL WELFARE

Walter I. Trattner
University of Wisconsin-Milwaukee
and
W. Andrew Achenbaum
Carnegie-Mellon University

1. SYNTHESES AND OVERVIEWS

1.1. THEMATIC

1. Axinn, June and Herman Levin. "Social Change and Social Work: Lessons from the Past, Implications for the Future." Journal of Social Welfare, Vol. 4, Nos. 2-3 (Winter, 1977), 27-35. In the belief that the social work profession "needs to maintain readiness to participate in shaping social programs" and be "involved with framing economic legislation", the authors consider the lessons of American social welfare history in exploring the potential of social work's contribution to reform in light of President Jimmy Carter's proposed revamping of the welfare system.

2. Axinn, June and Herman Levin. Social Welfare: A History of the American Response to Need. Second Edition, New York: Harper and Row, 1982. A general survey of American social welfare history from the colonial period to the present with selected documents at the end of each chapter. Values and attitudes are explored as well as the political and economic forces that have brought about particular social welfare policies and programs, which have fluctuated between individual service and social reform. The first edition paid special attention to blacks and veterans; the second edition pays particular attention to women as well.

3. Berkowitz, Edward and Kim McQuaid. Creating the Welfare State: The Political Economy of Twentieth-Century Reform. New York: Praeger Publishers, 1980. The thesis of this work is that between 1900 and 1950 private businessmen and public officials operating on both the state and national levels created the American social welfare system. The authors succeed in demonstrating that private businessmen played an important role in American

social welfare history.

4.   Boyer, Paul. Urban Masses and Moral Order in America, 1820-1920. Cambridge, Mass.: Harvard University Press, 1978. An excellent and important synthesis of urban philanthropy between the Jacksonian era and 1920, in which the author argues that an urban moral or social control tradition, resulting largely from a fear of the city, dominated social welfare and reform during the century. In the 1920s, the urban moral-social control tradition began to fade, according to Boyer, as champions of urbanism, critics of small town life, and advocates of cultural pluralism all rejected the vision which had united reformers throughout the previous century--a vision rooted in nostalgia for an older, simpler way of life.

5.   Brandes, Stuart D. American Welfare Capitalism, 1880-1940. Chicago: University of Chicago Press, 1976. In this concise analysis of the efforts by corporate executives to nurture a pliable workforce and to check the growth of unions by providing company stores, libraries, and other benefits, Brandes concludes that welfare capitalism was "better than nothing at all." The extensive notes are worth further mining.

6.   Bremner, Robert H. American Philanthropy. Chicago: University of Chicago Press, 1960. A brief narrative on the American philanthropic tradition, the first of its kind which surveys voluntary activity in the fields of charity, religion, education, humanitarian reform, social work, war relief, and foreign aid. This book deals with donors, agitators, promoters of causes, and with numerous institutions and associations Americans have founded to conduct their philanthropic business, Bremner mainly is concerned with the reasons why so many Americans from colonial times to the present have felt an obligation to do good--and shows the various ways they have attempted to fulfill their obligation.

7.   Bremner, Robert H. From the Depths: The Discovery of Poverty in the United States. New York: New York University Press, 1956. A pathbreaking study of America's awakening and response to poverty as a social problem from the 1830s to the 1920s. This is not a history of economic distress, but rather an exceedingly creative and successful account of the factors that made Americans conscious of and sympathetic toward the misfortune of their fellow citizens from the pen of someone whose unabashed belief in social welfare programs as humanitarian progress reveals itself throughout the work. A must for all students of the subject, even those with other points of view.

8. Bremner, Robert H. "The State of Social Welfare His-
    tory." In The State of American History, ed. by Herbert
    J. Bass. Chicago: Quadrangle Books, 1970, 89–98. In
    this essay, delivered at the 1969 meeting of the O.A.H.
    as part of an appraisal of the state of American
    history, Bremner urged that historians of social welfare
    pay more attention to the viewpoint of the client and
    less to that of those who operate, administer, and
    finance social welfare services. He also called upon
    them "to serve the other branches of the discipline of
    which we are a part," and thus "lighten, enliven, and
    humorize the study of history."

9. Chambers, Clarke A. "America Discovers Pov-
    erty--Again." The Elizabeth Wisner Lecture, Tulane Uni-
    versity School of Social work, 1967. A look at the pov-
    erty problem in America in historical perspective (from
    the vantage point of 1967), which, in the author's opin-
    ion, suggests that in the current crusade poverty war-
    riors "can gather both insight and inspiration from
    scholars, educators, leaders, and workers of those
    earlier generations who recognized the needs, elaborated
    the practical and constructive programs, and fought for
    their inauguration."

10. Chambers, Clark A. "An Historical Perspective on Poli-
    tical Action vs. Individualized Treatment." In Per-
    spectives on Social Welfare, ed. by Paul E. Weinberger.
    New York: Macmillan, 1980. A penetrating discussion
    and evaluation, of the social reform and social ser-
    vice--or cause and function--dichotomy in social welfare
    placed in historical perspective.

11. Chambers, Clarke A. "Social Service and Social Reform:
    A Historical Essay." Social Service Review, Vol. 37,
    No. 1 (March, 1963), 76–90. Similar to his essay in
    Weinberger's Perspectives on Social Welfare, Chambers
    again demonstrates that, from its beginning, social wel-
    fare work has been engaged in both service to in-
    dividuals in need and social reform, or reconstruction
    of the social environment. Thus the profession is in a
    good position to draw insight and inspiration for the
    tasks ahead.

12. Coughlin, Bernard J. Church and State in Social
    Welfare. New York: Columbia University Press, 1965.
    An important and comprehensive study of the role of sec-
    tarian agencies in America's welfare system by someone
    who favors having the nation's churches play an even
    more active role in the field "in order to maintain the
    necessary balance between personal freedom and govern-
    ment power, between personal responsibility and govern-
    ment responsibility."

13. Davis, Allen F. "Social Welfare History." Reviews in
     American History, Vol. 2, No. 3 (Sept., 1974), 343-45.
     A review of Komisar's Down and Out and Trattner's From
     Poor Law to Welfare State which is a good his-
     toriographical article in which Davis calls upon social
     welfare history to "become a branch of the new social
     history in its search to document the lives of the anon-
     ymous poor. . . ."

14. Derthick, Martha. Policymaking for Social Security.
     Washington, D. C.: The Brookings Institution, 1979.
     Seeking to explain why the traditionally non-controver-
     sial Social Security program has come under widespread
     attack, the author, director of Government Studies at
     the   Brookings   Institution,   presents   a   thorough,
     well-balanced, and readable account of the program's
     history, focusing on the rationale and motives of the
     policymakers and shapers, as vulnerability, and the rea-
     sons why. Insofar as Derthick uses Social Security to
     demonstrate the advantages and limitations of the poli-
     tics of incrementalism, her work also analyzes amend-
     ments passed between 1950 and 1964. She does, however,
     deal with a larger time frame.

15. Feagin, Joe R. Subordinating the Poor: Welfare and
     American Beliefs. Englewood Cliffs, N.J.: Prentice-
     Hall, 1975. A compelling examination of current
     American attitudes toward poverty and the poor, and a
     revealing analysis of how they have become important
     tools in keeping the poor in their place and preserving
     the political and economic status quo. The villain for
     Feagin, is the age-old work ethic and the ideology that
     maintains that the individual alone ultimately is re-
     sponsible for economic fortune--or misfortune.

16. Friedman, Milton. Capitalism and Freedom. Chicago:
     University of Chicago Press, 1962. In this classic
     statement by a Nobel Laureate and one of the nation's
     leading conservative economists, Friedman argues that
     "competitive capitalism" is both a device for achieving
     economic growth and a condition for political freedom.
     His ideas on the advantages of a negative income tax,
     interestingly, were adopted by some liberal economists
     in the late 1960s an 1970s as a way to establish a fed-
     erally sponsored minimum income maintenance program.

17. Galper, Jeffrey H. The Politics of Social Services.
     Englewood Cliffs, N.J.: Prentice-Hall, 1975. A biting
     criticism of social work as a helping profession. Among
     other things, the profession supports present social ar-
     rangements which, in turn, destroy the well-being of
     many, according to Galper. Social work also patronizes
     clients and encourages their dependency, and values ex-
     pertise, or technical matters, rather than mass mo-

bilization and structural or political problems, according to the author.

18. Gaylin, Willard, Ira Glasser, Steven Marcus, and David Rothman. Doing Good: The Limits of Benevolence. New York: Pantheon Books, 1978. Four imaginative essays on dependency that ask and attempt to answer such questions as: do efforts to help the dependent often become coercive, and if so, why? What happens when the state assumes the role of parent? Are there ways of protecting the needy's rights and at the same meeting their needs? Can we have good care and liberty together, in other words? Taken together, these essays provide an important statement on the mode in concern, and fear, of "doing good"--and how and why they arose.

19. Graebner, William. A History of Retirement: The Meaning and Funcion of an American Institution, 1885-1978. New Haven: Yale University Press, 1980. This work, the first full-scale study of the subject, is one of the most recent and best examples of the newer revisionist, or social control, accounts. Simply stated, the thesis of this extremely well researched work is that retirement and pension plans developed not to serve the needs of the elderly but rather those of the marketplace; they were designed, in other words, to satisfy the demands of a capitalist economy for efficiency and social control rather than for the purposes of social justice.

20. Greenberg, Sanford N. "Invisible Poor and Forgotten Men: The Rhetoric of American Social Reform." Unpublished Ph.D. Diss., University of California, Berkeley, 1978. Using Michael Harrington's rediscovery of the invisible poor living in The Other America and his call for a federal war on poverty as representative of one tradition, and Richard Nixon's attack on that anti-poverty crusade and his forgotten American appeal in the 1968 presidential campaign as representative of the other, the author examines the longtime debate in American history between reformers who have sought to help the poor and others who have claimed that working-and middle-class Americans have been the forgotten victims of misguided attempts to eradicate poverty. The work concludes with a consideration of a possible alliance between the two.

21. Greenstone, David J. "Dorothea Dix and Jane Addams: From Transcendentalism to Pragmatism in American Social Reform." Social Service Review, Vol. 53, No. 4 (December, 1979), 527-59. An examination of the contributions of Dorothea Dix and Jane Addams to American social reform in terms of the political and philosophical commitments to American culture. The dif-

ferences between the two women according to Greenstone closely parallel the transition from the moral certainty and self reliance of Emerson's Transcendentalism to the collective action and moral inquiry of John Dewey's pragmatism.

22.   Grob, Gerald. "Reflections on the History of Social Policy in America." Reviews in American History, Vol. 7, No. 3 (Sept., 1979), 293-306. An important plea by Grob for historians to "delineate the contours and development of social policy in America," something they have not yet done for reasons he discusses in this article, which also is very critical of the social control school of social welfare history.

23.   Grob, Gerald. "The Social History of Medicine and Disease in America: Problems and Possibilities." Journal of Social History, Vol. 10, No. 4 (Summer, 1977), 391-409. After lamenting the lack of sound work in the area, Grob calls for the growth of the social history of medicine and disease in America as a specific field of specialization; he also provides suggestions for the directions such a new field might take, and the reasons why.

24.   Grob, Gerald. The State and the Mentally Ill. Chapel Hill: University of North Carolina Press, 1966. An excellent study of the Worcester (Massachusetts) State Hospital for the Insane, probably the nation's leading such institution, and of the interaction of psychiatric theory and practice, state policy, and public attitudes toward mental illness. Grob shows how therapy and administrative policy responded to pressures created by industrialization, urbanization, increasing ethnic heterogeneity, the growth of state authority, and the like.

25.   Grob, Gerald. "Welfare and Poverty in American History." Reviews in American History, Vol. 1, No. 11 (March, 1973), 43-52. A review essay of Mohl's Poverty in New York, Smith-Rosenberg's Religion and the Rise of the American City, and Rothman's The Discovery of the Asylum in which Grob talks about and analyzes scholarly concern with the fate of the poor and dependent in America and points out some of the shortcomings, and dangers, of the social control theory.

26.   Klein, Philip. From Philanthropy to Social Welfare. San Francisco: Jossey-Bass, 1968. A critical examination of the social work profession by a prominent social worker-educator who calls upon his colleagues to become reformers and presents some novel suggestions for reorganizing training programs in the academic structure in order to reorient professional organization and purpose and produce desperaterly needed new leaders with wisdom and courage.

27.   Leiby, James. <u>A History of Social Welfare and Social
       Work in the Unites States</u>. New York: Columbia Uni-
       versity Press, 1978. A general overview of American so-
       cial welfare history from 1815 to the present designed
       primarily to show how policies and agencies came into
       being and changed over time. The work contains an ex-
       cellent bibliography.

28.   Leiby, James. "Social Work and Social History: Some
       Interpretations." <u>Social Service Review</u>, Vol. 43, No. 3
       (Sept., 1969), 310-18. An interesting and perhaps un-
       usual plea by a social welfare historian in the 1960s
       for social workers to spend more time addressing the
       "technical" and "scientific" problems of their en-
       terprise. Based, too, on the notion that America is be-
       coming increasingly homogeneous, Leiby suggests that so-
       cial welfare would continue to receive increased public
       sympathy and financial support.

29.   Lubove, Roy. "Economic Security and Social Conflict in
       America." Part I, <u>Journal of Social History</u>, Vol. 1,
       No. 1 (Fall, 1967), 61-87; Part II, Vol. 1, No. 4 (Sum-
       mer, 1968), 325-50. According to Lubove, the social in-
       surance movement launched in the early twentieth century
       marked a decisive episode in American social welfare
       history, for in marked contrast to the reform tradition
       of the past with its emphasis upon economic independence
       and mobility, social insurance advocates addressed them-
       selves to the requisites of security in a wage-centered,
       industrial economy. This study focuses on that clash
       between social insurance goals on the one hand, and the
       ideology and institutions of voluntarism upon the social
       insurance movement. An excellent study which forms the
       basis for chapter one of Lubove's work on <u>The Struggle
       for Social Security</u>.

30.   Lubove, Roy. <u>The Struggle for Social Security,
       1900-1935</u>. Cambridge, Mass.: Harvard University Press,
       1968. An excellent highly analytical study of the evo-
       lution and history of the concept of social security in
       America up to the time of the New Deal, a concept which
       provoked a great debate over such important issues as
       liberty, welfare, and the role of the state in a demo-
       cratic society. Lubove emphasized both the clash bet-
       ween the American tradition of voluntarism and the prin-
       ciples of social security and the bitter struggle within
       the social security movement itself between those who
       favored the preventive approach and those who saw the
       movement as a mechanism for income redistribution.

31.   McElroy, James L. "Social Control and Romantic Reform
       in Antebellum America: The Case of Rochester, New
       York." <u>New York History</u>, Vol. 58, No. 1 (Jan., 1977),

17-46. An examination, and analysis, of the influence of religious benevolence and social control upon radical reform in Rochester, N.Y., which tends to verify the seeming irony of a conservative, control-oriented crusade giving birth to a radical liberating movement--abolitionism.

32. Mencher, Samuel. "Ideology and the Welfare Society." Social Work, Vol. 12, No. 3 (July, 1967), 3-11. Meucher discusses the relationship between ideology and welfare policy and points out how current ideological differences have left unresolved several important social welfare issues.

33. Meyer, Stephen. The Five Dollar Day: Labor Management and Social Control in the Ford Motor Company, 1908-1921. Albany: State University of New York Press, 1981. In 1914, the Ford Motor Company introduced a profit-sharing plan to remedy the low productivity attributed to absenteeism, chronic turnovers, slowdowns, and problems associated with acclimating pre-industrial peasants to a "modern" factory. This study examines the Americanization and home improvement tactics employed by the company's management. As such, it offers a broader scope to the realm of "welfare capitalism" than other studies provide.

34. Mohl, Raymond. "Mainstream Social Welfare History and Its Problems." Reviews in American History, Vol. 7, No. 4 (Dec., 1979), 469-76. A review of Leiby's A History of Social Welfare and Social Work in the United States in which Mohl discusses briefly the history of social welfare history, especially its emphasis on middle class reformers and other spokespersons for the welfare establishment and calls for a "new" social welfare history, one that views the subject from "the bottom up" rather than from top down.

35. Muraskin, William. A. "The Social Control Theory in American History: A Critique." Journal of Social History, Vol. 9, No. 4 (Summer, 1976), 559-69. Author uses a review essay of Rothman's The Discovery of the Asylum and Platt's The Child Savers as a vehicle to discuss the social control theory in American social welfare history--and concludes that for all its promise, the thesis suffers from serious flaws.

36. Piven, Frances F. and Richard A. Cloward. Poor People's Movements: Why They Succeed, How They Fail. New York: Pantheon, 1977. On the basis of several case studies of lower class protest movements in America since the Depression, Piven and Cloward argued that mass defiance rather than formal organizations per se achieved the

welfare gains of the 1930s and 1960s. The organizations
in fact, were rent by internal disputes, short-lived-
ness, and hence failure.

37. Piven, Frances F. and Richard A. Cloward. <u>Regulating</u>
     <u>the Poor: The Functions of Public Welfare</u>. New York:
     Pantheon, 1971. An essential, thought-provoking work,
     one of the best and certainly the most influential ex-
     ample of the social control interpretation of American
     social welfare history. In it, Piven and Cloward set
     forth their widely cited thesis that public officials
     expand the welfare roles in times of unemployment and
     social unrest in order to quell disorder or threatened
     disorder, then reduce those rolls in times of widespread
     employoment and aquiescence in order to perpetuate the
     work ethic and create a pool of marginal laborers, and
     thus preserve the capitalist system. Welfare patterns,
     then, are cyclical in nature and are controlled or mani-
     pulated, by the special interests in order to preserve
     their own advantage in society. While the work begins
     with discussion of the Middle Ages, it concentrates,
     heavily, on the American experience during the 1930s and
     the 1960s.

38. Pumphrey, Ralph E. "Compassion and Protection: Dual
     Motivations in Social Welfare." <u>Social Service Review</u>,
     Vol. 33, No. 1 (March, 1959), 21-29. In an effort to
     identify some unifying ideas to be utilized in an an-
     alysis of American social welfare history, Pumphrey ar-
     gues that two threads run through organized efforts to
     help the needy in America--compassion, or "efforts to
     alleviate . . . suffering, deprivation, or other un-
     desirable conditions," and protection, or "endeavors to
     prevent unwanted developments."

39. Rein, Martin. <u>Social Science and Public Policy</u>. New
     York: Penguin Books, 1976. In this series of lucid es-
     says on the relationship among values, the social
     sciences, and social policy, Rein makes a good case for
     an historical approach, particularly one that recognizes
     the need to select and tell a good story which high-
     lights and bridges gaps in our understanding of social
     issues.

40. Rescher, Nicholas. <u>Welfare</u>. Pittsburgh: University of
     Pittsburgh Press, 1972. This cogent analysis of the
     normative dimensions of "welfare" by one of America's
     leading philosophers underscores major continuities and
     changes in nuances and meanings of this elusive term
     over time.

41. Ridenour, Nina. <u>Mental Health in the United States</u>.
     Cambridge, Mass.: Harvard University Press, 1961. A
     capsule account, or description, of the mental health

movement in America from its origins in 1908 to some fifty years later written by a strong supporter of mental health groups

42.   Rimlinger, Gaston V. "Welfare Policy and Economic Development: A Comparative Historical Perspective." Journal of Economic History, Vol. 26, No. 14 (Dec., 1966), 556-71. Focusing on the impact of industrialization on production, the author emphasizes the positive effect social welfare measures have for the private economic sector, primarily in making available a sizable pool of skilled workers to manage a technologically advanced productive capacity. The government must develop welfare programs, in other words, according to Rimlinger, as a form of investment in human capital in order to ensure the adequacy of the labor force

43.   Rochefort, David A. "Progressive and Social Control Perspectives on Social Welfare." Social Service Review, Vol. 55, No. 4 (Dec., 1981), 569-92. An extremely useful and insightful article for all students of American social welfare history and historiography. The author reviews the major themes which make up both the "progressive" and the "social control" models of social welfare history and then develops a critique which identifies the major methodological shortcomings shared in common by the two models and points to the kinds of questions further work in the area must address.

44.   Rothman, David. Conscience an Convenience: The Asylum and its Alternatives in Progressive America. Boston: Little, Brown, 1980. In this exceedingly important work which speaks as much to contemporary policymakers as to historians, Rothman continues the storyu he started in The Discovery of the Asylum. Like the earlier book, this work focuses on attempts to reform the treatment of those institutionalized earlier, especially criminals, delinquents, and the mentally ill, between the years 1890 and 1930; it departs from its predecessor, however, in that it is less concerned with the social context of the institutions than with their internal history. The thesis of this work is that, while reformers introduced measures to improve penal and mental institutions, primarily by providing individualized treatment to their inmates, administrators--wardens, judges, hospital superintendents, and others--turned those measures to their own advantage in order to perpetuate the status quo, and thus preserve their authority. Conscience, in other words, lost out to convenience, and many unfortunate citizens are still paying the price. A brilliant analysis which must be contended with by all students of social welfare history.

45.   Rothman, David. The Discovery of the Asylum: Social
       Order and Disorder in the New Republic.   Boston:
       Little,   Brown,   1971.   In   this   very   influential
       prize-winning   work   Rothman   attempts   to   explain   two
       things: 1) why Americans in the Jacksonian era began
       resorting to institutions for the care and treatment of
       dependent   and   deviant   members   of   society--almshouses,
       orphanages,   insane   asylums,   reformatories,   and   peni-
       tentiaries,   and 2) why those institutions, which were
       intended   to be therapeutic in nature became, at best
       custodial,   and at worst, harmful, places.   According to
       Rothman,   the asylum was initiated to fulfill a dual
       role--to   insure   order   and,   at   the   same   time,   reha-
       bilitate its members, neither of which it could do; yet
       it persisted, for reasons the author makes clear in this
       very important work, and in his later one, Conscience
       and Convenience (1980).

46.   Rothman, David.   "Social Control: The Uses and Abuses
       of the Concept in the History of Incarceration."   Rice
       University Studies, Vol. 167, No. 1 (Winter, 1981),
       9-19.   A very thoughtful article which first goes into a
       history of the social control thesis and its effect on
       current thinking, and then pleads for its very careful
       and judicious use.

47.   Titmuss, Richard M.   Essays on the Welfare State.   New
       Haven: Yale University Press, 1958.   While the welfare
       state is good for those people who are poor, those who
       benefit most from it, especially the Social Security
       system, are members of the middle and upper classes, ac-
       cording to this expert.

48.   Trattner, Walter I.   From Poor Law to Welfare State: A
       History of Social Welfare in America.   2nd Edition, New
       York: The Free Press, 1979.   A general history of so-
       cial welfare in America from its European roots to the
       Carter administration; organized chronologically, it al-
       so has topical chapters on child welfare, the public
       health movement, the mental health movement, and the
       quest for professionalization.

49.   Trattner,   Walter I., ed.   Social Welfare or Social
       Control?   Some Historical Reflections on REGULATING THE
       POOR.   Knoxville: The University of Tennessee Press,
       1983.   A series of essays by social welfare historians
       which   raise   important   questions   about   the   so-called
       Piven and Cloward thesis.   The work also has an in-
       troductory essay that places Regulating the Poor in his-
       torical perspective and concludes with a spirited rebut-
       tal by Piven and Cloward.

50.   Wachtel, Howard M.   "Looking at Poverty From a Radical
       Perspective."   Review of Radical Political Economics,

Vol. 13, No. 3 (Summer, 1971), 1-19. The author argues that poverty is part of American capitalist society--a logical outcome of the interaction of "class, labor markets, and the state." Public policies to combat poverty have failed, he argues, because they do not challenge the institution of capitalism but seek to reform the individual poor person. Wachtel's interpretation differs from the liberal perspective of most socal welfare historians.

51.   Wilensky, Harold L. and Charles N. Lebeaux. Industrial Society and Social Welfare. New York: The Free Press, 1965. In this work, one of the most widely used in the field, the authors elaborate a multi-dimensional theory of the relationship between social welfare practices and the development of industrial society. They argue that industrialization has simultaneously determined the demand for, supply of, and organization of welfare services within modern social systems. First of all, social problems (old age dependency, unemployment, juvenile delinquency, etc.) directly result from industrialization and its impact on the economy and such traditional institutions as the family. At the same time, however, industrialization has stimulated the economic growth which makes possible the income for welfare expenditures. Finally, it also creates bureaucratic and hierarchical forms of organization that determine the way social welfare services are formally administered and delivered.

1.2. TEMPORAL.

52.   Annunziata, Frank A. "The Attack on the Welfare State from the New Deal to the New Left." Unpublished Ph.D. Diss., Ohio State University, 1968. Ever since its creation, the American welfare state has been denounced, both as a violation of the nation's individualist ethos and as a conservative guise to maintain an inequitable and unjust social and economic system. This thesis is an analysis of certain aspects of the opposition toward the welfare state during the past three decades, opposition from both the right and the left.

53.   Athey, Louis Lee. "The Consumers' Leagues and Social Reform, 1890-1923." Unpublished Ph.D. Diss., University of Delaware, 1965. An excellent study of the nation's various Consumers' Leagues which among other things, illustrates how the initiative of modestly sized reform groups during the Progressive era paved the way for new social legislation, such as child labor and minimum wage laws, protective legislation for women, and the like, and demanded the enforcement of existing statutes as well. Clearly, the Consumers' Leagues were effective in

promoting reform needed to ameliorate laboring conditions, especially for women and children, in a modern
industrial society.

54.   Bird, Frederick B. "The Poor Be Damned: An Analysis of
How Americans Have Perceived and Responded to the Problems of Poverty, 1885-1970." Unpublished Ph.D. Diss.,
General Theological Seminary of the Episcopal Church,
1973. Author analyzes the history of anti-poverty programs instituted by various public and private agencies
between 1885 and 1970 and concludes that, in general,
Americans have felt that the primary purpose of such
programs was to enhance the upward mobility of individuals (either through educational programs or by removing obstacles in their way); they have paid much less
attention to schemes designed to raise the poor's level
of wealth in relation to the rest of society. The work
concludes with a plea for the latter.

55.   Bremner, Robert H. The Public Good: Philanthropy and
Welfare in the Civil War Era. New York: Knopf, 1980.
A long awaited study from which Bremner's prior articles
on the subject were drawn. This interpretive history of
philanthropic and welfare activities in the period from
the 1830s to the 1880s centers on the formal helping efforts of private organizations and governmental agencies
and the interplay between the two. Not surprisingly,
the Civil War is viewed as a central event in shaping
those efforts; it not only enhanced voluntarism and public welfare but taught those administering both the need
for a rational, systematic, and orderly approach—and
hence helped usher in the era of "scientific
philanthropy."

56.   Burns, Eveline M. Social Security and Public Policy.
New York: McGraw-Hill, 1956. In this classic study of
the subject, the author analyzes the adoption and implementation of the Social Security system in America,
particularly its cash income provisions.

57.   Cavallo, Dominick. Muscles and Morals: Organized
Playgrounds and Urban Reform, 1880-1920. Philadelphia:
University of Pennsylvania Press, 1981. In this cultural history of an important section of urban Progressive reform, Cavallo examines the intellectual basis and
institutional strategies employed to strike a balance
between individualism and collectivism in shaping the
environment for children and adolescents. In so doing,
Cavallo shows the value and bias in viewing "social control" as a distinctive element of the reform impulse.

58.   Clayton, James L. "The Fiscal Limits of the
Warfare-Welfare State: Defense and Welfare Spending in
the United States Since 1900." The Western Political

Quarterly, Vol. 39, No. 3 (September, 1976), 364-89.
This essay documents various ways to measure and compare
defense and welfare expenditures since 1900. It suggests that we cannot continue to increase our rate of
welfare spending without a substantial increase in taxes
or national debt.

59.   Coll, Blanche D.   Perspectives in Public Welfare.
Washington, D.C.: Government Printing Office, 1969. A
succinct and informative review of poor relief policies
and practices from the medieval period through the
1920s. The chief points that emerge from the narrative
are the persistence of public outdoor relief as the
principal method of caring for the poor, and the persistence of criticism of such assistance.

60.   Connolly, Michael Padrick.   "An Historical Study of
Change in Saul D. Alinsky's Community Organization
Practice and Theory, 1939-1972." Unpublished Ph.D.
Diss., University of Minnesota, 1976. Saul Alinsky
(1909-1972) was one of America's most controversial community organizers. This thesis is particularly helpful
in explaining why Alinsky opted for non-violent conflict
tactics in the 1960s, rather than more radical options.

61.   Critchlow, Donald T.   "The Political Control of the Economy: Deficit Spending as a Political Belief,
1932-1952." The Public Historian, Vol. 3, No. 3
(Spring, 1981), 5-22. This article examines the relationship between electoral behavior and economic public
policy, primarily deficit spending, between the years
1932-1952. In so doing, the author demonstrates how
historians can contribute new analysis and understanding
of the complex problems involved in the evolution of
(economic) public policy.

62.   Davis, Allen F.   Spearheads for Reform: The Social
Settlements and the Progressive Movement 1890-1914 .
New York: Oxford University Press, 1967. A very favorable account of the settlement house movement in America, the men and women involved in it, and their relationship to the larger reform movement of the late nineteenth and early twentieth century. Davis concentrates
on the settlements in Boston, Chicago, and New York,
where the movement was strongest and most concerned with
reform. An account of idealistic, dedicated reformers,
one challenged later by members of the social control
school.

63.   Doyle, Don H.   "The Social Functions of Voluntary
Associations in a Nineteenth Century American Town."
Social Science History. Vol. 1, No. 3 (Spring, 1977),
333-55. This case study of the officers and functions
of voluntary associations in Jacksonville, Ilinois be-

tween 1825 and 1870 suggests that voluntary associations <u>collectively</u> helped to maintain stability, order, and well-being among an extraordinarily mobile and discordant population.

64. Duffy, John. <u>A History; of Public Health in New York City, 1625-1966,</u> 2 Vols. New York: Russell Sage Foundation, 1968-1974. A detailed two-volume account of public health in New York City from 1625 to 1966 which is the most thorough work of its kind for any American city--a major contribution.

65. Fox, Richard W. <u>So Far Disordered in Mind: Insanity in California, 1870-1930.</u> Los Angeles: University of California Press, 1978. An excellent study of the social and cultural meaning of insanity in California between 1870 and 1930, with a special focus on the twentieth century, a period of widespread change in medical and popular attitudes toward "mental illness" and in institutional modes of detention and treatment--a time when the "moral model" of deviant behavior was in the course of being displaced by the therapeutic model.

66. Funston, Richard. "The Double Standard of Constitutional Protection in the Era of the Welfare State." <u>Political Science Quarterly</u>, Vol. 90, No. 2 (Summer, 1975), 261-87. Because the Supreme Court since the New Deal has given greater priority to civil liberties than to property rights, the Court has no helped resolve the relationship between economic independence and individual freedom. This has had grievous consequences, argues Funston, for American justice in the welfare state.

67. Graham, Otis L., Jr. <u>Toward a Planned Society: From Roosevelt to Nixon.</u> New York: Oxford University Press, 1976. A historical study of the idea and practice of federal planning from the 1930s to the 1970s. Graham addresses the present and future policies in areas of natural resources, manpower, science and technology, and income.

68. Haller, Mark H. <u>Eugenics: Hereditarian Attitudes in American Thought.</u> New Brunswick, N.J.: Rutgers University Press, 1963. A detailed and objective history of the eugenics movement in America which deals mainly with its social consequences and provides a means for examining the place of science (heredity) in American social thought and history.

69. Heald, Morrell. <u>The Social Responsibilities of Business: Company and Community, 1900-1960.</u> Cleveland: Press of Case Western Reserve University, Press, 1970. In a (perhaps excessively) sympathetic analysis

of the ideas and activities of American businessmen in the twentieth century, Heald documents the initiatives corporations took in the community chest movement and (after World War II) in sponsoring educational and cultural activities. The treatment of the 1920s is especially useful for social welfare historians.

70. Heale, M. J. "From City Fathers to Social Critics: Humanitarianism and Government in New York, 1790-1860." Journal of American History, Vol. 58, No. 1 (June, 1976), 24-41. Humanitarian activities was one of the functions that the elite adopted as a consequence of its social position. To ascribe benevolent activities then, solely to the conservative temperament of an elite interested in maintaining the status quo, as members of the social control school do, is wrong according to Heale. It was civic stewardship, not social control, that motivated them.

71. Horlick, Allan S. Country Boys and Merchant Princes: The Social Control of Young Men in New York. Lewisburg, Pa.: Bucknell University Press, 1975. Casting around for agencies that would enable them to re-establish control of the social order that previously rested exclusively in their hands the business elite (especially merchants) created various social institutions particularly the YMCA, to regulate the conduct of newcomers to the city and normalize an environment that was getting out of control--and threatening their profits. The work tends to support, in some ways, Paul Boyers' Urban Masses and Moral Order in America, 1820-1920.

72. Janowitz, Morris. The Last Half-Century: Societal Change and Politics in America. Chicago: University of Chicago Press, 1978. This magisterial survey of major trends in American society since the 1920s rests on a sophisticated model of social control. Social-welfare historians will find chapters 1-3, 5, 12-14 particularly useful. They may also profitably read an earlier and more concise statement of Janowitz's thesis in his Social Control of the Welfare State (Chicago: University of Chicago Press, 1976).

73. Karl, Barry D. "Philanthropy, Policy Making, and the Bureaucratization of the Democratic Ideal." Daedalus, Vol. 105, No. 4 (Fall, 1976), 129-49. This essay traces the notion of the "bureaucrat" from Weber's (neutral) usage to its current (negative) connotations. Using philanthropy as a case study, Karl shows how bureaucrats during the past century have assumed a role as political mediators as they advance their professional interests.

74. Klebaner, Benjamin J. Public Poor Relief in America, 1790-1860. New York: Arno Press, 1976. A recent

publicaton of what was a significant and pioneering doctoral dissertation, completed in 1952, on public poor relief between 1790 and 1860. While no longer an indispensable source, this detailed account of welfare beliefs and practices in early nineteenth century America still is worth reading.

75. Kolko, Gabriel. Wealth and Power in America. New York: Praeger, 1962. Kolko argues, and demonstrates, that inequalities in the distribution of income and wealth in the United States had not changed since 1939--or even 1910; those in the lowest income groups have received a decreasing share of the nation's wealth during the past fifty years, so that the poor remain, and likely will increase in number in the future.

76. Leffler, Keith B. "Minimum Wages, Welfare, and Wealth Transfers to the Poor." The Journal of Law and Economics, Vol. 21, No. 2 (October, 1978), 345-58. Applying an econometric model to U.S. aggregate data (1950-1973), Leffler argues that minimum wages may not hurt the poor. Indeed, as welfare advocates suggest, minimum wages may be a technique of lowering the cost of establishing eligibility for more and more generous public welfare programs.

77. Leiby, James. "Amos Warner's American Charities, 1894-1930." Social Service Review, Vol. 37, No. 14 (Dec., 1963), 441-55. A look a the classic American Charities (1894) and its author, Amos Warner, in an effort to answer th question: What was it about the work--and American social welfare--that made it virtually no revision when new editions appeared in 1908 and 1919, but made it old-fashioned and even outdated by 1930? Leiky suggests an answer to the question, but does not analyze its causes.

78. Leiby, James. Charity and Correction in New Jersey: A History of State Welfare Institutions. New Brunswick, N.J.: Rutgers Univ. Press, 1967. An analysis of how the state of New Jersey established, organized, and operated its services for dependent and delinquent citizens from the colonial period to 1959. The theme of the book is the transformation of ideas about "charity and corrections" into a system of public welfare.

79. Lewis, W. David. From Newgate to Dannemora: The Rise of the Penitentiary in New York, 1796-1848. Ithaca: Cornell University Press, 1965. The first extended treatment of American prison reform, one which takes into account the broader context of political economic, and cultural trends current in the early national and Jacksonian periods, especially the activities and motives of various penal reformers.

80. Lloyd, Gary A. Charities, Settlements, and Social Work: An Inquiry into Philosophy and Method, 1890-1915. New Orleans: Tulane University School of Social Welfare, 1971. A monograph dealing with a critical period in American social welfare history, the years between 1890 and 1915, when a large number of concerned people, whatever their differences, saw the need to develop a corps of trained professionals to help the needy. This work, though, does not really deal with the development of social work as a profession; rather, it is an attempt to explore what early social workers did in practice and to inquire into the philosophical rationale for those actions.

81. Lubove, Roy. The Professional Altruist: The Emergence of Social Work as a Career, 1880-1930. Cambridge, Mass.: Harvard University Press, 1965. The definitive study of the way in which the traditional practices of private charity organizations became outmoded as urbanization changed family and neighborhood life and new knowledge in the behavioral and social sciences gave deeper insight to understanding and influencing human behavior. An analysis, in other words, of the forces that reshaped philanthropy (and voluntarism) into a profession of social work, 1880-1930--and the consequences of that change. Another one of the books that must be read by all students of the subject.

82. Lubove, Roy. The Progressives and the Slums. Pittsburgh: University of Pittsburgh Press, 1962. A systematic analysis of the origins, nature, and influence of housing reform in America, and its relationship to the Progressive movement. On the whole, Lubove is rather critical of the housing reformers for being conservatives who looked upon housing reform as a key to social control, and for never really evolving a public philosophy of the city and urban planning, largely, according to Lubove, because they were anti-urban.

83. MacDonald, Maurice. Food Stamps and Income Maintenance. New York: Academic Press, 1977. A short history of the food stamp program (beginning with the Potato Control Act of 1935) in which the author concludes that 1) it acts like a cash transfer program which makes a substantial contribution toward reducing poverty, and 2) only a small percentage of those eligible to participate in the program (less than 40 percent) do so.

84. McKinley, Edward H. Marching to Glory: The History of the Salvation Army in the United States of America, 1880-1980. San Francisco: Harper & Row, 1980. Writing as a Salvationist and an historian, McKinley offers a

somewhat partisan account of the Army's beliefs, practices and accomplishments. Social welfare historians
should not ignore the role that the Salvation Army has
played in "modern" philanthropy, but they will have to
make the larger connections for themselves.

85.   Magnuson, Norris A. "Salvation in the Slums:
Evangelical Social Work, 1865-1920." Unpublished Ph.D.
Diss., University of Minnesota, 1968. A study of late
nineteenth and early twentieth century revival-
ists/evangelists who organized under the banner of
various little known religious groups and who, according
to the author, played an important role in social welfare. Combining conservative and revivalistic religion
with a progressive position on a variety of social issues, including women's rights, child labor, fair wages,
better working conditions, and the like, "they were an
important force for social welfare and are an index to
the mind of America during the Populist and Progressive
eras."

86.   Mayer, John A. "Private Charities in Chicago from
1871-1915." Unpublished Ph.D. Diss., University of
Minnesota, 1978. An analysis of the Pro-
testant-dominated private charities in Chicago from 1871
to 1915 which concludes, 1) that, whatever the motives,
the charities could not accomplish social control (for
there were too many other sources of financial aid in
the city), and 2) that they provided all sorts of useful
benefits to their middle and upper class supporters;
they served as useful outlets for otherwise "useless"
women, they allowed members of the middle and upper
classes to believe that the social and economic systems
were operating well and that there was no need for public bodies to get involved with the problem of poverty,
and the like.

87.   Merriam, Ida C. "Social Welfare in the United States,
1934-1954." Social Security Bulletin, Vol. 18, No. 10
(Oct., 1955), 3-14, 31. A summary of the development
and scope of the Social Security programmer in America,
1934-1954, which the author feels goes a long way toward
providing adequate provision for all individuals. While
it was by no means perfect--it had gaps and weak-
nesses--it had a solid foundation which could, and
would, be expanded both in scope and effectiveness.

88.   Monkkonen, Eric H. Police in Urban America, 1860-1920.
New York: Cambridge University Press, 1981. Whereas in
his previous book Monkkonen explored the evolution of
the "dangerous class"--the poor, homeless, ill, and
criminal--in this work he turned his attention to the
agency of urban government created to control that
class: the uniformed police. In it, he argues that

while the urban police were created to control crime and
other forms of disorderly behavior, they, in fact, were
the first widely available social service agency for the
poor, homeless, helpless, or lost. Prior to the Progressive era and the rise of voluntary and public social
service agencies, the police, according to Monkkonen
spent a significant portion of their time locating and
returning lost children, sheltering transient laborers,
providing lodging for drunks, intervening in family
squabbles, etc.

89.   Nash, Gary B. The Urban Crucible: Social Change,
Political Consciousness, and the Origins of the American
Revolution.   Cambridge,   Mass.:   Harvard   University
Press, 1979. In this synthesis of continuities and
changes in America's three largest cities (Boston, New
York, and Philadelphia), Nash documents the increasing
social stratificaton and inequality in early American
society. Changing economic conditions, and especially
rising insecurity, led both to growing lower class discontent and new institutional responses to poverty.

90.   Nelson, Daniel. Unemployment Insurance: The American
Experience, 1915-1935. Madison, Wis.: University of
Wisconsin Press, 1969. This carefully documented work
illuminates two decades of action (1915-1935) by economists, reformers, progressive businessmen, and some
union leaders to design a program to deal with the problem of unemployment. Despite those efforts, Americans
were slow to awaken to the problem, or at least do something about it, until the Depression. Nelson examines
how and by whom this general in difference was overcome,
and how the unemployment insurance legislation of the
mid-1930s reflected the interests and ideas of the many
groups and individuals who brought about its passage.

91.   Newcomer, Mabel. "Fifty Years of Public Support of
Welfare Functions in the United States." Social Service
Review, Vol. 115, No. 4 (Dec., 1941), 651-60. A very
clear, well written article, including facts and
figures, about the growth of public welfare, at all
levels, during the prior fifty years, from 1890 to 1940.

92.   Patterson, James T. America's Struggle Against Poverty,
1900-1981. Cambridge, Mass.: Harvard University Press,
1981. An extremely well researched and indispensable
history of American attitudes and policy toward poverty
and welfare in the twentieth century, especially since
the 1930s. Among many other things, Patterson undermines the social control thesis by demonstrating that
popular views on the subject do not always affect policy
nor is the system controlled by the elite; on occasion,
all sorts of other factors, including chance and the existence of a self-perpetuating welfare bureaucracy play

important roles. Useful, too, is the fact that the author places the American experience within the context
of international developments.

93.   Pickens, Donald. Eugenics and the Progressives. Nash-
       ville: Vanderbilt University Press, 1969. A diffiicult
       to read, poorly organized, and somewhat simplistic ac-
       count of hereditarian ideas from around 1870 to 1930
       (despite the title). Basically, the author argues that
       the eugenics philosophy flourished because of the pe-
       culiar concerns of Americans, especially progressives,
       to reconcile themes of fitness and uplift rather than
       because of its scientific credentials; thus, despite its
       shortcomings, it is a useful counterpoint to Mark
       Haller's close scientific approach to the subject.

94.   Riesenfeld, Stefan. "The Formative Era of American As-
       sistance Law." California Law Review, Vol. 143 (May,
       1955), 175-233. By far the most comprehensive and best
       account of the legal background and passage of all the
       colonial poor laws, one which clearly demonstrates that
       "public provision for the unfortunate and needy has been
       an essential ingredient of the American democratic creed
       and a fundamental component of the American fabric of
       government since colonial days."

95.   Rosenberg, Charles E. "And Heal the Sick: The Hospital
       and the Patient in Nineteenth Century America." Journal
       of Social History, Vol. 10, No. 4 (Summer, 1977),
       428-47. This article sketches the internal environment
       of the nineteenth century general hospital in an attempt
       to demonstrate that it was by no means a monolith con-
       trived for the imposition of social control; rather, it
       was a battleground for the conflicting values of tra-
       ditional stewardship and the priorities of an emerging
       medical profession which (thus) tended to buffer the
       hospitalized poor from both physicians and trustees,
       providing them with a large degree of psychological au-
       tonomy. Conditions would deteriorate for the sick poor
       in the late nineteenth and twentieth century.

96.   Rosenkrantz, Barbara Gutmann. Public Health and the
       State: Changing Views in Massachusetts, 1842-1936.
       Cambridge, Mass.: Harvard University Press, 1972. A
       fine piece of social history which, in large part is a
       history of the Massachusetts State Board of Health, es-
       tablished in 1869, the first such institution of its
       kind, to prevent unnecessary mortality and promote all
       aspects of public health.

97.   Schultz, Thomas W. "Our Welfare State and the Welfare
       Farm People." Social Service Review, Vol. 38, No. 2
       (June, 1964), 123-29. Arguing that the welfare state in
       America has not given to farmers the social services

rendered to needy urban dwellers, the author 1) recounts, briefly, the objectives of the late nineteenth century agrarian movements, 2) lists several social services that specifically benefit farm dwellers, 3) examines the social needs of farm people, and 4) analyzes the reasons for their neglect--a combination of internal and external political and cultural factors.

98.   Sinclair, Barbara Deckard. "The Policy Consequences of Party Realignment--Social Welfare Legislation in the House of Representatives, 1933-1954." American Journal of Political Science, Vol. 22, No. 1 (Feb., 1978), 83-105. Walter Dean Burnham's theory of the policy consequences of party realignments--that party realignments are the major source of non-incremental policy change in the American political system--is applied to social welfare legislation during the New Deal era and its aftermath, and is found to hold true, especially with regard to passage of the Social Security Act and the Fair Labor Standards Act. This, of course, has all sorts of implications for future change.

99.   Steiner, Gilbert Y. The Futility of Family Policy. Washington, D.C.: The Brookings Institution, 1981. This judicious account of American family policy since World War II argues that family patterns are simply too diverse, and family members responses to social policy too complex, to permit any single universal family policy to be established.

100.   Thernstrom, Stephen A. The Other Bostonians: Poverty and Progress in the American Metropolis, 1880-1970. Cambridge, Mass.: Harvard University Press, 1973. In many ways an elaboration and refinement of his earlier book and articles, The Other Bostonians goes beyond the immediate data to offer provocative hypotheses about changing patterns of mobility and shifts in the nature and dimensions of poverty in twentieth-century America.

101.   Tishler, Hace Sorel. Self-Reliance and Social Security, 1870-1917. Port Washington, N.Y.: Kenniat Press, 1971. A study of the evolution and significance of the social security movement in the United States in which the author seeks to show how the philanthropic activities of the years between 1870-1893 and the impact of the depression of the 1890s led to a revision of traditional ideas about self-reliance and a growing acceptance of the notion of collective responsibility, the first manifestations of which were adoption of workman's compensation and widow's pensions legislation in the early twentiety century. The work suggests, then, that neither late nineteenth century philanthropy nor the early twentieth century social security movement can be understood in the simplistic framework of individualism

vs. collectivism; the reformers apparently saw
individual security and social order as complementary,
or reciprocal needs.

102.   Travis, Anthony R. "The Impulse Toward the Welfare
       State: Chicago, 1890-1932." Unpublished Ph.D. Diss.,
       Michigan State University, 1971. After analyzing the
       social progressive coalition and the welfare system it
       built and administered in Chicago, 1890-1932, the author
       concludes that the welfare state originated not during
       the New Deal but in the Progressive era. Further, it
       came about not as a response to an upwelling of popular
       demand but rather a desire by a alliance of corporate
       businessmen, professionals, and reformers to create a
       society that was congenial to its interests and ideals.
       In other words, it originated in large part out of a de-
       sire to control the working class.

103.   Tyack, David and Michael Berkowitz. "The Man Nobody
       Liked: Toward a Social History of the Truant Officer,
       1840-1940." American Quarterly, Vol. 29, No. 11
       (Spring, 1977), pp. 131-54. The image of the truant of-
       ficer simultaneously resembled that of a policeman, min-
       ister, social worker, salesman, psychologist, and a
       child-accounting executive. Truant officers, however,
       represent yet another type of "street-level bureaucrat"
       who sought to help the poor as they maintained social
       order.

104.   Viswanthan, Narayan. "The Role of American Public Wel-
       fare Policies in th United States, 1930-1960." Un-
       published Ph.D. Diss., Columbia University, 1961. A
       study of the American Public Welfare Association de-
       signed to assess th role of private welfare organi-
       zations in public policy-making. Created in 1930 to co-
       ordinate and improve the activities of public welfare
       organizations throughout the nation, the A.P.W.A. did
       play an important role in shaping public welfare poli-
       cies throughout the United States, according to the au-
       thor.

105.   West, Margarida P. "The National Welfare Rights Move-
       ment: Social Protest of Welfare Women (1966-1976)."
       Unpublished Ph.D. Diss., Rutgers University, 1978. This
       dissertation is a study of the factors that led to the
       decline of the National Welfare Rights Organizatioon and
       protest movement. The central thesis, or major con-
       clusion, is that "the internal and external conflicts,
       stemming from class, race, and sex contradictions, as
       well as changes in the sociopolitical climate,
       interacted to bring about the loss of people and money,
       and the downfall of the protest movement."

106.   Wilensky, Harold. The Welfare State and Equality:

Structural   and   Ideological   Roots   of   Public
Expenditures.   Berkeley: University   of   California
Press, 1975. An important work in which the author en-
gages in a cross-sectional analysis of sixty-four countries in an effort to isolate "structures and ideological roots of public expenditures" in order to explain differences in absolute levels of welfare spending
among nations—and concludes that "economic growth and
its demographic and bureaucratic outcomes are the root
causes of the general emergence of the welfare state."
In short, differences in overall effort are related less
to political and ideological factors than to levels of
economic development (as Kirsten Gronbjerg also suggested in her Mass Society and the Extension of Welfare,
1960-1970).

107.   Wylie, Mary S. "The Images of Sickness and Health in
America: Medical Thought, 1776-1800 and 1835-1865." Unpublished Ph.D. Diss., American University, 1981. In
this dissertation, the medical views of the two periods
are analyzed and compared to determine the relationship
of medical language to more general political and social
concerns of each period. The author concludes that by
the mid-nineteenth century, the nation's doctors believed that the nation and its people had declined in
strength, purity, and energy—and that their future was
in danger.

108.   Yellowitz, Irwin. "The Origins of Unemployment Reform
in the United States." Labor History. Vol. 9, No. 3
(Fall, 1968), 330-60. An examination of how a small
group of "social progressives" carried through the first
serious campaign for unemployment reform in the United
States two decades before the New Deal. In so doing, it
discusses the scope and sources of the reformers' plans,
the nature of the opposition, and the reasons why it
failed.

1.3. (AUTO)BIOGRAPHIES

109.   Abbott, Edith. "The Hull House of Jane Addams." Social
Service Review, Vol. 26, No. 3 (Sept., 1952), 334-38. A
first-hand account of the early days of Hull House—and
the early residents and their concerns, including
Florence Kelley, Julia Lathrop, Alice Hamilton, George
Hooker, and others.

110.   Abbott, Edith. Some American Pioneers in Social
Welfare. Chicago: University of Chicago Press, 1937.
A useful collection of documents related to the begin-
nings of social services in America as viewed through
the activities of Benjamin Rush, Benjamin Franklin,
Thomas Eddy, Stephen Girard, Samuel Gridley Howe,
Dorothea Dix, and Charles Loring Brace, "pioneers with
social vision who outran their years."

111. Addams, Jane. <u>My Friend, Julia Lathrop</u>. New York:
      Macmillan, 1935. An exceedingly favorable biography
      which   just   covers   Julia   Lathrop's   earlier
      (pre-Children's Bureau) years, when the two women worked
      together in Illinois. More a portrait of Lathrop's per-
      sonal qualities and characteristics—a woman who "was
      attracted to social work as a statesman"—than an ac-
      count of her many activities, the work was found in
      manuscript form right after Jane Addams's death.

112. Addams, Jane. <u>The Second Twenty Years at Hull-House</u>.
      New York: Macmillan, 1930. A continuation of the au-
      thor's earlier work, <u>Twenty Years at Hull-House</u>, which
      deals less with her activities at Hull-House than with
      her reflections on the domestic and world affairs of the
      prior twenty years—the woman's movement, the peace
      movement, World War I, Prohibition, immigration restric-
      tions, etc. In short, a much more philosophical work
      than the earlier one by someone who had not lost her
      idealism despite all that occurred between 1910 and 1930.

113. Addams, Jane. <u>Twenty Years at Hull-House</u>. New York:
      Macmillan, 1910. One of the most famous and widely read
      works which, in effect, is an autobiography and a his-
      tory of the founding and early years of Hull-House and
      the   settlement   house   movement.   Like   many   auto-
      biographies, however, parts of the work are suspect.
      Students of the subject should consult Allen Davis's
      <u>American Heroine</u> as well.

114. Aptheker, Herbert. "DuBois on Florence Kelley." <u>Social
      Work</u>, Vol. 11, No. 4 (Oct., 1966), 98-100. A brief but
      glowing eulogy delivered by Willian E.B. DuBois at a
      memorial service following Florence Kelley's death in
      1932, with introductory remarks by Aptheker, who re-
      ferred to Kelley as "one of the outstanding white pio-
      neers of the early twentieth century in the battle
      against Jim Crowism." In his tribute to her, DuBois
      proclaimed that "save for Jane Addams there is not an-
      other social worker in the United States who has had
      either her insight or her daring, so far as the American
      Negro is concerned."

115. Athey, Louis Lee. "Florence Kelley and the Quest for
      Negro Equality." <u>Journal of Negro History</u>, Vol. 54, No.
      4 (Oct., 1971), 249-61. Another very good article on
      Florence Kelley's commitment to, and quest for, Negro
      equality. According to Athey, who here recounts and
      evaluates her activities on behalf of Negro equality,
      Florence Kelley helped to create the tradition of pro-
      test against racial discrimination and segregation which
      was to effect a revolt of major proportions in American
      society in the mid-twentieth century—the civil rights

movement.

116.   Bartlett, Harriet M. "Ida M. Cannon: Pioneer in Med-
       ical Social Work." Social Service Review, Vol. 49, No.
       2 (June, 1975), 208-29. A glowing tribute to Ida
       Cannon, an early social work leader, who made a major
       contribution to the building of the profession—its or-
       ganization, its educational base, and its practice, es-
       pecially in hospital settings.

117.   Beers, Clifford. A Mind That Found Itself: An
       Autobiography. New York: Longmans, Green, 1909.
       Beer's famous autobiography which provides a graphic de-
       scription of his mental collapse, the inhumane treatment
       to which he was subjected (in both private and public
       institutions), his recovery, and his determination to
       radically change the system of caring for the mentally
       ill. The work stimulated great interest in the subject,
       and Beers, of course, carried out his plans.

118.   Blumberg, Dorothy M. Florence Kelley: The Making of a
       Social Pioneer. New York: Kelley, 1967. A useful ac-
       count of the social, intellectual, and personal factors
       that shaped Florence Kelley's thought and action early
       in her career, especially the years 1884-1894, when she
       encountered socialism (and friendship with Friedrich
       Engels) and served as Illinois factory inspector and
       Hull-House resident.

119.   Brinkley, Alan. Voices of Protest: Huey Long, Father
       Coughlin, and the Great Depression. New York: Knopf,
       1982. In this important study of radical protest during
       the Great Depression, Brinkley focuses on the
       anti-centrist ideology that appealed to those who found
       their hard-won status in a middle class world of modest
       accomplishments threatened by Roosevelt's reformist pro-
       grams and ideals. Studying Long and Coughlin thus en-
       ables Brinkley to delve into the objectives and al-
       ternatives to FDR's social welfare agenda.

120.   Broderick, Francis L. Right Reverend New Dealer: John
       A. Ryan. New York: Macmillan, 1963. A full-length
       biography of the "political priest" who became the fore-
       most Catholic spokesperson for social justice.
       Broderick not only recounts Ryan's accomplishments but
       his failures and weaknesses as well. An admirable work
       that clearly shows Ryan's influence on the great social
       changes of the 1930s.

121.   Cannon, Ida. On the Social Frontier of Medicine:
       Pioneering in Medical Social Service. Cambridge,
       Mass.: Harvard University Press, 1952. In 1905 Richard
       C. Cabot, a young, enthusiastic, welfare-minded phy-
       sician, initiated the medical social service department

at the Massachusetts General Hospital. Ida Cannon
joined him in 1906 and remained at the hospital in
charge of that division for the next forty years. The
story of those four decades forms the basis of this interesting work.

122.   Cassedy, James H. Charles V. Chapin and the Public
        Health Movement. Cambridge, Mass.: Harvard University
        Press, 1962. An excellent, well written and meti-
        culously researched biography of Dr. Charles V. Chapin
        which is both the story of this distinguished leader's
        life and a history of the public health movement in
        America as well, especially the fight for water puri-
        fication, better garbage disposal, the prevention of
        tuberculosis and other communicable diseases, the col-
        lection of vital statistics, the reduction of infant
        mortality, and the introduction of school health work,
        all of which Chapin pioneered in.

123.   Chambers, Clarke A. Paul U. Kellogg and The Survey.
        Minneapolis: University of Minnesota Press, 1972. A
        joint biography of an editor, Paul U. Kellogg, and the
        journal he edited, The Survey, which provides all sorts
        of insights into social work, social welfare policy, and
        political and social reform in the United States during
        the first half of the twentieth century--a very im-
        portant chapter in the history of American social de-
        velopment.

124.   Charles, Searle F. Minister of Relief, Harry Hopkins
        and the Depression. Syracuse: Syracuse University
        Press, 1963. A sympathetic study of Harry Hopkins' re-
        lief work in the 1930s with emphasis on the three most
        important   federal   relief   agencies--the   Federal
        Emeregency Relief Administration, the Civil Works Ad-
        ministration   and   the   Works   Progress/Projects   Ad-
        ministration. While it is a fairly good summary of fed-
        eral relief efforts during the Depression decades, the
        work supplies surprisingly little insight into Hopkins's
        personality   or   contributons   in   the   area   of   ad-
        ministration.

125.   Clark, Clifford. "Religious Beliefs and Social Reforms
        in the Gilded Age: The Case of Henry Whitney Bellows."
        New England Quarterly, Vol. 43, No. 1 (March, 1970),
        59-78. Bellows' religious beliefs interacted with such
        other interests as those of family, occupation, and
        class to shape his attitudes toward social reform, es-
        pecially his work with the U.S. Sanitary Commission
        during the Civil War and civil service reform after it.
        His long and varied career from the 1840s to the 1880s
        illustrates the tensions which sometimes existed between
        the religious beliefs and the social aspirations of
        genteel reformers, according to Clark.

126.   Cooper, Robert I. "William Rhinelander Stewart and the Expansion of Public Welfare Services in New York State, 1882-1929." Unpublished Ph.D. Diss., City University of New York, 1969. A study of William Rhinelander Stewart, a commissioner and longtime president of the New York State Board of Charities, who, motivated by compassion and civic duty, in many ways was an important impetus to the expansion of the Empire State's public welfare responsibilities and services--and helped create the foundation for today's concern for the underpriviliged.

127.   Cornelius, Sandra Sidford. "Edward Thomas Devine, 1867-1948: A Pivotal Figure in the Transition from Practical Philanthropy to Social Work." Unpublished Ph.D. Diss., Bryn Mawr College, 1976. As its title indicates, this thesis recounts the major views and activities of the founder of Charities and a president of the National Conference of Charities and Correction.

128.   Cross, Robert D. "The Philanthropic Contributions of Louisa Lee Schuyler." Social Service Review, Vol. 35, No. 3 (Sept., 1961), 290-301. While, for the most part, it was middle class women who played important roles in late nineteenth and early twentieth century American social welfare, occasionally an upper class one did, too; one such woman was Louisa Lee Schuyler, a real aristocrat. No mere Lady Bountiful, however, her life work merged a vicarious awareness of suffering, initiative from the upper class, and the desire for rational investigation that would eventuate in many social reforms.

129.   Curti, Merle. "Jane Addams on Human Nature." Journal of the History of Ideas, Vol. 22, No. 2 (April-June, 1966), 240-53. A successful effort to place Jane Addams within the context of American intellectual history. Curti does not attempt to elevate Addams into a major figure in the nation's intellectual life, but he argues that, while justice has been done her heart and her social vision, it has not been done her mind, which illuminated in sensitive and often keen ways major movements of thought in her time.

130.   Dain, Norman. Clifford Beers: Advocate for the Insane. Pittsburgh: University of Pittsburgh Press, 1980. This excellent, carefully researched and long needed work is both a biography of Clifford Beers and a history of the mental health movement he founded. Drawing on Beers's case records and unpublished manuscripts, the author reconstructed in a believable way the complex man who emerged from psychosis and institutionalization to found the National Committee for Mental Hygiene, which spearheaded a drive for the prevention of mental illness as well as better treatment of those already

victimized by it.

131. Davis, Allen F. <u>American Heroine: The Life and Legend of Jane Addams</u>.. New York: Oxford University Press, 1973. A very important, detailed, and well researched work that accomplishes precisely what it was designed to do--systematically and persuasively separate the real Jane Addams from the mythical Jane Addams. While Davis tarnishes the myth of "St. Jane," it nevertheless still is a favorable account of Jane Addams and her public and private lives, one that tells the reader a great deal about American society from 1889 to 1935 as well.

132. Devine, Edward T. <u>When Social Work Was Young</u>. New York: Macmillan, 1939. Personal recollections of Devine's early years as a charity/social worker. Actually, the work begins with Devine's early life as background for the story of his career in charity and social work during the late nineteenth and early twentieth century. Except for a final summarizing chapter, the work concludes with an account of relief efforts after the San Francisco fire.

133. Duffus, Robert. <u>Lillian Wald, Neighbor and Crusader</u>. New York: Macmillan, 1938. A very admiring account of Lillian Wald and her dedication to the poor, one which outlines the interaction of her settlement house to the social conditions surrounding it.

134. Farrell, John C. <u>Beloved Lady: A History of Jane Addams' Ideas on Reform and Peace</u>. Baltimore: Johns Hopkins University Press, 1967. A study of Jane Addams' intellectual development, especially her ideas on settlement house work, educaton, urban recreation, and war and peace. Farrell paints Addams as an intelligent, widely read woman who had a gift for molding and reworking the ideas of others; her real genius lay in translating ideas into action.

135. Goldmark, Josephine. <u>Impatient Crusader: Florence Kelley's Life Story</u>. Urbana, Ill.: University of Illinois Press, 1953. An adulatory biography of Florence Kelley by one of her fellow workers which emphasizes her early crusades for child labor laws, minimum wage and maximum hours statutes, and industrial health control--and completely glosses over the controversy or sore spots that Kelley frequently provoked. Still, a useful work about a woman of indefatigable energy and extraordinary accomplishments.

136. Hall, Helen. <u>Unfinished Business; in Neighborhood and Nation</u>. New York: Macmillan, 1971. This is the story of the author's thirty-four years--from the midst of the Depression until her retirement in 1967--at the Henry

Street Settlement House, an absorbing, and revealing,
picture of life among the poor.

137.   Hamilton, Alice. Exploring the Dangerous Trades.
Boston: Little, Brown, 1943. An exciting autobiography
of a pioneer investigator of occupational diseases in
industry whose work in social service led her from Hull
House to the Health Committee of the League of Nations.
Some of her descriptions of men and women at work, however, especially in the smelting and enamelling trades
in Pittsburgh and elsewhere, are rather grim.

138.   Harmon, Sandar D. "Florence Kelley in Illinois."
Journal of the Illinois State Historical Society, Vol.
74, No. 3 (Autumn, 1981), 163-78. An appreciative account of Florence Kelley's Illinois years as a Hull H
House resident and the state's first factory inspector
where she not only left an impressive record to the
state but developed and honed various skills (in lobbying, investigating, meeting the public, establishing a
national reputation, etc.) that stood her in good stead
as she expanded the scope of her work as general secretary of the National Consumers' League after 1899.

139.   Hijiya, James A. "Four Ways of Looking at a Philan-
thropist: A Study of Robert Weeks de Forest."
Proceedings of the American Philosophical Society, Vol.
124, No. 6 (1980), 404-18. An examination of Robert W.
deForest, a man who took part in many social organizations and movements and who, according to the author,
"may represent as well as anybody the time and place in
which he lived." Actually, the author studied deForest
in order to throw light on a number of important subjects, including the revolt against formalism, the progressives and the slums, the triumph of conservatism,
the search for order, philanthropy, and the evolution of
taste in America.

140.   Huthmacher, J. Joseph. Senator Robert F. Wagner and the
Rise of Urban Liberalism. New York: Atheneum, 1968.
In this major biography of one of America's most distinguished social-welfare reformers, Huthmacher elucidates
the prototypical response of twentieth-century liberals
to problems of social security, unemployment and poverty
from the Progressive period through Truman's first administration.

141.   Johnson, Alexander. Adventures in Social Welfare:
Being Reminiscences of Things, Thoughts and Folks During
Forty Years of Social Work. Fort Wayne: Fort Wayne
Publishing Co., 1923. A useful autobiography that
deals with the many facets of Johnson's career--his work
in organized charity (in Cincinnati and Chicago), his
work as a member of the Indiana State Board of

Charities, his work as long-time Secretary of the
National Conference of Charities and Correction, his
work in early social work education (at the New York
School of Philanthropy), and his work for the American
Red Cross during World War I.

142.   Kesselman, Steven. The Modernization of American
Reform: Structures and Perceptions. New York:
Garland, 1979. On the basis of his case study of six
reform intellectuals--Henry George and Edward Bellamy,
Jane Addams and Herbert Croly, and Rexford Tugwell and
Thurman Arnold--Kessleman traces changing responses to
the problems associated with industrialization from the
Gilded Age through the New Deal. The book highlights
the polarity between ideal orders and "real" conditions
that confronted these members and the intellectual
milieu in which they formed their ideas.

143.   Kurzman, Paul. Harry Hopkins and the New Deal. Fair
Lawn, N.J.: R.E. Burdick, 1974. Like Charles' work,
this too, is no full-length biography; rather it is a
study of Hopkins' role in the New Deal's relief efforts
written by someone interested primarily in public administration, from the vantage point of the early
1970s. In the author's words, it is an attempt to capture the spirit and achievements of Harry Hopkins; "in
an era where the Watergate scandal shadows the performance of an Administration, it may well be worthwhile
to review, and remember an innovator in government who
resolutely set the highest standards of probity for himself and all who worked with and for him." In any
event, since the author primarily is interested in public administration and Hopkins influence on the decision
making process of the decade, it emphasizes the very
things lacking in the Charles study.

144.   Lane, James B. "Jacob A. Riis and Scientific Philanthropy During the Progressive Era." Social Service
Review, Vol. 47, No. 1 (March, 1973), 32-48. This most
interesting and revealing article is based on study of
the interrelationship and methodological conflict between urban reform and scientific philanthropy during
the Progressive era, as exemplified by Jacob Riis and
the New York Charity Organization Society. The theories
and tactics of urban reconstruction used by Riis are
contrasted favorably with those or organized charity
spokesperson Josephine Shaw Lowell and housing tech-
nician Lawrence Veiller. The author concludes by pointing out that although the methods of the latter two won
out, and professionalism triumphed, they did not work
and Riis' emphasis on neighborhood organization and the
democratization of urban planning are now being revived.

145. Levine, Daniel. Jane Addams and the Liberal Tradition.
      Madison, Wis.: The State Historical Society, 1971. The
      thesis of this book is that Jane Addams was an important
      moving force in the transition of America from a lais-
      sez-faire to a general welfare state. Perhaps more than
      anyone else, Levine contends, she convinced Americans
      that the welfare ideology and state were both right and
      practical. She was not an original thinker, rather she
      was a retailer of reform, a publicist and a persuader.
      She, almost singlehandedly, according to the author,
      convinced Americans (both inside and outside of govern-
      ment) of the seriousness of the nation's social problems
      and the need for change—and then pointed the direction
      those changes should take. As an aside, implicit in
      this work, then, is the notion that the origins of the
      welfare state are not in the New Deal but rather in the
      progressive years.

146. Lewis Verl S. "Stephen Humphreys Gurteen and the Ameri-
      can Origins of Charity Organization." Social Service
      Review, Vol. 40, No. 2 (June, 1966), 190-201. An at-
      tempt to clarify the role of Gurteen in the estab-
      lishment of the charity organization movement, and to
      rectify the mistaken notion that he began his clerical
      career in England, where he first came into contact with
      organized charity. According to Lewis, Gurteen's cleri-
      cal career began and ended in America, and his as-
      sociation with the London Charity Organization Society
      was limited to visits made there after he had estab-
      lished himself in Buffalo, New York.

147. Patterson, James T. "Mary Dewson and the American Mini-
      mum Wage Movement." Labor History, Vol. 5, No. 2
      (Spring, 1964), 134-52. Mary Dewson, whose career in
      social work vaulted her into the top echelons of New
      Deal women politicians, was a representative female re-
      former. Her role in the quest for minimum wages for
      women is used here by the author as a case study for un-
      derstanding the minimum wage movement from its birth in
      the Progressive era, through its trials in the 1920s, to
      its success in the New Deal period—and the improtant
      link as well between the social justice and the women's
      rights movements.

148. Rader, Frank J. "Harry Hopkins, the Ambitious Cru-
      sader." Annals of Iowa, Vol. 44, (Fall, 1977), 83-102.
      Arguing both that Hopkins has received short shrift from
      American historians and that his chief interpreter,
      Robert Sherwood (Roosevelt and Hopkins, 1951), painted a
      flat, one-dimensional and incorrect portrait of Hopkins
      as a man who "merely exchanged one crusade for another,"
      Rader seeks to rectify both those shortcomings. In the
      end, he concludes that Hopkins was a "complex,
      multi-layered individual" who was no lightweight func-

tionary, "but rather an ambitious and talented public servant who saw great opportunities in public service to help mankind and advance his own career."

149. Reynolds, Bertha C. An Uncharted Journey: Fifty Years of Growth in Social Work. New York: Citadel Press, 1963. Both an autobiography of an important social worker who was a controversial figure in the profession (primarily because of her continuing interest in social reform as opposed to individual treatment) and a history of social work and social welfare during the period from 1940 to 1954.

150. Schlabach, Theron F. Edwin E. Witte: Cautious Reformer. Madison, Wis.: State Historical Society, 1969. An excellnt account of the "cautious reformer" and "father of social security" in America, which, in effect, is a history of the welfare state. Witte's varied career was inseparable from many of the major developments in social welfare from the progressive period through the New Deal. A very helpful book, especially for those interested in the history of social insurance and social security in America.

151. Schwartz, Harold. Samuel Gridley Howe: Social Reformer, 1801-1878. Cambridge, Mass.: Harvard University Press, 1956. A good, well-written biography of the many-faceted reformer driven by a deep compassion for the unfortunate and afflicted, especially the deaf an dumb and the blind, whose early treatment is especially well covered in this useful work.

152. Scott, Anne F. "Jane Addams and the City." Virginia Quarterly Review, Vol. 43, No. 1 (Winter, 1967), 53-60. Jane Addams was an exceptionally perceptive observer and analyst of urban life--and its problems. In fact, according to Scott, she was the pre-eminent urban interpreter of her time: "the corpus of her writings on the city would provide, even today, a useful introduction to the study of American urban hitory and sociology."

153. Scudder, Vida D. On Journey. New York: Dutton 1937. A charming autobiography of someone who truly lived the Christian life. While much of the work deals with her life as a professor of English literature at Wellesley, there is interesting material on her other activities, and achievements, including her social settlement work.

154. Shapiro, Edward. "Robert A. Woods and the Settlement House Impulse." Social Service Review, Vol. 52, NO. 2 (June, 1978), 215-26. A convincing article on Robert A. Woods and the founding of South End House, Boston's first social settlement, established in 1891. According

to Shapiro, the primary goal of the settlement house's founders, all of whom shared nostalgic feelings for the older small New England town, was to restore communal harmony to a community plagued with diversity and conflict. Thus, it was a conservative institution.

155.   Shea, Mary M. "Patrick Cardinal Hayes and the Catholic Charities in New York City." Unpublished Ph.D. Diss., New York University, 1966. As the title implies, this is a study of Hayes's endeavors in the area of welfare, to which he was deeply committed. Known as the "Cardinal of Charity," throughout his career Hayes worked to extend existing Catholic charitable agencies and organizations, create new ones as needed, coordinate their operation, and cooperate with public agencies to meet pressing problems, especially during the Great Depression. At the time of his death in 1938 his Archdiocese was hailed as a model in the organization and provision of Catholic charitable services.

156.   Simkhovitch, Mary K. Neighborhood: My Story of Greenwich House. New York: Norton, 1938. The reminiscences of one of the founders of Greenwich House which not only provides a history of that institution but throws light on the whole development of the settlement idea. A work that takes its place alongside Jane Addams' Twenty Years at Hull-House and Lillian Wald's House on Henry Street.

157.   Stewart, William Rhinelander, ed. The Philanthropic Work of Josephine Shaw Lowell. New York: Macmillan, 1911. A compilation of many of Josephine Shaw Lowell's writings, including her Civil War diary, letters, and speeches, which provide good insight into her ideas and activities.

158.   Szasz, Ferenc M. and Ralph F. Bogardus. "The Camera and the American Social Conscience: The Documentary Photography of Jacob A. Riis." New York History, Vol. 55, No. 14 (Oct., 1974), 409-36. Through his books, articles, and especially his travelling lantern slide shows, Jacob Riis added the camera to the tools of social reform. He was according to the authors, the first, and perhaps the foremost, of America's documentary photographers. From 1890 onward, thanks in large part to him, the camera would be an essential piece of equipment for those who would remake society in the name of a higher good.

159.   Taylor, Eleanor K. "The Edith Abbott I Knew." Journal of the Illinois State Historical Society, Vol. 70, No. 3 (Aug., 1977), 178-84. An interesting personal reminiscence of Edith Abbott during her teaching and writing days at the University of Chicago's School of Social

Service Administration, by an admiring former graduate
assistant.

160.   Taylor, Graham. Chicago Commons Through Forty Years.
Chicago: University of Chicago Press, 1936. A vivid
and moving account by a veteran social worker of the
early years of the settlement house he founded and the
people he drew to it. The work also includes a discussion by Taylor's daughter, then the head resident, of
the settlement's work at the time of publication, and an
account by another staff member of its educational efforts.

161.   Taylor, Graham. Pioneering on Social Frontiers.
Chicago: University of Chicago Press, 1930. After
training as a clergyman, Graham Taylor concluded that
religion and social activism were inseparable; as a result, he used his position as head of the Chicago Theological Seminary to train generations of students in the
principles of the social gospel. He also founded
Chicago Commons, one of the nation's most well known
settlement houses. In this autobiographical account, he
details his long involvement with social welfare.

162.   Taylor, Lea D. "The Social Settlement and Civic Respon-
sibility--The Life Work of Mary McDowell and Graham
Taylor." Social Service Review, Vol. 28, No. 12 (March,
1954), 31-40. In an avowed effort to revive the settlement idea at a time when it was not very popular, the
author discusses the thought and outreach activities of
two of Chicago's more well known and highly regarded
pioneer settlement house figures--Mary McDowell and
Graham Taylor.

163.   Taylor, Lloyd C. "Josephine Shaw Lowell and American
Philanthropy." New York History, Vol. 44, No. 4 (Oct.,
1963), 336-64. A rather favorable, uncritical survey of
Josephine Shaw Lowell's many social welfare acti-
vities--as a member of the New York State Board of
Charities, as head of the New York Charity Organization
Society, and in a number of other capacities as well.
The author concludes that "her legacy of ideas have con-
tinued to stimulate the growth of American humani-
tarianism."

164.   Trattner, Walter I. Homer Folks: Pioneer in Social
Welfare. New York: Columbia University Press, 1968. A
study of many aspects of late nineteenth and twentieth
century social welfare history--child welfare, public
welfare, public and mental health, etc.--as seen through
the life and career of Homer Folks, "whose significance
and record of achievements spanning half a century" according to the author, "are unmatched in the annals of
American humanitarianism."

165. Wade, Louise C. Graham Taylor: Pioneer for Social
      Justice. Chicago: University of Chicago Press, 1964.
      An excellent biography of the "conscience of Chicago,"
      as Graham Taylor was called. The complete story of his
      many activities for social justice--and a history of
      early twentieth century Chicago as well.

166. Wald, Lillian D. The House on Henry Street. New York:
      Holt, 1915. Like Jane Addams' Twenty Years at
      Hull-House, this, too, is a record of twenty years of
      settlement activity. More than a book of reminiscences
      or human interest stories, it provides a good picture of
      the breadth of settlement work and offers discussions of
      many of the social problems of the day.

167. Wald, Lillian D. Windows on Henry Street. Boston:
      Little, Brown, 1934. Largely a continuation of the au-
      thor's earlier work, The House on Henry Street, one
      which records twenty more years of social progress in a
      changing Lower East Side of New York City.

168. Williams, Howell V. "Benjamin Franklin and the Poor
      Laws." Social Service Review, Vol. 18, No. 1 (March,
      1944), 77-91. Thanks, in part, to his laissez-faire
      convictions and his belief that the fear of want was
      necessary to get people to work, as well as his con-
      viction that all who wanted to do so could prosper in
      America, Franklin opposed public poor relief and ad-
      vocated repeal of the poor laws.

169. Wilson, Howard E. Mary McDowell: Neighbor. Chicago:
      University of Chicago Press, 1928. A tribute to rather
      than a critical examination of Mary McDowell's remark-
      ably useful life. Wilson recounts the story of her in-
      fluence in securing protection for Chicago packing-house
      employees, in combating racial discrimination and
      hostility, in providing for better garbage removal, and
      in bringing about many other reforms.

170. Winslow, C. E. A. The Life of Hermann M. Biggs.
      Philadelphia: Lea and Febiger, 1929. As excellent bio-
      graphy of a man who, with a handful of others, did more
      than anyone else between the seventeenth and twentieth
      centuries to prevent the spread of disease and advance
      public health. Biggs' accomplishments, primarily in the
      development of modern sanitation and the administrative
      control of preventable disease, are placed in historical
      perspective. No better medical biography and history of
      public health has been written.

171. Woods, Eleanor. Robert A. Woods: Champion of
      Democracy. Boston: Houghton Mifflin, 1929. A bio-
      graphy, or rather a memorial, to the founder and di-

rector of Boston's South End House, a man who contributed a great deal to human welfare in Massachusetts,
and elsewhere. The story is told largely in Woods own
words--with extracts from his correspondence, books,
reports, addresses, etc.--supplemented by the memories
of his wife and co-workers.

1.4. DOCUMENTARIES

172.   Abbott, Edith, ed. Public Assistance. Chicago: University of Chicago Press, 1940. A compilation of documents
on public relief divided into the following sections,
each of which is preceded by an excellent interpretive
essay: Principles of Public Responsibility, The Old
Poor Law in the Twentieth Century, Local Responsibility
and Medical Care, State Grants-in-Aid, and Federal Aid
and Emergency Relief. An important source of primary
materials.

173.   Abbott, Edith. "Social Insurance and/or Social
Security." Social Service Review, Vol. 8. No. 3 (Sept.,
1934), 537-40. A description of the differences and
similarities between social insurance and social
security and a plea for a system of coverage for the
hazards of life that covers all in need, not just those
who can afford to contribute to it, whatever it is
called.

174.   Abbott, Grace, ed. From Relief to Social Security.
Chicago: University of Chicago Press, 1941. A collection of documents about the history of public welfare
and some theoretical problems involved in the transition
from relief to social security--which makes it of interest to students of social problems as well as to those specializing in public welfare administration.

175.   Abbott, Grace. "Recent Trends in Mothers' Aid." Social
Service Review, Vol. 8, No. 12 (June, 1934), 191-220. A
history of mothers' aid legislation and what it was designed to do (end the separation of mothers and children
on the grounds of poverty alone) which, in effect, was a
plea for federal assistance to the state pro-
grams--something, of course, that would occur a year
later with passage of the Social Security Act. Federal
funds, Abbott wrote, among other things, would improve
standards in the more backward states and tend to equal-
ize costs of the programs.

176.   Alinsky, Saul. Reveille for Radicals. New York:
Random House, 1946. A classic that described the work
and beliefs of the notorious community organizer who
stressed conflict and giving the poor the power to speak
for themselves. Actually, it is both a recounting of
Alinsky's early organizational experiences and a state-

ment of his faith in the ability to implement the nation's democratic ideals--through the creation of "people's organizations."

177.   Armstrong, Barbara N.   Insuring the Essentials   New York: Macmillan, 1932. A very useful legal and economic analysis of minimum wage legislation and a careful and clearly presented description of the steps taken by various governments around the world, to insure their citizens against the hazards of an industrial society, including workmen's compensation, health insurance, old age and invalidity insurance, survivors insurance, and unemployment insurance. An objective account in which the author does not really come out in favor of any specific program(s) for the United States.

178.   Brown, Esther. Social Work as a Profession. New York: Russell Sage Foundation, 1935. One of the best and most influential statements on the nature and importance of social work as a profession, one that influenced a generation of people to choose social work as a career.

179.   Brown, Josephine C. Public Relief, 1929-1939. New York: Holt, 1940. Still the most comprehensive and fully documented (but partisan) book on public relief during the Great Depression, one which includes a wealth of information on all phases of the battle between proponents of private charity vs. those of public assistance, between those who favored local and then state as opposed to federal aid, between those who supported work rather than home relief, etc. A vast storehouse of data that was carefully compiled and analyzed, both from a theoretical and a practical perspective, by a strong supporter of federal aid.

180.   Bruno, Frank J. Trends in Social Work, 1874-1956: A History Based on the Proceedings of the National Conference of Social Work. New York: Columbia University Press, 1957. The authorized history of the National Conference, based entirely on its proceedings. Nevertheless, it is a good general survey of how social workers gradually accumulated knowledge and experience, provided for the education of personnel, established professional standards of performance, developed scientific methods of operation, responded to growing needs in the community, and emerged as an important social force in society.

181.   Burns, Eveline M. The American Social Security System. Boston: Houghton Mifflin, 1949. A thorough, thoughtful, and readable work from someone who has excellent command of the material which depicts the main characteristics of the various social security programs then in operation in America, the differences among them, and

their relationships to each other.

182.   Byington, Margaret. Homestead: The Households of a
Mill Town. University of Pittsburgh: The University
Center for International Studies, 1974. This reprint of
one of the original volumes of the Pittsburgh Survey,
underwritten by the Russell Sage Foundation (in 1910),
not only describes the welfare network and priorities
established by immigrant families after the Homestead
Steel Strike of 1892, but also reveals the assumptions
and methods of "Progressive" experts.

183.   Carroll, Douglas G. and Blanche D. Coll. "The Baltimore
Almshouse: An Early History." Maryland Historical
Magazine, Vol. 66, No. 2 (Summer, 1971), 135-52. A history of the Baltimore Almshouse, 1768-1819, written by
Thomas W. Griffith (1767-1838), published for the first
time. The manuscript is largely a chronicle of legislation, administrative arrangements, and other factual
data, but it also contains a considerable amount of
material about dependency and its causes and reveals attitudes that reflect the general thinking of the
Baltimore community at that time.

184.   Colcord, Joanna and Ruth Mann, eds. The Long View:
Papers and Addresses by Mary E. Richmond. New York:
Russell Sage Foundation, 1930. A selection from the
more important papers written by Mary Richmond, many of
them previously unpublished. Read in their entirety,
the papers provide a record of her developing philosophy
of social work.

185.   Davies, Stanley P. Social Control of the Mentally
Deficient. New York: Crowell, 1930. A classic in the
field, which begins with a history of efforts made to
study the problem of mental deficiency, or feeble-
mindedness, as it was called, and emphasizes the value
of the social institution, or training colony, as a so-
cializing force.

186.   Deutsch, Albert. The Mentally Ill in America. New
York: Doubleday, 1937. A social history of the care
and treatment of the mentally ill in America from
colonial times to the mid-1930s--an excellent work con-
sidering it was the first of its kind.

187.   Devine, Edward T. The Spirit of Social Work. New
York: Macmillan, 1911. A collection of addresses by
one of the leading figures in American social welfare
history. In this volume can be found his views on a
variety of social problems facing the American people at
the time, including the changing nature of social work
as it strove for professional recognition.

188.   Epstein, Abraham. Insecurity: A Challenge to America:
        A Study of Social Insurance in th United States and
        Abroad. New York: Smith and Haas, 1933. A com-
        prehensive volume on social insurance from a persistent
        and untiring advocate of such measures. Not only does
        Epstein discuss the great risks which modern workers
        face, and thus the need for social insurance, but he
        also analyzes the experiences of other countries and
        goes on to present his own plan in light of those ex-
        periences. Generally considered the best treatise on the
        subject at that time.

189.   Hopkins, Harry L. Spending to Save. New York: Norton,
        1936. Although probably written by one of his staff
        members, this work--the only book to bear his name--can
        be taken as an accurate portrayal of Harry Hopkins' pub-
        lic views on the welfare state--the mature ideas of a
        man who literally put the federal government into the
        business of relief giving.

190.   Hull-House Residents. Hull-House Maps and Papers. New
        York: Crowell, 1895. A book of essays by Hull House
        residents (patterned after Charles Booth's minute
        studies of the London poor) that describe the economic,
        social, residential, and cultural problems of the poor,
        overcrowded neighborhoods of Chicago's near west side.
        The contributors include such important social reformers
        as Florence Kelley, Julia Lathrop, Ellen Gates Starr,
        Charles Zueblin as well as Jane Addams and others. The
        work is accompanied by large detailed maps relating eth-
        nic groups to wage information on a house by house basis.

191.   Hunter, Robert. Poverty: Social Conscience in the
        Progressive Era. New York: Macmillan, 1904. In this
        influential study of the American urban poor which
        caused something of a sensation when it was published in
        1904, Hunter defined poverty in a new way--as de-
        privation relative to a standard of living that was
        necessary for industrial eficiency--and provided stati-
        stics that indicated that some ten million Americans
        (out of a population of about eighty million) lived
        below that standard. He also described the "poverty
        syndrome," the relationship between economic de-
        privation, physical debility, and mental difficulties,
        and called for preventive reforms that would help those
        already deprived from falling further into dependency. A
        true classic in the field.

192.   Jernegan, Marcus W. Laboring and Dependent Classes in
        Colonial America, 1607-1783. Chicago: University of
        Chicago Press, 1931. A remarkable attempt to study the
        lives of the neglected long before the advent of the
        so-called new social history: it views history from the
        bottom up, in other words. As far as the poor are   con-

cerned, Jernegan stresses application of the Elizabethan
Poor Law principles in the colonies and reasonably good
treatment of those in need.

193.   Jorns, Auguste. The Quakers as Pioneers in Social
Work. New York: Macmillan, 1931. Originally published
in German in 1912, this work portrays a picture of
Quakers as great disinterested humanitarians, promoters
of social welfare and spiritual happiness--a far different picture than that portrayed in the James work.

194.   Kelley, Florence. Some Ethical Gains Through
Legislation. New York: Macmillan, 1905. A precis of
legislative and judicial decisions concerning the rights
of children, women, laborers, and consumers, all clearly
presented and discussed--another one of the classics to
come out of this period.

195.   Kelso, Robert W. Poverty, New York: Longmans, Green,
1929. An important work not only because it defines
poverty, estimates its extent in 1929, and discusses the
causes and suggested remedies of the problem, but because it was a wholesome antidote to the preoccupation
with psychiatric factors among social workers at the
time.

196.   Kelso, Robert. W. "The Transition from Charities and
Correction to Public Welfare." Annals of the American
Academy of Political and Social Science. Vol. 105 (Jan.,
1923), 21-25. An analysis of the creation of the State
Boards of Charities and their evolution into Departments
of Public Welfare. Useful for an understanding of the
state of public welfare in the mid-1920s.

197.   Lowell, Josephine Shaw. Public Relief and Private
Charity. New York: Putnam's, 1894. A small book from
the pen of the spokesperson of the organized charity
movement in America "in which the principles underlying
our science of the modern methods of charity can be
found clearly stated." In her opinion, of course,
"dealing with the poor and degraded has become a
science."

198.   Lynd, Robert S. and Helen Merrell Lynd. Middletown: A
Study in Modern American Culture. New York: Harcourt,
Brace & World, 1956. A pioneering study of Muncie,
Indiana, in the 1920s, originally published in 1929,
which sheds valuable insights on community life in "modern" America. part 6--"Engaging in Community Activities"--deals at length with the role of local government promoting welfare. Readers should also read
Middletown in Transition (1937), especially chapter 4,
which deals with the initial impact of the Depression on
prevailing attitudes an activities in this area.

199.   McKinley, Charles and Robert Frase. Launching Social
        Security. Madison, Wis.: University of Wisconsin
        Press, 1970. Although published in 1970, this work was
        completed in 1941. It is an account of the problems,
        and solutions to those problems, that grew out of the
        day-to-day operating of the Social Security Adminis-
        tration, 1935-1937. Its chief contributions are the in-
        sights it offers into the personalities, policies, and
        politics that were part of launching such an agency.

200.   Meriam, Lewis. Relief and Social Security. Washington,
        D. C.: The Brookings Institution, 1946. The most
        thorough study conducted to that date of the entire is-
        sue of public relief and old age and unemployoment in-
        surance, including the questions of financing and ad-
        ministering those programs, from a critic of the prin-
        ciples of social security and the system itself .

201.   Nathan, Maud. The Story of an Epoch Making Movement.
        Garden City, N.Y.: Doubleday, 1926. An intimate but
        business-like history of the origin, development, and
        success of the National Consumers' League and its cam-
        paign to improve the working conditions of women and
        children, especially in department stores.

202.   Pacey, Lorene M., ed. Readings in the Development of
        Settlement Work. New York: Association Press, 1950. A
        collection of forty papers written by different in-
        dividuals over a forty year period which, taken to-
        gether, present a clear picture of the principles and
        the development of social settlement work. The work,
        which is organized chronologically, contains some of the
        most vivid writings of settlement leaders, including
        Jane Addams, Vida Scudder, Mary McDowell, Graham Taylor,
        and others.

203.   President's Committee on Recent Social Trends. Recent
        Social Trends, 2 Vols. New York: McGraw-Hill Book Com-
        pany, 1933. This is one of the earliest and most am-
        bitious attempts by the federal government to marshall
        social science expertise in diagnosing and dealing with
        the challenges confronting "modern" America. Its chap-
        ters on the family, welfare and health offer a marvelous
        perspective on "expert" assumptions in the 1930s.

204.   Ravenel, Mazyck, ed. A Half-Century of Public Health.
        New York: American Public Health Association, 1921. A
        collection of essays on the history of public health,
        broadly defined, from 1871-1921, written by leading au-
        thorities on the subject(s). An indispensable source on
        the subject--and an excellent guide to the state of the
        field at the time.

205. Richmond, Mary E. <u>Friendly Visiting Among the Poor.</u>
      New York: Macmillan, 1909. A well known and widely
      read "handbook" for beginning friendly visitors which
      contains lists of supplementary readings at the end of
      each chapter that serve as useful guides to the liter-
      ature of that day--from the charity organization society
      viewpoint.

206. Richmond, Mary E. <u>Social Diagnosis.</u> New York: Russell
      Sage Foundation, 1917. The first major treatise in book
      form on social casework theory and method--a classic
      which immediately won widespread acclaim and played a
      major role in the professionalization of social work.

207. Riis, Jacob. <u>How the Other Half Lives: Studies Among
      the Tenements of New York.</u> New York: Scribner's,
      1890. One of the most famous and influential works of
      its kind--a vivid (and, at the same time, im-
      pressionistic) series of sketches of what life was like
      in the wretched slums of New York which, more than any-
      thing else, made Americans aware of the human side of
      poverty and the need for tenement house reform.

208. Rubinow, Isasc. <u>The Quest for Security.</u> New York;
      Holt, 1934. A classic and very influential discussion
      of the social problems exacerbated by the Depression,
      including poverty, dependency, unemployment, illness,
      etc., and a rationale for a social insurance program
      which apparently played a major role in creating the en-
      vironment conducive to the expansion of welfare pro-
      grams, including passage of the Social Security Act.

209. Rubinow, Isaac. <u>Social Insurance.</u> New York: Holt,
      1913. Recognized as the standard textbook on the sub-
      ject for more than twenty years, this work, one of the
      first and certainly the most important of its kind, grew
      out of a series of lectures delivered in 1912 at the New
      York School of Philanthropy. It dealt with insurance
      against all the major causes of poverty--accidents, il-
      lness, premature death, old age, and unemployment.

210. Warner, Amos. <u>American Charities.</u> New York: Crowell,
      1894. Published for the first of many times in 1894,
      this work was a landmark, both because of its content
      and its method; it suggested that social and economic
      factors were important causes of poverty and it was the
      first real attempt at an empirical, or "scientific"
      study of the subject.

211. Watson, Frank D. <u>The Charity Organization Movement in
      the United States.</u> New York: Macmillan, 1922. Be-
      ginning with a sketch of its antecedents in Europe, the
      author traces the history of the charity organization

movement in the United States. He discusses both its failures and its successes, indicates the social and economic forces that shaped its growth, and analyzes its spirit.

212. Woods, Robert A., ed. The City Wilderness. Boston: Houghton Mifflin, 1918. A collection of essays on the South End district of Boston, its problems, and proposed remedies for those problems, including improved educational opportunities for children, destruction of wretched tenements, attacks on prostitution, the cooperation and federation of charitable organizations, settlement houses, and churches, etc.

213. Woods, Robert A. The Neighborhood in Nation-Building: The Running Comment of Thirty Years at the South End House. Boston: Houghton Mifflin, 1923. A volume of articles and addresses written and delivered by Woods over a period of thirty years dealing chiefly with the methods and results of settlement house work, especially those at Boston's South End House. Another important source for understanding both the aims and achievements of settlement houses.

214. Woods, Robert A. and Albert J. Kennedy. The Settlement Horizon: A National Estimate. New York: Russell Sage Foundation, 1922. A comprehensive account of the work of settlement houses from their inception in England in the 1880s, through the early 1920s. The authors review the history of the settlement house, evaluate its accomplishments, and survey the social problems not yet attacked by the institution.

1.5. CLASSIC CASE STUDIES

215. Brown, Roy. Public Poor Relief in North Carolina. Chapel Hill: University of North Carolina Press, 1928. One of the first scholarly studies of welfare, which focuses on the relief system in North Carolina from its beginnings to the twentieth century. Brown contends that the public response to poor relief in the South was in many respects comparable to that of the Northern states.

216. Bruce, Isabel C. and Edith Eickhoff. The Michigan Poor Law. Chicago: University of Chicago Press, 1936. One of the classic studies undertaken at the University of Chicago School of Social Service Administration, this work examines the evolution of poor law and welfare programs in Michigan from their inception through the early Depression years.

217. Creech, Margaret. Three Centuries of Poor Law

Administration: A   Study   of   Legislation   in   Rhode
Island.   Chicago: University   of   Chicago   Press,   1936.
This   industrious   and   exhaustive   study   traces   the   development   of   poor   laws   in   Rhode   Island   over   three   centuries,   from   the   time   the   colony   was   founded   to   the
mid-1930s.

218.   Heffner, William C.   History of Poor Relief Legislation
in Pennsylvania, 1682-1913.   Cleona Pa.:   Holzapfel,
1913.   One   of   the   first   studies   of   its   kind   which   among
other   things,   pointed   out   the   need   for   similar   studies
of   other   states.   Cumbersome   in   style   and   descriptive   in
approach,   it   is   most   useful   as   a   "time"   piece.

219.   Kelso, Robert W.   The History of Public Poor Relief in
Massachusetts, 1620-1920.   Boston: Houghton   Mifflin,
1922.   Another   very   good   early   study   based   on   careful
consideration   of   original   sources.   An   important   addition   to   the   literature   in   its   day   which   gave   special
consideration   to   the   evolution   of   the   law   of   settlement
and   the   work   of   the   state   department   of   public   welfare.

220.   Schneider, David M.   The History of Public Welfare in
New York State, 1609-1866.   Chicago: University   of
Chicago   Press,   1938.   Perhaps   the   best   of   the   state
studies   conducted   at   the   University   of   Chicago's   School
of   Social   Service   Administration.   The   work   covers   the
colonial   period   to   the   end   of   the   Civil   War,   with   heavy
emphasis   on   developments   in   New   York   City.

221.   Schneider, David M. and Albert Deutsch.   The History of
Public Welfare in New York State, 1867-1940.   Chicago:
University   of   Chicago   Press,   1941.   A   companion   piece   to
the   earlier   volume   which   starts   where   the   other   one   left
off--with   creation,   in   1867,   of   New   York's   Board   of
State   Commissioners   of   Public   Charities,   and   goes
through   1940.   Taken   together,   they   provide   a   very   good
account   of   public   welfare   in   the   Empire   State,   despite
the   lack   of   much   analysis.

222.   Shaffer,   Alice,   Mary   W.   Keefer,   and   Sophonisba
Breckinridge.   The Indiana Poor Law.   Chicago: University   of   Chicago   Press,   1936.   Another   of   the   monographs
to   come   out   of   the   University   of   Chicago's   School   of   Social   Service   Administration,   this   is   one   of   the   best
studies   of   the   evolution   of   welfare   in   a   midwestern
state   from   its   founding   through   the   mid-1930s.

223.   Wisner, Elizabeth.   Public Welfare Administration if
Louisiana.   Chicago: University   of   Chicago   Press,
1930.   Another   and   one   of   the   better   studies   done   at   the
University   of   Chicago's   School   of   Social   Service   Administration.   This   one   traces   the   evolution   of   welfare
in   this   southern   state   for   a   period   of   125   years,   from

1.6.   TEXTBOOKS, READERS, BOOKS OF DOCUMENTS, BIBLIOGRAPHIES

224.   Breckinridge, Sophonisba, ed. Public Welfare
Administration in the United States. Chicago: University of Chicago Press, 1938. A collection of documents
that went through numerous editors designed to illustrate the problems connected with administring public
welfare. For the most part, the documents are 1) reports of legislative or investigative committees
pointing out the kind and volume of the need for which
provision is to be made, 2) statutes by which the establishment of a public welfare agency is authorized, 3)
reports of the authorities set up under such statutes,
and 4) discussions in national conferences evaluating
those agencies and proposing their further development
or alteration.

225.   Bruel, Frank R. and Steven J. Diner. Compassion and
Responsibility: Readings in the History of Social
Welfare Policy in the United States. Chicago: University of chicago Press, 1980. A collection of articles
on American social welfare history that have appeared in
the Social Service Review over the last half century.
Also useful is a complete list of the articles on social
welfare history that have appeared in the SSR since its
inception in 1927, printed at the end of the book, which
is designed for courses on social welfare policy.

226.   Clarke, Helen I. Social Legislation. Second Edition,
New York: Appleton-Century Crofts, 1957. A pioneer
survey of the law pertaining to the family and the poor
which makes frequent reference to judicial decisions and
places both the legislation and judicial decisions in
historical perspective.

227.   Crampton, Helen M. and Kenneth K. Keiser. Social
Welfare: Institution and Process. New York: Random
House, 1970. A textbook-like work which explores the
history and philosophy of social welfare institutions
and their relationship to other social institutions in
the United States. Emphasis is on the role of social
work in various interrelated social welfare institutions.

228.   Ferman, Louis A., Joyce L. Kornbluth, and Alan Haker,
eds. Poverty in America: A Book of Readings. Ann
Arbor: University of Michigan Press, 1965. A book of
essays from economists, sociologists, social psycho-
gists and psychiatrists, which provides an opportunity
for taking stock of the "facts" on poverty at the time
and evaluating the proposed needs and possibilities for

future research and action in the field.

229. Friedlander, Walter A. Introduction to Social Welfare. Fourth Edition, Englewood Cliffs, N.J.: Prentice-Hall, 1974. This work explains how social welfare concepts and services developed from tradition, experience, and social change. Part I deals with the development of social welfare in England and the United States from the Elizabethan Poor Law of 1601 to World War II.

230. Gilbert, Neil and Harry Spect, eds. The Emergence of Social Welfare and Social Work. Itasca, Illinois: Peacock Publishers, 1976. A book of readings intended to introduce students to important ideas associated with the emergence and growth of social welfare and social work, including the changing nature of responsibility society assumes for the welfare of its citizens, the needs and problems that emanate from existing social arrangements, and the development of professionalism in social work.

231. Lubove, Roy, ed. Poverty and Social Welfare in th United States. New York: Holt, Rinehart and Winston, 1972. A collection of readings on poverty and social welfare in America designed for undergraduate courses on the subject which begins with an excerpt from Robert Hunter's Poverty and contains several selections under each of the following headings: Poverty and Benevolence; The Voluntary Tradition; Social Security in the Twentieth Century, and War on Povertyy.

232. Mandell, Betty Reid, ed. Welfare in America: Controlling the "Dangerous Classes." Englewood Cliffs, N.J.: Prentice-Hall, 1975. A collection of essays by various scholars on such subjects as work and manpower programs, the social services, income, wealth, manpower, birth control, medicine, child welfare, criminal justice, etc., which seek to demonstrate that welfare services are designed not to help the poor but rather to keep them in their place; take together, they provide graphic evidence of the system's inequities.

233. Miles, Arthur P. An Introduction to Public Welfare. Boston: D.C. Heath, 1949. A widely used textbook which attempts to explain the complexities of public welfare administration through a study of the development of the doctrine of public responsibility for the dependent. Part I of the work concentrates on the "historical background" of public assistance in America.

234. Pumphrey, Ralph and Muriel Pumphrey, eds. The Heritage of American Social Work: Readings in Its Philosophical and Institutional Development. New York: Columbia University Prss, 1961. An outdated but still handy book of

documents designed to be of general interest to social
workers and students of social work arranged more or
less chronologically and containing extensive intro-
ductions to each period.

235. Romanyshyn, John M. Social Welfare: Charity to
Justice. New York: Random House, 1971. A general work
written for undergraduate students seeking to understand
the nature and place of social welfare in American society. While the work affirms the significance of humanitarianism in explaining the development of American
social welfare policy, and hence falls within the progressive camp, the author also indicates that such
policy has been "constrained by the structure and values
of capitalism;" thus social control perspectives are incorporated.

236. Rothman, David and Sheila Rothman, eds. On Their Own:
The   Poor   in   Modern   America.   Reading,   Mass.:
Addison-Wesley, 1972. A very useful collection of documents illuminating the history of poverty and the poor
in Modern America which treats the subject, in part at
least, from the point of view of the poor themselves,
both in urban and in rural areas. The work also contains a lengthy introductory essay written by the editors which interprets the history of poverty in America
from the colonial period to the present.

237. Sheppard, Harold L., ed. Poverty and Wealth in
America. Chicago: Quadrangle Books, 1970. A collection of readings on the subject of poverty taken from
the New York Times from the Great Depression through the
1960s. For the most part, they describe the nature of
poverty and discuss proposed short-term solutions to the
problem; there is almost no theory or any sort of conceptual framework.

238. Smith, Russell E. and Dorothy Zietz. American Social
Welfare Institutions. New York: Wiley, 1970. An overview of social welfare and social work history with a
view to the future of both, written by two social reform-minded social work educators who favor various income maintenance programs and urge social workers to become advocates of the poor.

239. Stevens, Robert B., ed. Income Security: Statutory
History of the United States. New York: Chelsea House
Publishers, 1970. This important book of documents
traces federal involvement in providing income security,
particularly between 1935 and 1969. Compiled by a Yale
professor of law, the volume includes excerpts from congressional hearings, legislative drafts, and policy
proposals.

240.   Wildavsky, Aaron. <u>Speaking Truth to Power; The Art and Craft of Policy Analysis</u>. Boston: Little, Brown & Co., 1979. This is a textbook on how policy-makers in the United States go about their business by one of this nation's leading students of policy analysis. As such, it offers students of social welfare history valuable insights into the assumptions, language, and techniques of the field.

241.   Zald, Mayer N., ed. <u>Social Welfare Institutions</u>. New York: Wiley, 1965. A very useful collection of readings that details the development, structure, and operation of welfare organizations and institutions. Written from a sociological perspective, the work communicates basic concepts through a study of their specific applications to welfare. Especially useful are two introductory essays on the history of social welfare by Robert Bremner and Asa Briggs.

2.   PERIOD PIECES.

2.1.   COLONIAL.

242.   Bernhard, Virginia. "Cotton Mather and the Doing of Good: A Puritan Gospel of Wealth." <u>New England Quarterly</u>, Vol. 49, No. 2 (June, 1976), 225-41. An article on Cotton Mather's <u>Bonifacius</u>, or <u>Essays to Do Good</u>, published in 1710 in an unsuccessful effort to throw "oil on the troubled waters of social instability." Mather's pleas to do good, inform against sinners, and contribute to the poor could not preserve conformity and the traditional social order.

243.   Bernhard, Virginia, "Poverty and the Social Order in Seventeenth Century Virginia." <u>Virginia Magazine of History and Biography</u>, Vol 85, No. 2 (April, 1977), 141-55. Seventeenth-century Virginia was not merely a land of profit-mad planters, as is often portrayed, according to Bernhard; rather, it was a community with a social conscience which did not consider poverty a sin and willingly made provision for its destitute members. Indeed, poverty drew together those who relieved it, particularly planters, who thus had the opportunity to play the role of the English country gentleman.

244.   Creech, Margaret. "Some Colonial Case Histories." <u>Social Service Review</u>, Vol. 9, No. 4 (Dec., 1935), 699-730. Although "case records" were unknown to administrators of poor relief in colonial America, it is possible of course, to assemble separate items from town and council meeting reports and thus put together what, in effect, may be considered "social histories." Used in conjunction with the poor law, these socal histories

provide information on the methods used to raise funds
for the poor, the care given to them, and the ways in
which it was administered. These useful, early case
histories were constructed from the records of colonial
Rhode Island.

245. Heyrman, Christine L. "A Model of Christian Charity:
The Rich and the Poor in New England, 1630-1730." Unpublished Ph.D. Diss., Yale University, 1977. An account of shifting social attitudes toward poverty and
the poor between first and third generation New
Englanders. Whereas members of the first generation believed that poverty was an inevitable phenomenon over
which the poor had little control and thus showed compassion toward them, their grandchildren blamed the poor
for their condition and feared and hated them, largely,
according to Heyrman, because of clerical anxiety over
increasing wealth. Clergymen depicted the poor as idle,
immoral and irreligious in an effort to exert some control over the well--to-do by convincing them of the need
for benevolent-reformist acts.

246. Jernegan, Marcus W.   "Poor Relief in Colonial
Virginia." Social Service Review, Vol. 3, No. 1 (March,
1929), 1-18. A favorable account of parish relief
(within the context of the English Poor Law of 1601) in
Colonial Virginia--and the development of county responsibility as a result of the American Revolution and
separation of church and state. Relief clearly was
adequate and given with regard to the feelings of the
recipients, according to Jernegan.

247. Jernegan, Marcus W. "The Development of Poor Relief in
Colonial America." Social Service Review, Vol. 5, NO. 4
(June, 1931), 175-98. An early study of the subject by
one of the real pioneers in the field who concludes
that, in North and South alike, the colonists "accepted
responsibility for support of their poor and there is
little evidence of real suffering for lack of support."

248. Jones, Douglas. "The Strolling Poor: Transiency in
Eighteenth-Century Massachusetts." Journal of Social
History, Vol. 8, No. 3 (Spring, 1975), 18-54. By the
late eighteenth century, a modern society was beginning
to emerge in Massachusetts, and with it, more mo-
bility--and transiency. This essay examines transiency
at this time, seeking to determine its magnitude, the
social and economic characteristics of the transients,
and the legal response to them.

249. Klebaner, Benjamin J.   "Pauper Auctions: The New
England Method of Public Poor Relief." Essex Institute
Historical Collection. Vol. 91 (1955), 195-210. It was
not uncommon in the early nineteenth to auction off to

the lowest bidder the care of paupers not confined to public institutions; by the 1850s, however, the practice had virtually disappeared.

250.   Klein, Randolph S. "Medical Expenses and the Poor in Virginia." Journal of the History of Medicine. Vol. 30, No. 1 (July, 1975), 160-66. An interesting discussion of the effects of illness and medical expenses upon colonists in Virginia which suggests that the question of whether medical treatment is a human right, or a privilege, was unresolved then, just as it is today.

251.   Lee, Charles R. "This Poor People: Seventeenth-Century Massachusetts and the Poor." Historical Journal of Massachusetts. Vol. 9, (Jan., 1981), 41-50. An analysis of the poverty cases that came before town and county officials in Massachusetts between 1630 and 1719 indicates a clear connection between public responses to poverty adnd the factor of age. In general, those who received aid tended to be older persons while those who were not given assistance tended to be younger persons.

252.   Mackey, Howard. "The Operation of the English Old Poor Law in colonial Virginia." Virginia Magazine of History and Biography, Vol 73 (Jan., 1965), 29-40. The author of this article arrives at the unsurprising conclusion that parish poor relief in Virginia was not novel: "Even a partial examination of Virginia vestry records indicates," he wrote, "that parish poor relief was nothing more nor less than the overseas operation of the Old Poor Law. In fact if not in name, the poor law of Elizabeth applied to Virginia throughout almost the entire colonial period."

253.   Mackey, Howard. "Social Welfare in Colonial Virginia: The Importance of th English Old Poor Law." Historical Magazine of the Protestant Episcopal Church. Vol. 36, No. 4 (Dec., 1965), 357-82. Very similar to Mackey's other article under a slightly different title. Does demonstrate, however, that the colony's parishes performed the welfare function well; the colonists took good care of their less fortunate neighbors.

254.   Narrett, David Evan. "Patterns of Inheritance in Colonial New York City, 1664-1775: A Study in the History of the Family." Unpublished Ph.D. Diss., Cornell University, 1981. On the basis of all 1,572 wills made by residents of New York City during the colonial period, Narrett is able to draw fascinating inferences about kin ties, wealth, age, literacy, ethnic bonds, and the growing significance of English law. Rural-urban comparisons are also offered.

255.   Nash, Gary B. "Poverty and Poor Relief in

Pre-Revolutionary Philadelphia." William and Mary Quarterly, Vol. 33, No. 1 (Jan., 1976), 3-30. An extremely important article that sheds a lot of light on the extent and nature of the poverty problem in pre-Revolutionary Philadelphia (and by implication in other cities throughout the colonies). Nash demonstrates that contrary to popular views, the problem was real—about 25 percent of all free men were poor or near poor by the standards of that time—and that it was caused largely by modernization; hence, it was not an occasional problem but a systematic one, one that was getting worse rather than better.

256.   Parkhurst, Eleanor. "Poor Relief in a Massachusetts Village in the Eighteenth Century." Social Service Review, Vol 11, No. 3 (Sept., 1937), 446-64. Colonial records from the town of Chelmsford which provide important information regarding methods of administering the poor laws in an eighteenth-century Massachusetts town.

257.   Schneider, David M. "The Patchwork of Relief in Provincial New York, 1664-1775." Social Service Review, Vol. 12, No. 3 (Sept., 1938), 464-94. While the poor relief system in New York after it became an English colony was patterned closely on the mother country's, it was fairly repressive in practice and characterized by a general lack of uniformity, according to Schneider.

258.   Waters, John J. "Family, Inheritance, and Migration in Colonial New England: The Evidence from Guilford, Connecticut." The William and Mary Quarterly, Vol. 39, No. 1 (January, 1982), 64-86. Fortified by his use of anthropological theories on kinship patterns and his reconstitution of eighteenth-century family trees in Guilford, Connecticut, Waters underscores the close link between rhetoric and reality in family decisions concerning marriage, inheritance, and care of the old folks.

259.   Watson, Alan D. "Public Poor Relief in Colonial North Carolina." North Carolina Historical Review, Vol. 54, No. 4 (Oct., 1977), 347-66. A very good article on public relief in colonial North Carolina which demonstrates that there, too, the poor were well cared for; a good deal of time, money, and effort was expended on helping the needy.

260.   Wiberly, Stephen. "Four Cities: Public Poor Relief in Urban America, 1700-1775." Unpublished Ph.D. Diss., Yale University, 1975. A study of Boston, New York, Philadelphia, and Charleston during the first seventy five years of the eighteenth century indicates that approximately 20-40 percent of the population was poor during that time. It further suggests that a sense of

community existed between the poor and those better off, and that therefore there was a lack of class conflict.

261.   Wisner, Elizabeth. "The Puritan Background of the New England Poor Laws." Social Service Review, Vol. 19, No. 3 (Sept., 1945), 381-90. While it is true that the American poor laws were patterned after their English predecessors, it also is true, as Wisner demonstrates, that due to New World conditions they were not always administered the way they were in England.

2.2. REVOLUTIONARY AND EARLY NATIONAL

262.   Alexander, John K. Render Them Submissive: Responses to Poverty in Philadelphia, 1760-1800. Amherst, Mass.: University of Massachusetts Press, 1980. The thesis of this fine study is that because of a real rise in class antagonism and erosion of lower class deference, the elite in Philadelphia during the Revolutionary period worked to keep the laboring poor in check by using poor relief, medical assistance, and education as instruments of discipline and moral management; the upper class in other words, sought to render the poor submissive in order to defuse what they perceived as a potential danger from below.

263.   Epstein, Batsheva Spiegel. "Patterns of Sentencing and heir Implementation in PHiladelphia City and County, 1795-1829." Unpublished Ph.D. Diss., University of Pennsylvania, 1981. On the basis of a stratified random sample of Walnut Street Jail sentence documents, Epstein concludes that sentences were judicious and designed to fit the crime. The offenders' socio-economic characteristics were generally ignored in implementing sentences, though discrimination probably occurred at the arrest and indictment stages. Poverty became a social equalizer among inmates.

264.   Grigg, Susan. "The Dependent Poor of Newburyport, 1800-1830." Unpublished Ph.D. Diss., University of Wisconsin, 1978. This is a case study of persons who received public assistance (outdoor relief, indoor relief, and home placement) in Newburyport, Mass. during the first three decades of the nineteenth century which emphasizes gender as a key factor in the process.

265.   Heale, M. J. "Humanitarianism in the Early Republic: The Moral Reformers of New York, 1776-1825." Journal of American Studies, Vol. 2, No. 2 (Oct., 1968), 161-75. Many humanitarian activities were undertaken in the large commercial centers of the early republic. While most of these were armed at the moral reformation of the alleged degenerate, some were designed to change en-

vironmental influences and bring about social reform, presaging the great reform crusades of the mid-nineteenth century.

266.   Heale, M. J. "The New York Society for the Prevention of Pauperism, 1817-1823." New York Historical Society Quarterly, Vol. 55, NO. 2 (April, 1971), 153-72. An examination of the N.Y.S.P.P. which tries to demonstrate that the organization was more than a mere moral reform agency; its members saw the need to improve social conditions, and worked to do so.

267.   James, Sydney V. A People Among Peoples: Quaker Benevolence in Eighteenth Century America. Cambridge, Mass.: Harvard University Press, 1963. Book is designed to explain how and why the Quakers became spokespersons for virtue in public affairs and undertook all sorts of social welfare and social service projects between the 1750s and 1815. They did so, according to James, not out of humanitarianian reasons but because such activities compensated for a loss of political power and helped to maintain their group identity and norms; in short, Quaker "humanitarianism" was not a matter of disinterested benevolence.

268.   Main, Jackson Turner. The Social Structure of Revolutionary America. Princeton: Princeton University Press, 1965. A pioneering examination of the economic class structure of Revolutionary America based on tax and probate records which suggested that property was widely dispersed and easily attainable and that wages were high and poverty low. America was, in his words, "the best poor man's country in the world."

269.   Mohl, Raymond A. "Humanitarianism in the Preindustrial City: The New York Society for the Prevention of Pauperism, 1817-1823." Journal of American History, Vol. 57, No. 3 (December, 1970), 576-99. In this case study of the attitudes, assumptions, and activities of the politicians, professionals and merchants who attempted to eliminate pauperism while reducing relief costs, Mohl details the shift from rational humanism to moral stewardship, which typifies reform efforts in the antebellum period.

270.   Mohl, Raymond A. "Poverty in Early America, A Reappraisal: The Case of Eighteenth-Century New York City." New York History, Vol.50, No. 1 (Jan., 1969), 5-27. Through a study of poor laws and their administration, public relief expenditures and institutions, mutual aid societies and other private welfare organizations and other sources, Mohl concludes that colonial America was not a land of opportunity for all of its residents; indeed, widespread poverty was a

fact of life, especially in urban areas.

271.   Mohl, Raymond A. <u>Poverty in New York, 1783-1825</u>. New
        York: Oxford University Press, 1971. The main thesis
        of this exceedingly well researched and well written
        book is that during the half century or so after the
        American Revolution rapid change destroyed the stable
        and orderly society of the eighteenth century. In re-
        sponse to that and all sorts of other disturbing social
        and economic changes, including an alarming increase in
        poverty and welfare expenditures, urban leaders created
        a variety of charitable and reform organizations that
        were less humanitarian in nature than mechanisms for re-
        storing order and stability to society. Moralism, in
        short, superseded benevolence; public responsibility and
        private charity were transformed into effective tech-
        niques for social control.

272.   Nash, Gary B. "Urban Wealth and Poverty in
        Pre-Revolutionary America." <u>Journal of Interdisciplinary
        History</u>, Vol. 6, No. 4 (Spring, 1976), 545-84. This
        article, similar to the author's other one cited under
        the colonial period, challenges some generally accepted
        notions regarding urban social and economic development
        in Revolutionary America. Nash argues that there was a
        real decline in wealth and a rise in urban poverty at
        the time. In fact, he says, those conditions may have
        contributed significantly to the growth of revolutionary
        sentiment.

273.   Resch, John P. "Federal Welfare for Revolutionary War
        Veterans." <u>Social Service Review</u>, Vol. 56, No. 2 (June,
        1982), 171-95. The 1818 Revolutionary War Pension Act,
        designed to assist impoverished Continental army
        veterans, combined features of a pension plan and a poor
        law. Approximately 20,000 veterans applied for benefits
        under the measure, which included a means test; their
        claims produced a national survey of poverty conditions
        experienced by a large number of elderly men and their
        families. This article examines the pension act and
        provides the first systematic study of the claimants and
        their households who sought relief under the act.

274.   Smith, Billy Gordon. "Struggles of the 'Lower Sorts':
        The Lives of Philadelphia's Laboring People, 1750 to
        1800." Unpublished Ph.D. Diss., University of
        California at Los Angeles, 1981. Building on ideas and
        concerns set forth in Gary Nash's research into urban
        life during the Revolutionary period, Smith demonstrates
        that lower-class, laboring Philadelphians struggled con-
        stantly to ward off deprivation, disease and death.
        These demographic and economic parameters greatly af-
        fected their family life, and circumscribed their pro-
        spects for upward mobility.

275.   Virgadamo, Peter R. "Charity for a City in Crisis: Boston, 1740-1775." Historical Journal of Western Massachusetts, Vol. 10, No. 1 (Jan., 1982), 22-33. Arguing that the charitable impulse in the American colonies has been slighted by historians, the author then goes on to discuss the matter in Boston, 1740-1775, where it was great both in terms of large donations to meet emergencies and in the steady work of small benevolent societies. The thesis of the article, however, is that charity in the colonies developed a significance beyond the amount of financial aid given to the poor; it helped to break down the barriers of localism and proved to be a spur to national unity

276.   Williams, William H. "The Industrious Poor and the Founding of the Pennsylvania Hospital." Pennsylvania Magazine of History and Biography, Vol. 97, No. 4 (Oct., 1973), 431-43. A study of the Pennsylvania Hospital, the first such institution in colonial America, founded in Philadelphia in 1751 by Dr. Thomas Bond with the support of Benjamin Franklin, some Quaker merchants, and a number of other public spirited people. As the author shows, the main impulse behind the support the hospital received grew out of a desire to help, in particular, those poor who showed respect for the work ethic.

2.3. ANTEBELLUM AND CIVIL WAR

277.   Banner, Lois W. "Religious Benevolence as Social Control: A Critique of an Interpretation." Journal of American History, Vol. 60, No. 1 (June, 1973), 23-41. Contrary to the claims of others, the religious humanitarians had little conscious desire to control society or to resurrect an older social order in which clerical wisdom was supreme, according to Banner. Rather, they wanted to ensure the success of the American republic and to ultimately attain a stable democratic order.

278.   Bremner, Robert H. "The Impact of the Civil War on Philanthropy and Social Welfare." Civil War History, Vol. 12, No. 4 (Dec., 1966), 293-303. The war had a great impact on philanthropy and social welfare, in both the North and the South, according to Bremner. Although the crisis created a large amount of need, both public and private agencies responded accordingly; indeed, receipts of private benevolent societies and expenditures of public agencies as well rose to new highs during the war, as assistance was showered on both those in and out of uniform. The Civil War, then, proved to be an important link in American social welfare history.

279.   Bremner, Robert H. "The Prelude: Philanthropic

Rivalries in the Civil War." Social Casework, Vol, 49, No. 2 (Feb., 1968), 77-81. This brief article deals with the rivalries among organizations and individual philanthropists serving soldiers during the Civil War. Rather than dealing with sniping and bickering, however, Bremner examines the different styles of benevolence that were practiced or advocated during the conflict. The subject of this article, then, is the conflict, not between rival agencies but between different conceptions of philanthropy.

280.   Clement, Priscilla F. "The Philadelphia Welfare Crisis of the 1820s." Pennsylvania Magazine of History and Biography, Vol. 55, No. 2 (April, 1981), 150-65. In the belief that most of the poor were needy due to moral failings, primarily intemperance, Philadelphians in the 1820s abolished home relief and turned instead to the poorhouse, which they thought would serve both to reduce relief expenditures and punish the destitute. They also reduced the number of Guardians of the poor and lengthened their term of service in an effort to make them more efficient.

281.   Coll, Blanche D. "The Baltimore Society for the Prevention of Pauperism, 1820-1860." American Historical Review, Vol. 161, No. 1 (Oct., 1955), 77-87. A brief account of the Baltimore Society for the Prevention of Pauperism—an agency ahead of its time, according to the author—designed to encourage further research in the subject of such charitable institutions and their sponsors.

282.   Escott, Paul D. "The Cry of the Sufferers: The Problem of Welfare in the Confederacy." Civil War History. Vol. 23, No. 3 (Sept., 1977), 228-40. In addition to its many other problems, the Confederacy suffered from a major poverty/welfare problem. This article presents some new findings on Conferate welfare activities and suggests that the welfare problem was a central one in the Confederacy, contributing, among other things, to desertion in the army and southern disaffection with the war.

283.   Glassberg, Eudice. "Philadelphians in Need: Client Experience with Two Philadelphia Benevolent Societies, 1830-1860." Unpublished Ph.D. Diss., University of Pennsylvania, 1979. A study of two mid-nineteenth century benevolent societies, the Union Benevolent Association, a moral reform agency, and the Philadelphia Society for the Employment and Instruction of the Poor, or social reform agency, which reveals that, under the pressure of massive population increases and periodic economic dislocations, the ideological distinctions between the two became blurred.

284.   Griffin, Clifford. <u>Their Brothers' Keeper: Moral
        Stewardship in the United States, 1800-1865</u>. The story
        of do-gooders, or stewards of God, as they called them-
        selves, who between 1800-1860 feared the new forces of
        America life, especially new moral standards and the de-
        cline of religion, and believed that the spread of the
        Protestant gospel and morality would not only save the
        souls of their fellow citizens but would restore to so-
        ciety stability and order, sobriety and safety.

285.   Heale, M. J. "Patterns of Benevolence: Associated
        Philanthropy in the Cities of New York, 1830-1860." <u>New
        York History</u>, Vol. 57, No. 1 (Jan., 1976), 53-79. As-
        sociated charity (as opposed to spontaneous benevolence)
        emerged in antebellum America as a means of adapting the
        traditional conception of charity to the imperatives of
        an urban social order plagued by rapid growth and vast
        change, including widespread immigration. Designed to
        drive the "undeserving poor" from the streets, the
        effort failed.

286.   Klebaner, Benjamin J.   "Poverty and Its Relief in
        American Thought: 1815-1861." <u>Social Service Review</u>,
        Vol. 38, No. 4 (Dec., 1964), 382-99. An investigation
        of the American literature on pauperism between 1815 and
        1861 which focuses on the explanations offered for pov-
        erty and proposals for dealing with it, including dis-
        cussion of the merits of public assistance versus
        private charity.

287.   Klips, Stephen A. "Institutionalize the Poor: The New
        York City Almshouse, 1825-1860." Unpublished Ph. D.
        Diss., City University of New York, 1980. An analysis
        of poverty and social welfare in New York City from 1825
        to 1860 which is very critical of the role the city
        played in dealing with the poverty problem, particularly
        the development of a system of wretched institutions to
        isolate and remove the poor from the larger urban
        community.

288.   Knights, Peter R. <u>The Plain People of Boston,
        1830-1860: A Study in City Growth</u>. New York: Oxford
        University Press, 1971. As one of the first products of
        the so-called "new urban history," Knights' analysis of
        wealth and mobility in antebellum Boston provides so-
        cial-welfare historians with aggregate data with which
        to compare their own hypotheses and case studies. The
        volume's ultimate usefulness is limited by the author's
        decision to "provide data," and not offer hypotheses
        about the extent of poverty in Boston.

289.   Lasch, Christopher. "Origins of the Asylum." In <u>The
        World of Nations: Reflections on American History</u>,

Politics, and Culture. New York: Knopf, 1974, 3-17.
In this very important theoretical essay, Lasch rejects
the Rothman and Grob assertions that external pressures
were the crucial elements in the failure of asylums,
particularly in their transformation from reformative
curative to custodial institutions. Instead, borrowing
heavily from Erving Goffman's theory of the "total institution," Lasch argues that the institution never de-
generated; thanks to its organization and structure, it
was flawed from the outset.

290.   Lubove, Roy. "The New York Association for Improving
the Condition of the Poor," New York Historical Society
Quarterly, Vol. 43, No. (July, 1959), 307-28. An excellent analyltical study of the N.Y.A.I.C.P., from its
founding in 1843 through its formative years over the
next two decades, in which the author concludes that the
organization's significance was twofold: 1) as testimony to the anxiety which middle class Americans felt
over the increasing urban destitution at the time, and
2) as a revelation of the tension that characterized the
middle class crusade against that poverty.

291.   Rosenkrantz, Barbara and Maris A. Vinovskis.   "Caring
for the Insane in Ante-Bellum Massachusetts." In Kin
and Communities: Families in America, ed. by Allan J.
Lichtman and Joan R. Challinor. Washington, D.C.:
Smithsonian Institution, 1971, 187-218. An essay that
addresses one of the most notable trends in the modernization of American society--the assumption of responsibility for family welfare by organizations outside the
family, in this case mental institutions. Using sophisticated methods of multi-variate analysis as well as
more traditional methods, the authors document the shift
away from family to institutional care demonstrate the
importance of age as a factor in treatment, and discuss
the rather dreary history of the asylum in nineteenth
century America.

292.   Schlossman, Steven L.   "The 'Culture of Poverty' in
Ante-bellum Social Thought." Science & Society, Vol.
38, No. 2 (Summer 1974), 150-66. Far from being a new
conceptual tool, this essay argues that the "culture of
poverty" idea first emerged in its currently recog-
nizable form in the late 1840s as zealous middle-class
citizens called for public intervention to ensure that
foreign-born youth did not wreak havoc in antebellum
urban centers.

293.   Thomas, John L.   "Romantic Reform in America,
1815-1865." American Quarterly, Vol. 17, No. 4 (Winter,
1965), 656-81. Thomas argues that progressive and per-
fectionist impulses imbued antebellum reformers; the desire for social control, in other words, was not the

motivating impulse.

294.   Trattner, Walter I.   "The Federal Government and Social
Welfare in Early Nineteenth Century America."   Social
Service Review, Vol. 50, NO. 2 (June, 1976), 243-55.
This article, which deals with federal assistance to two
charitable institutions--the Connecticut Asylum for the
Deaf and dumb, in 1819 and the Kentucky Deaf and Dumb
Asylum, in 1826--suggests that the origin of the welfare
state antedates the New Deal by more than a century.

295.   Zainalden, Jamil S. and Peter Tyor.   "Asylum and Society: An Approach to Institutional Change."   Journal
of Social History, Vol. 13, No. 1 (Fall, 1971), 23-48.
This article deals with the same subject Rothman, Grob,
Lasch, and others have explored, namely, why Americans
began resorting to asylums in the 1830s and 1840s, and
why those asylums changed from therapeutic to custodial
institutions.   Rather than providing answers to those
questions, the authors discuss some of the limitations
of the earlier works on the subject, and suggest the
kinds of questions that need to be asked, and answered,
in the future.   Future studies, they contend, must pay
strict attention to the "inner/history" of asylums, must
substitute case analyses for aggregate data and broad
overviews, in order to provide a fuller and more accurate picture of the role of the institution and why it
changed over time.

2.4. POSTBELLUM

296.   Becker, Dorothy G..   "Exit Lady Bountiful: The
Volunteer and the Professional Social Worker."   Social
Service Review, Vol. 38, No. 1 (March, 1964), 57-72.   An
explanation of the historical roots of professional social work's resistance to the use of direct-service
volunteers, which stems largely from the lingering image
of the "friendly visitor."

297.   Bremner, Robert H.   "Scientific Philanthropy."   Social
Service Review, Vol. 30, No. 2 (June, 1956), 168-73.   An
excellent brief examination of the methods by which some
concerned citizens in the Gilded Age sought to make
charity more a matter of the head than the heart, a
scientific rather than an emotional response--and the
ways in which their efforts influenced later developments, both in social work and social reform.

298.   Fine, Sidney.   Laissez-Faire and the General Welfare
State: A Conflict in American Thought, 1865-1901.   Ann
Arbor, University of Michigan Press, 1956.   An older but
still very useful intellectual history of the late nineteenth century which traces the revolution and blos-

soming of the laissez-faire philosophy among some academics, businessmen, and public officials—and the rise of opposition to that position by reformers and political economists who favored a more active role by the state and federal governments.

299. Gutman, Herbert C. "The Failure of the Movement by the Unemployed for Public Works in 1873." Political Science Quarterly, Vol. 80, No. 2 (June, 1965), 254-77. Shortly after the 1873 depression began, workers in many large cities challenged the emerging laissez-faire philosophy and asked for public employment and other considerations from local and state authorities—without success. According to Gutman, the urban middle and upper classes did not really care about the poor's woes and resented and feared their organized efforts to violate the "laws of progress." More important, because these demands attracted the support of immigrants and socialists, and came shortly after the Paris Commune, they conjured up images of enormous potential violence and destruction—and hence violent opposition.

300. Huggins, Nathan I. Protestants Against Poverty: Boston's Charities, 1870-1900. Westport, Conn.: Greenwood Press, 1971. A clear, detailed description of the impact of social and economic change—primarily mass immigration and rapid industrialization—on Boston's private charities during the last three decades of the nineteenth century—especially the emergence of "scientific charity," and its failure.

301. Kaplan, Barry J. "Reformers and Charity: The Abolition of Public Outdoor Relief in New York City, 1870-1898." Social Service Review, Vol. 52, No. 2 (June, 1978), 202-14. An excellent article on the abolition of public home relief in late nineteenth century New York City—and its consequences. Public home relief was terminated, in large part, to reduce corruption and the power of Tammany Hall. However, as the author demonstrates, this led to a reduction in the city's welfare services which, in turn, ironically, allowed Tammany Hall to fill the gap and intensify its image as a friend of the poor, and hence its power.

302. Larsen, Lawrence H. "Nineteenth-Century Street Sanitation: A Study of Filth and Frustration." Wisconsin Magazine of History, Vol. 52, No. 3 (Spring, 1969), 239-47. An interesting account of the problems of street sanitation (including garbage collection, sewerage, etc.) in nineteenth century American cities, with emphasis on New York—due, in large part, to the "horse age." The article contains some excellent illustrations.

303. Leiby, James. "State Welfare Institutions and the

Poor." Social Casework, Vol. 49, No. 2 (Feb., 1968), 90-95. An account of the "division of interest" in late nineteenth and early twentieth century American social welfare between members and supporters of the state boards of charities and emerging professional social workers.

304.   Monkkonen, Eric H. The Dangerous Class: Crime and Poverty in Columbus, Ohio, 1860-1885. Cambridge, Mass.: Harvard University Press, 1975. This work seeks to test quantitatively the widely held and asserted belief that urban and industrial growth were causal factors in the increase in crime and poverty in nineteenth century America. Briefly stated, the author concludes that although urban and industrial growth did affect crime and poverty, it was more in their structure than in their quantity; indeed, apparently there was no overall increase in either phenomenon as the city of Columbus grew and industrialized.

305.   Pratt, John W. "Boss Tweed's Public Welfare Program." New York Historical Society Quarterly, Vol. 45, No. 4 (Oct., 1961), 396-411. While those who pay some tribute to the Tweed Ring usually point to the personal favors and gifts its leaders provided to New York City's needy--random gifts of groceries, coal, etc.--Pratt emphasizes the public welfare the Ring systematically administered--especially public aid to parochial schools and private charities--in a successful attempt to gain and hold the allegiance of the city's poor. In so doing, the organization definitely cared for the needs of th city's underprivileged and helped to soften some of the rigors of urban life years before the majority of Americans were persuaded that the public had a continuing responsibility for the welfare of society's unfortunates.

306.   Rauch, Julia. "The Charity Organization Movement in Philadelphia." Social Work, Vol. 21, No. 1 (Jan., 1976), 55-62. A study of the founding of Philadelphia's charity organization society that seeks to answer such questions as why the organization developed as it did, what factors influenced its operation (as well as development), and what lessons, if any, can we learn from it today? The work sheds light, among other things on the apparent relationship between economic cycles and relief systems--light which tends to raise questions with the so-called Piven and Cloward thesis.

307.   Reinders, Robert C. "Toynbee Hall and the American Settlement Movement." Social Service Review, Vol. 56, No. 1 (March, 1982), 39-54. Although Toynbee Hall in London, founded in 1885, served as a direct impetus to the early settlement houses in America--indeed, American

settlements imitated its form and many of its prac-
tices--by 1900 the American movement not only dwarfed
its English predecessor but differed from it significantly. This is an analysis of those differences and
how and why they came about.

308.   Rhines, Charlotte Cannon. "A City and Its Social Prob-
        lems: Poverty,   Health   and   Crime   in   Baltimore,
        1865-1875."   Unpublished Ph.D. Diss., University of
        Maryland, 1975.   Agreeing with many of the themes set
        forth in Sam Bass Warner's The Private City:
        Philadelphia   in   Three   Periods   of   Its   Growth
        (Philadelphia: University of Pennsylvania Press, 1969),
        this thesis underscores the limits and ultimate failure
        of a piecemeal approach to welfare that relied upon a
        tradition of voluntarism.

309.   Saveth, Edward N.   "Patrician Philanthropy in America:
        The Late Nineteenth and Early Twentieth Centuries."
        Social Service Review, Vol. 54, No. 1 (March, 1980),
        76-91. An analysis of the roles played by three late
        nineteenth   patrician   philanthropists--Josephine   Shaw
        Lowell, Robert Treat Paine, and Joseph Lee--which sug-
        gests that, in general, they distrusted poor people and
        felt that poverty was mainly a consequence of personal
        failings.   Nevertheless, they felt a responsibility to
        serve the poor. Social work professionalism, however,
        which they supported, ironically tended to reduce their
        role in philanthropy.

310.   Schneider, David M. and Albert Deutsch.   "The Public
        Charities of New York: The Rise of State Supervision
        after the Civil War." Social Service Review, Vol. 15,
        No. 1 (March, 1941), 1-23. A study of the origin and
        early history of New York's State Board of Charities
        which, the authors argue, was not a sudden, un-
        precedented development but rather the culmination of
        many older forces in society, including the proli-
        feration of public welfare agencies and the ongoing cen-
        tralization of public administrative processes.

311.   Sicherman, Barbara.   "The Paradox of Prudence: Mental
        Health in the Gilded Age." Journal of American History,
        Vol. 62, No. 4 (March, 1976), 890-912. A study of
        Gilded Age definitions of mental health, which differ
        from those in vogue during earlier and lter periods, in
        order to gain insight into the cultural ethos of the
        period.

312.   Speizman, Milton D.   "The Radicals and the Poor."
        Social Casework, Vol. 49, No. 2 (Feb., 1968), 102-112.
        A review of the explanations of poverty, and its pro-
        posed cures, by a number of American radicals--Henry
        George, Laurence Gronland, Edward Bellamy, Henry

Demarest Lloyd, Eugene Debs, and Emma Goldman—which suggests that many of their ideas have been realized. America needs its radicals, who serve a useful purpose, according to Speizman; they push the nation "toward important goals upon which all decent persons do agree."

313.   Speizman, Milton D. "Poverty, Pauperism and Their Causes: Some Charity Organization Views." Social Casework, Vol. 46, No. 3 (March, 1965), 142-49. Extracted from the author's dissertation, this article is an overview of the views held by the leaders of organized charities regarding the causes of poverty, with little new that is added.

314.   Trattner, Walter I. "Louisa Lee Schuyler and the Founding of the State Charities Aid Association." New York Historical Society Quarterly, Vol. 51, No. 3 (July, 1967), 233-48. Few voluntary organizations in American history have contributed as much both to the health and welfare of the people of New York State and the nation and to the principle that public and private aid must work together for the public welfare, as did the New York State Charities Aid Associaion. This article examines, and places in historical perspective, the early history of that organization and its founder and organizer, Louisa Lee Schuyler (1835-1926).

2.5. PROGRESSIVE

315.   Boer, Albert, The Development of United South End Settlements. Boston: United South End Settlements, 1966. A brief account, or chronology, of past events and activities of the United South End Settlements of Boston written by a current staff member who concentrated on the work of the organization's pioneers.

316.   Burnham, John C. "Psychiatry, Psychology, and the Progressive Movement." American Quarterly, Vol. 12, No. 14 (Winter, 1960), 457-65. A study of the two professions that deal with the human psyche—psychology and psychiatry—and their intimate relationship to the progressive movement prior to World War I. The work not only is an interesting brief history of those professions but contributes to a broader view of progressivism by suggesting that the reform movement was not limited to politics, economics, and social philsophy; rather, it permeated all endeavors of middle class Americans.

317.   Chambers, Clarke A. and Andrea Hinding. "Charity Workers, the Settlements, and the Poor." Social Casework, Vol. 49, No. 2 (Feb., 1968), 96-101. An account of those who spoke for the poor in the latter

nineteenth and early twentieth century—social workers and their organizations who, according to the authors, awakened the nation to the causes and consequences of poverty and proposed constructive (although usually only partial) programs for its alleviation and cure.

318.   Davis, Allen F. "The Social Workers and the Progressive Party, 1912-1916." American Historical Review, Vol. 69, No. 3 (April, 1964), 671-88. An account of why many social workers supported Theodore Roosevelt's bid for the Presidency in 1912 and the important contributions they made to the Progressive Party and the 1912 campaign, particularly with regard to the social justice planks of the party platform.

319.   Davis, Allen F. "Welfare Reform and World War I." American Quarterly, Vol. 19, No. 3 (Fall, 1967), 516-33. This article questions something that for a long time simply was accepted as true, namely, the notion that World I killed the progressive movement. As Davis here demonstrates, many progressives, especially those concerned with social justice matters, felt the war could be used as an instrument of reform, and in many ways their feelings, and wishes, proved to be true. The war did not kill progressivism; on the contrary, in a number of important ways, progressivism flowered under the impact of the wartime experience. What happened afterwards, however, is another story.

320.   Davis, Allen F. and Mary Lynn McCree, eds. Eighty Years at Hull House. Chicago: Quadrangle Books, 1969. A book of photographs and excerpts from the writings of key founders, residents, critics, and supporters of Hull House which, taken together, trace the changing problems and programs of the institution from its founding (in 1889) to the late 1960s.

321.   Graebner, William. "Federalism in the Progressive Era: A Structureal Interpretation of Reform." Journal of American History, Vol. 64, No. 2 (September, 1977), 331-57. During a political economy in which interstate competition and federalism worked at cross purposes, the movement for uniform state legislation reached its fullest development in the areas of child labor, workmen's compensation, and mine safety. The case for uniformity was also made in other Progressive legislation.

322.   Howe, Barbara. "The Emergence of the Philanthropic Foundation as an American Social Institution, 1900-1920." Unpublished Ph.D. Diss., Cornell University, 1976. This thesis traces the rationale and formative experiences of the Rockefeller and Carnegie Foundations and other philanthropic institutions in the early twentieth century.

323.   Kalberg, Stephen. "The Commitment to Career Reform: The Settlement Movement Leaders." Social Service Review, Vol. 49, NO. 4 (Dec., 1975), 608-25. By studying the early leaders of the settlement house movement who became career activists and reformers, the author of this study attempts to define the forces that led to long-term commitment to activism. The enduring commitment of the individuals studies is analyzed in terms of the beliefs and attitudes predominant in their families and factors that may have reinforced their commitment once they had chosen to become career activists. The final section of the paper compares and contrasts leaders in the student and civil rights movements of the 1960s with the career activists in this study.

324.   Kirschner, Don S. "The Ambiguous Legacy: Social Justice and Social Control in the Progressive Era." Historical Reflections, Vol. 2, No. 1 (Summer, 1975), 69-88. This article begins by outlining both the progressive and the social control interpretations of early twentieth century social reform, and then asks which is correct? The author concludes that, in perspective, "both impulses [social reform and social control] appear to have been genuine and . . . basic. Because they were contradictory, they generated a tension in many of the reformers that had important consequences for the Progressive era."

325.   Kusmer, Kenneth L. "The Functions of Organized Charity in the Progressive Era: Chicago as a Case Study." Journal of American History, Vol. 60, No. 3 (Dec., 1973), 657-78. A very sympathetic and sometimes incorrect look at the organized charities which, in the author's view, not only spawned professional social work but performed many other important functions well into the twentieth century--until the Great Depression, which marked the end of voluntaristic charity and the beginning of an age of public welfare.

326.   Numbers, Ronald L. Almost Persuaded; American Physicans and Compulsory Health Insurance, 1912-1920. Baltimore: Johns Hopkins University Press, 1978. This interesting monograph is a study of the medical profession's reaction to the issue of compulsory health insurance, 1912-1920. As the title implies, whereas initially the nation's physicans endorsed the concept, by 1920 they had changed their minds--for a number of reasons analyzed by the author, chief of which, however, he feels was money: medical men opposed health insurance, in other words, to protect their own pocketbook, and for other reasons as well, made clear in this well written and well researched work.

327.   Reagan, Patrick D.   "The Ideology of Social Harmony and
        Efficiency: Workmen's   Compensation   in   Ohio,
        1904-1919."   Ohio History, Vol. 90, No. 14 (Autumn,
        1981), 317-31. The successful drive for workmen's com-
        pensation legislation in Ohio, 1904-1919, stemmed, ac-
        cording to Reagan, from the growth and implementation of
        an ideology of mutual accomodation between the State
        Federation of Labor and the state's Manufacturers' As-
        sociation, one that included a whole set of concepts
        popular during the Progressive era.   This in-
        terpretation, then, varies somewhat from other recent
        studies of the subject, especially Weinstein's and
        Lubove's, which argue that the "reform" grew out of the
        desire of the business community to cut production costs
        and rationalize labor-management relations.

328.   Vecoli,   Rudolph.   "Sterilization: A   Progressive
        Measure?"   Wisconsin Magazine of History, Vol. 43, No. 3
        (Spring, 1960), 190-202. A study of the political, med-
        ical, and sociological thinking that led to one of
        Wisconsin's most controversial laws--the sterilization
        statute of 1913, a eugenic measure designed to deal with
        those   considered   socially   inadequate.   In   essence,
        Vecali argues that the statute (and others like it) was
        not inconsistent with the major tenets of progressivism;
        hence the enactment of such measures by sixteen states
        between the years 1907-1917.

329.   Wade, Louise C. "The Heritage from Chicago's Early Set-
        tlement Houses."   Journal of the Illinois State
        Historical Society, Vol. 60, No. 4 (Winter, 1967),
        411-41. An attempt to remind social workers of the so-
        cial activism of their predecessors--pioneer settlement
        house residents--at a time when the newly created VISTA
        program and other current measures were "breathing new
        life into the settlement goals of residence, research,
        and reform." The "old-fashioned settlement ministry of
        understanding deserves a new lease on life," Wade
        concluded.

330.   Watts, Phyllis A. "Casework Above the Poverty Line:
        The Influence of Home Service in World War I on Social
        Work."   Social Service Review, Vol. 38, No. 3 (Sept.,
        1964), 303-15. An attempt to indicate the indebtedness
        of professional social work to the American Red Cross'
        Home Service Division, created during World War I to
        provide casework services to uprooted soldiers and their
        families. Home service casework, or casework "above the
        poverty line," the author maintains, tested and expanded
        social work theory and practice and facilitated social
        work's shift from a socioeconomic to a psychological
        base, thereby helping it achieve professional statues.

331. Weinstein, James. "Big Business and the Origins of Workmen's Compensation." Labor History, Vol. 8, No. 2 (Spring, 19697), 156-74. An examination of the process whereby big business came to sponsor workmen's compensation legislation, and its striking legislative success between the years 1911-1920, when every state in the Union, with the exception of six southern ones, adopted such measures. That sweeping achievement, according to Weinstein, was made possible by the concerted activity of the National Civic Federation, with the strong support of its big business affiliates. It represented a growing maturity and sophistication on the part of many large corporation leaders who had come to understand (as Theodore Roosevelt often told them) that social reform truly was conservative.

332. Woods, Robert A. and Albert J. Kennedy, eds. Handbook of Settlements. New York: Russell Sage Foundation, 1911. Compiled at the height of the settlement house movement by a couple of its most effective members and organizers, this work is the most comprehensive list of settlement houses throughout the United States, one that enumerates the activities of each. A very useful document.

2.6. THE 1920s AND THE GREAT CRASH.

333. Alexander, Leslie B. "Social Work's Freudian Deluge: Myth or Reality." Social Service Review, Vol. 46, No. 4 (Dec., 1972), 517-38. This article provides a comparison of primary and secondary literary sources on social work theory and practice in the 1920s which challenges the notion that the profession was inundated with Freud's ideas during the prosperity decade. Indeed, the evidence seems to suggest just the opposite--that psychoanalytic theory influenced an elite minority fringe rather than the main body a theory and practice in the 1920s.

334. Betten, Neil. "The Great Depression and the Activities of the Catholic Worker Movement." Labor History, Vol. 12, No. 2 (Spring, 1971), 243-58. This essay traces the work of Peter Maurin, Dorothy Day, and others in the Catholic Worker Movement in stressing the disparity between American realities and Catholic ideals, thereby rekindling social reform activities that had been dormant in the 1920s.

335. Chambers, Clarke A. Seedtime of Reform: American Social Service and Social Action, 1918-1933. Minneapolis: University of Minnesota Press, 1963. In this important full-length study from which his article of the subject was extracted, Chambers clearly demon-

strates that the period between the Armistice and the
Great Depression was not a wasteland for reform, as was
widely believed. Indeed, not only did reform survive,
but it witnessed a subtle advance from the prevention of
social ills to more constructive measures aimed at the
creation of a more secure and abundant life for all.
The work is a valuable corrective to the history of a
complex decade.

336.   Chepaitis, Joseph B.   "Federal Social Welfare Pro-
        gressivism in the 1920s." Social Service Review, Vol.
        46, 1No. 2 (June, 1972), 213-29. A rather simplistic
        account   of   the   enactment   and   demise   of   the
        Sheppard-Towner Act which stresses the role of women in
        both. Chepaitis argues that passage of the measure re-
        sulted from the power women acquired when they were
        granted the franchise, and its demise coincided with and
        explains the weakened clout of female voters by the end
        of the 1920s.

337.   Field, Martha H.   "Social Casework Practice During the
        Psychiatric Deluge." Social Service Review, Vol. 54,
        No. 4 (Dec., 1980), 482-507. After examining the re-
        cord, the author concludes that the prevalent assumption
        that a "psychiatric deluge" swept casework practice
        after World War I simply is not true. Although
        psycho-dynamic formulations began to appear in the case-
        work literature about 1918, psychodynamics did not
        really enter agency practice until the post World War II
        period. Further, adoption of the practice occurred
        slowly and unevenly; there was no deluge. This work, of
        course, tends to coincide with or at least complement,
        the Alexander article on the same subject.

338.   Fox, Bonnie.   "Unemployment Relief in Philadelphia,
        1930-32: A Study of the Depression's Impact on Volun-
        tarism." Pennsylvania Magazine of History and
        Biography, Vol. 93, No. 1 (Jan., 1963), 86-108. The au-
        thor used Philadelphia's experience in trying to meet
        the needs of its unemployed citizens and a case study in
        the "breakdown of local resources," which led many so-
        cial workers, and others, to solicit from the states,
        and even the national government, additional funds for
        the emergency. They realized, as she put it, that "a
        national problem could not be alleviated by local means."

339.   Lemmons, J. Stanley.   "The Sheppard-Towner Act: Pro-
        gressivism in the 1920s." Journal of American History,
        Vol. 55, No. 4 (March, 1969), 776-86. A study of the
        Sheppard-Towner Act which refers to it as both an ex-
        ample of progressivism in the 1920s and "a link in the
        chain of ideas and action from Roosevelt to Roosevelt,"
        Theodore to Franklin. The major thesis of the article,
        however, is that, although passed during the Harding ad-

ministration, the act was a product of the progressive movement, not merely, or even largely a product of female suffrage, as Chepaitis argues.

340.   Orme, John G. and Paul Stuart. "The Habit Clinics: Behavioral Social Work and Prevention in the 1920s." Social Service Review, Vol. 55, No. 2 (June, 1981), 242-56. A description of a group of social agencies in Massachusetts in the 1920s--Habit Clinics--in which social workers used new casework methods to alleviate, and prevent, behavioral problems of preschool children. The agencies illustrate many of the important forces in the history of social welfare in the 1920s, including casework becoming the "nuclear skill" of the emerging profession of social work, the development of the family service agency as a distinct organizational form, the emergence of federated fundraising and federal support for state social and health services, the education and training of social workers, etc.

341.   Perlman, Helen Harris. "Freud's Contribution to Social Work." Social Service Review, Vol. 31, No. 2 (June, 1957), 192-202. A very positive account, or assessment, of Freud's contributions to social work, and social workers, from a strong proponent and theorist of psychiatric casework. In general, Freud's ideas expanded social welfare goals, enhanced its practice, and purged social workers of their moralism and self-righteousness, according to the author.

342.   Romasco, Albert U. The Poverty of Abundance: Hoover, the Nation, the Depression. New York: Oxford University Press, 1964. A rather skillful analysis of the various efforts of the Hoover administration, and the American people, to arrest the Depression--and the ways in which the old institutions and methods failed to do so.

2.7.   NEW DEAL AND WORLD WAR II.

343.   Alexander, Leslie B. and Milton D. Speizman. "The Union Movement in Voluntary Social Work." In The Social Welfare Forum. New York: Columbia University Press, 1980, 179-87. An interesting look at the birth, growth, and virtual death of a union movement in voluntary social work, especially among Jewish social workers in Jewish agencies. The movement, which was synonymous with the Social Service Employees Union (S.S.E.U.) locals of the United Office and Professional Workers of America, a C.I.O. affiliate, was born out of the Great Depression and the resulting upsurge of the C.I.O.

344.   Braeman, John, Robert H. Bremner, and David Brody, eds.

The New Deal, 2 Vols. Columbus: Ohio State University Press, 1975. An important collection of essays which not only assess the current literature on the New Deal but point to promising lines of inquiry for social welfare historians. Among other things, the volumes help to elucidate the growing pre-eminence of the federal government in dealing with major social issues.

345.   Bremer, William W. "Along the 'American Way': The New Deal's Work Relief Programs for the Unemployed." Journal of American History, Vol. 62, No 3 (Dec., 1975), 636-52. A discussion of the New Deal's work relief programs and why the social work community and the administration favored them over direct assistance. Work relief was seen by both as the "American Way," chiefly because it made public assistance something earned rather than merely granted by charity, and because it thereby infused symbols of respectability into the stream of relief. There is no mention, however, of the more radical members of the social work profession, and others who were quite critical of the administration's work relief programs for one reason or another.

346.   Chapman, Richard Norman. "The Contours of Public Policy, 1939-1945." Unpublished Ph.D. Diss., Yale University, 1976. Despite FDR's desire to bolster New Deal initiatives with a Keynesian program, the President opted for a defensive strategy amid political, fiscal, and international pressures to cut back reform programs. This thesis should be read as an alternate to the argument set forth in Geoffrey Perret's Days of Sadness, Years of Triumph (1973).

347.   Clement, Priscilla F. "The Works Progress Administration in Pennsylvania, 1935 to 1940." The Pennsylvania Magazine of History and Biography, Vol. 95, No. 2 (April, 1971), 244-60. An interesting case study of the W.P.A. in Pennsylvania, 1935-1940, which attempts to answer the question of what happens to federal-state relationships when an agency of the federal government assumes considerable authority for what had been a state function—the granting of relief. According to the author, a great deal of friction, or conflict, resulted over both political and financial matters.

348.   Crouse, Joan M. "Transiency in New York State: The Impact of the Depression Decade, 1929-1940." Unpublished Ph.D. Diss., State University of New York-Buffalo, 1981. The purpose of this study was to use an examination of the clash during the depression decade of the heroic American image of the "man on the move," or pioneer, and the tramp, or "bum"—the wanderer, stranger, intruder, or pioneer without a frontier—to study federal-state cooperation in public re-

lief. In other words, this really is a study of the concept of social responsibility for the transient. The author found that for a while, especially between 1933-35, the federal government assumed responsibility for these people; after that, decentralization of social services occurred and responsibility for indigent transients reverted to the locality, with devastating consequencies for these people.

349.   Fisher, Joel. The Response of Social Work to the Depression. Boston: G.K. Hall and Co., 1980. This work does not really deal with social work's response to the Depression. Rather, it is an account of the profession's left wing during the Depression, a small group of people, including the author, who comprised what was known as the Rank-and-File Movement. Rank-and-Filers, who sought a fundamental reorganization of society, attacked both the aims and achievements of FDR and the New Deal and the social work establishment on virtually every issue during that troubled time. Written from the perspective of the radical left, this is an extremely useful book which enlarges and enlivens the reader's understanding of the period and many of its leading characters--and serves as a good reminder of the radical heritage of the social service profession.

350.   Hendrikson, Kenneth E. "Relief for Youth: The Civilian Conservaiton Corps and the National Youth Administration in North Dakota." North Dakota History. Vol. 48, (Fall, 1981), 17-27. The agricultural economy of North Dakota was in near collapse when President Roosevelt took office in March, 1933; in most areas of the state more than one-third of the people needed assistance and in some sections the figure was nearly 90 percent. The administration's Civilian Conservation Corp and National Youth Administration alleviated the situation greatly--and while their demise in the early 1940s is understandable, it nevertheless is tragic; if they had been kept in operation, perhaps the history of our more recent work relief efforts would not be so bleak, the author concludes.

351.   Hirshfeld, Daniel. Last Reform: Campaign for Compulsory Health Insurance from 1932-1943. Cambridge, Mass.: Harvard University Press, 1970. This is the best account of efforts by social welfare reformers and liberal Democrats to implement a federal health-care program as a major part of the social legislation associated with the New Deal. Hirshfeld also discusses Progressive antecedents for this drive.

352.   Jones, John F. "The Use of Volunteers in American So-

cial Welfare During the Depression." Unpublished Ph.D.
Diss., University of Minnesota, 1968. This study explores the extent and nature of volunteer participation
in public and private non-sectarian social welfare organizations during the Depression, 1929-41, and concludes that no single pattern prevailed. There is a
final chapter on the theory of volunteer participation
in which the author proposes a model that would allow
maximum use of volunteers in social welfare.

353.   Kimberly, Charles M. "The Depression in Maryland: The
        Failure of Voluntarism." Maryland Historical Magazine,
        Vol. 70, No. 2 (Summer, 1975), 189-202. As the title
        aptly states, this is a study of the "failure of volun-
        tarism" in Maryland during the Depression. While at the
        outset of the crisis, in Maryland, as elsewhere, busi-
        nessmen and others repeatedly expressed confidence that
        the economy was fundamentally sound--and that private
        charity and balanced budgets represented the appropriate
        response to the problem--within two years they were ac-
        cepting federal aid; the failure of the private sector
        forced them to turn to the federal government for
        assistance.

354.   Lambert, C. Roger. "Man and Plenty: The Federal Sur-
        plus Relief Corporation and the AAA." Agricultural
        History, Vol. 46, No. 3 (July, 1972), 390-400. This es-
        say traces the conflicting goals and almost whimsical
        motives underlying the creation of the FSRC between 1933
        and 1935 to deal with the paradox of producing surpluses
        while millions went hungry in the depths of the Great
        Depression.

355.   Maxwell, John C.   "Social Welfare Attitudes in
        California During the Thirties." Unpublished Ph.D.
        Diss., University of California, Los Angeles, 1971.
        This is a study of the changes that occurred at the
        local and state levels when the Depression challenged
        existing social welfare attitudes and programs in
        California, changes, as the author demonstrates, that
        were determined mainly by businessmen and politicians.
        Nevertheless, he found that the notion--mythical
        notion--that the individual should be able to sustain
        himself, was discredited, at least temporarily.

356.   May, Marion I. "The Paradox of Agricultural Abundance
        and Poverty: The Federal Surplus Relief Corporation,
        1933-35." Unpublished Ph.D. Diss., University of
        Oklahoma, 1970. A history of the Federal Surplus Re-
        lief Corporation, 1933-35, which, in effect, is a his-
        tory of how the United States Government responded
        during that time to the twin problems, and em-
        barrassment, of agricultural surpluses and human
        hunger. According to May, the F.S.R.C. manifested New

Deal humanitarianism and concern for the forgotten man
(not the power of big agriculture, as others would
maintain)--and served as a good example of cooperative
federalism during an emergency. It, however, didn't
solve the nation's problems. The agency's main importance, the author asserted, aside from the benefits
it distributed at the time, was that it established a
pattern of federal food distribution that later would be
expanded, and thus represented an important step toward
the welfare state.

357.   Morgan, Thomas S. "A Step Toward Altruism: Relief and
Welfare in North Carolina, 1930-1938." Unpublished
Ph.D. Diss., University of North Carolina, 1969. A history of North Carolina's efforts to meet the needs of
its citizens during the Depression, a relatively successful story after a slow start. By 1938, the author
concludes, thanks in part to federal prodding, most welfare programs in the state, including those under the
social security program, were placed in operation by a
considerably expanded welfare department which was beginning to funciton smoothly.

358.   Phillips, Norma K. "Social Work, Government and Social
Welfare: The Social Security Act." Unpublished Ph.D.
Diss., Yeshiva University, 1981. The author of this
study uses the Social Security Act as a vehicle for examining a number of things, chief of which was the
relationship between the social work profession and the
federal government during the Depression. She concludes
that the nature of that relationship was a reciprocal
one, in which each accomodated to and was influenced by
the other. Despite conflicts within the profession, the
official social work organization assumed a moderate
ideological position in relation to the federal government, putting the profession in a position to utilize
opportunities for expansion of professional activity and
jurisdiction that were made available by the new federal
programs.

359.   Schwartz, Bonnie Fox. "Social Workers and New Deal
Politicians in Conflict." Pacific Historical Review,
Vol. 42, No. 1 (Feb., 1973), 53-73. According to the
author of this article, confrontation and conflict
rather than accomodation and mutual interests best describe the relationship between New Deal politicians and
professional social workers, as each group had different
approaches toward the administration of relief. Social
workers favored private charity and non-partisan professional administration, while politicians saw charitable
services as an opportunity to both aid the needy and
build up their party organizations. The Civil Works
Administration, in particular, became a battleground for

these opposing forces.

360. Witte, Edwin C. The Development of the Social Security
      Act. Madison, Wis.: University of Wisconsin Press
      1963. Basically, this is a rather dull legislative case
      study which describes, step-by-step, the process by
      which the goals of the President's Committee on Economic
      Security were achieved. Still, it is a valuable docu-
      ment for understanding how the Social Security Act was
      developed and passed--and it does give a clear picture
      of an important man at work, the author of this work who
      was the Committee on Economic Security's executive
      director.

361. Trolander, Judith. The Settlement Houses and the Great
      Depression. Detroit: Wayne State University Press,
      1975. The book's central thesis is that settlement
      house acceptance of the Community Chest principle as a
      basis for funding--often necessitated by the De-
      pression--resulted in constraints which inhibited social
      action initiatives. Since Chicago and New York were the
      only cities in which settlement houses refused to af-
      filiate with Community Chest organizations, a major
      theme of the book is the contrast between the wil-
      lingness of the leaders in those cities to support so-
      cial action and the reluctance of most leaders in other
      cities to do so.

362. Trout, Charles H. Boston, the Great Depression, and the
      New Deal. New York: Oxford University Press, 1977.
      This case study underscores the significance of "local
      obstacles"--political factionalism, bureaucratic machi-
      nations, and competing special interests--that limited
      the impact of New Deal initiatives during the Great De-
      pression. Reviewers have questioned the represen-
      tativeness of Boston's experiences.

363. Wallis, John Joseph and Daniel K. Benjamin. "Public
      Relief and Private Employment in the Great Depression."
      Jounal of Economic History, Vol 41, No. 1 (March, 1981),
      97-102. The authors here argue, and demonstrate, that
      federal relief programs in the 1930s did not, as is
      widely believed, produce lower employment in the pri-
      vate sector; they merely helped the poor who otherwise
      would have been unemployed.

2.8. POSTWAR.

364. Berkowitz, Edward and Kim McQuaid. "Welfare Reform in
      the 1950s." Social Service Review, Vol. 54, No. 1
      (March, 1980), 45-58. Just as others have argued that
      the 1920s was no wasteland for reform, here Berkowitz
      and McQuaid argue that, contrary to popular opinion,

welfare expansion and reform did not die in the 1950s either. On the contrary, even conservatives agreed on the necessity for both, even federal spending for welfare. Disagreement existed only over what to finance. In the end, most money went to Social Security and vocational rehabilitation programs.

365. Burns, Eveline M. "Further Needs in Social Security Legislation in the Field of the Social Insurances." Social Serivce Review, Vol. 25, No. 3 (Sept., 1951), 283-88. A "taking stock" of the Social Security Act and where it needs to go in light of the 1939 and 1950 amendments. It needed to go, according to Burns, in the direction of disability and health insurance as well as broader unemployment and retirement coverage—and she pleaded with social workers to take the initiative in the effort to expand the program and improve its coverage.

366. Corson, John T. "Social Security and the Welfare State." Social Service Review, Vol. 24, No. 1 (March, 1954), 8-12. Writing from the vantage point of 1954, when the welfare state was in disfavor with many people, the author asks, is the Social Security system necessary and worth preserving? Is it providing too much security and destroying individual initiative? Are we trading security for personal freedom? Corson answers the first question with a resounding yes, and the latter two with a no! In fact, he argues for more welfare services and programs, not less, in order to attain security for all citizens, including some sort of guaranteed minimum income.

367. Galbraith, John Kenneth. The Affluent Society. Boston: Houghton Mifflin, 1958. The well known Harvard economist's best-selling critique of existing economic ideas and attitudes, especially the so-called productivity ethic, which is important for students of social welfare because it reflected the misguided but widely held view that poverty in America, in Galbraith's words, is no longer "a massive affliction [but] more nearly an after thought."

368. Miles, Rufus E., Jr. The Department of Health, Education, and Welfare. New York: Praeger, 1974. An attempt to explain how and why the U.S. Department of Health, Education, and Welfare grew so quickly to its enormous size—the largest department in the world, expenditure wise—what social and political forces shaped it, who its leading figures have been, and how it is organized and managed.

369. Morgan, James N., et al. Income and Welfare in the United States. New York: McGraw-Hill, 1962. A highly

detailed and technical study based on interviews with 2,800 families which explores the redistribution of income through regular programs such as Social Security, private pensions, public welfare, etc. While nothing of great significance emerges, th analylsis does provide some interesting insights into the ways in which a number of factors affect income, especially education.

2.9. GREAT SOCIETY.

370. Ball, Robert M. "Is Poverty Necessary?" Social Security Bulletin, Vol. 28, No. 8 (Aug., 1965), 18-24. A perfect reflection of the mid-1960s: the statement that in America the aboliton of want no longer is a problem of economic capacity. The problem according to Ball, is one of making sure that all parts of the population have an opportunity to work and have a continuing income when work is not possible.

371. Brauer, Carl M. "Kennedy, Johnson, and the War on Poverty." Journal of American History, Vol. 69, No. 1 (June, 1982), 98-119. An excellent analysis of the history, operation, consequences, and lessons of the so-called War on Poverty which, among other things, demonstrates that President Kennedy had been planning the program prior to his death, and that President Johnson adopted it due to the circumstances of his assumption of the office. It also explains, clearly, why the program favored human services and seeking to change individuals over economic transfers and economic equality, and clearly refutes the Piven and Cloward assertion that the measure was designed to control the poor, primarily to win black votes in the 1964 presidential election.

372. Briar, Scott. "Welfare From Below: Recipients' Views of the Welfare System." California Law Review, Vol. 54, No. 2 (May, 1966), 370-85. A description of the findings of a study on welfare recipients' views of themselves and the welfare system which indicates that, in general, welfare recipients have rather conservative views, including the notion that assistance is a privilege rather than a right; they view themselves as suppliants rather than as rights-bearing citizens. The author then goes on to suggest why that is so—mainly because public welfare agencies and their staff members, social workers, encourage and reinforce attitudes of submissiveness and suppliance on the part of recipients.

373. Burke, Vincent and Vee Burke. Nixon's Good Deed: Welfare Reform. New York: Columbia University Press, 1974. A fascinating, well written, play-by-play account of the intrigue and infighting in Nixon's proposed Family Assistance Plan (F.A.P.) and the development of

the Supplemental Security Income program (S.S.I.), including a discussion of the merits and drawbacks of
each, the latter of which succeeded and the former of
which failed.

374.   Clark, Kenneth and Jeanette Hopkins. A Relevant War
Against Poverty: A Study of Community Action Programs
and Observable Social Change. New York: Harper and
Row, 1970. An important case study of the first two
years of the community action concept in practice, which
argues that means were confused with ends in the Johnson
program. The work is especially useful in highlighting
class dynamics within the black community.

375.   Cloward, Richard A. and Frances F. Piven. "The Weight
of the Poor: A Strategy to End Poverty." The Nation
(May 2, 1966), 510-17. Piven and Cloward's famous
plan, or attempt, to get the poor to adopt the tactics
of the civil rights movement in an effort to create a
political crisis which, they hoped, would lead to enactment of legislation for a guaranteed annual income and
an end to poverty. It was predicated on the assumption
that if all those eligible for but not receiving welfare
would seek it, it would overwhelm and break down the existing welfare system and lead to creation of some sort
of a federal system based upon guaranteed annual incomes
for all those in need. This article and other efforts
did help organize the poor and create the National Welfare Rights Organization--but, needless to say, not the
end result the authors of the article sought.

376.   Cohen, Henry. "Poverty and Welfare: A Review Essay."
Political Science Quarterly, Vol. 87, No. 4 (Dec.,
1972), 631-50. An interesting, and useful, review essay
of some ten books on the subject of poverty, indicating
widespread concern over, or at least interest in, the
subject of welfare and income maintenance, primarily the
result of staggering increases in the number of people
on public assistance since the early 1960s. After
reviewing the books, the author concludes that America
needs a multi-program strategy to attack the problem,
which is deep and complex and not susceptible to quick,
easy solutions. Yet, he said, we are a wealthy nation
with a deep national concern for the problem, and that
is hopeful.

377.   Cohen, Wilbur J. "A Ten-Point Program to Abolish
Poverty." Social Security Bulletin, Vol. 31, No. 12
(Dec., 1968), 3-13. Cohen's "farewell address" as secretary of the Department of Health, Education, and Welfare before the onset of the Nixon administration--an
exceedingly optimistic appraisal of the poverty problem
and the chances of eliminating it: "The Nation," he
wrote "has the economic capacity, the technological

capability, and the intellectual resources" to do so within the next decade, and he offered a plan to implement that goal.

378. Donovan, John C. The Politics of Poverty. New York: Western Publishing, 1967. A readable but rather sketchy and superficial review of the Economic Opportunity Act of 1964 and the political issues involved in the first two years of its operation. Donovan attempts to demonstrate how irrational the decision–making process was, how the administration (wittingly or unwittingly) created hopes for winning the war against poverty without developing a supporting program for the purpose, and how President Johnson failed miserably to fight two wars simultaneously, one at home and one in Vietnam, and abandoned the former.

379. Elman, Richard. The Poorhouse State. New York: Pantheon, 1966. A passionate polemic which portrays what it means and how it feels to be poor and subject to all sorts of indignities. "We must," Elman writes, "seek out ways to vest dependency with decency, to provide assistance without humiliation." A grim work that makes a very important point—that the central premise of the nation's welfare system, the notion that the poor are temporary unfortunates who can be lured or dragooned into becoming self-supporting citizens, is false.

380. Gilbert, Charles E. "Policy-Making in Public Welfare: The 1962 Amendments." Political Science Quarterly, Vol. 81, No. 2 (June, 1966), 196-224. A history of the 1962 amendments to the Social Security Act, considered by many to be a fundamental change in policy because of their acceptance of the social work doctrine about the need for "services" in public assistance. The author discusses the important substantive issues involved and argues that the amendments were a combination of bureaucratic survival tactics in the face of criticism, the inertial progress of professionalism, and a recognition of the changing nature of dependency and a fresh attack on chronic poverty. Thus a study of the amendments, in the author's opinion, helps us better understand how public welfare has been and is shaped by traditional, political, and professional forces all of which are related.

381. Goldberg, Gertrude S. "New Directions for the Community Service Society of New York: A Study of Organizational Change." Social Service Review, Vol. 54, No. 2 (June, 1980), 184-219. An account of the Community Service Society's decision, in 1971, to end individual and family casework services and turn, instead, to community organization and social reform, one that draws conclusions, among other things, about the functions of

trustees, professionals, and administrators and about the knowledge necessary for effecting organizational change.

382. Gordon, Margaret S. The Economics of Welfare Policies. New York: Columbia University Press, 1963. An attempt to stimulate interest in the economic issues of welfare policy through a brief description of social welfare programs in America and their history, including an analysis of the effects of such programs on income distribution.

383. Gronbjerg, Kirsten. Mass Society and the Extension of Welfare, 1960-1970. Chicago: University of Chicago Press, 1977. An empirical study inspired by the "welfare crisis" of the 1960s in which the author attempts to explain why the AFDC rolls, the primary public assistance program in America, expanded so greatly at that time. On the basis of an examination of AFDC payments on a state-by-state basis during the decade, she concludes that expansion, for the most part, was tied to modernization, or advanced industrialization: the modernization process liberalizes social welfare programs through the creation of a conductive set of attitudes among the citizenry involving "a sense of common identity" and "mutual responsibility." If true, this would tend to refute the so-called Piven and Cloward thesis, for it would be evolution of mass society rather than outbreaks of mass disorder which accounts for the precipitous AFDC increase in the 1960s.

384. Gronbjerg, Kirsten, David Street and Gerald Suttles, eds. Poverty and Social Change. Chicago: University of Chicago Press, 1978. This little collection of essays succinctly and coherently summarizes the major thoughts and social welfare developments associated with the Great Society. The bibliography is indispensable for research in the period.

385. Harrington, Michael. The Other America: Poverty in the United States. New York: Macmillan, 1962. A very readable and moving survey of the poverty problem in America, including a discussion of who the poor are, why they are not seen, and how they can be helped, which quickly became a classic and supposedly played a role in initiating the War on Poverty. Must reading for all!

386. Kahn, Alfred. "Social Services in Relation to Income Security." Social Service Review, Vol. 39, No. 14 (Dec., 1965), 381-89. A discussion of what historically has been a central question for social work policy and planning--the relationship of social services to income security, and whether or not public relief investigators also should be the service provider, or caseworker, an

old charity organization tradition, one acepted by the
1962 amendments to the Social Security Act. The author
concludes that they should not--that modern society
needs separate well developed and soundly administered
income security and social service systems.

387.   Keyserling, Leon. Progress or Poverty: The United
        States at the Crossroads. Washington, D.C.: Conference
        on Economic Progress, 1964. Based on the assumption
        that with its resources and technology America can elim-
        inate poverty, and that its persistence therefore is
        "shocking and shameful," this work spells out clearly
        practical steps that can be taken to remedy the situ-
        ation. An appendix includes a good summary of the Eco-
        nomic Opportunity Act of 1964.

388.   Larner, Jeremy and Irving Howe, eds. Poverty: Views
        from the Left. New York: Morrow, 1968. Twenty essays
        (many of which appeared earlier in Dissent) which probe
        into the War on Poverty from economic, sociological,
        political, and practical points of view and which, on
        the whole, indict that war as a total failure. Poverty,
        the authors agree is a national shame which requires
        more massive, and radical remedies.

389.   Levitan, Sar A. The Great Society's Poor Law: A New
        Approach to Poverty. Baltimore: Johns Hopkins Univer-
        sity Press, 1969. An excellent monograph that provides
        a comprehensive treatment of the enactment of the Eco-
        nomic Opportunity Act and the first two years of its
        operation. An informed, judicious, and prudent work by
        a sympathetic author who nevertheless emphasizes
        failures over successes and makes recommendations for
        the future, including efforts to augment the E.O.A. and
        improve its efficiency.

390.   Levitan, Sar A. and Robbert Taggart. The Promise of
        Greatness. Cambridge, Mass.: Harvard University Press,
        1975. An important book which attempts to document the
        actual changes that occurred as a result of the Great
        Society's welfare programs, in which the authors deal
        with, statistically, in successive chapters, the effect
        of legislation in the areas of welfare, health care,
        low-income housing, education, manpower programs, and
        civil rights. They conclude that the results of the
        programs were, on the whole, positive and that the
        nation came a long way toward eradicating poverty.

391.   Lewis, Oscar. The Children of Sanchez. New York:
        Knopf, 1961. The author's famous work in which he out-
        lined his controversial "culture of poverty" ar-
        gument--the notion that poverty is not only a state of
        economic deprivation but a way of life, something that
        affects the very personality of the slum dweller, re-

markably stable and persistent, passed down from
generation to generation along family lines, and cutting
across national borders.

392. Macdonald, Dwight. "Our Invisible Poor." New Yorker
Magazine, Vol. 38, (Jan. 19, 1963), 82-132. A review
essay of Michael Harrington's The Other America (an
"excellent" and "important" book) and a number of other
works on the subject in which the author concludes, "The
problem is obvious: the persistence of mass poverty in
a prosperous country. The solution is also obvious: to
provide, out of taxes, the kind of subsidies that have
always been given to the public schools (not to mention
the police and fire departments and the post office),
subsidies that would raise incomes above the poverty
level, so that every citizen could feel he is indeed
such." Until that is done, "the shame of the other
America will continue."

393. May, Edgar. The Washed Americans. New York: Harper
and Row, 1964. A graphic attempt by a concerned journalist to place the problems of public welfare in clear
perspective. He examines the negative public attitude
toward welfare and its recipients, and blames not only
those who prefer to look the other way but others as
well, including social workers and supporters of social
agencies who theoretically have assumed responsibility
for helping the poor. Unfortunately, however, while
strong on what is wrong with the system, the work is
weak on proposed remedies.

394. Miller, Herman P. Rich Man, Poor Man: A Study of
Income Distribution in America. New York: Cromwell,
1964. In this important work, the author interprets income distribuiton in America in relation to occupation,
education, religion, race, age, health, and family--and
finds an increased disparity between the haves and
have-nots during the prior twenty years. The chief barriers to a more equitable distribution of wealth, he
feels, are racial discrimination, insufficient private
and public investment, and inflation.

395. Miller, S. M. and Martin Rein. "Poverty and Social
Change." American Child, Vol. 46, No. 3 (March, 1964),
10-15. The authors argue that the notion that poverty
can and will be eliminated by increasing welfare benefits and funds to social service agencies, and by expanding educational and employment opportunities, is
false; these things only will permit society to continue
doing what it has done in the past. It is necessary,
they declare, to change society's social institutions so
that they are more effectively responsible to the needs
of the poor.

396.   Moynihan, Daniel P.   "The Crisis in Welfare."   The
        Public Interest, No. 10 (Winter, 1968), 3-29.   A dis-
        cussion of the 1967 Amendments to the Social Security
        Act which the author referred to as both "the first pur-
        posively punitive welfare legislation in the history of
        the American national government" and "the first deli-
        berate anti-civil rights measure of the present era."
        The targets of the legislation, weak and abandoned women
        and helpless and innocent children, are also without
        precedent according to Moynihan.   Yet, he concludes, in
        some way the legislation is useful, for it brought into
        the open the mounting crisis of the American welfare
        system, which needs to be reassessed and revamped, es-
        pecially by the adoption of some sort of family al-
        lowance.

397.   Moynihan, Daniel P.   Maximum Feasible Misunderstanding:
        Community Action in the War on Poverty.   New York: The
        Free Press, 1969.   An elaboration of the most dis-
        tinctive feature of the Economic Opportunity Act--the
        provision that its programs be carried out with "the
        maximum feasible participation" of the residents of the
        communities   involved--intended   to   dispel   mis-
        understanding about that provision and the reasons for
        its inclusion in the legislation.   The author, who
        helped draft the legislation, sees the War on Poverty as
        lost, in part, because of the misguided notions of in-
        tellectuals who insisted on arousing poor people, es-
        pecially blacks to insist on carrying out the letter of
        the law.   An extremely distressing book in that the au-
        thor spends a good deal of time decrying militancy on
        the part of the poor and their supporters in community
        action programs provided for by the legislation.

398.   Moynihan, Daniel P.   The Politics of a Guaranteed
        Income: The Nixon Administration and the Family
        Assistance Plan.   New York: Vintage Books, 1973.
        Moynihan here describes in minute detail, what happened
        to the Family Assistance Plan, which he proposed to
        Nixon, while it was under discussion in the ad-
        ministration and under consideration at congressional
        hearings--and again claims that it was killed by li-
        berals who he claims were beholden to their con-
        stituencies of social workers, self-seeking spokesmen
        for the underprivileged and welfare recipients in
        high-payment states.   A polemical work which absolves
        Nixon of all shame for defeat of the measure, something
        many other knowledgeable people refuse to do.

399.   Moynihan, Daniel P.   "The Professionalization of Re-
        form."   The Public Interest, No. 1 (Fall, 1965), 6-16.
        There are two aspects of the War on Poverty that dis-
        tinguish it from earlier movements, or programs, of its
        kind, according to Moynihan: it arose from within the

federal government rather than from the demands of the poor, and it was conceived by professional social welfare leaders using new and sophisticated analytic tools. This "professionalization of reform," he argues, i leading to the development of a profoundly new society in America, one Moynihan does not seem to be certain he likes.

400.   Ornati, Oscar. Poverty Amid Affluence. New York: Twentieth Century Fund, 1966. An examination of the indices of poverty in America, including income distribution, education, housing, illness, employment, and "types" of poverty, and suggestions for a "true" attack on it, well documented with statistics.

401.   Orshansky, Mollie. "Counting the Poor: Another Look at the Poverty Profile." Social Security Bulletin, Vol. 28, No. 1 (Jan., 1965), 3-29. A description of a method used to define equivalent incomes at a poverty level for a large number of different family types. A summary picture of groups who fell below the poverty level on the basis of their 1963 incomes also is provided.

402.   Orshansky, Mollie. "Measuring Poverty." The Social Welfare Forum, 1965. New York: Columbia University Press, 1965, 211-23. The author here questions the measurements which have been used to calculate poverty and reviews those measurements in order to show differences and similarities in the presentation of poverty statistics.

403.   Pious, Richard M. "The Phony War on Poverty in the Great Society." Current History, Vol. 61, No. 363 (Nov., 1971), 266-72. The author argues that the Economic Opportunity Act, or War on Poverty, failed for a variety of reasons, one of which was that it was conducted as a sitzkrieg rather than a blitzkrieg—"a phony war of stalemate and standstill." What was needed was not the paltry handouts of the Great Society, according to the author, but rather a fundamental commitment to spend the funds necessary to provide real opportunity for social mobility in the inner cities and depressed rural areas—something we did not get.

404.   Plotnick, Robert and Felicity Skidmore. Progress Against Poverty: A Review of the 1964-1974 Decade. New York: Academic Press, 1975. This important addition to the poverty literature is an appraisal of the nation's progress in eliminating poverty during the ten years after the War on Poverty was declared. The authors conclude that in absolute terms, progress was made. Progress also was made in relative terms, but not quite as much. Further, poverty actually declined little with regard to income, or cash; however, if in-kind benefits

are included, substantial progress can be demonstrated. Both the poverty gap and the poverty incidence are sharply diminished.

405.   President's Commission on Income Maintenance Programs. Poverty Amidst Plenty: The American Paradox. Washington, D.C.: Government Printing Office, 1969. This is the famous Report of the President's Commission on Income Maintenance Programs, or the so-called Heineman Commission, which, after twenty-two months of study, found severe poverty in America, especially among members of all minority groups. The problem of poverty, the Commission went on to state, must be dealt with by the Federal Government—through construction of a system that would give all Americans economic security, chiefly through the creation of a universal supplement program whereby the federal government would make cash payments to all needy members of the population, without any strings attached, including mandatory work requirements.

406.   President's National Advisory Commission on Rural Poverty. The People Left Behind. Washington, D.C.: Government Printing Office, 1967. The Report of the President's National Advisory Commission on Rural Poverty, which assembled the facts on rural poverty in America—for the most part untouched by most anti-poverty efforts, including the War on Poverty—and made specific recommendations designed both to give immediate aid to the rural poor and to attack the causes of their poverty—recommendations that called for action by all levels of government and by private individuals and groups as well, including creation of a national policy "designed to give residents of rural America equality of opportuonity with all other citizens, including equal access to jobs, medical care, housing, educaion, welfare, and all other public services."

407.   Ritz, Joseph P. The Despised Poor: Newburgh's War on Welfare. Boston: Beacon Press, 1966. A calm, coherent, and carefully documented account of the "war" on welfare costs and recipients unleashed in 1961 by Joseph M. Mitchell, Newburgh, N.Y.'s city manager. The work, which is very critical of Mitchell and sympathetic to the needy, actually goes much further; it goes deeply into Mitchell's background and motivation and probes the roots of the public apathy to the incident and conservative hostility towards urbanization and social change.

408.   Ryan, William. Blaming the Victim. New York: Vintage Books, 1971. A good, well written, highly readable analysis (by a clinical psychologist) of how Americans prefer to blame the victims of poverty rather than examine the inequalities of their society.

409.   Schorr, Alvin. Explorations in Social Policy. New
        York: Basic Books, 1968. This collection of essays re-
        flects the prevailing hopes and qualms by leading policy
        analysts about the ways in which major pieces of social
        welfare legislation were conceived, implemented and ev-
        aluated during Lyndon Johnson's Great Society initiative.

410.   Seligman, Ben B. Permanent Poverty: An American
        Syndrome. Chicago: Quadrangle Books, 1968. A useful
        overview, or synthesis, of poverty in America by a con-
        cerned but "defeated" labor economist who concludes his
        survey of the problem--and the various categories of the
        poor--by implying that the problem, and their plight, is
        permanent, and that little can be done about either.

411.   Steiner, Gilbert Y. Social Insecurity. Chicago: Rand
        McNally, 1966. A discussion of the nation's various
        public assistance program which provides a good deal of
        insight into the "politics" of welfare and policy making
        by a critic of the system who favors reversing the "ser-
        vices" approach with the relief, or aid, one.

412.   Stern, Philip M. and George deVincent. The Shame of a
        Nation. New York: Ivan Obolensky, 1965. A rather sen-
        sitive and moving photographic essay on modern American
        poverty. The authors have put together a very moving
        portrait of the poor--their lives, their environments,
        their problems, their needs, their lot in an affluent
        society.

413.   Sundquist, James L., ed. On Fighting Poverty:
        Perspectives From Experience. New York: Basic Books,
        1969. This edited collection attempts to review the
        origin and development of antipoverty policies, par-
        ticularly the Community Action Program. It is written
        largely by supporters of and participants in the War on
        Poverty.

414.   Theobald, Robert. The Challenge of Abundance. New
        York: Mentor Books, 1962. An economist examines the
        dangers and opportunities presented by America's economy
        of abundance, proposing a number of changes in a variety
        of policies and practices, particularly a new plan for
        better income distribution.

415.   Theobald, Robert, ed. The Guaranteed Income. Garden
        City, N.Y.: Doubleday, 1966. The authors of the
        various papers in this work examine the notion that
        government should guarantee each citizen an income to
        live with dignity--and, in general, support the prin-
        ciple. They cover such wide-ranging topics as auto-
        mation, the means test, and the social, cultural, and
        psychological aspects of a guaranteed income, and in the

appendix include a special proposal for such a measure.

416.   Tobin, James. "The Case for an Income Guarantee." The Public Interest, No. 4 (Summer, 1966), 31-41. In an effort to conquer poverty there are two basic strategies—"structural" and "distributive." The former concentrates on changing the poor so that they (allegedly) can earn decent incomes, while the latter assures every family a decent standard of living regardless of its earning capacity. Both strategies are essential; they really are complementary, not competitive. Thus far, according to the author, we have emphasized the structural, especially in the War on Poverty. That war will not be won, however, he argues, with implementation of a distributive policy as well.

417.   Valentine, Charles A. Culture and Poverty: Critique and Counter-Proposals. Chicago: The University of Chicago Press, 1968. Valentine's cogent critique of the "culture of poverty" concept exposes biases and flaws in the intellectual and ideological fundations of War on Poverty initiatives in the 1960s. In so doing, he exposes the errors in confounding poverty, ethnicity, class, and race.

418.   Youngdahl, Benjamin E. Social Action and Social Work. New York: Association Press, 1966. In this volume, the author, a leading social worker and social work educator, clearly indicates that he believes the first responsibility of social workers and the profession is to social reform, or social action, as opposed to social "service." Professsional social work, he argues, must be the "conscience of the community," and its skills and insights must be put to work in the achievement of civil liberties, civil rights, a peaceful world, and the like.

2.10.   THE CONTEMPORARY PERIOD.

419.   Anderson, Martin. Welfare. Stanford University: Hoover Institution, 1978. This monograph, which provided the intellectual basis for many of President Reagan's proposed welfare "reforms," critiques the strengths and weaknesses of the Great Society from a neo-conservative perspective. It is worth noting that Anderson believes that the Great Society succeeded in winning the war on poverty; now, however, its bureaucratic excesses must be pruned.

420.   Califano, Joseph A., Jr. Governing America. New York: Simon and Schuster, 1980. An insider's account of Carter's efforts to reform the welfare system, written by the secretary of H.E.W. whom the President fired in 1979. Though the analysis is often self-serving,

Califano nonetheless offers cogent comments about the difficulties inherent in reforming, much less transforming, American social-service delivery systems, Social Security, and health programs.

421.   Duignan, Peter and Alvin Rabushka, eds. The United States in the 1980s. Stanford University: Hoover Instituion, 1980. This "neo-conservative" volume reflects the agenda on domestic and foreign policies articulated by the Reagan administration. The articles on welfare and health care are particularly interesting: they should be read in conjunction with the Brookings Institution report, Setting National Priorities.

422.   Gans, Herbert J. More Equality. New York: Random House, 1973. A collection of essays about the prospects and problems of attempting to achieve greater equality of results in American society since 1960. The volume is particularly useful in analyzing the motives and assumptions of reformers. As such, it implicitly links its thesis to larger issues in American social welfare history.

423.   Gilbert, Neil. "The Future of Welfare Capitalism." Society, Vol. 18, No. 5 (Sept.-Oct., 1981), 18-37. This essay deftly and persuasively exposes the fallacy of distinguishing between public and private welfare initiatives in "modern" America since the spheres of responsibility overlap so greatly.

424.   Lynn, Lawrence E. and David deF. Whitman. The President as Policymaker: Jimmy Carter and Welfare Reform. Philadelphia: Temple University Press, 1981. A detailed review of the acrimonious controversy between experts in the Department of Health Education, and Welfare and members of the Department of Labor over the design of President Carter's proposed Better Jobs and Income Program.

425.   Morgan, James N., et al. Five-Thousand Families, 5 Vols.. Ann Arbor: Institute of Social Research, 1974ff. This massive data base traces changes in the demographic and socio-economic conditions and opinions expressed by the heads of a cross-section of post-1960 American society. Among other things, these volumes explode the myth of a "culture of poverty" by showing that changes in household structure, members' employment, and taxes and new regulations alternately lift families over (or drop them below) the official poverty line.

426.   Owen, Henry and Charles L. Schultze, eds. Setting National Priorities: The Next Ten Years. Washington, D.C.: The Brookings Institution, 1976. This "neo-liberal" statement of past successes and failures

and forecast of future developments should be read as a companion to The United States in the 1980s, edited by Duignan and Rabushka. This volume emphasizes the pivotal role that federal policymakers will continue to play in promoting the commonwealth in general and welfare reform in particular.

427.   Ozawa, Martha. "S.S.I.: Progress or Retreat?" Public Welfare, Vol. 32, No. 2 (Spring, 1974), 33–40. An attempt to review the S.S.I. program (the 1972 Social Security Amendments, or Supplemental Security Income for the Aged, the Disabled, and the Blind) which, according to the author, contains both progressive and regressive features and, most importantly, can have adverse effects on Social Security recipients.

428.   Piven, Frances F. and Richard A. Cloward. "Notes Toward a Radical Social Work." In Radical Social Work, ed. by Roy Bailey and Mike Brake. New York: Pantheon, 1976, vii–xlviii. In their introduction to the American edition of this work, Piven and Cloward set forth their views on the question of what constitutes radical social work, lambast professional education as a major obstacle to its development, and plead with students and social workers to defy the system.

429.   Piven, Frances F. and Richard A. Cloward. The New Class War: Reagan's Attack on the Welfare State and Its Consequences. New York: Pantheon Books, 1982. The authors' most recent work, one which deviates somewhat from their past writings. Briefly, the thesis of this work is that the business–oriented leaders who came to power with the election of Ronald Reagan to the Presidency in 1980 are trying to dismantle the welfare state, but, will fail to do so, mainly because the developments in American society which brought the welfare state into being (primarily a variety of permanent income.maintenance entitlements) are sufficient to ensure its persistence. Regulating the Poor, then, which describes a cyclical pattern of providing aid and then cutting it back, characterizes the past, not the future, according to the authors of this work.

3.   SALIENT VARIATIONS.

3.1.   LOCAL, STATE, REGIONAL

430.   Baghdadi, Mania K. "Protestants, Poverty, and Urban Growth: A Study of the Organization of Charity in Boston and New York, 1820–1865." Unpublished Ph.D. Diss., Brown University, 1975. This thesis explores contradictions in the charity workers' viewpoints, 1820–1860, such as a desire to restore an imagined, in-

formal village community through the use of formal
bureaucratic organizations, and an attempt to integrate
moralism and environmentalism.

431.   Becker, Dorothy G. "The Visitor to the New York City
Poor, 1843-1920." Social Service Review, Vol. 35, No. 1
(Dec., 1961), 382-96. A review of the history of the
New York Association for Improving the Condition of the
Poor in order to clear up some misunderstandings about
the organization, especially with regard to its decline
and its contributions to professional soial work, which
the author claims have been underestimated in the past.

432.   Brown, Elizabeth G. "Poor Relief in a Wisconsin County,
1846-1866: Administration and Recipients." American
Journal of Legal History, Vol. 20 No. 2 (April, 1976),
79-117. The county poorhouse in Waukesha County,
1846-1866, functioned primarily as an institution that
provided short-term emergency care for individuals and
families who could not care for themselves. Such care
was given honestly, efficiently, and fairly personally.

433.   Clement, Priscilla F. "The Response to Need: Welfare
and Poverty in Philadelphia, 1800-1850." Unpublished
Ph.D. Diss., University of Pennsylvania, 1977. The
study is designed to examine how the city's public welfare system and private charities responded to the needs
of the indigent between 1800 and 1850. The conclusion
is, not very well. Welfare officials were always motivated by a spirit of economy; they emphasized the cheap-
est programs and sought to reduce the relief rolls by
making the welfare program as unattractive as possible.

434.   Ettling, John. The Germ of Laziness: Rockefeller
Philanthropy and Public Health in the New South.
Cambridge, Mass.: Harvard University Press, 1981. This
study explores the role of corporate philanthrophy and
scientific commissions in dealing with the problem of
hookworm disease during the Progressive era. In stressing the significance of rural evangelical Protestantism
that inspired the scientists and reformers, Ettling offers an alternative to the quasi-Marxian, social-control
model set forth by E. Richard Brown in Rockefeller
Medicine Men (University of California Press, 1979).

435.   Fleckner, John A. "Poverty and Relief in Nineteenth-Century Janesville." Wisconsin Magazine of
History, Vol. 61, No. 4 (Summer, 1978), 279-99. This
case study of a Wisconsin city whose population grew
from 3,000 in 1850 to nearly 11,000 in 1890 emphasizes
the extent to which the poor were encouraged and were
able to fend for themselves in caring for their needs.
Philanthropic and community-based resources are also described here.

436. Franklin, John Hope. "Public Welfare in the South During the Reconstruction Era, 1865-1880." <u>Social Service Review</u>, Vol. 44, No. 4 (Dec., 1970), 3<u>79-92</u>. During the Reconstruction era the southern states, for the first time, provided public welfare services on a large scale to a wide variety of needy people--the poor, including orphans and widows, the insane, the deaf and dumb, the blind, etc. However, most of the energies and resources of the region were expended in an effort to establish and maintain separate institutions for the black and white races, which inevitably meant inferior facilities for the former slaves.

437. Hosay, Myron P. "The Challenge of Urban Poverty: Charity Reformers in New York City, 1835-1890." Unpublished Ph.D. Diss., University of Michigan, 1969. A study of a group of N.Y.C. charity workers who, in attempting to meet the problem, went through several phases--from moral reform, to social reform ,back to moral reform (thanks largely to late nineteenth century hereditarian ideas and large scale immigration), and eventually to despair. Their departure from the field paved the way for professional social work.

438. Krueger, Thomas D. <u>And Promises to Keep: The Southern Conference for Human Welfare, 1938-1948</u>. Nashville: Vanderbilt University Press, 1967. The story of the Southern Conference for Human Welfare, a popular front organization which was created to initiate cures for the economic and social ills of the South, including those of its poor agricultural and urban workers. Before collapsing in 1948, thanks in large part to the disenchantment of labor and its more left-wing elements, the Conference had helped to improve the region's antiquated and oppressive economic and social system, demonstrating that the South had many spokespersons for its dispossessed residents.

439. McCarthy, Kathleen D. <u>Noblesse Oblige: Charity and Cultural philanthropy in Chicago, 1849-1929</u>. Chicago: University of Chicago Press, 1982. This monograph traces the distinctive criteria, composition, and techniques of four generations of civic stewards--"antebellum volunteers, Gilded Age plutocrats, progressive iconoclasts, and Jazz Age donors and dilettantes"--who created and managed Chicago's non-sectarian welfare organizations and institutions before the New Deal.

440. Mertz, Paul E. <u>New Deal Policy and Southern Rural Poverty</u>. Baton Rouge: Louisiana State University, <u>1978</u>. Besides corroborating the prevailing thesis that the New Deal failed to transform the longstanding condition of rural poverty, Mertz sharpens the difference

between relief and rehabilitation in dealing with the South's rural poor.

441. O'Keefe, Dominic Francis. "The History of Home Relief in New York City, 1938 through 1967." Unpublished Ph.D. Diss., New York University, 1978. By uncovering changes in home-relief recipients and rising caseload responsibilities, this thesis is able to describe how the original objectives of Home Relief have changed since the Great Depression.

442. Rosen, Bernard. "Social Welfare in the History of Denver." Unpublished Ph.D. Diss., University of Colorado, 1976. This case study describes the nature of dependency and patterns of relief in 19th century Denver. Some attempt is made to relate the laissez-faire attitudes of the city's economic elite with prevailing welfare practices.

443. Shifflett, Crandall A. "Shadowed Thresholds: Rural Poverty in Lomsa County, Va., 1860-1900." Unpublished Ph.D. Diss., University of Virginia, 1975. This thesis analyzes the response to poverty by blacks and whites in a rural Virginia county where formal social welfare institutions were lacking—and suggests that the family served as the adaptive mechanism for members of both races. Slavery clearly had not destroyed the vitality of the black family, according to the author.

444. Walch, Timothy. "Catholic Social Institutions and Urban Development: The View from Nineteenth Century Chicago and Milwaukee." Catholic Historical Review, Vol. 64, No. 1 (Jan., 1978), 16-32. An examination of early nineteenth century Chicago and Milwaukee which illustrates how the accidents of local urban development (particularly the early arrival of Catholics) and community self-interest contributed to the significant involvement of the Catholic Church in the area of urban social welfare—schools, hospitals, and asylums for the needy.

445. Wisner, Elizabeth, Social Welfare in the South: From Colonial Times to World War I. Baton Rouge: Louisiana State University, 1970. A good, concise history of poverty and treatment of the poor in the South over a three-hundred year span, from colonial times to World War I. Especially interesting are the discussions of Dorothea Dix's work on southern treatment of the mentally ill and the relief effort launched by the Freedmen's Bureau.

446. Wright, Conrad E. "Christian Compassion and Corporate Beneficence: The Industrialization of Charity in New England 1720-1810." Unpublished Ph.D. Diss., Brown Uni-

versity, 1980. Between the 1720s and 1810 charity, as New Englanders thought about and practiced it changed in a number of important ways. This thesis seeks to describe and account for those changes, the most important of which, according to the author, was the instituionalization of charity; that is, the change from charity being considered a private, personal matter to it being conceived of as a corporate, public obligation.

3.2. RACIAL/ETHNIC.

447.   Anders, Gary C. "Dependence and Underdevelopment: The Political Economy of Cherokee Native Americans." Unpublished Ph.D. Diss., University of Notre Dame, 1978. This work attempts to provide a new insight into the problem of American Indian poverty and underdevelopment by examining the applicability of a new theoretical model of dependency to a case study of the Oklahoma Cherokees. The major hypothesis, which is confirmed by the empirical data developed in the case study, is that the Cherokees and other Indian tribes with similar experiences have been involuntarily integrated into a system of economic and political relations which are best understood as internal colonialism, and that the operation of that system has, over time, given rise to an Indian political economy characterized by dependence and underdevelopment. The study, then, lends support for a more general acceptance of dependency theory as an explanation for the Indians' underdevelopment.

448.   Batchelder, A. "Poverty: The Special Case of the Negro." American Economic Review, Vol. 55, No. 12 (May, 1965), 530-40. The author points to five economic considerations which distinguishes black from white poverty, and then argues that the investment of capital in programs for the Negro poor would be more productive of results.

449.   Berkhofer, Robert F., Jr. The White Man's Indian. New York: Knopf, 1978. This impressive volume traces images of the American Indian from Columbus to the mid-1970s. After tracing continuities and changes in imagery in literature, art, philosophy, religion, anthropology, and the social sciences, Berkhofer turns to public policy issues. In his discussion of acculturation and detribalization of the nineteenth and twentieth century reservation, he treats social welfare issues.

450.   Blassingame, John W. The Slave Community: Plantation Life in the Antebellum South. New York: Oxford University Press, 1972. In this important work, the author examines the ways that blacks became enslaved, their

process of acculturation in the American South, and their ties to their African heritage. He shows how the slave was able to control parts of his or her own life while wearing the mask of submissiveness required by the harshe realities of the plantation regime. Indeed, the book's central theme is that the slave gained a sense of worth in the quarters where he spent most of his time free from white surveillance, and that this relative freedom helped the slave to preserve his personal autonomy and create a culture which has contributed a good deal to America life and thought--a good antidote to Moynihan and others who have argued that slavery emasculated black males and destroyed the black family.

451.   Brophy, William A. and Sophie D. Aberle, eds. The Indian: America's Unfinished Business. Oklahoma: University of Oklahoma Press, 1966. The final report of the Commission on the Rights, Liberties and Responsibilities on the American Indian, established in 1957 to appraise the condition of the nation's Indian population. It discusses the history of government relations with Indian tribes, describes the present condition of various tribes, discusses what is being done to help them, and makes suggestions for doing so. An important document which summarizes Indians' problems with compassion and skill.

452.   Buroker, Robert L. "From Voluntary Association to Welfare State: The Illinois Immigrants' Protective League, 1908-1926." Journal of American History, Vol. 58, No. 3 (December, 1971), 643-60. Building on the interpretive overviews published by Samuel Hays, Arthur Mann, Roy Lubove and Robert Wiebe, Buroker argues that in its leadership and activities, the IPL was a "proto-bureaucratic association" that was a vital foundation in the evolution of the American welfare state, particularly in the development of "modern" public bureaucracies.

453.   Clark, Kenneth. Dark Ghetto. New York: Harper and Row, 1965. A scholarly, impassioned examination of the Negro ghetto--Harlem--covering the social dynamics, the psychology, pathology, education, and public structure of the community, one which clearly destroys the fallacy that the inhabitants of the area are responsible for their condition. An indispensable work.

454.   Diner, Steven J. "Chicago Social Workers and Blacks in the Progressive Era." Social Service Review, Vol. 44, No. 4 (Dec., 1970), 393-410. This essay explores the relationship between social workers and blacks in Chicago between the years 1900 and 1920. In a city settled by some thirty different nationality groups, leading social workers not only discovered many simi-

larities between poor blacks and poor white immigrants but were impressed as well by the unique problems faced by the former because of racial discrimination, according to Diner; they sought to discover the place of blacks in a pluralistic society.

455.   Fishel, Leslie H. "The Negro in the New Deal Era." Wisconsin Magazine of History, Vol. 48, No. 2 (Winter, 1964-65), 111-26. While Franklin Roosevelt was the most attractive President for American Negroes since the Civil War, FDR's actual commitments to the black person were slim, as Fishel here demonstrates; he was more a symbol than an activist. His compassion, although real, was tempered by his background, by the enormity of the decisions he faced, and especially by political considerations.

456.   Glassberg, Eudice. "Work, Wages and the Cost of Living: Ethnic Differences and the Poverty Line, Philadelphia, 1880." Pennsylvania History, Vol. 46, No. 1 (January 1979), 17-58. This case study, conducted as part of the Philadelphia Social History Project, gives a striking portrait of the needs and resources available to poor people in Philadelphia. Not surprisingly, the unemployed, Blacks, the aged, and female-headed households were among the city's most vulnerable.

457.   Graymont, Barbara. "New York State Indian Policy After the Revolution." New York History, Vol. 57, No. 4 (Oct., 1976), 438-74. An examination and analysis of the process by which the Iroquois--due to their weak military position, their abandonment by the British, their disunity, the conflicting sovereignties between Congress and New York State, the weakness and indifference of the federal government, and the insatiable land hunger of the New Yorkers--gave up almost all of their lands in central and western New York and thus became powerless and poverty-stricken.

458.   Hasson, Gail S. "Health and Welfare of Freedmen in Reconstruction Alabama." Alabama Review, Vol. 35, No. 2 (April, 1982), 94-111. A study of the medical activities of the U.S. Freedmen's Bureau in Alabama, which, under the direction of the compassionate Wager Swayne of Ohio, a one-legged Union veteran, did a fantastic job in aiding the black aged, ill, and disabled: by "providing health and welfare services that were unavailable from any other source, the bureau saved untold numbers of needy blacks from suffering and pain," according to the author.

459.   Holley, Donald. "The Negro in the New Deal Resettlement Program." Agricultural History, Vol. 45, No. 3 (July, 1971), 179-93. This essay documents one of the federal

government's successful attempts to deal with the needs of poor southern blacks amidst the disappointing legacy of race relations during the first stages of the New Deal. A comment by Robert Nipp, who joined the Farmers Home Administration (an offshoot of the F.S.A.) follows.

460.   Horton, James Oliver and Lois E. Black Bostonians: Family Life and Community Struggle in the Antebellum North. New York: Holmes and Meier, 1979. This book's significance to social welfare historians lies in its demonstration of the existence of a viable black community in antebellum Boston. Through their informal associations and voluntary organizations, blacks sought to help themselves and to protest the denial of access to social services in the city.

461.   Jackson, Philip. "Black Charity in Progressive Era Chicago." Social Service Review, Vol. 52, No. 3 (Sept., 1978), 400-417. This study focuses on Chicago, a typical northern city of the period where, like elsewhere, blacks were segregated and excluded from the organized charitable resources of the community; it describes both the urban welfare needs of blacks and the organizations they established to fill those needs--homes for the aged, young women, and juveniles, orphanages, social settlements, and the like.

462.   Johnson, Samuel Otis. "The Social Welfare Role of the Black Church." Unpublished Ph.D. Diss., Brandeis University, 1980. An examination of the role the black church has played in the area of social welfare which concludes: (1) it has played an important role; (2) the nature of that role has been affected by the locality of the church and the socio-economic background and education of its members and ministers; (3) there is a need for such work, and (4) the black church can and should do more in the area of social action.

463.   Jones, James H. Bad Blood: The Tuskegee Syphilis Experiment. New York: Free Press, 1981. This study recounts the purposes and horrifying implications of a Public Health Service study conducted in Macon County, Alabama, between 1932 and 1972 to investigate whether untreated syphilis affected baacks differently from whites. The case study offers a judicious assessment of what happens when unthinking decisions become institutionalized in unregulated bureaucracies.

464.   Kogut, Alvin B. "The Negro and the Charity Organization Society in the Progressive Era." Social Service Review, Vol. 44, No. 1 (March, 1970), 11-21. The policies, practices, and attitudes of the charity organization society are explored with regard to the Negro during the Progressive era and, not surprisingly, it is found that

such societies did very little for blacks, primarily, according to the author of this study, because they really were not social reform organizations, which provided the sort of help blacks needed, and also because of the racism present in the movement.

465. Kogut, Alvin B. "The Settlements and Ethnicity, 1890-1914." Social Work, Vol. 17, No. 3 (May, 1972), 22-31. Prior to World War I, settlements were closer to immigrants than any other American institution. This analysis of major settlements in Chicago, Boston, and New York City focuses on their policies and practices, which the author demonstrates were guided by such diverse, even contradictory, attitudes such as veiled racism and egalitarianism.

466. Leiby, James. "How Social Workers Viewed the Immigrant Problem, 1890-1930." In Current Issues in Social Work Seen in Historical Perspective. New York: Council on Social Work Education, 1962, 30-42. Social workers, according to Leiky, pretty much had the same interest in and attitude toward the immigrant problem as did the general American public. However, they did avoid simple-minded stereotypes and at least had some sort of method for looking at and analyzing the problem, which proved useful later on, especially in reducing the divisions that plagued Americans.

467. Levitan, Sar A., William B. Johnston, and Robert Taggart. Still a Dream: The Changing Status of Blacks since 1960. This cogent and judicious analysis evaluates the composite impact of federal social programs and civil-rights activities on Black America. Although the authors believe that significant progress has been made, they note serious gaps in existing legislation and offer a guarded prognosis for the future.

468. Lewis, Oscar. La Vida: A Puerto Rican Family in the Culture of Poverty--San Juan and New York. New York: Random House, 1965. A classic model of the new urban anthropology, La Vida discusses the individual and collective options and views of poor Hispanics in modern America. Lewis's discussion of the "culture of poverty" concept in the introduction is essential reading.

469. Mandle, Jay R. The Roots of Black Poverty: The Southern Plantation Economy after the Civil War. Durham: Duke University Press, 1978. This analysis of the breakdown of the plantation economy, "The Great Migration" of blacks and the development of share-tenancy provides a cogent argument about the economic roots of black poverty. Mandle's Marxist perspective sheds new light on the subject, though a comparison of white tenants' problems would have bolstered this work's overall

significance.

470.   May, J. Thomas. "A Nineteenth Century Medical Care Program for Blacks: The Case of the Freedmen's Bureau."
Anthropological Quarterly, Vol. 46, No. 3 (July, 1973),
160-71. The author uses admissions data from a fed-
erally-sponsored hospital for blacks (in Shreveport,
La.) in the 1860s as a way of pinpointing change in medical care policy. He found that changes reflected conflicts among sponsoring agencies--the Freedmen's Bureau
and the Union Army--rather than the actual needs of the
black population. Resolution of the conflict eventually
was achieved because both groups sought a common
end--re-establishment of social order through a revival
of the plantation economy, a lesson useful for analysis
of more recent social welfare programs, according to the
author.

471.   Miller, Herman P. Poverty and the Negro. Los Angeles:
University of California's Institute of Government and
Public Affairs, 1965. A monograph that highlights the
growing economic gap between whites and blacks and the
failure of the War on Poverty to really do anything
about it.

472.   Mohl, Raymond and Neil Betten. "Paternalism and Pluralism: Immigrants and Social Welfare in Gary, Indiana,
1906-1910." American Studies, Vol. 15, No. 1 (Spring,
1974), 5-30. The authors of this study argue that, despite belief to the contrary, most settlement houses served the interests of American society more than those of
the immigrants in their neighborhoods; they were, in
other words, agencies of social control, which was not
the case with International Institutes, at least in
Gary, Indiana, and by implication elsewhere as well.
They conclude this provocative article with a plea for
more research in the area to better determine the purposes and programs of early twentieth century social
agencies working in immigrant communities.

473.   Moore, Deborah Dash. "From Kehillah to Federation: The
Communal Functions of Federated Philanthropy in New York
City, 1917-1933." American Jewish History, Vol. 68, NO.
2 (December, 1978), 131-146. Seizing on the dislocations wrought by World War I, Federation leaders
sought to adapt Progressive business ideals to Jewish
communal organization. This institution remained vital,
though with a different mission, when the Great Depression struck.

474.   Moynihan, Daniel P. The Negro Family: The Case for
National Action. Washington, D.C.: U.S. Dept. of
Labor, 1965. The famous and exceedingly controversial
Moynihan Report, as it is widely known, a review of the

Negro family in America from the American Revolution to the time of publication, in which the author argues that the structure of the black family is unstable and matriarchal, a result of slavery and discrimination--and that unless family stability is increased, the Negro will not be able to take advantage of educational or economic opportunities. Moynihan's data and interpretations not only have been hotly challenged but pretty much discredited in the last few years.

475. Myrdal, Gunnar. <u>An American Dilemma: The Negro Problem and Modern Democracy, 2 Vols.</u> New York: Pantheon, 1972. Published originally in 1944, this work probably is the most influential analysis of black America ever written. Myrdal's conceptual framework, data, and discussion of the relationship between American values and public policies remain indispensable to social welfare historians.

476. Nieman, Donald G. <u>To Set the Law in Motion: The Freedman's Bureau and the Legal Rights of Blacks, 1865-1868.</u> Millwood, NY: KTO Press, 1979. An important study of the Freedman's Bureau, which suggest that the "retreat from reconstruction" was more the result of legal strictures and constitutional impediments than of racist attitudes.

477. Olds, Victoria. "The Freedmen's Bureau: A Nineteenth Century Federal Welfare Agency." <u>Social Casework,</u> Vol. 44, No. 5 (May, 1963), 247-54. A very favorable account which attempts to rehabilitate the Freedmen's Bureau as an important pioneer social work agency, one that achieved, for a while at least, an integrated program of family centered service for thousands of black and white citizens in the South adversely affected by the Civil War and the social, political, and economic chaos of the postwar years.

478. Parris, Guichard and Lester Brooks. <u>Blacks in the City: A History of the National Urban League.</u> Boston: Little, Brown, 1971. A long, detailed, and at times rather dull "official," or authorized, study of the National Urban League. Still, it is a useful introduction to the problems of blacks in urban America and what one organization has attempted to do about them.

479. Pleck, Elizabeth H. <u>Black Migration and Poverty in Boston, 1865-1900.</u> New York: Academic Press, 1979. This monograph documents and attempts to explain the extent to which black upward mobility was blocked by racism and structural limitations imposed in both the public and private sectors. Of particular interest is Pleck's chapter on the black family, which rejects the "pathology of black culture" thesis set forth by Daniel

Moynihan in his 1965 report.

480.   Pollard, Leslie J. "Black Beneficial Societies and the Home for the Aged and Infirm Colored Persons: A Research Note." Phylon, Vol. 41, No. 3 (Sept., 1980), 230-34. A call for more research, and scholarship on black benevolent societies—a response to a burning desire for racial uplift in antebellum America—especially in providing psychological and economic support to the black community.

481.   Rabinowitz, Howard. "From Exclusion to Segregation: Health and Welfare Services for Southern Blacks, 1865-1890." Social Service Review, Vol. 48, No. 3 (Sept., 1974), 327-54. Immediately after the Civil War, southern whites continued to exclude most blacks from public welfare services and facilities. That changed when the so-called Radical Republicans came to power; under their tutelage, the policy of exclusion was replaced by one of separate but equal treatment. Their successors, the "Redeemers," continued and often expanded the segregated facilities, but rarely provided equal treatment. As the period waned, then, the gap between the provisions made for the two races widened.

482.   Rainwater, Lee and William L. Yancy. The Moynihan Report: The Politics of Controversy. Cambridge, Mass.: Massachusetts Institute of Technology Press, 1967. An analysis and critique of the so-called Moynihan Report on the Negro family and a provocative essay on the role of social science research in the formulation of public policy. On the whole, the writers are Moynihan supporters and critics of government bureaucrats whom they accuse of opposing Moynihan in order to protect their vested interests (in the Department of Health, Education, and Welfare).

483.   Raphael, Alan. "Health and Social Welfare for Kentucky Black People, 1865-1870." Societas, Vol. 2, No. 2 (Spring, 1972), 143-157. This case study describes the limited success of the short-lived Freedmans' Bureau in attending to the health-care needs of blacks. After this institution's demise, however, local authorities and private physicians were indifferent to blacks' deplorable situation.

484.   Rawick, George. From Sundown to Sunup: The Making of the Black Community. Westport, Conn. Greenwood Press, 1972. Based primarily on slave narratives assembled by the Federal Writers Project in the 1930s, which the author edited, this pioneering work is a story of slavery which portrays blacks in the process of creating a vital culture rooted in African traditions and sustained in the face of oppression.

485. Roberts, Shirley J. "Minority-Group Poverty in Phoenix: A Socio-Economic Survey." The Journal of Arizona History, Vol. 14, No. 4 (Winter, 1973), 347-62. Throughout the twentieth century, Phoenix's poor have consisted of Mexicans, Indians, Blacks, Chinese, and aging native-white health seekers and migrant workers. Attitudes among the Anglo-American elite changed from indifference to concern around the 1940s, but the mode of life in South Phoenix did not change dramatically.

486. Romanofsky, Peter. ". . . 'To Rid Ourselves of the Burden . . .': New York Jewish Charities and the Origins of the Industrial Removal Office, 1890-1901." American Jewish Historical Quarterly, Vol. 64, No. 4 (June, 1975), 332-43. An interesting account of attempts by New York City Jews to relieve problems of poverty and need resulting from overcrowdedness and discrimination—in part by efforts to establish Jewish agricultural colonies outside the city.

487. Roper, Arthur F. "The Southern Negro and the NRA." Georgia Historical Quarterly, Vol. 64, No. 2 (Summer, 1980), 128-45. Despite the fact that the two areas that most greatly affected blacks, agriculture and domestic service, did not come under NRA codes, that measure really hurt them, largely through the loss of marginal jobs, thanks in large part to the closing up of many small businesses. No wonder blacks referred to the measure as the "Negro Removal Act."

488. Ross, Edyth L. "Black Heritage in Social Welfare: A Case Study of Atlanta." Phylon, Vol. 37, No. 4 (Dec., 1976), 197-307. A case study of the black response to need in Atlanta, Georgia (both in the form of treatment and prevention) which illustrates that the black population has a long history of developing creative and innovative ways of solving its social problems—and should help dispel the myth that blacks did nothing for themselves.

489. Thompson, Gregory C. "The Origins and Implementation of the American Indian Reform Movement: 1867-1912." Unpublished Ph.D. Diss., University of Utah, 1981. Between the end of the Civil War and the year 1912, a small group of Americans focused on a series of reforms aimed at aiding American Indians. How these people (either individually or in small groups, usually religiously affiliated) formed their movement, the traditions they drew upon, the people involved, the programs developed, and their successes and failures are the questions central to this study, which suggests that the "reformers" were united in the belief that the red man had to change if he was to survive in American society.

490.   Weeks, Philip and James B. Gidney. Subjugation and Dishonor: A Brief History of the Travail of the Native Americans. New York: Robert Krueger, 1981. An exceedingly well written and moving account of the white elite's cruel, inhumane treatment of the American Indian from the colonial period to the present; a work that brings to life both the human qualities and the tragedy of the American Indian.

491.   White, George C. "Social Settlements and Immigrant Neighbors, 1886-1914." Social Service Review, Vol. 33, No. 1 (March, 1959), 55-66. According to the author of this older "progressive" interpretation of the movement, the residents of social settlements were among the first Americans to appreciate the cultural heritage which foreigners brought to America and the first to combat the notion of assimilation. They originated a conception of the immigrant and his place in American society which stood in sharp contrast to the prevailing views of the period prior to World War I.

492.   Wilson, William J. The Declining Significance of Race. Chicago: The University of Chicago Press, 1978. This controversial monograph argues that due to recent social trends and the impact of federal welfare and educational intitiatives, class handicaps, not race per se, have become the major barrier for minorities trying to break out of the web of poverty.

493.   Young, Robert Allan. "Regional Development and Rural Poverty in the Navajo Indian Area." Unpublished Ph.D. Diss., University of Wisconsin-Madison, 1976. By integrating geographers' and economists' theories into a regional development model of the Navajo Reservation from 1868 to 1974, this thesis traces changes in Indian attitudes and behavior as well as the significance of federal intervention in altering the intratribal circumstances of this economically depressed area.

3.3. GENDER-SPECIFIC

494.   Amsterdam, Susan. "The National Women's Trade Union League." Social Service Review, Vol 56, No. 2 (June, 1982), 259-72. An examination of the origin, devlopment, and activities of the National Women's Trade Union League, 1903-1950, a social reform organization formed during the Progressive era to assist unorganized women become unionized and improve their working conditions. The article also presents biographical material to illustrate the divergent backgrounds of its members and concludes with an analysis of the current status of women in the labor force.

495.   Brumberg, Joan Jacobs and Nancy Tomes. "Women in the
Professions: A Research Agenda for American Historians." Reviews in American History, Vol. 10, No. 2
(June, 1982), 275-96. This essay reviews the literature
on the role of women in the evolution of social work and
other "helping professions," and explores why this important topic has been slighted recently by women's historians.

496.   Candela, Joseph L., Jr. "The Struggle to Limit the
Hours and Raise the Wages of Working Women in Illinois,
1893-1917." Social Service Review, Vol. 53, No. 1
(March, 1971), 15-34. A study of the attempt by reformers in the state of Illinois during the Progressive
era to secure labor legislation to protect female wage
earners--efforts that met with only limited success.
The work examines the ideas mobilized for and against
the proposed reforms in an attempt to discover more
fully the period's reform mentally.

497.   Dublin, Thomas. Women at Work. New York: Columbia
University Press, 1979. In this prize-winning study of
the transformation of work and community in Lowell,
Massachusetts from 1826 to 1860, Dublin reveals the
shared experiences and cultural values, blind spots,
ethnic rivalries, and difficulties experienced by Yankee
and then Irish women in this prototypical factory town.
Social welfare issues emerge from his discussion of
shifting labor practices.

498.   Freedman, Estelle B. Their Sister's Keeper: Women's
Prison Reform in America, 1830-1930. Ann Arbor: University of Michigan Press, 1981. This study explores
changes in th ideology and strategies set forth by
middle-class women reformers to deal with female offenders, who typically suffered abuse, neglect and poor
conditions in state institutions. While little attention is given to the actual background of women
criminals, Freedman succeeds in elucidating many points
of convergence and divergence between women's history
and welfare history.

499.   Melder, Keith. "Ladies Bountiful: Organized Women's
Benevolence in Early Nineteenth Century America." New
York History, Vol. 48, No. 3 (July, 1967), 231-54. A
consideration of the background, general pattern of development, and some of the consequences of women's voluntary welfare organizations during the first forty
years of the nineteenth century, the most important of
which were changes in attitudes toward the status of
women.

500.   Rauch, Julia B. "Women in Social Work: Friendly Visi-

tors in Philadelphia, 1880." Social Service Review,
Vol. 49 (June, 1975), 241-59. An examination of the
women affiliated with the Philadelphia charity organization society, based on census data, suggests that the
typical "friendly visitor" was an older, native-born
white woman from the city's upper socio-economic strata
who was looking for a role alternative after her children had matured. It further suggests that charity organization flourished in the late nineteenth century because feminist impulses coincided with conservative
class interests.

501.   Rousmaniere, John P. "Cultural Hybrid in the Slums:
The College Woman and the Settlement House, 1889-1894."
American Quarterly, Vol. 22, No. 1 (Spring, 1970),
45-66. A study of the origins of the first woman's settlement house in America that was stimulated by the
question, why did a particular group of women found such
an organization in 1889? The answer, according to the
author, is, because the settlement was functional for
college women—in four related ways: 1) it was a socially approved alternative to very few other service
activities; 2) it served as a "home" for young college
women in a hostile world; 3) it was a middle class out-
post that concretized an otherwise abstract sense of
uniqueness, and 4) as a voluntary organization, it articulated the college woman's sense of superiority over
other young women.

502.   Stansell, Mary Christine. "Women of the Laboring Poor
in New York City, 1820-1860." Unpublished Ph.D. Diss.,
Yale University, 1979. This study emphasizes the significance of conflicts over gender roles among poor women
in urban milieu. Due to their employoment options and
household circumstances, only married women in the
emerging working class could aspire to the cult of middle-class domesticity.

503.   Ware, Susan. Beyond Suffrage: Women in the New Deal.
Cambridge, Mass.:" Harvard University Press, 1981.
This study of the pivotal role played by Frances
Perkins, Eleanor Roosevelt, Molly Dewson and twenty-five
other women in shaping New Deal public policies sheds
new light on social welfare initiatives at the federal
level between 1910 and 1940.

3.4. CLASS.
504.   Cumbler, John T. "The Politics of Charity: Gender and
Class in Late Nineteenth Century Charity Policy."
Journal of Social History, Vol. 14, No. 1 (Fall, 1980),
99-111. It is the thesis of this interesting and
well-conceived study that charity in the smaller in-

dustrial cities was initially controlled by male elites and that as females moved into positions of control they altered the policies and the orientation of those organizations; they paid less attention to welfare cheaters and more to reform, especially regarding women and child-related matters.

505.   Gettleman, Marvin E. "Charity and Social Classes in the United States, 1874-1900." American Journal of Economics and Sociology, Vol. 22, No. 2 (April, 1963), 313-30, and Vol. 22, No. 3 (July, 1963), 417-26. A clear Marxist interpretation of the charity organization movement which, according to the author, was cloaked in the rhetoric of equality and Christianity but, in reality, was a class-based effort at social control, one which because of internal shortcomings and contradictions, had hopelessly failed by the turn of the century. Success could result only from a fundamental reform of society, something never visualized by these nineteenth century charity workers, according to the author.

506.   Gettleman, Marvin E. "Philanthropy as Social Control in Late Nineteenth Century America." Societas, Vol 5, No. 1 (Winter, 1975), 49-59. Another critical attack on late nineteenth century social welfare from the perspective of the left. Here, Gettleman argues that with the failure of the charity organization movement a new effort at social control was concocted, this time in the guise of professional social work. Professionalism, which would not advocate radical change but rather would deal with the victims of capitalism, operated as a brake on growing radicalism and an assurance to the business elite that their hegemony never would be seriously challenged.

507.   Hall, Peter. "A Model of Boston Charitable Benevolence and Class Development." Science and Society, Vol. 38, No. 4 (Winter, 1974-75), 464-77. A Marxist interpretation which argues that there was a direct relationship between nineteenth century charitable endowments (to colleges, hospitals, dispensaries, medical schools, etc.), merchant families who made those endowments, and the economic life of the state and nation. Charitable endowments, in other words, were useful to the economic elite; they provided a form of social control, one that would help transform American entrepreneurial activities into corporate capitalism.

508.   Rosenberg, Charles. "Social Class and Medical Care in Nineteenth-Century America: The Rise an Fall of the Dispensary." Journal of the History of Medicine and Allied Sciences, Vol. 29 No. 1 (Jan., 1974), 32-54. A study of the medical dispensary, a nineteenth century

institution which was both the primary means for providing the urban poor with medical care and a vital link
in the prevailing system of medical education. The author uses the dispensary to illustrate not only an important aspect of nineteenth century medicine and philanthropy but significant relationships between general
social needs and values and the narrower world of medical men and ideas.

509.   Thernstrom, Stephen A. Poverty and Progress: Social
Mobility in a Nineteenth Century City. Cambridge,
Mass.: Harvard University Press, 1964. This case study
of Newburyport, Mass., between 1850 and 1880, has had an
impact on historical thinking and methodology that goes
beyond its actual conclusions on nineteenth-century mobility patterns. It remains essential reading for social
welfare historians.

4. AGE-SPECIFIC AND LIFE-CYCLE STUDIES.
    510.   Achenbaum, W. Andrew. Old Age in the New World: The
    American Experience Since 1790. Baltimore: Johns
    Hopkins University Press, 1978. A condensation of the
    author's dissertation in which he traces the meanings
    and experiences of being old in the United States from
    1790 to the 1970s.

    511.   Bushman, Richard L. "Family Security from Farm to City,
    1750-1850." Journal of Family Hisory, Vol. 6, No. 3
    (Fall, 1981), 238-56. This important essay summarizes
    much of the literature on changes in familial duties and
    intergenerational exchanges necessitated by moving the
    household from an agrarian to an urban milieu.

    512.   Demos, John and Sarane Spence Boocock, eds., Turning
    Points: Historical and Sociological Essays on the
    Family. Chicago: University of Chicago Press, 1978.
    This valuable, interdisciplinary collection of essays
    focuses on the relationship between family dynamics and
    transitions offered by larger societal forces. It is a
    useful theoretical and bibliographic resource for social
    welfare historians.

    513.   Elder, Glen H. Jr. Children of the Great Depression:
    Social Change in Life Experience. Chicago: The Univer-
    sity of Chicago Press, 1974. In this longitudinal study
    of a Depression cohort of children from working and mid-
    dle-class homes, Elder not only offers a stunning in-
    terpretation of American character during the last
    half-century but also provides a splendid model of the
    family-cycle approach to the historical, social, and
    psychological development of a pivotal generation.

514.   Fischer, David Hackett. Growing Old in America. New
        York: Oxford University Press, 1977. The first
        full-length scholarly work to place the process of aging
        in America in historical perspective. Fischer argues
        that old age was venerated in colonial America; change
        began to occur, however, in the late nineteenth cen-
        tury. By the twentieth century, old age came to be held
        in contempt and a cult of youth developed. Fischer,
        though, pointing to recent interest in and concern for
        the elderly, suggests that we may be entering a new
        period characterized by a partnership between the old
        and young, and concludes by offering several suggestions
        to combat the social and economic disadvantages of the
        aged.

515.   Glasco, Laurence A. "The Life Cycles and Household
        Structures of American Ethnic Groups: Irish, Germans,
        and Native-born Whites in Buffalo, New York, 1855."
        Journal of Urban History, Vol. 1, No. 3 (May, 1975),
        339-64. Using a life-cycle approach, Glasco reveals how
        age and gender were related to processes of ethnic
        stratification and assimilation. In so doing, he sug-
        gests theoretical issues that affect the relationship of
        nineteenth-century social welfare responses to the needs
        of the immigrant poor.

516.   Hareven, Tamara K., Family Time and Industrial Time.
        New York: Cambridge University Press, 1982. This im-
        pressive case study of family life and work patterns
        among two generations of native-born and immigrant tex-
        tile workers employed by the Amoskeag Manufacturing Com-
        pany in Manchester, NH, between the 1880s and 1930s is a
        model of research and exposition. Its data on charity,
        kin assistance and public welfare are no less important
        than its theoretcal contributions.

517.   Hawes, Joseph M. Children in Urban Society: Juvenile
        Delinquency in Nineteenth Century America. New York:
        Oxford University Press, 1971. In this, the first con-
        temporary history of juvenile delinquency in nineteenth
        century America, the author argues that new ways of pre-
        venting delinquency arose not just as a result of
        changing social conditions but also as a reflection of
        new views on childhood and youth as phases of the life
        cycle.

518.   Kett, Joseph F. Rites of Passage: Adolescence in
        America, 1790 to the Present. New York: Basic Books,
        1977. This work is primarily concerned with the in-
        tellectual and social features of the transformation of
        the male life cycle which gave greater specificity and
        meanings to the concept of "adolescence" after 1850.
        Kett offers incisive comments about the role of various
        social welfare institutions--ranging from Sunday schools

to social workers' programs--in effecting this transformation.

519.   Mennel, Robert M. Thorns and Thistles: Juvenile
Delinquents in the United States, 1825-1940. Hanover,
N.H.: University Press of New England, 1973. An important and judicious study of institutional responses
to juvenile delinquency. Mennel stresses the significance of "scientific" inquiry in the ways reformers
defined and dealt with the problem.

520.   Schlossman, Steven L. Love and the American
Delinquent: The Theory and Practice of "Progressive"
Juvenile Justice, 1825-1920. Chicago: University of
Chicago Press, 1977. More than other historians of juvenile delinquency, Schlossman eschews an interpretation
that either emphasizes humanitarian-reformist impulses
or underscores repressive acts. Rather, he stresses the
structural elements of modernization that altered prevailing modes of handling wayward youth.

521.   Tilly, Louise A. and Miriam Cohen. "Does the Family
Have a History?" Social Science History, Vol. 6, No. 2
(Spring, 1982), 131-79. This judicious review of three
major approaches to doing family history--"demographic"
"sentiments," and "household economics"--provides the
student of social welfare history with a first-class introduction to the literature and source of references
for case studies in the United States and Western Europe.

522.   Vinovskis, Maris A. "Recent Trends in American Historical Demography: Some Metholological and Conceptual
Considerations." Annual Review of Sociology, Vol. 4
(1978), 603-627. This review essay by one of America's
foremost historical demographers summarizes the "state
of the art" in theories about the life cycle and family
cycle in past and present times. As such it offers invaluable methodological insights about the family for
students of social welfare history.

5.   THE AMERICAN EXPERIENCE IN COMPARATIVE PERSPECTIVE.

523.   Flora, Peter and Arnold Heidenheimer, eds. The
Development of Welfare States in Europe and America.
New Brunswick: Transaction Books, 1980. A collection
of essays on "modern" welfare history that conjoin historical trend analysis and cross-cultural comparisons.

524.   Furniss, Norman and Timothy Tilton. The Case for the
Welfare State: From Social Security to Social
Equality. Bloomington: Indiana University Press,
1977. In this comparative study, Furniss and Tilton
distinguish among three kinds of governmental in-

tervention--the corporate-oriented positive state (the United States), the social-security state (Great Britain), and the social-welfare state (Sweden)--in dealing with the issues of bureaucratic responsiveness and citizen participation in dealing with poverty. A case is made for the Swedish model.

525.   Mencher, Samuel. Poor Law to Poverty Program: Economic Security Policy in Britain and the United States. Pittsburgh: University of Pittsburgh Press, 1967. A very useful, comprehensive, and relatively dispassionate intellectual history of poverty and welfare policy in Great Britain and the United States from the age of mercantilism to the time of writing.

526.   Rimlinger, Gaston. "Welfare Policy and Economic Development: A Comparative Historical Perspective." Journal of Economic History, Vol. 26, No. 4 (Dec., 1966), 556-71. Rimlinger puts forth the hypothesis that the historic shift from poor relief to a modern welfare system in America and Europe is at least partly a "response to the rising productivity and increasing scarcity of labor." When labor was cheap and unskilled, welfare was meager and designed to control the poor, but in highly developed modern economies,he argues, labor is scarce and worth the expense of greater welfare care. While the article is not directly about unemployment, its argument is relevant to an evaluation of changing responses to unemployment.

527.   Rimlinger, Gaston. Welfare Policy and Industrialization in Europe, America, and Russia. New York: Wiley, 1971. Using both an historical and comparative approach, this analysis treats the evolution of basic welfare policies in the context of changing socio-economic development.

528.   Schneider, Saundra Kay. "The Evolution of the Modern Welfare State: A Comparative Analysis of the Development of Social Welfare Programs in the United States, Canada, and Western Europe." Unpublished Ph.D. Diss., State University of New York at Binghamton, 1980. Integrating theoretical, historical, and empirical data in this comparative social policy analysis, Schneider concludes that democratic political participation is the most important and constant stimulator to welfare-state programs.

529.   Woodroofe, Kathleen. From Charity to Social Work in England and the United States. Toronto: University of Toronto Press, 1962. The only general comparative survey of social work in the United States and England, this is a well written useful work (from the British perspective) that goes from "The English Origins" to

"Lady Bountiful in the New World" to "From Lady Bountiful to Social Welfare." Highly recommended as an introductory survey.

Chapter Two
CARING FOR THE INFANT AND CHILD

Walter I. Trattner
University of Wisconsin-Milwaukee

Issues Covered: Infant mortality, aid to dependent children, child labor, U.S. Children's Bureau, institutions, juvenile delinquency, children's courts.

1. SYNTHESES AND OVERVIEWS.

1.1. THEMATIC

530. Aries, Philippe. <u>Centuries of Childhood: A Social History of Family Life</u>. New York: Random House, 1960. An extremely important but controversial study of the development of ideas about children and child care between the Middle Ages and the early nineteenth century. The central thesis of the work is that the traditional child was happy because he was free to mix with people of many ages and classes. However, in the early modern period a special condition known as childhood was "invented," resulting in a tyrannical concept of the family which destroyed friendship and sociability and deprived children of freedom, inflicting upon them for the first time the rod and the prison cell.

531. Beales, Ross W. "In Search of the Historical Child: Miniature Adulthood and Youth in Colonial New England." <u>American Quarterly</u>, Vol. 27, No. 4 (Oct., 1975), 379-98. This article takes issue with the widely held belief that colonial Americans regarded children as "miniature adults" and recognized no stage of adolescence.

532. Finestone, Harold. <u>Victims of Change: Juvenile Delinquents in American Society</u>. Westport, Conn.: Greenwood Press, 1976. The title of this work is misleading; it does not deal with juvenile delinquents, but rather with theories of delinquency since the early 1800s, concentrating on three major twentieth century views—the Chicago School, the subcultural theorists, and the labeling theorists. While not a comprehensive review, or critique, of delinquency theory, it nevertheless is an important work that effective links such theory to broad historical developments.

533. Gil, David G. <u>Violence Against Children: Physical</u>

Child Abuse in the United States. Cambridge, Mass.: Harvard Univ. Press, 1970. Although most people claimed that child abuse was on the rise, there was an incredible lack of systematic information on the subject. This work was an attempt to fill that gap. Actually, the book presented a comprehensive report on a number of studies on physical abuse of children initiated in 1965 by the U.S. Children's Bureau.

534.   Gillis, John R. "Essay Review: Youth in History: Progress and Prospects." Journal of Social History, Vol. 7, No. 2 (Winter, 1974), 201-07. A collective book review of Oscar and Mary Handlin's Facing Life, Joseph Hawes' Children in Urban Society, Jack Hall's Juvenile Reform in the Progressive Era, Robert Mennel's Thorns and Thistles, and Anthony Platt's The Child Savers; useful for an understanding of the "state" of the scholarly knowledge on the subject in the mid-1970s.

535.   Hawes, Joseph. Children in Urban Society: Juvenile Delinquency in Nineteenth Century America. New York: Oxford University Press, 1971. A "progressive" account of nineteenth century urban America's treatment of juvenile delinquents, as told largely through the story of various reformers, all of whom are taken at face value--a story of a series of successful steps taken by selfless altruists that culminate in the creation of the juvenile court, the supposed embodiment of the view that wayward youth are not members of stereotyped groups but are "people" with particular difficulties who stand in need of individual treatment.

536.   Mennel, Robert M. Thorns and Thistles: Juvenile Delinquents in the United States, 1825-1940. Hanover, N.H.: University Press of New England, 1973. An exceptionally well researched analysis of society's changing perceptions of and solutions to the problem of juvenile delinquency. Mennel is much less prone to heap praise on the "reformers" than was Hawes perhaps in part because he carries the story to 1940, by which time criticisms of earlier reforms had begun to appear. In any event, this is a very good study with an exceptionally useful last chapter on modern theories of delinquency.

537.   Platt, Anthony M. The Child Savers: The Invention of Delinquency. Chicago: University of Chicago Press, 1977. Focusing on the process by which certain acts came to be labeled deviant or criminal, Platt analyzes the late nineteenth and early twentieth century child-saving movement, including establishment of the juvenile court, and contends that it was not a benign effort to liberate and dignify youth but rather a punitive and intrusive one to control the lives of lower

class urban youngsters—and to provide career opportunities outside the home for middle-class women.
One of the most important and influential of the social
control works, it must be read by all students of child
and social welfare.

538.   Ryerson, Ellen. The Best-Laid Plans: America's
Juvenile Court Experiment. New York: Hill and Wang,
1978. An extremely important and lucid study of the institutional and intellectual history of the juvenile
court movement which demonstrates that it was the
creature of shifting social perceptions and reformist
positions over a long period of time. It is clear from
this study that the origin of the court should not be
judged from the vantage point of its later failures—and
thus, in many ways, serves as a corrective, or at least
a counterpoint, to the Platt book.

539.   Schlossman, Steven. Love and the American Delinquent:
The Theory and Practice of "Progressive" Juvenile
Justice, 1825-1920. Chicago: University of Chicago
Press, 1977. A clear, readable, and relatively sophisticated analysis of attempts to deal with juvenile delinquents in America, from 1825 to 1920. If "love" has
not always characterized those efforts, neither has re-
pressiveness, according to Schlossman. Urbanization,
industrialization, disorder (real or imagined), progressive ideology, and other factors all have affected
efforts to socialize wayward youth.

1.2. TEMPORAL
540.   James, Arthur W. "Foster Care in Virginia, 1679-1796."
Public Welfare, Vol. 8, No. 3 (March, 1950), 60-64. An
interesting account of boarding dependent and neglected
children in foster homes at public expense in Virginia
from 1679 to 1796.

541.   Meditch, Andrea. "In the Nation's Interest: Child Care
Prescriptions, 1890-1930." Unpublished Ph.D. Diss.,
University of Texas-Austin, 1981. This dissertation analyzes child-rearing advice literature produced in the
United States between 1890-1930. It argues that during
the period the literature encoded a process by which
human beings were presumed to pass from the state of
nature to the state of culture, or "civilization." At
the same time, the power to define the terms of the debate and control the knowledge considered relevant to
socialization shifted from the lay populace (mothers) to
an emergent professional subclass, which, in turn, led
to, or was accompanied by, the breakdown of the family
as the fundamental unit of society; it was superseded by
the relationship of the "individual" to the in-

stitutional context and the "state."

542.   New York Children's Aid Society. The Crusade for the
Children: A Review of Child Life in New York During
Seventy-Five Years, 1853-1928. New York: Children's
Aid Society, 1928. An historical sketch of the New York
Children's Aid Society which pays special attention to
the early days of its work and pays tribute to Charles
Loring Brace and his son, each of whom headed the or-
ganization for thirty-seven and a half years.

543.   Padernacht, Robert Z. "The Contributions of the New
York Association for Improving the Condition of the Poor
to Child Welfare." Unpublished Ph.D. Diss., St. John's
University 1976. This study traces and analyzes the
child welfare activities of the N.Y.A.I.C.P. and its relation to the child welfare movement in America from its
founding in 1843 through 1939, when it ended its existence as an independent organization by merging with
the city's C.O.S. to form the Community Service Society
of New York.

544.   Speizman, Milton D. "Child Care: A Mirror of Human
History." Children and YOuth Services Review, Vol. 3
(1981), 213-32. Asserting that child care in any period
of history can be understood best as a reflection of society itself during that era, and that therefore when
children are treated cruelly or indifferently people of
all ages are treated similarly and vice versa, Speizman
then goes on to survey the history of child care in
America from the colonial period to the present in an
effort to document that assertion; an interesting, well
written, and useful essay.

545.   Tiffin, Susan. "Charity's Children: The Welfare of Dependent and Neglected Children in the United States,
1890-1920." Unpublished Ph.D. Diss., Unversity of New
South Wales (Australia), 1978. A study that primarily
seeks to explain why destitute and dependent children
caused so much concern among late nineteenth and early
twentieth century Americans, and concludes that it was
not merely for humanitarian reasons: "Anxious Americans, who feared increasing stratification and conflict,
looked to the successful socialization of children to
ensure a stable future." Indeed, in the author's
opinion, in most cases the needs of children were sub-
ordinated to the needs of American society as in-
terpreted by controlling groups.

546.   Tillman, Elvena B. "The Rights of Childhood: The
National Child Welfare Movement, 1890-1919." Unpublished Ph.D. Diss., University of Wisconsin, 1968.
Another study of the national child welfare move-
ment--its origin, development, philosophy, and

leaders—which arrives at a totally different conclusion from the Tiffin work. According to the author of this study, the moving force behind the child welfare movement was the belief by a number of dedicated people that all children had rights that needed to be promoted and protected by society.

547.   Zelizer, Viviana A. "The Price and Value of Children: The Case of Children's Insurance. American Journal of Sociology, Vol. 86, No. 5 (March, 1981), 1036-56. An analysis of the development of children's insurance in the U.S., 1875-1920, particularly the legislative struggle between child insurers and child savers who opposed the insuring of children—and the victory of the former, demonstrating the complex relationship between the human and the market value of children.

1.3. (AUTO)BIOGRAPHIES

548.   Abbott, Edith. "Grace Abbott: A Sister's Memories." Social Service Review, Vol. 13, No. 3 (Sept. 1939), 351-408. A review of Grace Abbott's activities from her childhood in Nebraska to her service as Chief of the U.S. Children's Bureau.

549.   Abbott, Edith. Some American Pioneers in Social Welfare: Select Documents with Editorial Notes. Chicago: Unviersity of Chicago Press, 1937. Documented biographies of seven pioneers in the history of social welfare, including Stephen Girard and Charles Loring Brace, important figures in the area of child welfare.

550.   Addams, Jane. "A Great Public Servant, Julia C. Lathrop." Social Service Review, Vol. 6, No. 2 (June, 1932), 280-85. A brief tribute to Julia Lathrop expressed through a discussion of her many activities, especially, however, her tenure as Chief of the U.S. Children's Bureau.

551.   Campbell, D'Ann. "Judge Ben Lindsey and the Juvenile Court Movement, 1901-04." Arizona and the West, Vol. 18 (Spring, 1976), 5-20. A favorable account of Lindsey and the early juvenile court movement placed within the context of the so-called Progressive movement. The author, however, does point out the possible abuses in the system, which eventually led to the Gault decision.

552.   Flynn, Frank T. "Judge Merrit W. Pinckney and the Early Days of the Juvenile Court in Chicago." Social Service Review, Vol. 28, No. 1 (March, 1954), 20-30. A tribute to Judge Merritt Pinckney, whose service to the Cook County Juvenile Court in the early twentieth century de-

monstrated, according to the author, that at a difficult
time when the court was in grave danger from attacks and
had numerous obstacles to overcome, a man of basic personal integrity was able to carry on in such a manner
that the court emerged stronger than it was before.

553.   Goldmark, Josephine.   Impatient Crusader: Florence
Kelley's Life Story.   Urbana, Ill.:   University of
Illinois Press, 1953. Few people worked as hard or contributed as much to the well-being of America's children
as Florence Kelley, the sharp-tongued reformer who has
been fairly well captured in this very favorable biography written by her friend and co-worker.

554.   Larned, J. N.   The Life and Work of William P.
Letchworth.   Boston: Houghton Mifflin, 1912.   An uncritical and very favorable biography of William P.
Letchworth, a successful businessman who became a
"student and minister of public benevolence" and whose
special interests during his twenty-three years as a
member of the State Board of Public Charities in the
latter nineteenth century were dependent and neglected
children, as well as the epileptic and insane; a story
of noble labors on their behalf.

555.   Larsen, Charles.   The Good Fight: The Life and Times of
Ben B. Lindsey.   Chicago: Quadrangle Books, 1972.   A
biography of the best known juvenile court judge in
America whose avante-garde position on a variety of social questions, including the sexual revolution, women's
liberation, trial marriage, and the revolt of youth,
made him a controversial figure of international prom-
inence.

556.   Lenroot, Katharine F.   "Friend of Children and of the
Children's Bureau."   Social Service Review, Vol. 22, NO.
4 (Dec., 1948), 427-30.   An excellent summary of
Sophonisba Breckinridge's contributions to child welfare, as a Chicago social worker and reformer, as dean
of the Chicago School of Civics and Philanthropy, as a
professor at the University of Chicago School of Social
Service Administration, and especially as a firm supporter of the U.S. Children's Bureau and author of many
of its studies on children and child welfare.

557.   Lenroot, Katharine.   "Sophonisba Preston Breckinridge,
Social Pioneer."   Social Service Review, Vol. 23, No. 1
(March, 1949), 88-92.   Another article by the former
Chief of the U.S. Children's Bureau which summarizes
Breckinridge's contributions to child welfare, this time
especially her research and writing, particularly on ju-
venile courts.

558.   Lindsey, Benjamin B.   Twenty-Five Years of the Juvenile

and Family Court of Denver. Denver: Ben B. Lindsey,
1925. A commemorative piece on the twenty fifth an-
niversary of the founding of juvenile court in Denver,
Colorado; part 1, an address by Lindsey on the history
of the court, is especially interesting and useful.

559.   Lundberg, Emma O. "Pathfinders of the Middle Years."
Social Service Review, Vol. 21, No. 1 (March, 1947),
1-34. An article on progress in the area of child welfare as reflected through the philosophy and work of
leaders in the field during the prior four or five dec-
ades--Walter E. Fernald, Kate Waller Barrett, H. H.
Hart, Florence Kelley, Julia Lathrop, R.R. Reeder,
William J. Kerby, J. Prentice Murphy, Grace Abbott, C.
C. Carstens, Martha P. Falconer, and David C. Adie.

560.   Lundberg, Emma O. Unto the Least of These: Social
Services for Children. New York: Appleton-Century,
1947. In addition to an assessment of the current state
of child welfare work and suggestions for extending and
improving it, the book contains useful biographical
sketches of approximately twenty leaders in the field,
many of which are duplicated in her Social Service
Review article, "Pathfinders of the Middle Years."

561.   Perkins, Frances. "My Recollections of Florence
Kelley." Social Service Review, Vol. 28, No. 1 (March,
1954), 12-19. A glowing personal recollection of
Florence Kelley's contributions to social welfare, with
emphasis on her work to eliminate child labor. Kelley,
according to Perkins, "effected basic changes in American life by her brilliant analysis of the need for social advance, by her selfless dedication, by her
grueling research and reliance on facts, and by her
courage and sense of personal responsibility."

562.   Slater, Peter G. "Ben Lindsey and the Denver Juvenile
Court: A Progressive Looks at Human Nature." American
Quarterly, Vol. 20, No. 2 (Summer, 1968), 211-33. A
study of Ben Lindsey's ideas on human nature and therapeutic treatment for its disorders, as well as his role
as a progressive spokesman on these and related matters. Unfortunately, the author attributes too much influence to Lindsey for changing the public's attitudes
toward juvenile delinquents and their treatment.

563.   Trattner, Walter I. Homer Folks: Pioneer in Social
Welfare. New York: Columbia University Press, 1968. A
full-length biography of this "pioneer in social welfare" who began as a child welfare worker and then
moved into virtually every other area of social welfare,
and whose significance and record of achievements, according to the author, "are unmatched in the annals of
American humanitarianism." Includes a lot of historical

material on all aspects of child welfare.

564.   Wright, Helen R. "Three Against Time: Edith and Grace
        Abbott and Sophonisba Breckinridge." Social Service
        Review, Vol. 28, No. 1 (March, 1954), 41-53. "Three
        against time" connotes the qualities the author feels
        characterized the three remarkable women discussed in
        this article--boundless energy, broad vision, and a
        burning desire to accomplish. Whatever their pecu-
        liarities and differences, all three shared those
        characteristics plus a passion for service and a dis-
        taste for injustice and inequality.

565.   Young, Imogene S. "Jane Addams and Child Welfare Re-
        forms, 1889-1899." Unpublished D.S.W. Diss., Catholic
        University of America, 1967. The author of this study
        collects, systematizes and conceptualizes the work of
        Jane Addams on behalf of child welfare reform,
        1889-1899, with emphasis on the fact that, in almost all
        cases--whether it be in health, education, child labor,
        recreation, or whatever--she saw the need for increased
        federal intervention.

1.4.   DOCUMENTARIES, INCLUDING PROCEEDINGS OF WHITE HOUSE CONFERENCES
        ON DEPENDENT CHILDREN

566.   White House Conference, 1909. Proceedings of the
        Conference on the Care of Dependent Children Held At
        Washington, D.C., January 25, 26, 1909. Washington,
        D.C.: Government Printing Office, 1909.

567.   White House Conference, 1919. Standards of Child
        Welfare: A Report of the Children's Bureau Conference,
        May and June, 1919. Washington, D.C.: Government
        Printing Office 1919.

568.   White House Conference, 1930. White House Conference on
        Child Health and Protection, 1930: Addresses and
        Abstracts of Committee Reports New York: D.
        Appleton-Century, 1931.

569.   White House Conference 1930. Dependent and Neglected
        Children; Report of the Committee on the Socially Handi-
        capped--Dependency and Neglect. New York: D.
        Appleton-Century, 1933.

570.   White House Conference, 1940. Proceedings: Including
        the General Report Adopted by the Conference.
        Washington, D.C.: Government Printing Office, 1940.

571.   White House Conference, 1940. Final Report of the White
        House Conference on Children in a Democracy.
        Washington, D.C.: Government Printing Office, 1942.

572. White   House   Conference,   1950.   <u>Proceedings   of   the</u>
<u>Mid-Century   White   House   Conference   on   Children   and</u>
<u>Youth, 1950.</u>   Raleigh, N.C.:   Health Publications In-
stitute, 1951.

573. White House Conference, 1960. <u>Proceedings of the Golden</u>
<u>Anniversary   White   House   Conference   on   Children   and</u>
<u>Youth.</u>   Washington, D.C.:   Government Printing Office,
1960.

574. White House Conference, 1970. <u>Profiles of Children.</u>
Washington, D.C.: Government Printing Office, 1970.

575. White   House   Conference,   1970.   <u>A   Report   to   the</u>
<u>President: White House Conference on Children, 1970.</u>
Washington, D.C.: Government Printing Office, 1971.

1.5. CLASSIC CASE STUDIES
576. Addams,   Jane.   <u>The   Spirit   of   Youth   and   the   City</u>
<u>Streets.</u>   New   York: Macmillan,   1909.   Jane   Addams'
classic work on the city's obligation to concern itself
with children's insatiable desire, and need, for play.
If that desire was recognized, and satisfied by cities
through the provision of adequate recreational facilities, the number of children who fall victim to "evil
ways" would diminish greatly, according to Addams.

577. Beard, Belle B. <u>Juvenile Probation.</u> New York: American, 1934.   A somewhat flawed analysis of the case records of five-hundred children placed on probation by
the Juvenile Court of Boston which nevertheless is useful for its description of the city's juvenile court and
probation system.

578. Brace, Charles Loring. <u>The Dangerous Classes of New</u>
<u>York   and   Twenty   Years   Work   Among   Them.</u>   New   York:
Wynkoop and Hallenbeck, 1872.   An autobiographical account which, in effect, is a history of the first twenty
years of the New York Children's Aid Society and its
pioneering efforts in the home placement of dependent
children.

579. Breckinridge,   Sophonisba   and   Edith   Abbott.   <u>The</u>
<u>Delinquent Child and the Home.</u> New York: Survey As-
sociates, 1912.   Using materials gathered from juvenile
court files, probation officers' records, interviews,
and the like, the authors here present one of the first
studies of the causes of juvenile delinquency, one which
set the standard for many others to follow; they concluded that the delinquent child generally came from a

troubled home in which poverty had brutalized or degraded the parents.

580.   Brown, James. "Child Welfare Classics." Social Service
Review, Vol. 34, No. 2 (June, 1960), 195-202. A survey
of the literature on child welfare in America during the
prior seventy-five years in order to identify what might
be called the "classics"--those works that had a critical influence in determining the shape of things to come
in the field.

581.   Clopper, Edward N. Child Labor in City Streets. New
York: Macmillan, 1912. In this little work, a classic
in the field, Clopper reviews some of the problems and
conditions surrounding young newsboys and bootblacks,
discusses the effects of those conditions, and proposes
legislative remedies.

582.   Cooper, John M. Children's Institutions. Philadelphia:
Dolphin Press, 1931. A study of programs and policies
in Catholic children's institutions in the United States
conducted under the auspices of the National Conference
of Catholic Charities and the Commonwealth Fund of New
York City.

583.   Deutsch, Albert. Our Rejected Children. Boston:
Little, Brown, 1950. A well known work which exposed
some of the deplorable conditions that existed in juvenile correctional institutions in the 1940s.

584.   Earle, Alice M. Child Life in Colonial Days. New
York: Macmillan, 1927. A descriptive account of child
life in the American colonies, with comparisons to conditions in England. One of the first such studies of
its kind it was originally published in 1899, in the
midst of the child welfare movement.

585.   Eliot, Thomas D. The Juvenile Court and the Community.
New York: Macmillan, 1914. An important work in its
day which placed the juvenile court movement in historical perspective for communities launching, or
seeking to launch, such institutions.

586.   Flexner, Bernard and Roger Baldwin. Juvenile Courts and
Probation. New York: Century Co., 1914. A work intended as a guide to judges, probation officers, and interested laymen which deals with the juvenile court and
its administration as well as some "probable lines of
development." Especially important since it was the
first comprehensive treatment of the subject.

587.   Folks, Homer. The Care of Destitute, Neglected and
Delinquent Children. New York: Macmillan, 1902. An
historical treatment and critique of child-caring in-

stitutions and agencies in the United States written by
the leading expert in the field—the first scholarly
history of child welfare in America and a real classic
in the field: "All subsequent histories of child welfare in the country are based on . . . Folks's work,"
according to James Brown, himself an authority on the
subject.

588.   Hart, Hastings. Cottage and Congregate Institutions for
Children. New York: Charities Publication Committee,
1910. The most widely used handbook for officers and
trustees of children's institutions which tells how to
organize such places, provides plans for their construction, discusses their arrangement, and the like.
Well illustrated with photographs.

589.   Hart, Hastings. Juvenile Court Laws in the United
States. New York: Charities Publication Committee,
1910. A summary of juvenile court legislation in the
United States (to 1908), a topical abstract of state
laws governing the trial and disposition of juvenile offenders, and the Monroe County (N.Y.) Juvenile Court Law
of 1910 published for use by judges, juvenile court personnel, and students of the subject.

590.   Hart, Hastings. Preventive Treatment for Neglected
Children. New York: Russell Sage Foundation, 1910. An
"accounting" of work for neglected children in the
United States through studies of a great many children's
institutions and a discussion of about one hundred
child-helping agencies.

591.   Healy, William. The Individual Delinquent. Boston:
Little, Brown, 1915. A criminology textbook based on a
study of the causes and conditions of delinquent tendencies as revealed in the Psychopathic Institute of the
Cook County Juvenile Court. A valuable reference work
for those concerned with understanding "progressive"
views of delinquency.

592.   Healy, William and Augusta F. Bronner. New Light on
Delinquency and Its Treatment. New Haven: Yale University Press, 1936. A real landmark which, on the basis
of careful intensive study of more than 200 children,
for the first time scientifically substantiated the
powerful effect of emotional drives in determining behavior.

593.   Lou, Herbert H. Juvenile Courts in the United States.
Chapel Hill: University of North Carolina Press, 1927.
Perhaps the best technical history of the development of
juvenile courts and the fight to maintain their status.
The organization of the courts as well as the procedures
engaged in prior to hearings and the working of the

courts in the 1920s are described in detail.

594. Mangold, George B. <u>Problems of Child Welfare</u>. New York: Macmillan, 1936. The third and greatly revised edition of a book first published in 1914. The many phases of child welfare problems and methods of treatment are discussed in this work designed for college students interested in social problems.

595. Markham, Edwin, Benjamin B. Lindsey, and George Creel. <u>Children in Bondage</u>. New York: Hearst's International Library, 1914. This classic provided a passionate account of what child labor really meant through vivid descriptions of conditions in cotton mills, coal mines, canneries, and sweat shops. The authors also discuss why children toiled, estimate the cost of the practice in terms of vice, crime, and disease, and conclude with two chapters on suggested remedies of the evil.

596. Minehan, Thomas. <u>Boy and Girl Tramps in America</u>. New York: Farrar and Rinehart, 1934. A first-hand study of one of the products of the Great Depression--homeless young vagrants who lived the life of vagabondage. A valuable account of why they left home, how they lived, how they got food and lodging, what they talked about, etc., by someone who lived with them for two years.

597. O'Grady, John. <u>Catholic Charities in the United States: History and Problems</u>. Washington, D.C.: National Conference of Catholic Charities, 1930. A good sourcebook for information on the development of Catholic social services for cildren during the prior century.

598. Riis, Jacob A. <u>The Children of the Poor</u>. New York: Charles Scribner's Sons, 1892. A companion piece, of sorts, to the author's more well known work, <u>How the Other Half Lives</u>.

599. Spargo, John. <u>The Bitter Cry of the Children</u>. New York: Macmillan, 1906. A plain unvarnished statement of what life was like for poor children in early twentieth century America--and a series of remedial suggestions, including federal supervision of infant food manufacture, free meals for school children, medical inspection in schools, and federal regulation of child labor. A real classic which had a profound impact in its day.

600. Thurston, Henry W. <u>Concerning Juvenile Delinquency: Progressive Changes in Our Perspectives</u>. New York: Columbia University Press, 1942. A rambling disorganized work which discusses juvenile delinquency from every angle--the court, the detention home, the jail,

the probation officer, the community, and the delinquent him or herself. Despite its limitations, the study still is useful as a source of ideas on the subject in the early 1940s.

601.   Thurston, Henry W. The Dependent Child: A Story of Changing Aims and Methods in the Care of Dependent Children. New York: Columbia University Press, 1930. One of the real classics by an expert in the field. This work traces methods of care for dependent and neglected children from the late medieval period to the 1920s, with emphasis on the period after 1850. Thurston's discussons of binding ut, almshouse care, orphan asylums, and placement in foster families are enlivened by quotations from contemporary sources, including numerous statements by children about their experiences in institutions and foster homes.

1.6.   TEXTBOOKS, READERS, BOOKS OF DOCUMENTS, BIBLIOGRAPHIES

602.   Abbott, Grace, ed. The Child and the State, 2 Vols. Chicago: University of Chicago Press, 1938. An indispensable source of original documents and interpretive introductory notes summarizing major events through 1935. Volume I deals with the legal status of the child in the family, apprenticeship, and child labor. Volume II treats the dependent and delinquent child and the children of unmarried parents.

603.   Breckinridge, Sophonisba, ed. The Family and the State. Chicago: University of Chicago Press, 1934. A very useful book of documents on the family and child welfare, especially legal matters concerning the relationship between parents and children, guardianship, adoption, etc.

604.   Breckinridge, Sophonisba, ed. Public Welfare Administration in the United States, Select Documents. Chicago: University of Chicago Press, 1927. A valuable collection of source materials relating to the organization and administration of public welfare legislation and agencies—at the local, state, and national levels—from the colonial period to the mid-twenties. The work is divided into chronological sections, each of which has an excellent introductory note.

605.   Bremner, Robert H., et al., eds. Children and Youth in America: A Documentary History, 3 Vols. Cambridge, Mass.: Harvard University Press, 1970-74. A documentary history of public policy toward children and youth in America from colonial times to the early 1970s. The documents, arranged topically within chronological periods, deal with such subjects as child

health, educaion, labor, dependency, delinquency, etc. An indispensable source for any student of the subject.

606. Clarke, Helen I., ed. Social Legislation--American Laws Dealing With the Family, Child, and Dependent. New York: Appleton-Century, 1940. A survey of the law pertaining to the family and the poor which not only summarizes the legislation but makes frequent reference to judicial opinions and places both the legislation and judicial opinions in their historical context. The work was designed to show the complexities of legal procedure, the way courts reason, the social problems to be met by legal means, and th interrelations between the law, the social sciences, and social work.

607. Costin, Lela B. Child Welfare: Practices and Policies. New York: McGraw-Hill, 1972. A textbook that presents concepts, policies, and practices in the field of child welfare in order to provide undergraduate students with background that will be useful for entering practice or pursuing graduate education.

608. Fredericksen, Hazel and Raymond Mulligan. The Child and His Welfare. San Francisco: W. H. Freeman, 1972. The chief purpose of this textbook is to provide a broad view of child welfare for prospective workers in the field. Part II provides a fair amount of historical material.

609. Kadushin, Alfred. Child Welfare Services. New York: Crowell, Collier, and Macmillan, 1967. A comprehensive study of the principal child welfare services as opposed to a manual on skills to deal with child welfare problems. Each chapter includes useful material on the historical development of the service.

610. White House Conference, 1970. An Annotated Bibliography on Children. Washington, D.C.: Government Printing Office, 1971.

611. Zietz, Dorothy. Child Welfare: Principles and Methods. New York: Wiley, 1959. While this work primarily is about the child with special needs and the programs and services that have been developed tomeet those needs, it contains a great deal of material on child welfare history from the English Poor Law of 1601 to the mid-twentieth century.

2. PERIOD PIECES

2.1. COLONIAL

    612.   Morgan, Edmund S. The Puritan Family: Religion and
Domestic Relations in Seventeenth Century New England.
New York: Harper and Row, 1966. An exceedingly important revisionist account that raises questions about
long-held views about children in seventeenth century
New England. Morgan shows that the doctrine of infant
depravity was accompanied by an increased concern for
the child and an interest in child psychology; although
the Puritans did not view the child as the embodiment of
an unspoiled human nature, they did view it as the heir
of the new era.

2.2. REVOLUTIONARY AND EARLY NATIONAL

2.3. ANTEBELLUM AND CIVIL WAR

2.4. POSTBELLUM

    613.   Clement, Priscilla Ferguson. "Families and Foster
Care: Philadelphia in the Late Nineteenth Century."
Social Service Review, Vol. 53, No. 3 (Sept., 1979),
406-20. A study of the late nineteenth-century home
placement work of Philadelphia's Home Missionary and
Children's Aid Societies which, according to the author,
despite not protecting their charges from ill treatment
nevertheless played a useful role; they permitted impoverished mothers and fathers to secure for their children the basic necessities of life which they could not
otherwise provide them.

    614.   Cordasco, Francesco. "Charles Loring Brace and the
Dangerous Classes: Historical Analogues of the Urban
Black Poor." Journal of Human Relations, Vol. 20, No. 3
(Third Quarter, 1972), 379-86. This essay suggests that
Charles Loring Brace's views and strategies regarding
the "dangerous classes" are echoed in the efforts of
contemporary reformers to deal with urban poverty, es-
pecially those of Daniel P. Moynihan.

    615.   Langsam, Miriam. Children West: A History of the
Placing-Out of the New York Children's Aid Society.
Madison, Wis.: State Historical Society, 1964. A brief
history of the New York Children's Aid Society,
1853-1890, which is quite favorable to the agency and
its controversial head, Charles Loring Brace.

    616.   Nelson, Kristine E. "The Best Asylum: Charles Loring
Brace and Foster Family Care." Unpublished Ph.D. Diss.,

University of California, Berkeley, 1980. This study places the home placement program of the New York Children's Aid Society within the social and economic context of early nineteenth century America and argues that home care was a function of changes in the nature of the family brought about by economic development. Brace's legacy to the present, which has endured, was a mixture of innovation and traditional practice.

2.5. PROGRESSIVE

617. Cavallo, Dominick. "Social Reform and the Movement to Organize Children's Play During the Progressive Era." History of Childhood Quarterly, Vol. 3, No. 4 (Spring, 1976), 509-22. This article drawn from the author's dissertation on the subject, deals with an aspect of "child saving" during the Progressive era ignored by many scholars--the movement to organize play and games of children especially the children of immigrants living in urban areas.

618. Holl, Jack M. Juvenile Reform in the Progressive Era: William R. George and the Junior Republic Movement. Ithaca, N.Y.: Cornell University Press, 1971. A highly imaginative examination of William R. George and the Junior Republic Movement within the context of American social and economic history, including the "anti-institutional" tendencies of the time. Hall's contribution is not so much to challenge the earlier portrayal of the reformers' motivations (as being "good" and progressive) as to point out contradictions inherent in their social thought and to highlight the disjuncture between their great aspirations and their actual achievements.

619. Jambor, Harold. "Theodore Dreiser, the Delineator Magazine, and Dependent Children: A Background Note in the Calling of the 1909 White House Conference." Social Service Review, Vol. 32, No. 1 (March, 1958), 33-40. A not totally accurate article which seeks to trace the origins of the 1909 White House Conference on Dependent Children and concludes that most of the credit should go to Theodore Dreiser and the Delineator Magazine.

620. McArthur, Benjamin. "The Chicago Playground Movement: A Neglected Feature of Social Justice." Social Service Review, Vol. 49, No. 3 (Sept., 1975), 376-95. Among the many problems plaguing cities at the turn of the century was that of inadequate play areas for children. Chicago became the first city to remedy that situation on a large scale, as this article makes clear. Its network of playground parks, which it was hoped would preserve the health and morals of children, solidify the home,

and inculcate a democratic ethos and thus ensure an orderly society, provided the model for similar projects
in many other cities.

621.   Mergen, Bernard. "The Discovery of Children's Play."
American Quarterly, Vol. 27, No. 4 (Oct., 1975),
399-420. There are three reasons for studying children's play, according to the author: 1) it is part of
the larger culture and socializaion process; 2) it may
indicate certain things about the personality of the
players, and 3) it helps provide an understanding of the
development of the social sciences and their impace in
America. This article touches on all three of the above
reasons for studying childrens play, but it deals most
fully with the third.

622.   Schlossman, Steven and Ronald Cohen. "The Music Man in
Gary: Willis Brown and Child-Saving in the Progressive
Era." Societas, Vol. 7, No. 1 (Winter, 1977), 1-18.
This article concentrates on a relatively obscure and
enigmatic reformer of the early twentieth century,
Willis Brown, whose activities in Gary, Indiana and
elsewhere shed light on the personalities, fears, and
ideas of the more famous child savers. Brown's career,
which suffered more setbacks than successes, suggests
that there is much to learn about child saving in the
Progressive era in scattered communities throughout
America.

2.6.   THE 1920s AND THE GREAT CRASH
623.   Coffman, Harold C. American Foundations: A Study of
Their Role in the Child Welfare Movement. New York:
Association Press, 1936. An analysis of the grants of
seventy-five foundations (with a combined capital of
more than $1 billion) during the decade of the 1920s in
order to determine how much money went for child welfare
and child welfare organizations.

624.   Schlossman, Steven. "Philanthropy and the Gospel of
Child Development." History of Education Quarterly,
Vol. 21, No. 3 (Fall, 1981), 275-99. This case study of
the philosophy and tactics of the Laura Spelman
Rockefeller Memorial in the 1920s sheds light on the relation between "child study" and "parent education" that
reflected and resulted from the malaise of middle-class
women in the 1920s. It suggests that philanthropic initiatives such as these prompted public policy makers to
value family-focused interventions.

2.7.   NEW DEAL AND WORLD WAR II

625.   Breckinridge, Sophonisba.   "Government's Role in Child
        Welfare." Annals of the American Academy of Political
        and Social Science, Vol. 212 (Nov., 1940), 42-50. An
        excellent detailed discussion and analysis of the many
        significant changes that occurred in the 1930s (largely
        as a result of the Depression and enactment of the So-
        cial Security Act) in the area of child welfare.

626.   Hanlan, Archie.   "From Social Reform to Social Sec-
        urity: The Separation of ADC and Child Welfare." Child
        Welfare, Vol. 45, No. 9 (Nov., 1966), 493-500. The di-
        vided opinions among social workers in the 1930s over
        proposed programs of federal aid and the political is-
        sues affecting the separtation of ADC from the
        service-oriented Children's Bureau are reviewed her in
        an effort to demonstrate that social work has a rich
        heritage of providing criticism of existing or proposed
        programs to aid the poor.

2.8. POSTWAR
627.   Bloch, Herbert A. and Frank T. Flynn. Delinquency: The
        Juvenile Offender in America Today. New York: Random
        House, 1956. A study of juvenile delinquency in the
        mid-1950s in which the authors discuss and analyze cri-
        tically the latest developments in the field--new ap-
        proaches for investigation, new methods of treatment,
        the most recent changes in probation techniques and
        policies, etc.

2.9. GREAT SOCIETY
628.   Briar, Scott. "Why Children's Allowances?" Social
        Work, Vol. 14, No. 1 (Jan., 1969), 5-12. A favorable
        examination of the case for children's allowances as one
        component of a broader program to eliminate poverty in
        America.

629.   Child Study Association of America. Children of
        Poverty--Children of Affluence. New York: Child Study
        Association of America, 1967. A work that seeks to an-
        swer some important questions about children, namely,
        how children of poverty and children of affluence re-
        semble each other, how they differ from each other, and
        what we can learn from both regarding the needs of all
        children and all families.

630.   Coles, Robert. Uprooted Children: The Early Life of
        Migrant Farm Workers. Pittsburgh: University of
        Pittsburgh Press, 1970. A vivid account, frequently in
        the words of migrant families, with whom the author
        lived for seven years, of what it means for a child to

live a rootless, transitory experience, always sur-
rounded by hard work, pain, and ridicule.

631.   Dembitz, Nanette. "The Good of the Child Versus the
        Rights of the Parent: The Supreme Court Upholds the
        Welfare Home-Visit." Political Science Quarterly, Vol.
        86, No. 3 (Sept., 1971), 389-405. A legal analysis of
        the U.S. Supreme Court's decision, in January, 1971, up-
        holding New York State's law requiring that welfare
        recipients permit home visits by welfare workers—its
        history, its nature, and its implications.

632.   Garfinkel, Irwin. "Negative Income Tax and Children's
        Allowance Programs: A Comparison." Social Work, Vol.
        13, NO. 4 (Oct., 1968), 33-39. A comparison of two
        methods of implementing a guaranteed annual income—the
        negative income tax and children's allowances—with re-
        spect to their cost and probable effectiveness; the au-
        thor strongly favors the former.

633.   Kahn, Alfred J. Planning Community Services for
        Children in Trouble. New York: Columbia University
        Press, 1963. An attack on the then current individual
        efforts to deal with and help troubled children which
        stresses the need for a total community system of ser-
        vices, one that includes coordination, case integration,
        and accountability.

634.   Kahn, Alfred J. "The Social Scene and the Planning of
        Services for Children." Social Work, Vol. 7, No. 3
        (July, 1962), 3-14. Pointing out that America was in
        the midst of a severe crisis in the area of child care,
        due not to the immorality of children but to rapid so-
        cial change in the nation's cities, Kahn here called for
        the creation of more social services and rehabilitative
        facilities which, in his opinion, "have become as neces-
        sary to the modern city as sanitation and a water
        supply."

635.   Meyer, Carol H. "The Impact of Urbanizaton on Child
        Welfare." Child Welfare, Vol. 46, No. 8 (Oct. 1967),
        433-42. An analysis of how the basic characteristics of
        urban life have changed patterns of living which, in
        turn, require changes in older child welfare practices
        (most of which were based on a rural culture) and the
        development of new ones, especially some that take cog-
        nizance of the value of the urban neighborhood as the
        best social unit to mitigate the depersonalization of
        city life.

636.   Orshansky, Mollie. "Children of the Poor." Social
        Security Bulletin, Vol. 26, No. 7 (July, 1963), 3-13. A
        reminder that as the nation grows richer the gap between
        the well-to-do and the poor widens—and many young chil-

dren suffer. All told, she estimated, "some 17–23 million youngsters, or from a fourth to a third of all children, are growing up in the gray shadow of poverty."

637. Pavenstedt, Eleanor, ed. The Drifters: Children of Disorganized Lower-Class Families. Boston: Little, Brown, 1967. This work describes research on thirteen severely disorganized families from a skid-row neighborhood in Boston; it provides many insights into the psychological and social handicaps of the disadvantaged and serves to increase understanding of their problems.

638. Schorr, Alvin L. Poor Kids: A Report on Children in Poverty. New York: Basic Books, 1966. Estimating that there are some 16 million American children living in poverty, Schorr here offers three programs to break the cycle--fatherless child insurance, a negative income tax, and allowances for preschool children. He then weighs the merits and demerits of each proposal and leaves to the reader the decision as to which is the best of the three.

639. Tobin, James. "Do We Want a Children's Allowance?" New Republic (November 25, 1967), 16–18. The author, a professor of economics at Yale University, points out that a number of well-intentioned people find "family" or "children's" allowances an attractive form of income supplementation, and then goes on to argue against them--largely on economic grounds. Instead, he advocates a better system of public assistance to adults in need with or without children, one which preserves both their dignity and their incentive to work.

640. Vadakin, James C. Children, Poverty, and Family Allowances. New York: Basic Books, 1968. An unabashed, uncritical argument for some sort of family allowance program--for all, regardless of income or employment status--as the best means of ending poverty in America.

641. Wickenden, Elizabeth. "The '67 Amendments: A Giant Step Backward for Child Welfare." Child Welfare, Vol. 48, No. 7 (July, 1969), 388–94. A discussion of how the 1967 Amendments to the Social Security Act reversed the basic principles that had supported public aid and child welfare services throughout the twentieth century. Basically, whereas mothers' pensions and the Social Security Act stressed the right to public support of needy children, the new law stresses the obligation of the state to remove children from the welfare rolls. Whereas the earlier measures stressed the child's right to a mother's care, the new law stresses the mother's obligation to work outside the home for the child's support. It is, in the author's opinion, "an unmitigated

disaster."

642.   Winston, Ellen. "The Shape of Things to Come in Child
        Welfare--The Broad Outline." Child Welfare, Vol. 45,
        No. 1 (Jan., 1966), 5-11. Pointing out that despite
        progress child welfare workers have not been able to
        keep pace with increasing needs, Winston calls for more
        effective preventive and rehabilitative measures and,
        above all, some sort of guaranteed minimum annual income
        "in order to assure a good home and family life to all
        needy children."

2.10. THE CONTEMPORARY PERIOD
        643.   Bridgeland, William M. and Edward A. Duane, eds.
                "Young Children and Social Policy." Annals of the
                American Academy of Political and Social Science, Vol.
                461 (May, 1982), 9-124. Although this special issue on
                young children and social policy fails to put current
                policy concerns into historical perspective, the
                contributors nevertheless identify key conceptual and
                political issues surrounding the debate over day care,
                head-start programs, and the value of public
                intervention into family matters. The citations are
                useful.

        644.   Schorr, Alvin L., ed. Children and Decent People. New
                York: Basic Books, 1974. A set of papers which examine
                America's child care system and, taken together, con-
                clude that, contrary to popular opinion, Americans
                really do not care about children--and certainly do not
                provide for them adequately.

        645.   Silverman, Marvin. "Children's Rights and Social
                Work." Social Service Review, Vol. 51, No. 1 (March,
                1977), 171-78. In its desire to protect the child, so-
                ciety has placed children in a disabled status in which
                they lack political rights, according to the author, who
                then examines the psycho-social consequences of that and
                offers suggestions for extending such rights; he also
                explores the resulting implications for social work.

        646.   Spector, Alan J. "The Deinstitutionalization of Child
                Welfare Services in Illinois: Social Change and Policy
                Change." Unpublished Ph.D. Diss., Northwestern Univer-
                sity, 1980. Between 1973 and 1974, hundreds of children
                who were wards of the state of Illinois were removed
                from institutions and placed in other settings. This
                study examines the development and implementation of
                that deinstitutionalization policy, a product of broad
                societal trends.

        647.   Steiner, Gilbert Y. The Children's Cause. Washington,
                D.C.: The Brookings Institution, 1976. An examination

of how federal legislation on behalf of children develops—how it is conceived and nurtured in Congress, in
the executive agencies, and by lobbyists on Capitol Hill.

648. Vinter, Robert D. Juvenile Corrections in the United
States. Ann Arbor: University of Michigan Press,
1975. An analysis of the residential services provided
by state agencies to young offenders in their care or
custody which tends to support the criticisms leveled
against traditional institutions and the argument that
community based corrections are more economical and
probably as effective.

3. SALIENT VARIATIONS

3.1. LOCAL, STATE, REGIONAL

649. Gibson, William. "A History of Family and Child Welfare
Agencies in Baltimore, 1849-1943." Unpublished Ph.D.
Diss., Ohio State University, 1969. A history of
non-sectarian welfare agencies in Baltimore from the
founding of that city's Association for Improving the
Condition of the Poor in 1849 to creation, in 1943 of
the Family and Children's Aid Society, with special emphasis on the positive influence Daniel Coit Gilman and
Johns Hopkins University had on many of the agencies.

650. Jacoby, George Paul. Catholic Child Care in Nineteenth
Century New York. Washington, D.C.: The Catholic University of America, 1941. A highly partisan account of
the origin and growth of Catholic child care in New York
City from its creation as a diocese in 1808 until the
end of the nineteenth century, the major thesis of which
is that the Catholic church continually developed new
methods to meet new needs.

651. Lisenky, William F. "An Administrative History of Public Programs for Dependent Children in North Carolina,
Virginia, Tennessee, and Kentucky, 1900-1942." Unpublished Ph.D. Diss., Vanderbilt University, 1962. A
study of child welfare in four southern states—North
Carolina, Virginia, Tennessee, and Kentucky—from 1900
to 1942, including emphasis on non-institutional care,
passage of mothers' aid legislation, creation of juvenile courts, administration of ADC under the Social
Security Act, etc. The author also goes into the problems, or defects, in the respective states, including
discrimination against black youngsters and inadequate
probation work.

652. Moran, Robert E. "The History of Child Welfare in

Louisiana, 1850-1960." Unpublished Ph.D. Diss., Ohio
State University, 1968. Only in the twentieth century
did Louisiana begin to make some real progress in the
area of child welfare; the chief beneficiaries of that
progress, however, were white youngsters in need.
Throughout the period under study, services to Negro
children lagged far behind those for whites.

653.   Romanofsky, Peter. "Saving the Lives of th City's
Foundlings: The Joint Committee and New York City Child
Care Methods, 1860-1907." New York Historical Society
Quarterly, Vol. 61, Nos. 1-2 (Jan./April, 1977), 49-68.
A history of child welfare, especially the treatment of
foundlings, in New York City from the mid-nineteenth to
the early twentieth century, with an emphasis on the
Joint Committee on the Care of Motherless Infants, created in 1898 to save the lives of the city's foundlings
by removing them from institutions and placing them in
private homes. New York City officials however, influenced by Catholic opposition to home placement, killed the Joint Committee and thereby "helped to make the
public care of dependent babies and foundlings, as it
had been before, regressive."

654.   Romanofsky, Peter. "The Public is Aroused: The
Missouri Children's Code Commisson, 1915-1919."
Missouri Historical Review, Vol. 68, No. 2 (Jan., 1974),
204-22. An account of the origins, operation, and effects of the Missouri Code Commission, especially enactment of the Missouri Code of 1919 which, according to
Romanofsky, gave that state the most progressive child
welfare laws in the United States--and served as a model
for many other states.

655.   Ross, Catherine J. "Society's Children: The Care of
Indigent Youngsters in New York City, 1875-1903." Unpublished Ph.D. Diss., Yale University, 1977. An examination of the evolution of programs for indigent
children in New York City--the switch from private to
public care and the change from institutional to home
care--in order to explore the conditions in which they
and their families lived, as well as the emergence of
modern attitudes toward social welfare and childhood."

656.   Salsgiver, Richard O. "Child Reform in Pittsburgh,
1890-1915: The Development of the Juvenile Court and
the Allegheny County Industrial and Training School for
Boys." Unpublished Ph.D. Diss., Carnegie-Mellon University, 1975. An exploration of the movement in
turn-of-the century Pittsburgh to establish a juvenile
court and then an industrial school for delinquent boys,
neither of which are viewed favorably by the author.
The court usually sent delinquent youngsters, especially
those from poor immigrant or black families, to the

"school," which quickly deteriorated into a punitive
custodial institution.

657.   Slater, Peter G. Children in the New England Mind.
        Hamden, Conn:" Archon, 1977. Based on diaries, bio-
        graphical works, journals, letters, theological tracts,
        and child development literature, this work is an ex-
        amination of changes in adult ideas about children
        during two hundred years of New England history, from
        the seventeenth to the nineteenth century. It con-
        centrates, in other words, on attitudes and perceptions
        rather than behavior. Unfortunately, it is lacking in
        analysis.

658.   Stanton, Mary. "The Development of Institutional Care
        of Children in California from 1769 to 1925." Social
        Service Review, Vol. 25, No. 3 (Sept., 1951), 320–31. A
        review of the history of institutional care of children
        in California with emphasis on the role of private agen-
        cies during the early years, and on the increasing im-
        portance of public agencies in the more recent period.

659.   Williams, Carol Wilson. "Guardianship: A Minimally
        Used Resource for California's Dependent Children: A
        Study in Policy, 1850–1978." Unpublished Ph.D. Diss.,
        University of Southern California, 1980. An historical
        analysis that attempts to document developments in
        California's public policy governing guardianship of
        children between 1850–1978 in the context of a changing
        social environment which affects dependent children.
        The study attempts to address such matters as the
        threats that have emerged regarding the practice, the
        policies and services that have been developed to safe-
        guard a child's right to a personal guardian, the so-
        cial, political and economic factors that have shaped
        developments of guardianship policy and the modi-
        fications that are needed in existing policy and ser-
        vices to make the practice an effective child care re-
        source.

660.   Williams, Thomas E. "The Dependent Child in
        Mississippi: A Social History, 1900–1972." Unpublished
        Ph.D. Diss., Ohio State University, 1976. This study
        examines the system of child welfare in Mississippi
        during the twentieth century and concludes that "child
        welfare programs dealing with the basic problem of eco-
        nomic deprivation without attempting to deal with the
        social ramificaions of poverty have been politically
        viable, socially acceptable, and the most successful
        programs for dependent children in Mississippi."

3.2. RACIAL/ETHNIC

661. Billingsley, Andrew and Jeanne M. Giovannoni. Children
      of the Storm: Black Children and American Child
      Welfare. New York: Harcourt Brace Jovanovich, 1972. A
      successful attempt to prove that racism has had tragic
      effects on black children and that an expression of that
      has been the child welfare system. The authors trace
      the history of child welfare in America, placing special
      attention on the most recent decades and call for badly
      needed reforms in the care and placement of black
      children.

662. Clark, Dennis. "Babes in Bondage: Indentured Irish
      Children in Philadelphia in the Nineteenth Century."
      The Pennsylvania Magazine of History and Biography, Vol.
      101, No. 4 (October, 1977), 475-486. This essay traces
      the persistence of a colonial practice despite the ex-
      pansion of public and private child-welfare bureaus and
      the Irish's rising socio-economic status in the latter
      half of the 19th century.

663. Frey, Cecil P. "The House of Refuge for Colored Chil-
      dren." Journal of Negro History, Vol. 66, No. 2
      (Spring, 1981), 10-25. A discussion of the House of
      Refuge for Colored Children in Philadelphia, which
      opened in 1850--the only nineteenth century northern in-
      stitution of its kind and clearly an effort at social
      control. The program of the institution, created and
      operated by whites, was designed to "restrain, to edu-
      cate, to impart morality, and to incarcerate potentially
      harmful [black] deviants." In other words, it served to
      remove black youngsters from the streets of Philadelphia
      and to retrain "them into an acceptance of the morality
      and standards" of the white founders of the institution.

664. Kiple, Kenneth F. and Virginia H. Kiple. "Slave Child
      Mortality: Some Nutritional Answers to a Perennial
      Puzzle." Journal of Social History, Vol. 10, No. 3
      (March, 1977), 284-309. Although there was a very high
      incidence of slave child, particularly slave infant,
      mortality relative to their white antebellum counter-
      parts, that was not due to planter mistreatment, ac-
      cording to the authors of this article. Rather, black
      children were "victims of a conspiracy of nutrition,
      African environmental heritage, and North American cli-
      matic circumstances," they conclude.

665. Moran, Robert. "The Negro Dependent Child in Louisiana,
      1800-1935." Social Service Review, Vol. 45, No. 1
      (March, 1971), 53-61. An account of the care and treat-
      ment of black dependent children in Louisiana from the
      antebellum period to the enactment of the Social Sec-
      urity Act--a tale of neglect, discrimination, and op-
      pression. Only in the more recent period were black
      children provided with the same type of care given white

youngsters, usually, however, in separate and inferior facilities.

666. Romanofsky, Peter. "'To Save . . . Their Souls': The
      Care of Dependent Jewish Children in New York City,
      1900-1905." Jewish Social Studies, Vol. 36, Nos. 3-4
      (July-Oct., 1974), 253-61. An account of the
      in-fighting and bickering among early twentieth century
      Jews and Jewish organizations to control the home place-
      ment of needy Jewish youngsters, which tended to retard
      the success of the operation. As a result, as
      Romanofsky demonstrates, it was not until much later,
      1915 and thereafter, that Jewish foster, boarding, and
      adoptive home programs flourished.

667. Scott, Rebecca. "The Battle Over the Child: Child Ap-
      prenticeship and the Freedmen's Bureau in North
      Carolina." Prologue, Vol. 10, No. 1 (Summer, 1978),
      101-13. A pretty standard account of white southerners
      using apprenticeship statutes to virtually re-enslave
      blacks in the postwar period, chiefly as a means of
      securing a cheap supply of labor. The author does show,
      however, that in North Carolina, at least, white agents
      of the Freedmen's Bureau were divided over these prac-
      tices; sometimes they allowed them to occur, illegally
      and unjustly, and at other times they did not.

3.3. GENDER-SPECIFIC

3.4. CLASS
      668. Dann, Martin E. "'Little Citizens': Working Class and
            Immigrant Childhood in New York City, 1890-1915."
            Unpublished Ph.D. Diss., City University of New York,
            1978. An examination of the ideological, experiential
            and institutional aspects of immigrant and working class
            childhood in urban America, with specific emphasis on
            New York City in the period 1890-1915. A fundamental
            concern is to understand the ways in which childhood was
            transformed and how that transformation affected the
            process of assimilation and social change.

4. AGE-SPECIFIC AND LIFE-CYCLE STUDIES

4.1. INFANT MORTALITY/CHILD HYGIENE
      669. Meckel, Richard A. "The Awful Responsibility of Mother-
            hood: American Health Reform and the Prevention of In-

fant and Child Mortality Before 1913." Unpublished
Ph.D. Diss., University of Michigan, 1980. This dissertation attempts to place the evolution of American
ideas on the prevention of infant and child mortality
within the changing socio-cultural milieu that gave them
shape and provided the rationale for their acceptance.
In reality, it is a study of a single argument—that
prevention could best be accomplished by educating
mothers in the proper care of their young. The study
begins in seventeenth century England and ends with the
early twentieth century Progressive baby-saving campaign.

670.   Melvin, Patricia Mooney. "Make Milwaukee Safe for
        Babies: The Child Welfare Commisison and the De-
        velopment of Urban Health Centers, 1911-1912." Journal
        of the West, Vol. 17, No. 2 (April, 1978), 83-93. As
        this article makes clear, the recent fascination with
        neighborhood health centers is not new; its roots go
        back at least to the early twentieth century when, in
        1911-1912, the city of Milwaukee pioneered in the mat-
        ter. This is an excellent study of the rise, and de-
        mise, of that pioneering venture.

671.   Romanofsky, Peter. "Infant Mortality, Dr. Henry Dwight
        Chapin and the Speedwell Society." Journal of the
        Medical Society of New Jersey, Vol. 73, (Jan., 1976),
        33-38. A tribute to Dr. Henry Dwight Chapin for his
        work in developing the Speedwell Society, a pioneering
        organization created in 1902 to place in private homes
        foundlings and illegitimate babies. While the society
        never operated throughout the country, it did influence
        the national movement to board out destitute and de-
        pendent infants, especially in the Metropolitan New York
        area.

672.   Romanofsky, Peter. "'To One Common End': The United
        States Public Health Service and the Missouri Child Hy-
        giene Movement, 1919-1921." Bulletin of the History of
        Medicine, Vol. 52, No. 2 (Summer, 1978), 251-65. Events
        related to World War I made Americans increasingly con-
        cerned about the physical and medical conditions of
        American children. This, in turn, led to the creation,
        in Missouri, of a Children's Code Commission which, was
        responsible for establishment of a Division of Child Hy-
        giene in its State Health Department. The Division of
        Child Hygiene, working in conjunction with the U.S. Pub-
        lic Health Service, helped reduce the state's infant
        mortality rate, especially in rural areas. World War I,
        then, promoted rather than retarded social progress, at
        least in this area.

4.2.   AID TO DEPENDENT CHILDREN (Mothers' Aid, Widows' Pensions)

673. Abbott, Grace. "Recent Trends in Mothers' Aid." Social
      Service Review, Vol. 8, No. 2 (June, 1934), 191-210. A
      review of the history of mothers' pension legislation
      and its administration from 1911 to 1934, with a plea,
      at the end, for such assistance to become part of a fed-
      eral grant-in-aid program.

674. Bell, Winifred. Aid to Dependent Children: New York:
      Columbia University Press, 1965. The most searching and
      best study of the subject by an astute critic of the
      program, especially its "suitable home" provisions and
      their discriminatory features.

675. Leff, Mark. "Consensus for Reform: The Mothers' Pen-
      sion Movement in the Progressive Era." Social Service
      Review, Vol. 47, No. 3 (Sept., 1973), 397-417. Mothers'
      pensions, precursors of today's Aid to Families with De-
      pendent Children, achieved remarkable legislative suc-
      cess during the early twentieth century; only social
      workers in some private agencies actively opposed them.
      This "consensus for reform" was due to the fact, ac-
      cording to the author, that the movement for their en-
      actment synthesized the Progressive era's concerns about
      children, widows, and the home.

4.3. ADOPTION
676. Madison, Bernice Q. "Adoption: Yesterday, Today, and
      Tomorrow--Part I." Child Welfare, Vol. 45, No. 5 (May,
      1966), 253-58; Part II, Vol. 45, No. 6 (June, 1966),
      341-48. In addition to a discussion of agency practice
      and research in the area, Part I provides a review of
      the history of adoption in the Unites States (including
      the legislation that established it as a legal prac-
      tice); Part II primarily discusses the future of adop-
      tion from the vantage point of the mid-1960s.

4.4. CHILD LABOR
677. Abbott, Grace. "Federal Regulation of Child Labor
      1906-1938." Social Service Review, Vol. 13, No. 3
      (Sept., 1939), 409-30. An account of efforts to control
      child labor through federal legislation from in-
      troduction of the first bill in 1906 to passage of the
      Fair Labor Standards Act in 1938.

678. Felt, Jeremy P. Hostages of Fortune: Child Labor
      Reform in New York State. Syracuse, N.Y.: Syracuse
      University Press, 1965. An excellent monograph that
      deals with child labor in New York State and efforts by
      the New York State Child Labor Committee to eliminate
      it, 1903-1942--a tale of sorrow, squalor, and some

success.

679.   Lumpkin, Katharine DuPre and Dorothy W. Douglas. Child
        Workers in America. New York: Robert M. McBride and
        Co., 1937. The first comprehensive scholarly study of
        child labor in America, replete with facts on every as-
        pect of the evil--its history, its social, economic, and
        human effects (including testimony from child laborers
        themselves), and efforts to abolish it.

680.   Speakman, Joseph M. "Unwillingly to School: Child
        Labor and its Reform in Pennsylvania in the Progressive
        Era." Unpublished Ph.D. Diss., Temple University,
        1976. A history of child labor reform in Pennsylvania
        during the Progressive era, in large part a success
        story, one with a twist, however. As the progressive
        period came to a close, child labor reform tended to be
        absorbed into the movement to make the child into an ef-
        ficient and well-trained worker. Concern for the child
        as a national asset in the competitive world, or market-
        place, in other words, came to replace earlier, more hu-
        manitarian, concerns, according to the author.

681.   Trattner, Walter I. Crusade for the Children: A
        History of the National Child Labor Committee and Child
        Labor Reform in America. Chicago: Quadrangle Books,
        1970. A monograph on the history of child labor and
        child labor reform in America, especially the efforts of
        the National Child Labor Committee to eliminate the
        evil, 1904-1960. Reform came, slowly, as much from
        technology as from the reformers' efforts, according to
        Trattner.

4.5. U.S. CHILDREN'S BUREAU

682.   Bradbury, Dorothy E. Five Decades of Action for
        Children: A History of the Childrens Bureau.
        Washington,D. C.: Children's Bureau, 1962. A good
        brief history of the Bureau written by the director of
        its Division of Reports, including creation of the
        Bureau, the early years (1912-21), the years of economic
        crisis (1921-33), the coming of the maternal and child
        welfare program (1934-40), the Bureau in wartime
        (1940-45), the postwar decade (1946-56), and moving into
        the sixties (1957-62).

683.   Covostos, Louis J. "Child Welfare and Social Progress:
        A History of the U.S. Children's Bureau, 1912-1935."
        Unpublished Ph.D. Diss., University of Chicago, 1976. A
        history of the U.S. Children's Bureau, 1912-1935, which
        furnishes an overview of the major ideas and trends con-
        cerning child welfare during that time; it also sheds
        light among other things, on conceptions of the family,

women, and the social work profession as well as the
problems encountered in operating a bureaucracy.

684.   Eliot, Martha M.   "Six Decades of Action for Children."
        Children Today, Vol. 1, No. 2 (March-April, 1972), 2-6.
        A brief sketch of the Bureau's history written by a
        former chief of the agency--with some comments on "the
        potential of the Bureau now and in the years ahead."

685.   Parker, Jacqueline and Edward Carpenter.   "Julia Lathrop
        and the Children's Bureau: The Emergence of an In-
        stitution."   Social Service Review, Vol. 55, No. 1
        (March, 1981), 60-77.   The critical task facing the
        newly created federal Children's Bureau was the es-
        tablishment of an institution that could survive re-
        curring appropriations crises.   How Julia Lathrop the
        first woman bureau chief in the federal government, de-
        fined its mission, selected operating goals from its
        statutory functions, and utilized a potent constituency
        network is the subject of this interesting article.

686.   Weiss, Nancy.   "Save the Children: A History of the
        Children's Bureau, 1903-1918."   Unpublished Ph.D. Diss.,
        University of California, Los Angeles, 1974.   A study of
        the formation and early history of the Children's Bureau
        viewed against the backdrop of the society in which it
        emerged.   Special attention is paid to the agency's
        place in the progressive movement.

687.   United States Childrens Bureau The, 1912-1972.   New
        York: Arno Press, 1974.   An original anthology which
        includes a variety of previously published works on the
        U.S. Children's Bureau by such people as Julia Lathrop,
        Grace Abbott, Dorothy Bradbury, and others.

4.6.   INSTITUTIONS FOR DEPENDENT, NEGLECTED, AND ORPHANED CHILDREN

688.   Buckingham,   Clyde.   "Early   American   Orphanages:
        Ebenezar and Bathesda."   Social Forces, Vol. 26, No. 3
        (March, 1948), 311-22.   A history of the care of or-
        phaned   youngsters   from   the   founding   of   America's
        earliest   orphanages   in   the   1730s   through   the
        mid-nineteenth century.

689.   Low,   Seth.   America's   Children   and   Youth   in
        Institutions,   1950-1960-1964:   A Demographic Analysis.
        Washington, D.C.:   Government Printing Office, 1965.
        This report provides useful statistical information con-
        cerning children in institutions and the   many different
        types of facilities in which they resided at the time.
        It also reviews current trends in the field, par-
        ticularly the provision of more specialized care and
        treatment of needy children, particularly the mentally

retarded.

690.   Pappenfort, Donnell M. and Dee Morgan Kilpatrick. "Child-Caring Institutions, 1966." Social Service Review, Vol. 43, No. 4 (Dec., 1969), 448-59. This article presents the findings of the first national survey of programs and services of children's institutions throughout the U.S. Puerto Rico, and the Virgin Islands. It identifies deficiencies in the child welfare system and summarizes the priorities of institution administrators for improving care.

691.   Patterson, R. S. and Patricia Rooke. "The Delicate Duty of Child-Saving: Coldwater, Michigan, 1871-1896." Michigan HIstory, Vol. 61, No. 3 (Fall, 1977), 195-219. The subject of this article is the early history of the State Public School for Dependent and Neglected Children, established in 1874 at Coldwater, Michigan. Designed to educate its wards "morally and mentally" and teach them "habits of industry," the institution was a successful venture that fulfilled the hopes and expectations of the founders. The author, however, refuses to take a stand on whether it was a humanitarian gesture or an effort at social control.

692.   Whittaker, James K. "Colonial Child Care Institutions: Our Heritage of Care." Child Welfare, Vol. 50, No. 7 (July, 1971), 396-400. Maintaining that some aspects of present-day theory and practice in the field of child welfare had their origins in America's colonial period, including the right of the state to remove children from the care of unfit parents, this article seeks to trace those features of child care earlier in American history that affected later developments, and why.

693.   Wolins, Martin and Irving Piliavin. Institutions or Foster Family: A Century of Debate. New York: Child Welfare League, 1964. A review of the literature from the middle of the nineteenth to the middle of the twentieth century on whether it is better to place children in institutions or in foster homes—and the implications of those debates for present practice.

4.7.   JUVENILE DELINQUENCY
694.   Fleisher, Belton M. The Economics of Delinquency. Chicago: Quadrangle Books, 1966. A fairly thorough and sophisticated statistical analysis of the relationships between income, unemployment, and delinquency.

695.   Fox, Sanford J. "Juvenile Justice Reform: An Historical Perspective." Stanford Law Review, Vol. 22 (1970), 1187-1239. A general survey of juvenile justice

reform from the perspective that historically there have been three major reform movements concerning juvenile delinquents--opening up of the New York House of Refuge in 1825, institution of the juvenile court in Illinois in 1899, and the Gault decision by the U.S. Supreme Court in 1967. In tracing these developments, the author does not always agree with other interpretations of them, especially Pickett's views on the first and Platt's on the second. The work ends with some conjecture on possible limitations on reform in the post-Gault era.

696.   Klempner, Jack and Roger D. Parker. Juvenile Delinquency and Juvenile Justice. New York: Franklin Watts, 1981. The authors of this recent work discuss the nature of the current juvenile justice system, which they clearly state does not work, analyze its origins and development, examine its limitations, and propose possibilities for its improvement.

697.   Langley, Michael H. and H. B. Drone. "Juvenile Justice: Reneging on a Sociological Obligation." Social Service Review, Vol. 47, No. 4 (Dec., 1973), 561-70. An examination of the extent to which the juvenile justice system is working properly. After evaluating the system at three levels--the legal or political, the social scientific, and the treatment--the authors conclude it is not working the way it is supposed to and suggest that new approaches and methods are necessary.

698.   Lemert, Edwin M. "Juvenile Justice--Quest and Reality." Trans-Action, Vol. 4, No. 8 (July-August, 1967), 30-40. It is Lemert's contention that humanitarian concerns have led to faulty justice for children. The family, even one disturbed by conflict, morality problems, divorce, or death, is best suited for nurturing children into stable adults; thus the flow of cases into juvenile courts must be stopped, according to the author.

699.   Schlossman, Steven. "Traditionalism and Revisionism in Juvenile Correctional History." Reviews in American History, Vol. 2, No. 1 (March, 1974), 59-64. A review article on Joseph Hawes' Children in Urban Society and Robert Mennel's Thorns and Thistles which the author uses as the basis for an excellent historiographical essay on crime and punishment, especially juvenile delinquency, in American history.

700.   Sutton, John R. "Stubborn Children: The Social Origins of Child-Regulation in the Juvenile Justice System." Unpublished Ph.D. Diss., University of California, Davis, 1981. This study uses both qualitative and

quantitative historical data to analyze both the origins
and the spread of key juvenile justice reforms among the
states, especially the emergence of the "status offender," or non-criminal juvenile offender, as a
specialized category of deviant in modern American law.
In general, the study concludes that innovations that
have differentiated among juvenile offenders have resulted from the efforts of reform groups to establish
preventive institutions, and through those institutions
to maintain the power to define juvenile deviance.

4.8.   CHILDREN'S COURTS

701.   Bryant, Keith. "The Juvenile Court Movement." Social
Science Quarterly, Vol. 49, No. 2 (Sept., 1968),
368-76. A case study of the successful effort by Ben B.
Lindsey and Kate Barnard, an Oklahoma social worker, to
create a juvenile court system for that state.

702.   Curtis, George B. "The Juvenile Court Movement in
Virginia: The Child Savers, 1890-1973." Unpublished
Ph.D. diss., University of Virginia, 1973. A history of
the juvenile court movement in Virginia which concentrates 1) on the concept of parens patriae and the
difficulties it ran into in the twentieth century and 2)
its leader for more than forty years, Judge James Hoge
Ricks, whose greatest task was to allay popular fear of
the delinquent child and the courts "soft" procedures.

703.   Handler, Joel F. "The Juvenile Court and the Adversary
System: Problems of Function and Form." Wisconsin Law
Review, Vol. 1965 , No. 1 (Winter, 1965), 7-51. Handler
analyzes the positions for and against "judicializing"
the procedures in juvenile courts--introducing adversary
procedures to determine the statutory status and disposition of delinquents--and concludes that neither is
adequate for determining the issue; he then proposes introducing adversary procedures at the administrative
level of the process with provisions for judicial control and supervision.

704.   Kahn, Alfred. A Court for Children. New York:
Columbia University Press, 1953. A provocative and controversial account of the juvenile court movement in
general and the New York City children's court in particular, which spared no detail in discussing what was
wrong with the court--and what needed to be done to
remedy it, including the provision of legal safeguards
to children, the need for more qualified staff members,
and the need for better probation services and the money
to support them.

705.   Neigher, Alan. "The Gault Decision: Due Process and

the Juvenile Court." Federal Probation, Vol. 31, No. 4
(Dec., 1967), 8-18. While the author concedes that the
Gault decision will have a positive impact on the future
of juvenile courts in America, he also argues in this
good review of precisely what that decision said and did
not say, that it is neither a panacea for children in
difficulty nor an onerous burden for juvenile law enforcement officers.

706.   Rosenheim, Margaret K., ed. Justice for the Child: The
Juvenile Court in Transition. New York: The Free
Press, 1962. A collection of ten papers, each of which
is well written and highlights one or more of the then
current issues surrounding the juvenile court, which,
taken together, comprised a valuable addition to the
literature on the subject. They synthesize the widespread disillusionment with the court, the belief that
it never lived up to its promise. The work allegedly
was a critical force leading to the Supreme Court's
famous Gault decision.

707.   Rosenheim, Margaret K. ed. Pursuing Justice for the
Child. Chicago: University of Chicago Press, 1976. A
successor to the editor's earlier volume on the subject
which covers a spectrum of issues with regard to the juvenile justice system in America, particularly the
place, purpose, and future of the juvenile court--and
again voices concern with the institution, more with the
way in which it has operated than with the institution
itself. Unfortunately, however, the work lacks any real
blueprint for change.

4.9.   CORRECTIONAL INSTITUTIONS
708.   Mennel, Robert M.   "'The Family System of Common
Farmers':   The Origins of Ohio's Reform Farm,
1840-1858." Ohio History, Vol. 89, No. 2 (Spring,
1980), 125-56; "The Family System of Common Farmers':
The Early Years of Ohio's Reform Farm, 1858-1884, Vol.
89, No. 3 (Summer, 1980), 279-322. An excellent two
part series on the origin and early history of the Ohio
Reform School for Boys, 1858-1884, the first American
institution to combine a decentralized cottage building
plan with an agricultural work regime. This is much
more than an institutional history; Mennel skillfully
uses a study of the so-called Ohio Reform Farm to analyze the development of attitudes and policies toward
juvenile delinquency and related problems in nineteenth
century America.

709.   Pickett, Robert S. House of Refuge: Origins of
Juvenile Reform in New York State, 1815-1857. Syracuse,
N.Y.: Syracuse University Press, 1969. The first

full-length account of America's first institution for
juvenile delinquents, which opened its doors on Jan. 1,
1825. The author traces the background and early history of the institution and compares it to successors in
Boston and Philadelphia. Although a relatively narrow
work, it still is an important chapter in antebellum
child welfare history.

710.   Stewart, Joseph M. "A Comparative History of Juvenile
        Correctional Institutions in Ohio." Unpublished Ph.D.
        Diss., Ohio State University, 1980. This is a com-
        parative study of Ohio's two state supported juvenile
        correctional institutions--the Boys' and Girls' In-
        dustrial Schools, created in the mid-nineteenth century
        to be sources of order and stability in the lives of ju-
        veniles who presumably were in need of a stern hand of
        authority. It seeks to show how the institutions de-
        veloped, how they compared to each other, and most im-
        portant, how they treated the children committed to
        their care.

711.   Teeters, Negley K. "The Early Days of the Philadelphia
        House of Refuge." Pennsylvania History, Vol. 27, No. 2
        (April, 1960), 165-87. The author describes and an-
        alyzes the creation (in 1828) and early history of the
        Philadelphia House of Refuge, the nation's third such
        institution, and places it within the context of the
        broad welfare movement.

712.   Whittaker, James K. "Nineteenth Century Innovations in
        Delinquency Institutions." Child Care Quarterly, Vol.
        2, No. 1 (Spring, 1973), 14-24. Some observations on
        selected nineteenth century examples of delinquency
        treatment in an attempt to place current efforts in the
        field into historical perspective--and demonstrate that
        not all late nineteenth century institutions were
        prison-like settings dedicated to punishment; at least
        some were engaged in developing creative, innovative
        methods for dealing with the problem and its causes.

5. THE AMERICAN EXPERIENCE IN COMPARATIVE PERSPECTIVE

Chapter Three

ADDRESSING THE PROBLEMS OF YOUTH

Robert Mennel
University of New Hampshire

Issues Covered: Delinquency, juvenile justice, schools and
  institutions, childrens rights.

1. SYNTHESES AND OVERVIEWS

1.1. THEMATIC

713. Cloward, Richard and Lloyd Ohlin. Delinquency and
Opportunity: A Theory of Delinquent Gangs. New York:
Free Press, 1960. Emphasizing the lack of opportunity
for young people in the post-World War II American
slums, this study keyed the Mobilization for Youth Program in New York City (1958) and also influenced planning for Lyndon B. Johnson's War on Poverty.

714. Conley, John A. "Criminal Justice History as a Field of
Research: A Review of the Literature, 1960-1975."
Journal of Criminal Justice, Vol. 5 No. 1 (Spring,
1977), 13-28. Includes a short section on juvenile delinquency bemoaning the absence of "conceptual interpretations" but also ignoring numerous relevant
volumes.

715. Faust, Frederic and Paul J. Brantingham, eds. Juvenile
Justice Philosphy. St. Paul, West, 1981. Includes an
essay on the history and development of the juvenile
court stressing the multiplicity of factors in its creation. Contrary to revisionist scholars, the authors
see undirected social forces interacting with en-
vironmentalist legal philosophy combining to produce an
institution appropriate to a newly industrialized nation.

716. Ferdinand, Theodore N. "History and Policy in Juvenile
Justice." In Inciardi, James A. and Charles E. Faupel,
eds. History and Crime: Implications for Criminal
Justice Policy. Beverly Hills: Sage, 1980. The parens
patriae doctrine usefully rationalizes the state's concern with juvenile delinquents but too often has been
used as a catch-all or has been inflexibly applied.

717. Fox, Sanford T. "Juvenile Justice Reform: An Historical Perspective." Stanford Law Review. Vol. 22
(June, 1970), 1187-1239. A law professor's perceptive
analysis of the ever-broadening legal basis for the

reform school and the juvenile court. Emphasizes the
creation and operation of the parens patriae doctrine,
and the inconsequential nature of much nineteenth
century juvenile crime.

718. Hagen, John. "The Legislation of Crime and De-
      linquency: A Review of Theory, Method and Research."
      Law and Society Review, Vol. 14, No. 3 (Spring, 1980),
      603-628. Analysis of case studies in a number of social
      control areas, including delinquency. Critical of the
      scholarly tendency to draw simplistic conclusions, em-
      phasizing instead the plurality of interests shaping and
      utilizing laws.

719. Hawes, Joseph M. Children in Urban Society: Juvenile
      Delinquency in Nineteenth Century America. New York:
      Oxford University Press, 1971. A survey of definitions
      and institutional responses from 1800 through the early
      juvenile court, including discussion of popular fic-
      tional treatment of delinquency. Professor Hawes be-
      lieves that the proliferation of preventive methods and
      programs illustrates increasing awareness of children as
      individuals.

720. Ignatieff, Michael. "State, Civil Society and Total
      Institution: A Critique of Recent Social Histories of
      Punishment." In, Norval, Morris and Michael Tonry,
      eds. Crime and Justice: An Annual Review of Research,
      Vol. 3. Chicago: University of Chicago Press, 1981. A
      thoughtful essay charging recent historians with over-
      simplifying the social control ideology of those who es-
      tablished prisons and reform schools in the nineteenth
      century. Future scholars should avoid imputing con-
      spiratorial rationality to the ruling class yet also
      avoid returning to the "hyper-idealist" style of earlier
      writers.

721. Jeronimus, Virginia N. "An Historical Analysis of the
      Community Approach to Delinquency Prevention. Un-
      published Ph.D. Diss., University of California,
      Berkeley, 1978. Delinquency prevention programs have
      failed consistently since their inception in the 1820s
      because of the social control motivations of middle
      class and upper class reformers. Even the community
      action programs of the Chicago sociologists (1930s) and
      the War on Poverty planners have failed "to confront the
      inequalities in our society."

722. Lasch, Christopher. Haven in a Heartless World: The
      Family Beseiged. New York: Basic Books, 1977. A fas-
      cinating diatribe directed mainly at the modern thera-
      peutic professions whose aim is not to provide relief
      but to make their clients expert-dependent. This "in-
      vasion," according to Lasch is one of the stigmata of

late capitalist society.

723.   Mennel, Robert M. "Attitudes and Policies Toward
Juvenile Delinquency in the United States: A Historiographical Review." In Norval Morris and Michael
Tonry, eds. Crime and Justice: An Annual Review of
Research, Vol. 4, Chicago: University of Chicago Press,
1982. An assessment of recent literature, critical of
the social control interpretations, dominant since the
late 1960s. Urges more use of the case study of the
comparative approach and more attention to the
Post-World War II era.

724.   Mennel, Robert M. Thorns and Thistles: Juvenile
Delinquents in the United States, 1825-1940. Hanover,
N.H.: University Press of New England, 1973. A survey
of institutional developments and youthful responses
from the origins of the first reform schools through the
advent of modern professional study.

725.   Pisciotta, Alexander W. "Corrections, Society and Social Control in America: A Metahistorical Review of the
Literature." Criminal Justice History, Vol. 2 (1981),
109-130. Bemoans both the paucity of historical treat-
ments of crime and delinquency and the failure of researchers to explicate their a priori assumptions. By
making assumptions clear and testing competing interpretations in the process of supporting their own
positions, historians can contribute to the search for
truth in this part of their discipline.

726.   Platt, Anthony M. The Child Savers: The Ivention of
Delinquency. 2nd ed., Chicago: University of Chicago
Press, 1977. A revisionist case study of child-saving
philanthropy in late nineteenth century Chicago as a
preface to an explanation of the beginning of the
Illinois juvenile court, the first of its kind. Limited
by the author's conspiratorial view of history, which
overstates the influence of the philanthropic women from
Hull House, who helped to create the court, presenting
them as agents of corporate capitalism.

727.   Rendelman, Douglas. "Parens Patriae: From Chancery to
the Juvenile Court." South Carolina Law Review, Vol.
23, No. 2 (1971), 205-59. A gracefully written piece
arguing (contra Sanford Fox) that parens patriae served
a positive purpose in that reforms schools removed children from the abusive and discredited poor relief
system, especially the almshouses. The Juvenile Court
did the same and also extended awareness of the social
nature of delinquency but the court, like the reform
schools before it, has fallen far short of providing the
care to which poor families are entitled.

728.   Rothman, David. <u>Conscience and Convenience: The Asylum</u>
        <u>and its Alternatives in Progressive America</u>. Boston:
        Little, Brown, 1980. A continuation of <u>Discovery of the</u>
        <u>Asylum</u> from the 1860s to World War II.
        Community-centered organizations--juvenile courts, pro-
        bation, parole and mental health clinics--based upon the
        ideal of individualized treatment supplement the dis-
        credited institutions. Alas, the new approach also
        falls short because of professional careerism and
        political pressure.

729.   Rothman, David. <u>The Discovery of the Asylum: Social</u>
        <u>Order and Disorder in the New Republic</u>. Boston:
        Little, Brown, 1971. Best-known study of the origin and
        proliferation of prisons, reform schools, almshouses,
        insane asylums and orphan asylums. Viewed as a response
        to (urbanism and) social decay by elite reformers
        seeking to recapture the pre-Revolutionary War order.
        Increasing diversity of inmates due to immigration plus
        the limited tolerance of asylum founders gave the in-
        stitutions a custodial character by the time of the
        Civil War.

730.   Ryerson, Ellen. <u>The Best-Laid Plans: America's</u>
        <u>Juvenile Court Experiment</u>. New York: Hill and Wang,
        1978. A thinly researched study of reformers' and pro-
        fessionals' attitudes from the optimism of the Pro-
        gressive era to the current period of disillusion and
        reduced goals symbolized by the Gault decision (1967).

731.   Schlossman, Steven L. <u>Love and the American</u>
        <u>Delinquent: The Theory and Practice of "Progressive"</u>
        <u>Juvenile Justice, 1825-1920</u>. Chicago: University of
        Chicago Press, 1977. A general analysis of doctrine
        followed by examinaton of the development of the
        Wisconsin reform school system and the juvenile court in
        Milwaukee. The excellence of Schlossman's case study
        derives from his use of court and institution records
        and his linkage of local efforts to the larger reform
        movements of the era.

732.   Schultz, T. Lawrence. "The Cycle of Juvenile Court His-
        tory." <u>Crime and Delinquency</u>, Vol. 19, No. 4 (Oct.,
        1973), 457-76. A rejoinder to revisionist portraits of
        the court by Platt and Fox. Notes the willingness of
        parents to use the court and the importance of voluntary
        agencies and informal procedures in the early years.

1.2. TEMPORAL
733.   Bondavelli, Bonnie Jean. "A Socio-Historical Study of
        Juvenile Justice." Unpublished Ph.D. Diss., University
        of Missouri, Columbia, 1977. Uses the juvenile court in

Illinois, established in 1899, as a case study of the relationship between law and theory. The biggest change has occurred since 1960 when labelling and conflict theories challenged the benevolent intent of the court and led to a more legalized court and a narrower definition of delinquency. Support for these recent changes may be weakening.

734.   Deutsch, Albert. The Mentally Ill in America. 2nd ed., New York: Columbia University Press, 1949. A progressive view of the subject from the colonial period to World War II. A useful reference source with material on the definition and treatment of afflicted young people.

735.   Finestone, Harold. Victims of Change: Juvenile Delinquents in American Society. Westport Conn.: Greenwood Press, 1976. Focuses on twentieth century developments particularly the oral histories of the Chicago sociologists Clifford Shaw and Henry D. McKay. Finestone, who once served as research sociologist with the Illinois Institute for Juvenile Research, is critical of Shaw's reluctance to construct a social theory. Finestone's own enthusiasm is labelling theory.

736.   Haller, Mark H. Eugenics: Hereditarian Attitudes in American Thought. New Brunswick, N.J.: Rutgers University Press, 1964. Excellent monograph on the development of a science and its application to social problems in the early twentieth century. Restrictive marriage laws, immigration reduction, special schools for the mentally handicapped and sterilization laws were all products of this new construct. Eugenics encouraged pessimistic definitions of crime and delinquency.

737.   Handlin, Oscar and Mary F. Handlin. Facing Life: Youth and the Family in American History. Boston: Little Brown, 1971. A well written survey made especially interesting by vignettes from the lives of diverse young people but marred somewhat by the authors' preoccupation with the abuse of freedom by contemporary youth during the demonstrations and marches of the 1960s.

738.   Horlick, Allan Stanley. Country Boys and Merchant Princes: The Social Control of Young Men in New York. Lewisburg, Pa., Bucknell University Press, 1975. Valuable study of a nineteenth century urban elite demonstrating the ambiguities of social control. Organizations such as the YMCA served both to prevent young men from going astray and to demonstrate willingness to endorse charitable activity by socially aspiring businessmen.

739.   Macleod, David I. "Good Boys Made Better: The Boy

Scouts of America, Boys' Brigades, and YMCA Boys Work, 1880-1920." Unpublished Ph.D. Diss., University of Wisconsin, 1973. A study of the growth of diverse youth groups. Macleod notes the influence of G. Stanley Hall's pedagogy which was based on the belief that directed group experiences could turn dangerous "natural instincts" toward altruistic activity. The appeal was not aimed and delinquents, however, but at early teen-agers, cautiously exploring the world outside the home but not yet ready for the enticements and miseries of high school years.

740.   Pelton, L. H., ed. Social Context of Child Abuse and Neglect. New York: Human Sciences Press, 1981. A historical and contemporary overview of the juvenile court's involvement with abused and neglected children and child welfare agencies. Originally the juvenile court had placement jurisdiction but the agencies gained all but the formality after passage of the Social Security Act. Recently, federal aid and the children's and parent's rights movements have combined to give the juvenile court a more active role.

741.   Pisciotta, Alexander W. "Saving The Children: The Promise and Practice of Paren Patriae, 1838-98." Crime and Delinquency, Vol. 28, No. 3 (July, 1982), 410-25. The nineteenth century reform schools promised parental care but they delivered cruel punishment, compulsory Protestantism and an exploitive labor system. The children protested through violence and escape but the parental doctrine survived until the 1960s because it was transferred from the institutions to the juvenile court in the early twentieth century.

742.   Rosenberg, Carroll S. Religion and the Rise of the American City: The New York City Mission Movement, 1812-1870. Ithaca: Cornell University Press, 1971. The relationship between Protestantism and the slums. The tenacity of belief in individual culpability rather than social causation and the variety of institutional efforts predicated upon same.

743.   Tyor, Peter L. "Segregation or Surgery: The Mentally Retarded in America, 1850-1920." Unpublished Ph.D. Diss., Northwesteren University, 1972. Because of the nature of their incapacities, the mentally handicapped have always been equated with children but, in the latter nineteenth century, under the impact of industrialization, urbanization and immigration, their actions were characterized as menacing and delinquent. This led to policies of permanent custody and sterilization, some of which were carried out in institutions for children.

744.   Vincent R. F. "Expanding the Neglected Role of the
        Parent in the Juvenile Court." Pepperdine Law Review,
        Vol. 4 (1976-77), 523-41. A history of laws that pun-
        ished parents for the delinquent acts of their chil-
        dren. These are related to the 1976 California law en-
        abling the court to make direct orders to parents re-
        garding their children. A cautious and precise ap-
        plication is urged due to past failures. The last issue
        of the Pepperdine Law Review, Volumes 4 (1976-77)
        through 8 (1979-80), is devoted to the legal issues of
        delinquency and child abuse.

745.   Wohl, R. Richard. "The 'Country Boy' Myth and Its Place
        in American Culture: The Nineteenth Century
        Contribution." Perspectives in American History, Vol. 3
        (1969), 77-158. A brilliant article containing a per-
        ceptive analysis of Charles Loring Brace and the New
        York Children's Aid Society (1853). Wohl relates the
        placing-out policies of the CAS to Brace's admiration of
        German family life acquired during a tour of the
        continent.

746.   Zimring, Franklin E. "American Youth Violence: Issues
        and Trends." In Norval Morris and Michael Tonry, eds.
        Crime and Justice: An Annual Review of Research, Vol 1,
        Chicago: University of Chicago Press, 1979. Census and
        arrest data suggest that violent youth crime increased
        more than the youth population in the 1960s but has re-
        mained generally stable in the 1970s with the exception
        of increases in the rate of aggravated assault. The
        data, however, are too ambiguous to lend sanction to the
        rising popularity of punitive policies.

1.3.   (AUTO)BIOGRAPHIES
747.   Drost, Walter H. David Snedden and Education for Social
        Efficiency. Madison: University of Wisconsin Press,
        1967. An informative biography of the pedagogue who
        popularized industrial and manual training in the early
        twentieth century and promoted reform schools because
        their routines purported to emphasize vocationalism.

748.   Flynn, Frank T. "Judge Merrit W. Pinckney and the Early
        Days of the Juvenile Court in Chicago." Social Serivce
        Review, Vol. 28, No. 1 (March, 1954), 20-30. A positive
        portrait of a judge of one of the more significant
        courts. Stresses his efforts to resist political
        spoilsmen and to administer both juvenile justice and
        mothers' pensions.

749.   Huber, Frances. "The Progressive Career of Ben B.
        Lindsey, 1900-1920." Unpublished Ph.D. Diss.,
        University of Michigan, 1963. Another favorable

portrait of the juvenile court judge and his transit from the courtroom to the larger political arena. Emphasizes the importance of the 1912 election and Lindsey's support of Theodore Roosevelt and the Bull Moose Party.

750. Hughes, Helen MacGill, ed. The Fantastic Lodge: The Autobiography of a Girl Drug Addict. Boston: Houghton Mifflin, 1961. A searing portrait of the ways in which conventional society stigmatized drug users principally through treatment programs designed to fail. By indicating the political forces sustaining deviance, "Janet Clark's" story went beyond the traditional limits of oral history. This account was originally transcribed by Howard S. Becker whose Outsiders: Studies in the Sociology of Deviance (1963) was a pioneer study in the area of labelling theory.

751. Larsen, Charles. The Good Fight: The Life and Times of Ben B. Lindsey. Chicago: Quadrangle, 1972. Admiring but comprehensive biography of the most famous juvenile court judge.

752. Ross, Dorothy. G. Stanley Hall: The Psychologist as Prophet. Chicago: University of Chicago Press, 1972. Definitive biography of the founder of the child study movement and originator of modern delinquency study. Includes informative discussion on the emergence of educational psychology, the concept of adolescence, and the American response to psychoanalysis.

753. Rowles, Burton, J. The Lady at Box 99. Greenwich, Conn.: Seabury Press, 1962. A journalistic but informative biography of Miriam Van Waters, the leading figure in early twentieth century female corrections. Van Waters' Youth in Conflict (1925) was a popular plea for understanding delinquency, especially among girls victimized by the double-standard.

754. Schlossman, Steven L. "G. Stanley Hall and the Boys Club: Conservative Applications of Recapitulation Theory." Journal of the History of the Behavioral Sciences, Vol. 9, No. 2 (April, 1973), 140-47. Analysis of the pioneer theorist of adolescence. Hall believed that the club movement could help boys through the "inevitable" rebelliousness which characterized the teenage years.

755. Slater, Peter G. "Ben Lindsey and the Denver Juvenile Court: A Progressive Looks at Human Nature." American Quarterly, Vol. 20, No. 2 (Summer, 1968), 211-33. A perceptive analysis of the Judge's social thought stressing his "uneasy compromise" regarding the criminal responsibility of juveniles between environmental factors

and character defect. Slater views Lindsey as a representative Progressive.

1.4. DOCUMENTARIES
756. Bettelheim, Bruno. Love is Not Enough: The Treatment of Emotionally Disturbed Children. New York: Free Press, 1950. The renowned psychiatrist recounts the day-to-day life of the University of Chicago Sonia Shankman Orthogenic School, the institution which he made famous. See also his Truants from Life (1955).

757. Murphy, J. Prentice. "The Juvenile Court at the Bar." Annals of the American Academy of Political and Social Science, Vol. 145, No. 1 (Sept., 1929), 80-97. A compendium of early criticism. Some lawyers were concerned about the absence of legal safeguards but the predominant note, sounded by social workers, was that the court should be expanded through other agencies such as the family court and the guidance clinic.

1.5. CLASSIC CASE STUDIES
758. Cohen, Albert K. Delinquent Boys: The Culture of the Gang. New York: Free Press, 1955. Classic study of the cultural, sociological and psychological origins of delinquency. Cohen's assessment of the delinquent subculture as an alternate value system for those denied status by conventional middle class society proved especially influential among social planners of the Great Society.

759. Fink, Arthur E. The Causes of Crime. Philadelphia: University of Pennsylvania Press, 1938. An older study but still useful because of discussion of the development of European criminology in the nineteenth century, especially the anthropometrical studies of Lombroso, Tarde and Quetelet which gave an impetus to deterministic definitions of delinquency. Also explains the significance of Franz Boas' anthropological studies which provided a rejoinder for environmental and social causationists.

760. Glueck, Sheldon and Eleanor. One Thousand Delinquents: Their Treatment by Court and Clinic. Cambridge: Harvard University Press, 1934. An older but still significant study because it was one of the first to question the value of mental hygiene clinics in the prevention of delinquency. The ensuing conflict between the Gluecks and William Healy of Boston's Judge Baker Center appears prophetic to the contemporary period.

761. Healy, William. The Individual Delinquent. Boston:
      Little Brown, 1915. The pioneering work of the psycho-
      logical case study approach by the founder of the child
      guidance clinic movement.

762. Shaw,   Clifford.   Delinquency   Areas.   Chicago:
      University of Chicago Press, 1929. Classic ecological
      statement by the University of Chicago sociologist.

763. Thomas, William I. The Unadjusted Girl. Boston:
      Little Brown, 1923. Classic study by the University of
      Chicago sociologist relating delinquency to unfulfilled,
      status-based wishes.

764. Thomas, William I. and Dorothy S. Thomas. The Child in
      America. New York: Knopf, 1929. An early but in-
      formative survey of child study programs in the United
      States and Canada by the famous team of sociologists.

765. Thrasher, Frederic M. The Gang: A Study of 1,313 Gangs
      in Chicago. Chicago: University of Chicago Press,
      1927. Group delinquency linked to the Chicago theory of
      urbanization.

766. Van Waters, Miriam. Youth in Conflict. New York:
      Republic, 1925. A study of twelve cases from the Los
      Angeles Juvenile Court designed to analyze the causes of
      juvenile delinquency. The author traces the problem to
      parental indifference and social indifference to the
      value of childhood.

1.6. TEXTBOOKS, READERS, BOOKS OF DOCUMENTS, BIBLIOGRAPHIES
      767. Abbott, Grace, ed. The Child and the State. 2 vols.
            Chicago: University of Chicago Press, 1938. A still
            valuable documentary history by the former Chief of the
            U.S. Children's Bureau (1921-34). Emphasis upon ju-
            dicial   and   administrative   actions   affecting   ap-
            prenticeship and child labor, child welfare, delinquency
            and the legal relations of children to parents and other
            adults in the American community from the colonial
            period to the New Deal.

      768. Bremner, Robert H., ed. Children and Youth in America:
            A Documentary History. 3 vols. Cambridge: Harvard
            University Press, 1970-74. The most complete col-
            lection, tracing all aspects of public provision for
            children including education, labor, dependency, de-
            linquency and child health from the colonial period to
            1972. Special topics such as the problems of slave,
            Indian and immigrant children are also treated.
            Editorial comments introduce each volume and major
            section.

769.   Cabot, P.S. de Q, ed. Juvenile Delinquency: A Critical
        Annotated Bibliography. New York: H.W. Wilson, 1946.
        Concentrates on the period from 1914 to 1944 and thus
        contains many abstracts of studies by psychiatrists, so-
        ciologists and social workers. Includes a subject index.

770.   Culver, Dorothy C., ed. Bibliography on Crime and
        Criminal Justice, 1927-37. 2 vols. New York: H.W.
        Wilson, 1934, 1939. Includes significant, annotated re-
        ferences on delinquency, juvenile courts and early
        modern research on youth problems.

771.   Gibbons, Don C. Delinquent Behavior. 3rd ed.
        Englewood Cliffs, N.J.: Prentice-Hall, 1981. A leading
        text. Examines major facets of youthful law-
        breaking--statistics, legal processes, causation
        theories and treatment programs. Includes expanded
        coverage of female delinquency and new correctional ap-
        proaches such as diversion, youth-service bureaus and
        community-based residential facilities. International
        patterns of delinquency are summarized.

772.   Gordon, Michael. Juvenile Delinquency in the American
        Novel, 1905-1965. Bowling Green, Ohio: Bowling Green
        University Popular Press, 1971. A compendium of plots
        including many little known ones.

773.   Greenberg, David F., ed. Crime and Capitalism:
        Readings in Marxist Criminology. Palo Alto,
        California: Mayfield, 1981. Focuses on adult crime but
        includes material on delinquent gangs "for their con-
        tribution to the 'terminal crisis' of capitalism." Con-
        clusion includes suggestions for Marxist criminologists
        to enable them to put their ideas into practice.

774.   Hall, John C., ed. Major Issues in Juvenile Justice
        Information and Training: Readings in Public Policy.
        Columbus, Ohio: Academy for Contemporary Problems,
        1981. Includes a variety of articles some with his-
        torical sections. Three articles discuss the role of
        waiver in the juvenile court. Since the Kent and Gault
        decisions, waiver has become formalized and increasingly
        utilized in adjudication of serious crimes. This trend
        conforms to the rising popularity of the prevention
        theory of punishment as opposed to the rehabilitative
        theory popular in the first half of the twentieth
        century.

775.   Kuhlman, Augustus Frederick, ed. A Guide to Material on
        Crime and Criminal Justice. New York: H.W. Wilson,
        1929. A still useful compilation, including a biblio-
        graphy of various writings on reform schools and the
        juvenile court.

776.   McCarthy, Francis Barry and James G. Carr. <u>Juvenile Law</u>
        <u>and Its Processes: Cases and Materials</u>. Indianapolis:
        Bobbs-Merrill, 1980. A well done law school text with a
        historical section. Includes materials from the ju-
        venile justice standards project of the American Bar As-
        sociation and the Institute of Judicial Administration.

777.   Noshpitz, Joseph D., ed. <u>Basic Handbook of Child</u>
        <u>Psychiatry</u>. 4 vols. New York: Basic Books, 1979. A
        compendium of expert opinion. Vol. 3 (Therapeutic
        Interventions) and Vol. 4 (Prevention and Current
        Issues) are the most relevant to this chapter. See es-
        pecially essay by Robert J. Marshall, "Antisocial
        Youth" (Vol. 3, 536-54) which includes a comprehensive
        bibliography.

778.   Remick, Cecile P. <u>An Annotated Bibliography of Works on</u>
        <u>Juvenile Delinquency in America and Britain in the</u>
        <u>Nineteenth Century</u>. Philadelphia: R. West, 1976. A
        partially annotated compilation of primary and secondary
        sources. Includes notations on child raising manuals
        and on papers read at the annual meeting of the National
        Conference of Charities and Correction.

779.   Taft, Jessie. <u>The Dynamics of Therapy</u>. 2nd ed. New
        York: Dover Books, 1962. Text by a leading psychiatric
        social worker. Jessie Taft believed that relationship
        therapy--developing a healthy emotional bond between
        therapist and child--could help prevent juvenile
        delinquency.

780.   Tomkins, Dorothy Campbell (Culver), ed. <u>Court</u>
        <u>Organization and Administration</u>. University of
        California, Berkeley: Institute of Governmental
        Studies, 1973. A bibliography which includes a section
        on the family court.

781.   Tomkins, Dorothy Campbell (Culver), ed. <u>Juvenile Gangs</u>
        <u>and Street Groups: A Bibliography</u>. University of
        California, Berkeley: Institute of Governmental
        Studies, 1966. A comprehensive work by the premier bib-
        liographer of crime and delinquency. Includes refer-
        ences to group delinquency throughout the world, drawn
        from United Nations and foreign government sources.

2. PERIOD PIECES

2.1. COLONIAL
      782. Bailyn, Bernard. <u>Education in the Forming of American</u>

Society. Chapel Hill: Universtity of North Carolina Press, 1960. Seminal historiographical essay tracing the impact of social and economic forces upon colonial family life and relating this change to the growth of institutions of all kinds in the nineteenth century.

783. Flaherty, David. "Laws and the Enforcement of Morals in Early America." Perspectives in American History, Vol. 5 (1971), 203-56. The intertwining of Mosaic biblical law and common law explains much about the subsequent growth of equity in American law and the broad juris- diction of children's institutions relying upon it.

784. Smith, Abbot E. Colonists in Bondage: White Servitude and Convict Labor in America, 1607-1776. Chapel HIll: University of North Carolina Press, 1947. The variety of circumstances governing transfer of criminals and delinquents from England to the colonies.

2.2. REVOLUTIONARY AND EARLY NATIONAL

785. Heale, Michael J. "Humanitarianism in the Early Republic: The Moral Reformers of New York, 1776-1825." Journal of American Studies. Vol. 2, No. 2 (Oct., 1968), 161-75. An excellent group portrait of the founders of the first reform schools, temperance societies and charity schools. Heale emphasizes the reformers' mix- ture of utilitarian and moral motives displayed in the New York House of Refuge's Benthamite punishment and re- ward system and its devotion to daily preaching and exhortation.

2.3. ANTEBELLUM AND CIVIL WAR

786. Banner, Lois. "Religious Benevolence as Social Control: A Critique of an Interpretation." Journal of American History, Vol. 60, No. 1 (June, 1973): 23-41. A rejoinder to Clifford Griffin and others. Banner ac- knowledges reformers' fear of democracy and devotion to capitalism but urges consideration of sectarian com- petition and millenialist ideas as reformatory motives. Thus, benevolent and reformatory institutions were em- blematic of efforts to insure the success of the new Republic rather than attempts to control society.

787. Crandall, John C. "Patriotism and Humanitarian Reform in Children's Literature, 1825-60." American Quarterly, Vol. 21, No. 1 (Spring, 1961), 3-22. A new genre emerges to inform young audiences of adult purposes. The workings of reform schools were pointedly outlined.

788. Davies, John D. Phrenology: Fad and Science. New

Haven: Yale University Press, 1955. A dispassionate
analysis of a "science" of the 1830s and 1840s which
drew conclusions about character and behavior by examining the shape and protuberances of individual
skulls. Phrenologists enjoyed visiting reform schools,
drawing pessimistic conclusions about new inmates and
optimistic conclusions about those nearing release.

789. Griffin, Clifford S. Their Brothers' Keepers: Moral
Stewardship in the United States, 1800-1965. New
Brunswick, New Jersey: Rutgers University Press, 1960.
Comprehensive study of early nineteenth century reformers. Christian duty combined with social fears and
anxieties caused urban elites to establish institutions
for dependent and delinquent persons, including special
institutions for children.

790. Katz, Michael B. The Irony of Urban School Reform:
Educational Innovation in Mid-Nineteenth Century
Massachusetts. Cambridge: Harvard University Press,
1968. Significant case study illustrating the social
control interpretation of educational institutions. Includes a chapter on the Massachusetts Reform School for
Boys (Westborough) showing the transition from voluntary
philanthropy to state enterprise.

791. Laurie, Bruce. "Fire Companies and Gangs in Southwark:
The 1840s." In Davis, Allen F. and Mark Haller, eds.,
The Peoples of Philadelphia: A History of Ethnic Groups
and Lower-Class Life, 1790-1840. Philadelphia: Temple
University Press, 1973. An interesting perspective on
lower class life. Fire-laddies may have avoided delinquency because of the political power of their
companies.

792. Pickett, Robert S. House of Refuge: Origins of
Juvenile Reform in New York State, 1815-1857.
Syracuse: Syracuse University Press, 1969. The early
history of the first American institution. Emphasizes
the process through which philanthropic impulses assumed
institutional form and the constant political conflict
surrounding the operation of quasi-public philan-
thropies. Pickett places the refuge in the context of
reform school development in other U.S. cities.

793. Teeters, Negley K. "The Early Days of the Philadelphia
House of Refuge." Pennsylvania History, Vol. 27, No. 2
(April, 1960): 165087. An informative description from
the progressive point of view.

2.4. POSTBELLUM
794. Langsam, Miriam Z. Children West: A History of the

Placing Out System of the New York Children's Aid
Society, 1853-1890. Madison: State Historical Society
of Wisconsin, 1964. A modern account of Charles Loring
Brace's anti-institutional solution to urban delinquency
in the latter nineteenth century, a rather favorable one
based largely on the New York Children's Aid Society's
records.

795.   Monkkonen, Eric H. The Dangerous Class: Crime and
Poverty in Columbus, Ohio, 1860-1885. Cambridge:
Harvard University Press, 1975. An empirical study not
dealing directly with delinquency but valuable because
it suggests that fear of crime was due in good part to
fear of strange persons, of whom columbus had plenty,
rather than numbers of offenses, of which Columbus had
less per capita than its rural hinterland.

2.5. PROGRESSIVE
796.   Holl, Jack M. Juvenile Reform in the Progressive Era:
William R. George and the Junior Republic Movement.
Ithaca: Cornell University Press, 1971. Excellent
study of an "anti-institutional" institution of the
early twentieth century. The Republics were based upon
a degree of inmate self-government and a "free enterprise" labor economy--ideas which still enjoy some
currency despite numerous examples of their abuse by
inmate-defined power structures.

797.   Mennel, Robert M. "Origins of the Juvenile Court:
Changing Perspectives on the Legal Rights of Juvenile
Delinquents." Crime and Delinquency, Vol. 18, No. 11
(Jan., 1972), 68-78. Emphasizes the transformation and
revitalization of the parens patriae doctrine by the ju-
venile court in the early twentieth century.

798.   Schlossman, Steven L. and Ronald Cohen. "The Music Man
in Gary: Willim Brown and Child Saving in the Progressive Era." Societas, Vol. 7. No. 1 (Winter, 1977),
1-18. A judge, not unlike the mythical Harold Hill,
tries to stem truancy and delinquency by establishing a
panoply of good works collectively labeled Boyville. He
failed and then disappeared but showed the kinder side
of progressive child-saving.

2.6. THE 1920s AND THE GREAT CRASH
799.   Faris, Robert E. L. Chicago Sociology, 1920-1932.
Chicago: University of Chicago Press, 1970. An en-
lightening account of the famous academic department and
the place of delinquency and crime research within it.

800. Levine, Murray and Adeline Levine. <u>A Social History of</u>
      <u>Helping Services</u>. New York: Appleton-Century Crofts,
      1970. A positive portrayal of the origins of clinics
      for delinquent children in the context of the mental
      hygiene movement.

2.7. NEW DEAL AND WORLD WAR II
      801. Flack, Bruce. "The American Youth Commission." Un-
            published Ph.D. Diss., Ohio State University, 1969. An
            account of a major project of the American Council on
            Education. The Commission monitored New Deal programs
            such as the CCC and conducted other studies on the needs
            and problems of youth in the Depression.

      802. Witmer, Helen L. <u>Psychiatric Clinics for Children</u>. New
            York: The Commonwealth Fund, 1940. An early, in-
            formative study quite favorable to the therapeutic ideal.

2.8. POSTWAR
      803. Davies, Stanley P. <u>The Mentally Retarded in Society</u>.
            New York: Columbia University Press, 1959. A survey
            showing the emergence of a more positive policy toward
            integrating patients, including youths, into the com-
            munity. An earlier study by Davies was entitled:
            <u>Social Control of the Feebleminded</u> (1923).

      804. Eissler, K. R., ed. <u>Searchlights on Delinquency</u>. New
            York: International Universities Press, 1949. A col-
            lection of articles expressing faith in psychotherapy as
            a solution to delinquency. The high noon of this mode
            of treatment.

      805. Fine, Benjamin. <u>1,000,000 Delinquents</u>. Cleveland:
            World, 1955. Famous expose by the education editor of
            the <u>New York Times</u>. Uses oral interviews to emphasize
            both the magnitude of the problem and the humanity of
            the youths. Fine stresses social causes and urges sup-
            port for community action programs.

      806. McCorkle, Lloyd W., Albert Elias, and F. Lovell Bixby.
            <u>The Highfields Story: An Experimental Treatment Project</u>
            <u>for Youthful Offenders</u>. New York: Henry Holt, 1958.
            Therapy based on "guided group interaction" in the New
            Jersey reformatory system in the 1950s. Proclaimed suc-
            cessful in dealing with hard core delinquents but never
            widely applied due to expense and political opposition.

      807. Polsky, Howard. <u>Cottage Six</u>. New York: Russell Sage,
            1962. The difficulties of applying "milieu therapy" in
            a 1950s reform school. The routine emphasized manipu-

lating the youths' emotional capacities into socially
acceptable channels through peer pressure and individually focused treatment by counselors in a family
setting. Not unlike the Victorian cottage reform
schools except in devotion to a historical professional
culture.

808.   Redl, Fritz and David Wineman. Children Who Hate: The
Disorganization and Breakdown of Behavior Controls. New
York: Free   Press,   1965.   Major   study   by   two
psychiatrists. An important document to those who interpret delinquency principally as a personality disorder. Inspired by the work of August Aichorn,
especially Wayward Youth (1935).

809.   Rosenheim, Margaret K., ed. Justice for the Child: The
Juvenile Court in Transition. New York: Free Press,
1962. One of the last significant collections of
articles expressing the hope that the juvenile court and
allied agencies could still bear the burden of the
juvenile justice system.

810.   Virtue, Maxine B. Public Services to Children in
Michigan. Ann Arbor: University of Michigan Press,
1952. One of the first comprehensive, critical
studies. Questions the benevolent intent of the juvenile court, particularly the probation system which
returned children to the supervision of the same officer
who had brought them into court.

2.9. GREAT SOCIETY

811.   Lemert, Edwin M. Social Action and Legal Change:
Revolution within the Juvenile Court. Chicago: Aldine,
1970. An important case study (California) systematically outlining the incongruity between the familial
pretensions and increasingly impersonal and bureau-
cratized procedures of the juvenile court. Importance
of the demands of social work agencies and the
California Youth Authority are stressed. An argument
for deinstitutionalization in order to maintain the integrity and future prospects of youths appearing in
court.

812.   Marris, Peter and Martin Rein. Dilemmas of Social
Reform: Poverty and Community Action in the United
States. Rev. ed. Chicago: Aldine, 1977. Study of the
tangled underbrush of congressional politics and pro-
fessional advocacy leading to the Great Society's War on
Poverty. The authors probe the origins of community
action in the activist anti-delinquency programs of the
Ford Foundation.

813.   Moore,   John.   "Controlling   Delinquency: Executive,
        Congressional and Juvenile, 1961-64." In Frederic N.
        Cleaveland,   ed.,   Congress   and   Urban   Problems.
        Washington: Brookings Institution, 1969.   A sharply-
        worded portrait of bureaucratic infighting during the
        formative years of federal policy.

814.   Morris, Joe.   First Offender.   New York: Funk and
        Wagnalls, 1970.   An account of 1960s programs designed
        to keep delinquents in the community and to utilize vol-
        unteers to supplement professional supervision.

815.   Moynihan, Daniel P.   Maximum Feasible Misunderstanding;
        Community Action in the War on Poverty.   New York: Free
        Press, 1969.   A bitter chronicle of the conflict and
        disorganization within the community action programs of
        Kennedy/Johnson War on Poverty.   Moynihan particularly
        blames social scientist advocates of community control
        who ignored the ease with which street-corner poli-
        ticians and their allies monopolized power in the
        anti-delinquency programs of the late 1950s.   The de-
        cline of Mobilization For Youth, a Manhattan project,
        foretold later problems.

816.   Ohlin, Lloyd, Robert Coates, and Alden Miller.   "Radical
        Correctional Reform: A Case Study of the Massachusetts
        Youth   Correctional   System."   Harvard   Educational
        Review, Vol. 44, No. 1 (Feb., 1974):   74-111.   A favor-
        able account of pioneer efforts to close custodial in-
        stitutions and to develop community-based care and
        corrections.

817.   Olson, Gayle C.   "Law Enforcement and Juvenile
        Delinquency Prevention: An Historical Federal, State
        and Local Perspective."   Unpublished Ph.D. Diss.
        University of California, Santa Barbara, 1981.   A sig-
        nificant portion of this work analyzes the efforts of
        the federal government to prevent delinquency following
        passage of the 1961 Act.   Studies the operation of the
        Office of Juvenile Justice and Delinquency Prevention.
        It is likely that the Federal government has been no
        more or no less successful than were th earlier pre-
        ventive efforts of state and local governments or
        private organizations.

818.   President's   Commission   on   Law   Enforcement   and
        Administration of Justice.   Juvenile Delinquency in a
        Free Society.   Belmont, California, 1968.   A call for
        federal action by a blue-ribbon panel.

2.10.   THE CONTEMPORARY PERIOD

819.   Allen, Francis A. The Decline of the Rehabilitative
        Ideal: Penal Policy and Social Purpose. New Haven:
        Yale University Press, 1981. A gracefully written syn-
        thesis (the 1979 William A. Storrs lectures at Yale Law
        School) warning that the current punitive emphasis can
        also lead to tyrannical government interventions against
        blameless members of society. Achieving social justice
        brings its own rewards. For a more positive statement
        of this philosophy see his The Borderlands of Criminal
        Justice (1964).

820.   Bartollas, Clemens, Stuart J. Miller and Simon Dinitz.
        Juvenile Victimization: The Institutional Paradox. New
        York: John Wiley, 1976. A case study (Ohio) of a
        "total institution" drawing on the theories of Erving
        Goffman, Amitai Etzioni and others to conclude that the
        institution helps no one, not even the staff but may be
        necessary to protect society from violently dangerous
        young men.

821.   Empey, Lamar T., ed. The Future of Childhood and
        Juvenile Justice. Charlottesville: University Press of
        Virginia, 1979. A highly valuable collection. The
        editor provides a historical introduction and a concise
        summary, noting that current reforms such as the chil-
        drens' rights movement do not necessarily denote pro-
        gress. The essays by Richard Farson (Children's
        Rights), Kingsley Davis (Demographic Changes), James F.
        Short Jr. (Social Contexts) and Franklin Zimring
        (Jurisprudence of Adolescence) are particularly useful.

822.   Empey, LaMar T. and Maynard L. Erickson. The Provo
        Experiment: Evaluating Community Control of
        Delinquency. Lexington, Mass.: D.C. Heath, 1972. A
        detailed comparison between two groups, one in-
        stitutionalized and the other treated in the community,
        concludes that the latter approach offers more hope in
        combatting delinquency. A cautious summary calling for
        more research.

823.   Esler, Anthony, ed. The Youth Revolution: The Conflict
        of Generations in Modern History. Lexington, Mass.:
        D.C. Heath, 1974. A compendium debating the social
        force of generational conflict. Contributors disagree
        with each other on the degree of group consciousness and
        action and the value of youth rebellions.

824.   Fisher, Stanley Z. "'Families with Service Needs': The
        Newest Euphemism?" Journal of Family Law, Vol. 18, No.
        1 (1979-89), 1-77. An informative review of the back-
        ground and dimensions of a controversy over the best way
        to treat status offenders (runaways, truants, "in-
        corrigible" youths). Formerly called PINS (Persons in
        Need of Supervision), these children can avoid court

jurisdiction in the post-Gault era since they are neither ostensibly abused nor overtly dangerous. The National Council of Juvenile Court and Family Court Judges wants to bring them under court scrutiny as members of "Families with Service Needs." The author prefers to treat them as delinquents since the rehabilitative ideal has been discredited.

825.   Florida-Deinstitutionalization of Status Offenders-A Case Study. Washington, D.C.: Arthur D. Little, 1977. An LEAA-funded study by the famous think tank. Similar study conducted in Iowa. As mandated by state law, most status offenders were diverted from court. The problem seemed to be providing them with useful and non-stigmatizing care.

826.   Fox, Sanford T. Modern Juvenile Justice: Cases and Materials. 2nd ed. St. Paul: West, 1981. A law school textbook comprised of articles, official reports and cases. Outlines recent changes such as the increasing importance of diversion and, at the same time, the waivering of violent and repeated offenders to adult tribunals. Courts increasingly intervene on behalf of abused children. Includes comparative material on Swedish and Scottish systems.

827.   Gold, Martin and Oliver C. Moles. "Delinquency and Violence in Schools and Communities." In Inciardi, James A. and Anne E. Pottieger, eds. Violent Crime: Historical and Contemporary Issues. Beverly Hills: Sage, 1978. Using statistics from the 1960s and 1970s, the authors contend that violence in the schools has not increased. Rather, people think it has increased. Research, they believe, should plumb this myth.

828.   Harvard Educational Review, Vol. 43, No. 4 (Nov., 1973), 481-704 and Vol. 44, No. 1 (Feb., 1974), 1-212. These two issues are devoted to the rights of children and cover many subjects including students' rights, juvenile justice, foster care, abused and neglected children and hyperkinetic children. The authors are generally favorable toward according children more legal rights and providing resources to insure that children receive equal care and treatment. Children are seen as equal persons under the law with rights as opposed to needs, which connote dependency.

829.   James, Howard. Children in Trouble: A National Scandal. New York: David McKay, 1970. Originally a series of articles in the Christian Science Monitor, this book fueled support for private and government-supported therapeutic programs in the 1970s.

830.   Lerman, Paul. Community Treatment and Social Control.

Chicago: University of Chicago Press, 1975. The therapeutic vogue of the 1970s is beset by a familiar paradox--the desire of reformers to advertise an innovative approach while not appearing lenient toward the objects of their affection. Nonetheless, the author advocates restrictions on restraining institutions and support for efforts to provide young people with non-coercive aid.

831.   Offer, Daniel, Richard C. Marohn, and Eric Ostnow. The Psychological World of the Juvenile Delinquent. New York: Basic Books, 1979. Psychological study still has its adherents. The children are categorized as 1) impulsive 2) narcissistic 3) empty-borderline 4) depressed borderline and, different therapies are prescribed for each type.

832.   Preliminary National Assessment of the Numbers and Characteristics of Juveniles Processed in the Juvenile Justice System. Washington: Government Printing Office, 1981. The latest statistics as aggregated by the American Justice Institute, National Juvenile Justice Assessment Center in Sacramento. In 1977, 2.5 million persons under 18 were arrested or were referred to the juvenile justice system. Of these, 90 percent were formally arrested by the police and 50 percent were given informal dispositions and dismissed. Of the 1.2 million cases referred to the prosecutor's office, 42 per cent were dismissed, primarily due to lack of evidence.

833.   Radzinowicz, Sir Leon and Marvin E. Wolfgang, eds. Crime and Justice, 3 vols. 2nd ed. New York: Basic Books, 1977. Though focusing mainly on the adult population, there are several interesting contributons on delinquency. These are the essays by Roger Hood and Richard Sparks on "Subcultural and Gang Delinquency" (Vol. I) and Wolfgang's essay on "Crime in a Birth Cohort" (Vol. III).

834.   Rosenheim, Margaret K., ed. Pursuing Justice for the Child. Chicago: University of Chicago Press, 1976. A response to the critics of the juvenile court in the post-Gault era. Expresses the hope that the court will still play an important, if admittedly less-central role in the care of delinquent children.

835.   Sandhu, Harjit S. Community Corrections: New Horizons. Springfield, Illinois: Charles C. Thomas, 1981. Includes analysis of the origins of probation and community-based delinquency prevention programs such as the Chicago Area Project. Various residential and non-residential programs are described and compared and the Community Treatment Project in California is

analyzed as a successful example.

836. Schur, Edwin M. <u>Radical Nonintervention: Rethinking the Delinquency Problem</u>. Englewood Cliffs, N.J.: Prentice-Hall, 1973. A forceful statement of protest against the traditional juvenile justice system as intentionally discriminatory against children generally but especially children from the poorer classes. A leading influence in the children's rights movement of the 1970s which narrowed the jurisdiction of the juvenile court.

837. U.S. Comptroller General. <u>Report to Congress: How Federal Efforts to Coordinate Programs to Mitigate Juvenile Delinquency Proved Ineffective</u>. Washington: Government Printing Office, 1975. Self-explanatory: the end of government intervention begun so optimistically in the Kennedy-Johnson era.

3. SALIENT VARIATIONS

3.1. LOCAL, STATE, REGIONAL

838. Alonzo, Frank O. "The History of the Mississippi Youth Court System." <u>Journal of Mississippi History</u>, Vol. 39, No. 2 (May, 1977), 133-53. A descriptive case study beginning with the Industrial and Training School Act (1916) and covering the establishment of juvenile courts (1940) and separate family courts (1964).

839. Curtis, George. "The Juvenile Court Movement in Virginia." Unpublished Ph.D. Diss., University of Virginia, 1973. Emphasizes the contradictions of the <u>parens</u> <u>patriae</u> doctrine—was the child a threat hence deserving oppression, or a future responsible adult hence requiring care? Analysis is built around a study of the state's foremost juvenile court judge, James Hoge Ricks, and stresses the additional conflicts generated by these racial relationships.

840. Grignano, Innocenzio A. "The Industrial and Training School Concept in Allegheny County: An Historical Analysis." Unpublished Ph.D. Diss., University of Pittsburgh, 1975. An interesting study from the perspective of Pittsburgh where no local institutions for delinquents existed from 1873 (when the Western House of Refuge moved to Cannonsburg) until 1909 when state law mandated the establishment of an industrial school organized on a cottage basis. This school eventually was phased out in the early 1970s after a conflict-filled history.

841. Haller, Mark H. "Urban Crime and Criminal Justice: the Chicago Case." Journal of American History, Vol. 57, No. 3 (Dec. 1970), 619-35. An examination of the complex interrelations of crime, criminal justice, and reform in Chicago, 1900-1930, which emphasizes, among other things, the weakness of the reforms--largely be cause "they lived outside the intellectual and geographical communities they wished to change."

842. Leiby, James. Charity and Correction in New Jersey: A History of State Welfare Institutions. New Brunswick, N.J.: Rutgers University Press, 1967. The most comprehensive state study. Contains informative material on the development of the juvenile corrections systems.

843. Mennel, Robert M. "The Family System of Common Farmers: The Origins (part I) and Early Years (part II) of Ohio's Reform Farm." Ohio History, Vol. 83, Nos. 2 and 3 (Spring and Summer, 1980), 125-56 and 279-322. The rise and fall of a pioneer cottage and farm school and the claiming force of local and state political culture upon same.

844. Parker, Graham. "The Juvenile Court: The Illinois Experience." University of Toronto Law Journal, Vol. 26, No. 3 (1976), 253-306. A case study of the first court emphasizing the importance of the clinic established by William Healy in 1909 with the philanthropic support of Ethel Dummer. Disputes Christopher Lasch's contention that early court founders and social workers were "engineers" but accuses them of lacking flexibility in their diagnoses. The court thus became overbureaucratized and the stage was set for the contemporary legal rights movement.

845. Pisciotta, Alexander W. "The Theory and Practice of the New York House of Refuge, 1857-1935." Unpublished Ph.D. Diss., Florida State University, 1979. A carefully researched case study of the disjunction between promise and practice which the author finds support for in the histories of institutions of other states.

846. Remick, Cecil. "The House of Refuge of Philadelphia." Unpublished Ed.D. Diss., University of Pennsylvania, 1975. A case study stressing social control motives of founders and the similarity of attitudes between Philadelphians and reformers in other American east coast cities and in England. Covers the colonial period as well as the nineteenth century when the institution was founded (1826). Includes discussion of the separate refuge established for black children in 1850.

847. Richette, Lisa A. The Throwaway Children.

Philadelphia: J. B. Lippincott, 1969. A passionate indictment   of   the   juvenile   justice   system   of
Philadelphia. Calls for a Youth Services Bureau to
replace the juvenile court.

848.   Salsgiver,   Richard.   "Child   Reform   in   Pittsburgh,
        1890-1915: The Development of the Juvenile Court and
        the Allegheny County Industrial and Training School for
        Boys."   Unpublished   Ph.D.   Diss.,   Carnegie-Mellon
        University, 1975. The interplay between factions of re-
        formers leading to new institutions for delinquents.
        "Moral reformers," those favoring institutional reform,
        won over advocates of placing out but the industrial
        school soon became custodial and punitive.   Includes a
        group profile of both the managers and students of the
        school.

849.   Silverman, Edgar. "The Juvenile Court for the District
        of Columbia: An Historical View of Its Development from
        1937 to 1957." Unpublished D.S.W., Catholic University
        of America, 1971. A case study of a large court under
        two judges with contrasting philosophies.   Fay Bentley
        (1934-1948) emphasized social work services while Edith
        Cockrill (1948-57) stressed the administration of ju-
        stice.   Cockrill conflicted with social agencies but in
        her emphasis upon the legal rights of children proved
        prophetic.

850.   Slater, Peter G. Children in the New England Mind: In
        Death and In Life. Hamden, Conn.: Shoe String Press,
        1977.   An informative study of the decline of the
        Calvinist belief that the child's nature was tainted
        with original sin and the rise of enlightenment and ro-
        mantic ideas emphasizing the child's malleability or in-
        nate goodness.   These prepared the way for a spate of
        institutional activity in the 1830s and 40s.

851.   Stewart, Joseph M. "A Comparative History of Juvenile
        Correctional Institutions in Ohio."   Unpublished Ph.D.
        Diss., Ohio State University, 1980. The first century
        of the boys and girls State reform schools in Ohio.
        Despite   a   shift   from   agricultural   to   industrial
        training, both institutions were primarily custodial
        after the late nineteenth century. Following a national
        trend, the Boys Industrial School was closed in 1980.

852.   Thavenet, Dennis. "Wild Young' Uns in their Midst':
        The Beginning of Reformatory Education in Michigan."
        Michigan History, Vol. 60, No. 3 (Fall, 1976), 240-59.
        The origins of a state reform school, emphasizing the
        social problems of Detroit and the reliance upon earlier
        efforts in eastern states.

853.   Wirkkala, John. "Juvenile Delinquency and Reform in

Nineteenth Century Massachusetts: The Formative Era in
State Care, 1846-1876." Unpublished Ph.D. Diss., Clark
University, 1973. An informative case study tracing the
emergence of "affective" discipline in the early history
of two state reform schools in Massachusetts,
Westborough (boys) and Lancaster (girls). The new style
sought control by manipulation of emotions rather than
by corporal punishment.

854.   Zimmermann, Hilda Jane. "Penal Systems and Penal Re-
        forms in the South since the Civil War." Unpublished
        Ph.D. Diss., University of North Carolina, 1947. A com-
        prehensive examination of the convict lease system and
        the state and county farms which replaced it in the
        1890s. Children, unless they were black, were usually
        pardoned since institutions for delinquents did not
        exist.

3.2. RACIAL/ETHNIC

855.   Abell, Aaron I. American Catholicism and Social
        Action: A Search for Social Justice, 1865-1950. South
        Bend, Ind.: University of Notre Dame Press, 1963. A
        thorough work. Includes discussion of efforts to es-
        tablish Catholic children's institutions which were, in
        part, a response to the nativist policies of the house
        of refuge and other asylums.

856.   Brown, Claude. Manchild in the Promised Land. New
        York: Macmillan, 1965. Major autobiography focusing on
        the pain and conflict of growing up in Harlem. The au-
        thor spent time in several children's institutions and
        these experiences are graphically portrayed.

857.   Freeman, Ira Henry. Out of the Burning: The Story of a
        Boy Gang Leader. New York: Crown, 1960.
        Autobiographical account of a black youth from
        Bedford-Stuyvesant who survived, according to his own
        account, by luck. Not a sophisticated study but a dis-
        illusioning one which sets the background for the crit-
        icisms of therapeutic institutions in the 1960s and
        1970s.

858.   Petterson, J. R. "Education, Jurisdiction, and
        Inadequate Facilities as Causes of Juvenile Delinquency
        Among Indians." North Dakota Law Review, Vol. 48, No. 4
        (Summer, 1972), 661-94. Reviewed historically and in
        the context of government oscillation between policies
        of assimilation and self-determination toward Indians,
        alternating between federal, state and tribal au-
        thority. The unhappy transition between special
        boarding schools and the public schools is emphasized.

3.3. GENDER-SPECIFIC

859. Brenzel, Barbara M. "Domestication as Reform: A Study of the Socialization of Wayward Girls, 1856-1905." Harvard Educational Review. Vol. 50, No. 2 (May, 1980), 196-213. A portion of the thesis, cited below, focusing on the characteristics of the inmates. Notes that girls were often incarcerated for marginal offenses or because of familial conflicts and that treatment was sometimes beneficial.

860. Brenzel, Barbara M. "The Girls at Lancaster: A Social Portrait of the First Reform School for Girls in North America, 1856-1905." Unpublished Ed.D. Diss., Harvard University, 1978. The only major study of its kind, this thesis presents a balanced view of the factors involved in the establishment and operation of the institution.

861. Freedman, Estelle B. Their Sisters' Keepers: Women's Prison Reform in America, 1830-1930. Ann Arbor: University of Michigan Press, 1981. Focuses entirely upon adult institutions and stresses the prevalence of the custodial philosophy and other special discriminations against women prisoners. A useful companion to studies of delinquent girls.

862. Melder, Keith. "Ladies Bountiful: Organized Women's Benevolence in Early Nineteenth Century America." New York History, Vol. 68, No. 2 (July, 1967), 231-55. The role of women in the establishment of houses of refuge, missionary groups and insane asylums.

863. Sagarin, Edward, ed. Taboos in Criminology. Beverly Hills: Sage, 1980. The rise of violent crime among women and the influence of intelligence and race upon delinquency are two of the major subjects where research is opposed by major political and social interests. Delinquency research concluding positively about the value of incarceration is another.

864. Schlossman, Steven L. and Stephanie Wallach. "The Crime of Precocius Sexuality: Female Juvenile delinquency in the Progressive Era." Harvard Educational Review, Vol. 48, No. 1 (Feb., 1978), 65-94. A critical portrait of Miriam Van Waters and other female penologists who view themselves as liberating young women, by individual treatment and community placement, from the toils of custodial institutions.

865. Tappan, Paul. Delinquent Girls in Court. New York: Columbia University Press, 1947. Significant early case study (New York City) criticizing the juvenile court for

denying due process of law. Loose administrative application of legal classifications led to the girls' effective stigmatization among metropolitan welfare
agencies, hence blocking their return to community life.

3.4. CLASS
   866.   Liazos, Alexander. "Class Oppression: The Functions of
          Juvenile Justice." The Insurgent Sociologist, Vol. 1,
          No. 1 (Fall, 1974), 12-24. Self-explanatory.

4. AGE-SPECIFIC AND LIFE-CYCLE STUDIES

4.1. CHILD NURTURE
   867.   Steere, Geoffrey H.   "Changing Values in Child
          Socialization: A Study of United States Child-Rearing
          Literature, 1865-1929." Unpublished Ph.D. Diss., Uni-
          versity of Pennsylvania, 1964. The change is from an
          "intuitive-religious" orientation to a "scientific-
          relativistic" orientation and is illustrative of wider
          change occuring in American society. The nineteenth
          century emphasized the laws of nature but made these
          indistinguishable from the will of God. The modern era
          interpreted values in psychological and sociological
          terms, though Freud's influence was not as great as
          might be expected. Philosophical relativism completed
          this "inner revolution."

   868.   Wishy, Bernard. The Child and the Republic: The Dawn
          of Modern American Child Nurture. Philadelphia: Uni-
          versity of Pennsylvania Press, 1968. A study of the
          nineteenth century literature on the subject stressing
          adult fears. In the antebellum period, the anxiety was
          expressed as concern about the "redeemable" child in a
          Christian Republic. After the war, fear of pluralism
          made adults wonder if the child could indeed be a
          "redeemer" of the promise of American industrialization.

4.2. ADOLESCENCE
   869.   Demos, John and Virginia Demos. "Adolescence in His-
          torical Perspective." Journal of Marriage and the
          Famile, Vol. 31, No. 4 (Nov., 1969), 632-38. Ex-
          planation of the growth of the concept from the colonial
          period to the present noting particularly the importance
          of G. Stanley Hall's work in the late nineteenth century.

   870.   Kett, Joseph F.   Rites of Passage: Adolescence in

America, 1790 to the Present. New York: Basic Books,
1977. An informative survey of "both the social experience and society's perception of young people." Includes analysis of economic and demographic changes
which shaped awareness of the age group and transformed
youths from producers to consumers.

4.3. THE SCHOOLS

871.   Baker, Keith and Robert J. Rubel, eds. Violence and
Crime in the Schools. Lexington, Mass.: Heath
Lexington Books, 1980. Historical roots of and statistical evidence for increased school violence. Federal
legislative (especially the Juvenile Justice and Delinquency Prevention Act of 1974), executive and judicial
actions are described.

872.   Braden, Carole L. Compulsory School Attendance Laws and
the Juvenile Justice System. Huntsville, Texas: Institute of Contemporary Corrections an Behavioral
Sciences, 1978. The relationship studied in historical
context. Current alternatives to schooling and correctional intervention are outlined.

4.4. CHILDREN'S RIGHTS

873.   Binder, Arnold. "The Juvenile Justice System: When
Pretense and Reality Clash. American Behavioral
Scientist, Vol. 22, No. 6 (July, 1979), 621-52. The
continuing story of a failure. The reform schools and
the juvenile courts did not provide parental care and
the post-Gault era promises little more since the effects of decisions granting rights to children has been
to treat young criminals like adults and to limit the
range of behaviors subject to court jurisdiction or any
other public supervision.

874.   Mabbutt, Fred R. "Juveniles, Mental Hospital Commitment
and Civil Rights: The Case of Parkham V. J. R."
Journal of Family Law, Vol. 19 (1980-81), 27-64. A review of recent cases concluding that children do not
have the same rights as adults, principally the right to
an adversarial hearing before a neutral tribunal, and
that commitment often results in tragedy. A plea for
equal treatment.

875.   Prescott, Peter S. The Child Savers: Juvenile Justice
Observed. New York: Alfred A. Knopf, 1981. A bleak
portrait of the New York City Family Court by a Newsweek
journalist. Doubtful about the benefits of legal safeguards to delinquents, flowing out of the Supreme

Court's Gault decision (1967), but even more pessimistic about the value of the supervisory role and therapeutic programs of the court.

876.   Stenger, Robert L. "Expanding Constitutional Rights of Illegitimate Children, 1968-1980." Journal of Family Law, Vol. 19, No. 1 (1980-81), 407-44. A review of Supreme Court decisions, the cumulative effect being the liberalization of status. State and federal laws, es pecially the Social Security Act have all been affected by the equal protection interpretations of the Court's majority.

877.   U.S. Senate Judiciary Committee. Constitutional Rights of Children. Washington, D. C.: Government Printing Office, 1978. Subcommittee on the Constitution summary of Supreme Court decisions defining the protections afforded to children by the Constitution. The subject has been complicated by recent litigation offering constitutional protection to parents in guiding and directing their minor children but the government's greater authority over children is emphasized.

878.   Law and Contemporary Problems. Vol. 39, No. 3 (Summer, 1975), 1-293. The summer issue is devoted to Children and the Law. Edited by Robert H. Mnookin, a specialist in child custody adjudicaton, this volume considers how power and responsibility for children should be distributed between the child, the family and the state. Includes a discussion of legal trends and, in general favors the proposition that children should be able to decide more things for themselves.

4.5. DEINSTITUTIONALIZATION

879.   Klein, Malcolm W. "Deinstitutionalization and Diversion of Juvenile Offenders: A Litany of Impediments." In Norval Morris and Michael Tonry, eds. Crime and Justice: An Annual Review of Research, Vol. 1, Chicago: University of Chicago Press, 1979. A trenchant analysis of commmunity treatment programs. Among the reasons noted for the failure of programs to realize their goals is "net widening"--the sustained maintenance of clients in order to insure continued funding.

880.   Lipset, Seymour M. Rebellion in the University. Boston: Little, Brown, 1971. A perceptive study by a leading sociologist who is suspicious about the motivations of student activists of the 1960s. Contains several chapters of perceptive analysis on earlier student protests in Europe and America and some sobering data about popular reaction to college student protests.

881.   Newman, Graeme R., ed. Crime and Deviance: A
        Comparative Perspective. Beverly Hills: Sage Pub-
        lications, 1980. An excellent collection focusing on
        the problems of developing international categories of
        crime and delinquency statistics and of analyzing
        cross-cultural perceptions of deviance. The connection
        between delinquency and minority status is also studied.

882.   Parker, Graham. "The Juvenile Court Movement."
        University of Toronto Law School, Vol. 26, No. 2 (1976),
        140-72. The evolution of juvenile court law in
        Anglo-American context. In the U.S. the development is
        tied to the history of social welfare, in Great Britain
        to penal reform. Traces the origins of the American
        court in nineteenth century probation laws and stresses
        the significance of local forces in shaping the
        institution.

883.   Resch, John P. "Anglo-American Efforts in Penal Reform,
        1850-1900: The Work of Thomas Barwicke Lloyd Baker."
        Unpublished Ph.D. Diss., Ohio State University, 1969.
        Baker's Gloucestershire reform school had of an less
        evangelical flavor than many early English institutions
        but it was a stopping-off place for American philan-
        thropists such as Roeliff Brinkerhoff, a founder of the
        Ohio Reformatory for young men. Baker's knowledge of
        continental reform schools such as Mettray and the Rauhe
        Haus and his advocacy of probation and parole rather
        than extensive incarceration were the drawing cards.

884.   Sanders, Wiley B., ed. Juvenile Offenders for a
        Thousand Years: Selected Readings from Anglo-Saxon
        Times to 1900. Chapel Hill: University of North
        Carolina Press, 1970. An interesting if eclectic col-
        lection of primary documents, particularly valuable on
        English attitudes and policies.

5. THE AMERICAN EXPERIENCE IN COMPARATIVE PERSPECTIVE
        885.   Bennett, James. Oral History and Delinquency: The
                Rhetoric of Criminology. Chicago: University of
                Chicago Press, 1981. An interesting analysis of the ap-
                plication of the technique in the Anglo-American world
                since 1800. Bennett emphasizes the generally con-
                servative character of the genre. By making the poor
                and delinquent familiar to middle class readers, jour-
                nalists like Mayhew and sociologists like Clifford Shaw
                encouraged complacency about the need for extensive
                social reform.

886.   Foucault, Michel. _Discipline and Punish: The Birth of the Prison._ New York: Pantheon, 1977. Although the focus of this study is the penitentiary, Foucault characterizes juvenile reformatories, particularly Frederic A. DeMetz's _colonie agricole_ at Mettray (1839), as important progenitors of the surveillance state. DeMetz utilized military drill and individual attention to seek the emotional allegiance of his inmates to law abiding behavior and conservative political values. He also in fluenced American reformers.

887.   Gillis, John R. _Youth and History: Tradition and Change in European Age Relations, 1770–Present._ New York: Academic Press, 1974. An interesting analysis concentrating mostly on England and Germany and portraying capitalist industrialization as the prime cause of adolescent miseries in the late nineteenth and early twentieth centuries. The patriarchal household was shattered and, class-oriented and adult-manipulated traditions were invented to keep youths in a state of dependency. Recent youthful protest, and sexual freedom movements are viewed in a positive light.

Chapter Four
RELIEVING THE DOMESTIC CRISES OF ADULTHOOD

Lilith R. Kunkel
Hiram, Ohio

Issues Covered: Mothers' pensions, mental/public health,alcoholism,
settlementhouses.

1. SYNTHESES AND OVERVIEWS

1.1. THEMATIC

888. Ackerknecht, Erwin W. A Short History of Psychiatry,
2nd ed., rev. New York: Hafner, 1968. A balanced
survey of medical ideas about mental illness and the
development of psychiatry.

889. Blocker, Jack S., Jr., ed. Alcohol, Reform and
Society: The Liquor Issue in Social Context. Westport,
Conn.: Greenwood Press, 1979. This anthology attempts
to integrate the study of alcohol and temperance with
the methods of the social sciences. The articles which
employ quantitative methods offer surprisingly few new
insights while the methodologically more traditional
articles by Engelmann, Kyvig, and Rubin provide valuable
information on the story of liquor control since the repeal of Prohibition. Jessup's "The Liquor Issue in
American History: A Bibliography" (pp. 259-279) will be
useful to researchers although her organization (books,
theses, and authors) is not the most helpful.

890. Blumberg, Leonard. "The Ideology of a Therapeutic Social Movement: Alcoholics Anonymous." Journal of
Studies on Alcohol, Vol. 38, No. 11 (Nov., 1977),
2122-43. The author traces the medical, psychological,
and religious origins of Alcoholics Anonymous. He compares A. A. to the Washington movement of the antebellum period.

891. Brenner, M. Harvey. Mental Illness and the Economy.
Cambridge, Mass.: Harvard University Press, 1973. A
study of the relationship between economic change and
mental hospitilization based on admissions data for the
Utica State Hospital (1841-1915) and private and state
hospitals in New York (1910-1967). Brenner finds that
the state of the economy and hospitalization rates are
inversely related--that admissions increase during hard
times and decrease as the economy improves.

892.   Dain, Norman. <u>Concepts of Insanity in the United States</u>
        <u>1789-1865</u>. New Brunswick, N.J.: Rutgers University
        Press, 1964. An important study of popular and scien-
        tific ideas about insanity and its treatment. Dain
        shows how social and economic trends shaped the develop-
        ment of American medical thought and defends Dorothea
        Dix's role in the creation of asylums.

893.   Davies, Stanley P. <u>The Mentally Retarded in Society</u>.
        New York: Columbia University Press, 1959. An attempt
        to present mental retardation in its social rather than
        its clinical aspects, particularly the relationship be-
        tween public opinion and action and the evolution of
        scientific knowledge. The work is built upon the au-
        thor's earlier work, <u>Social Control of the Mentally</u>
        <u>Deficient</u> (1930), but was expanded and updated.

894.   Fox, Richard W. <u>So Far Disordered in Mind: Insanity in</u>
        <u>California, 1870-1930.</u> Berkeley: University of
        California Press, 1978. Building on ideas set forth by
        Michel Foucault, Fox provides a compelling argument for
        claiming that the early twentieth century constitutes a
        watershed in the history of American mental health
        care. Of particular interest to social welfare his-
        torians is Fox's composite description of the insane
        being drawn largely from among blue-collar bachelors,
        widows, and the elderly.

895.   Goffman, Erving. <u>Asylums; Essays on the Social</u>
        <u>Situation of Mental Patients and Other Inmates</u>. Garden
        City, N.Y.: Doubleday, 1961. A major sociological in-
        terpretation which develops Goffman's theory of "total
        institutions." Goffman examines the internal dynamics
        of life in a mental hospital and shows that the in-
        stitution rather than the patients' illnesses is the
        crucial determinant of life in the institution. The ad-
        ministrators' desire to maintain order and ensure a
        smooth daily routine is at odds with their therapeutic
        goals and the medical-service model of the mental
        hospital.

896.   Grigg, Susan. "The Dependent Poor of Newburyport,
        1800-1830." Unpublished Ph.D. Diss., University of
        Wisconsin, 1978. This painstaking case study of persons
        assisted by Newburyport's overseers of the poor is im-
        portant for its examination of the economic problems of
        abandoned, divorced, and widowed women. Grigg finds
        that married men and widowed women were most likely to
        be assisted through outdoor relief while single men were
        most likely to be sent to the almshouse.

897.   Grob, Gerald. "Mental Illness, Indigency, and Welfare:
        The Mental Hospital in Nineteenth Century America." In
        <u>Anonymous Americans</u>, ed. by Tamara K. Harevan, Englewood

Cliffs, N.J.: Prentice-Hall, 1971, 250-79. Since the origins of the mental hospital were rooted in the social, cultural, and economic fabric of society as well as in medical and psychiatric developments, Grob uses an analysis of the mental hospital to try to understand the peculiar nature of American institutions in the nineteenth century. The author also approaches the mental hospital from the perspective of the inmate as well as that of the custodian and attacks the shortcomings of writing history from a middle class perspective.

898. Grob, Gerald N. Mental Institutions in America, Social Policy to 1875. New York: Free Press, 1973. Especially valuable for its discussion of the widening gap between the ideal institution and the reality of state mental hospitals and for its examination of class, ethnicity, and race in mental hospitals. Grob argues that from the beginning public hospitals embodied contradictory therapeutic and custodial or welfare functions. Rejecting social control as an explanation, he attributes the hospital's increasingly custodial character to the growth and heterogeneity of its population. Grob views the mental hospital as both a social and a medical institution, and places its development in the larger context of social history.

899. Jacobson, Paul H. American Marriage and Divorce. New York: John Wiley and Son, 1959. This study is one of the few attempts to compile historical statistics on American marriage and divorce. The author has collected data from widely scattered local and national sources. Social welfare historians will find the demographic data helpful in estimating poverty rates among women.

900. Kett, Joseph F. "Review Essay: Temperance and Intemperance as Historical Problems." Journal of American History, Vol. 67, No. 4 (March, 1981), 878-85. A useful review essay which places recent works by Rorabaugh, Tyrell, Blocker, Engelmann, Kyvig, and Kurtz in the context of historical writing.

901. Landis, Carney and Jane F. Cushman. "The Relation of National Prohibition to the Incidence of Mental Disease." Quarterly Journal of Studies on Alcohol, Vol. 34, No. 2 (June, 1973), 353-66. This study of admissions to New York mental hospitals since 1889 for alcohol psychoses attributes variations to changing admissions of men aged forty to sixty rather than to the effects of Prohibition.

902. Lasch, Christopher. "Origins of the Asylum." In The World of Nations: Reflections on American History, Politics, and Culture, New York: Vintage, 1974, 3-17. Lasch rejects explanations which blame public in-

difference or hostility for the failure of the asylum
and admonishes historians who identify with "en-
lightened" administrators. Drawing on Goffman's theory
of total institutions, he argues that the creation of
prisons and mental hospitals resulted in new forms of
repression. A well argued if not fully documented interpretation and a useful critique of Grob.

903.   Levine, Harry G. "The Discovery of Addiction: Changing
Conceptions of Habitual Drunkenness in American History." Journal of Studies on Alcohol, Vol 39, No. 1
(Jan., 1978), 143-74. Levine traces the development of
American thought about habitual drunkenness an finds the
origins of modern concepts of alcoholism in the late
eighteenth century.

904.   Lubove, Roy. The Professional Altruist: The Emergence
of Social Work as a Career, 1880-1930. New York:
Atheneum, 1969. Chapters 3 and 4 of this important
volume examine the relationship between psychiatry and
the development of social casework. Lubove argues that
this development was crucial to the professionalization
of social work. In so doing, he illuminates the role of
social workers in maintaining the mental health of their
clients and of paramedical professionals in caring for
the mentally ill.

905.   May, Elaine Tyler. Great Expectations: Marriage and
Divorce in Post-Victorian America. Chicago: University
of Chicago Press, 1980. One of a few recent works on
the history of divorce. This felicitously written, if
thinly researched study, attempts to put divorce in the
context of changing attitudes toward women, the family,
sex, and women's place in the economy. It is based on
an examination of Los Angeles divorce records of 1880
and 1920 and New Jersey records of 1920. May attributes
the the late nineteenth-century divorces to the failure
of marriage to live up to Victorian expectations; the
divorces of 1920 are attributed to new tensions resulting from new definitions of the family as a unit of
consumption and a place for personal fulfillment, the
popular cult of youth and romance, and the persistence
of Victorian attitudes and expectations. She is concerned with the reasons for divorce rather than with its
economic dimensions or its consequences for social welfare policy and practice.

906.   Mechanic, David. "The Development of Mental Health
Policy in the United States." In Mental Health and
Social Policy. Englewood Cliffs, N.J.: Prentice-Hall,
1980, 73-90. A useful survey of mental health policy
since the time of Pinel. Most useful for the period
since 1945.

907.   O'Neill, Wiliam L. <u>Divorce in the Progressive Era</u>. New
        Haven: Yale University Press, 1967. Based on the au-
        thor's 1963 doctoral dissertation, this book chronicles
        the increasing public acceptance of divorce during the
        Progressive Era. O'Neill argues that the rising divorce
        rate was a response to the comparatively recent de-
        velopment of the Victorian patriarchal family with its
        emotional intimacy and intensity. He contends that
        divorce, instead of signalling the decline of the family
        (as contemporary critics often claimed), served as an
        escape mechanism which allowed the family system to
        function. <u>Divorce in the Progressive Era</u> provides in-
        sight into the ideas influencing sociologists and social
        workers but says relatively little about the actual
        practice of divorce.

908.   Quen, Jacques M. and Eric T. Carlson, eds. <u>American
        Psychoanalysis: Origins and Development</u>. New York:
        Brunner/Mazel, 1978. A collection of twelve papers--for
        on the beginning of psychoanalysis in the United States,
        five on the development of psychoanalytic organizations
        and institutions, and three on the future of psycho-
        analysis--written by historians and psychoanalysts. The
        papers vary in quality but are generally useful for the
        study of mental health and illness in the twentieth
        century.

909.   Reverby, Susan and David Rosner, eds. <u>Health Care in
        America: Essays in Social History</u>. Philadelphia:
        Temple University Press, 1979. A brilliant and in-
        novative set of essays that turn medical history toward
        the so-called new social history and provide great in-
        sight into the origins of the socialization of health
        care institutions and the reform of medical education as
        well as background for an evaluation of escalating
        health care costs.

910.   Rorabaugh, W. J. <u>The Alcoholic Republic: An American
        Tradition</u>. New York: Oxford University Press, 1979.
        Rorabaugh uses a variety of sources to study the
        drinking behavior of antebellum Americans. His sta-
        tistics and literary sources indicate that the American
        consumption of liquor increased substantially between
        1800 an 1830. A final chapter attributes the rise of
        temperance after 1830 to a new generation which embraced
        self-restraint as a way of advancement. His conclusions
        are at times speculative and his portrayal of the tem-
        perance movement overemphasizes its unity.

911.   Rosen, George. <u>Madness in Society: Chapters in the
        Historical Sociology of Mental Illness</u>. Chicago: Uni-
        versity of Chicago Press, 1968. Collection of essays by
        a leading medical historian. Rosen's essay on "Ir-
        rationality and Madness in Seventeenth and

Eighteenth-Century Europe" (pps. 151-71) provides information of the European background of the movement to
reform care on the mentally ill. "Some Origins of Social Psychiatry; Social Stress and mental Disease from
the Eighteenth Century to the Present" (pps. 172-94) emphasizes the development of medical thought. "Psycho-
pathology of Aging: Cross-Cultural and Historical Approaches" (pps. 229-46) deals with the development of
medical ideas about old age.

912.   Rothman, David J. Conscience and Convenience, The
Asylum and its Alternatives in Progressive America.
Boston: Little, Brown, 1980. Two chapters in this
sequel to The Discovery of the Asylum tell the story of
mental hospitals and their progressive alter-
natives--out-patient clinics, psychopathic hospitals,
and mental hygiene programs. Rothman's concern here and
throughout the book is to show how reforms intended to
replace custodial institutions with individualized, community-based programs fell short of their goals. Ultimately, noninstitutional programs expanded the authority
of the state and institutions continued to dominate the
system. Readers may fault Rothman for skipping the
Civil War and Reconstruction instead of beginning where
his earlier work left off and for not describing the
larger social context of reform more fully.

913.   Rothman, David J. The Discovery of the Asylum: Social
Order and Disorder in the New Republic. Boston: Little
Brown, 1971. A major study of antebellum movements to
create institutions for the dependent and deviant.
Rothman's discussion of the insane asylume is out-
standing for its explication of the ideas underlying
this design and operation. If Rothman had taken his
study beyond the first generation of asylum history, he
would have attached less credibility to the medical
superintendents' claims of success. He portrays the
asylum as a response to the instability of Jacksonial
society--as an attempt not only to reform individual inmates but to restore order to the large society as well.

914.   Shryock, Richard H. National Tuberculosis Association,
1904-1954: A Study of the Voluntary Health Movement in
the United States. New York: National Tuberculosis Association, 1957. As the subtitle indicates, this is
much more than a mere history of the nation's first
national voluntary health organization dedicated to the
control of a specific public health problem; it is an
excellent account of an entire social movement which had
a marked positive impact on the nation's health and
welfare.

915.   Sicherman, Barbara. "The Uses of a Diagnosis; Doctors,
Patients, and Neurasthenia." Journal of the History of

Medicine, Vol. 32, No. 1 (Jan., 1977), 32-54. Sicherman
shows how the definition of neurasthenia (nervous weakness) as a somatic disease expanded the role of the
neurologist and allowed upperand middle-class patients
to find support and treatment outside the confines of
the asylum and without the stigma attached to diagnoses
such as insanity, hypochondria, or hysteria. Her
article demonstrates the impact of social and cultural
factors on the definition of mental illness and its
treatment.

916.   Tyrell, Ian R.   Sobering Up: From Temperance to
Prohibition in Antebellum America.   Westport, Conn.:
Greenwood Press, 1979. This study traces the complex
history of temperance from the early national period.
Tyrell documents the changing nature of the movement's
support, its varying methods and goals, and its internal
discord. He characterizes the temperance movement more
as an innovative, optimistic movement than as an effort
to control the lower classes. His study is based
largely on the Massachusetts (Worcester, in particular)
and New York movements.

1.2. TEMPORAL
917.   Blackmon, Dora M. E.   "The Care of the Mentally Ill in
America, 1604-1812." Unpublished Ph.D. Diss., University of Washington, 1964. Descriptive study of the care
and treatment of the insane in the original thirteen
colonies. The work traces the emergence of a medical
definition of insanity and the shift from care by the
community under poor laws to treatment in hospitals for
the insane.

918.   Burnham. John C.   Psychoanalysis and American Medicine,
1894-1918; Psychological Issues.   New York: International Universities Press, 1967. An analysis of the
diffusion of psychoanalytic theory in the United
States. Burnham describes the professional and scientific setting which received psychoanalysis and demonstrates how the resultant controversies changed psychoanalysis itself.

919.   Burnham, John C.   "The Struggle Between Physicians and
Paramedical Personnel in American Psychiatry,
1917-1941." Journal of the History of Medicine, Vol.
29, No. 1 (Jan., 1974), 93-106. This article traces the
rise and fall of the "mental hygiene team"--a group of
psychiatrists and nonmedical personnel who cooperated in
caring for the mentally ill. Burnham shows how
psychiatric theory and the professional aspirations of
nonmedical personnel impelled its development and how
the economic setbacks of the Depression cut short its

life.

920.   Byse, Clark. "Alcoholic Beverage Control Before Re-
        peal." Law and Contemporary Problems, Vol. 7, No. 4
        (Autumn, 1940), 544-69. Byse traces liquor control from
        colonial times with a view to identifying problems to be
        avoided in future legislation.

921.   Dain, Norman. Disordered Minds: The First Century of
        Eastern State Hospital in Williamsburg, Virginia
        1766-1866. Williamsburg: Colonial Williamsburg Foun-
        dation, 1971. A history of a pioneer, yet relatively
        unimportant, public mental hospital written for a
        general audience. Dain's book will interest historians
        for its analysis of the relationship between the com-
        munity and the hospital and for its discussion of the
        impact of slavery on the institution.

922.   Dannenbaum, Jed. "Drink and Disorder: Temperance Re-
        form in Cincinnati, 1841-1874." Unpublished Ph.D.
        Diss., University of California-Davis, 1978. This dis-
        sertation is a study of the Cincinnati temperance move-
        ment from the Washington period through the Women's
        Crusade. Dannenbaum sets the movement in the context of
        population growth and mobility, economic insecurity,
        nativism and anti-Catholicism, political trends, and
        changing sex roles. He sees temperance as a rational
        response to genuine social problems and characterizes
        reformers as egalitarian and liberal.

923.   Engelmann, Larry. Intemperance: The War Against
        Liquor. New York: Free Press, 1979. This study of de-
        fiance of the eighteenth amendment and the gradual col-
        lapse of enforcement is largely based on Michigan.

924.   Fox, Daniel. "Social Policy and City Politics: Tuber-
        culosis Reporting in New York, 1889-1900." Bulletin of
        the History of Medicine, Vol. 49, No. 2 (Summer, 1975),
        169-95. This is the story of a fight between the pro-
        ponents and opponents of compulsary notification, or
        case reporting, of tuberculosis, an important matter for
        historians for a number of reasons, not the least of
        which is that it exemplifies the use of techniques by
        bureaucracies and professional organizations to achieve
        measures for the general welfare. It also suggests that
        municipal government in America might not have been the
        "conspicuous failure" James Bryce labeled it in the
        1880s.

925.   Grob, Gerald N. The State and the Mentally Ill; A
        History of Worcester State Hospital in Massachusetts,
        1830-1920. Chapel Hill: University of North Carolina
        Press, 1966. This study views the history of one in-
        stitution as a reflection of American psychiatric prac-

tice and thought. It analyzes the development of state mental health policy and its impact on the hospital. It explores the extent to which the state at various times failed to live up to its responsibilities for the mentally ill and examines the reasons for this failure.

926.   Jiminez, Mary A. "Changing Faces of Madness: Insanity on Massachusetts, 1700-1850." Unpublished Ph.D. Diss., Brandeis University, 1981. Jiminez argues that New England colonists saw insanity as a manifestation of the supernatural and did relatively little to control or cure the insane. After 1776, however, two contradictory definitions developed--one emphasizing humane moral treatment and the other viewing insanity as a threat to the social order and resulting in the confinement of the insane in poorhouses and jails.

927.   Lender, Mark. "Jellinke's Typology of Alcoholism: Some Historical Antecedents." Journal of Studies on Alcohol, Vol. 40, No. 5 (May, 1979), 361-375. Lender finds the antecedents of the modern concept of alcoholism as a disease in the writings and work of members of the American Association for the Cure of Inebriates (later called the American Association for the Study of Inebriety).

928.   Meeker, Edward. "The Improving Health of the United States, 1850-1915." Explorations in Economic History, Vol. 9, No. 4 (Summer, 1972), 353-73. Thanks, in large part, to the sanitation movement the period from 1850 to 1915, one of rapid urbanization, witnessed unprecedented improvements in the health of Americans. Life expectancy rose dramatically, the crude death rate declined, and the number of fatalities from infectious diseases fell greatly.

929.   Rubin, Jay L. "Shifting Perspectives on the Alcoholism Treatment Movement, 1940-1955." Journal of Studies on Alcohol, Vol. 40, No. 4 (April, 1979), 376-86. This study of the relationship between the Yale Center of Alcohol Studies and the temperance movement revises the conventional wisdom that the relationship between the alcoholism treatment and temperance movements was adversarial.

930.   Shea, Christine Mary. "The Ideology of Mental Health and the Emergence of the Therapeutic Liberal State: The American Mental Hygiene Movement, 1900-1930." Unpublished Ph.D. Diss., University of Illinois, 1980. This dissertation examines the origins, development, and social ideology of the American Mental Hygiene Movement. It explores the collaboration between the industrial elite and liberal psychiatrists in that movement.

931.   Sicherman, Barbara. "The Quest for Mental Health in America, 1880-1917." Unpublished Ph.D. Diss., Columbia University, 1967. Sicherman's concern is with a movement which sought to expand and improve facilities for the mentally ill and protect the public's mental health. She examines the role of associations and professional societies in criticizing mental institutions and developing alternatives. Throughout the dissertation she is concerned with changing definitions of mental health and mental illness.

932.   West, Margarida P. "The National Welfare Rights Movement: Social Protest of Welfare Women (1966-1976)." Unpublished Ph.D. Diss., Rutgers, 1978. A history based on participant observation. The author's principal concern is with explaining the decline of the movement. West traces the impact of internal divisions within the national leadership and between national leaders and the general membership and examines the effects of conflict between the NWRO and welfare administrators, legislators, and adjudicators. Finally, she shows how changes in the general social and political climate undermined the movement.

1.3.   (AUTO)BIOGRAPHIES

933.   Abbott, Edith. "Grace Abbott and Hull House, 1908-1921." Social Service Review, Vol. 24, No. 3 (Sept., 1950), 374-94, and No. 4 (Dec., 1950), 493-518. Abbott has written a personal memoir of her sister's work with immigrants.

934.   Antler, Joyce. "After College What? New Graduates and the Family Claim." American Quarterly, Vol. 32, No. 4 (Fall, 1980), 409-34. Antler maintains that the role of the family in mediating between educated women and society's role prescriptions was not always negative. The decision to take up settlement work, while not without tensions and conflict, was supported by some families. Antler revises Christopher Lasch's explanation for Jane Addams' career in settlement work.

935.   Aptheker, Herbert. "DuBois on Florence Kelley." Social Work, Vol. 11, No. 4 (Oct., 1966) 98-100. This piece reproduces W.E.B. DuBois' reflections on Kelley's N.A.A.C.P. activities delivered at her 1932 memorial service.

936.   Bordin, Ruth. Women and Temperance: The Quest for Power and Liberty, 1873-1900. Philadelphia: Temple University Press, 1981. A study of Frances Willard and the rise, maturity, and decline of the Women's Christian

Temperance   Union.   Bordin   shows   how   women's
participation in the WCTU brought them into the feminist
cause.

937.   Dain, Norman.   <u>Clifford W. Beers: Advocate for the
       Insane</u>.   Pittsburgh: University of Pittsburgh Press,
       1980.   A study of the former mental patient who wrote <u>A</u>
       <u>Mind That Found Itself</u> and his part in the early twen-
       tieth-century mental hygiene movement.   Based on ex-
       tensive research in the Beers papers and other col-
       lections.   A significant contribution despite its nar-
       rative character.

938.   Davis, Allen F.   <u>American Heroine: The Life and Legend</u>
       <u>of Jane Addams</u>.   New York: Oxford University Press,
       1973.   This not entirely sympathetic biography chron-
       icles Addams's work at Hull House and her contributions
       to the settlementhouse movement.   Davis aims to separate
       the real Jane Addams from the myth and to understand her
       changing reputation.

939.   Fitzpatrick, Ellen F.   "Academics and Activists: Women
       Social   Scientists   an   the   Impulse   for   Reform,
       1892-1920."   Unpublished Ph.D. Diss., Brandeis Univer-
       sity, 1981.   This dissertation is a study of women
       activists who came to reform from the academic setting
       of the University of Chicago.   Fitzpatrick studies Edith
       Abbott, Sophonisba Breckinridge, Katharine Bement Davis,
       and Frances Kellor.

940.   Grob, Gerald N.   <u>Edward Jarvis and the Medical World of</u>
       <u>the Nineteenth Century</u>.   Knoxville: University of
       Tennessee Press, 1978.   Intellectual biography of a psy-
       chiatrist, social reformer, and statistician best known
       for   his   <u>Report   on   Insanity   and   Idiocy   in</u>
       <u>Massachusetts</u>(1855).   This work brought issues of class
       and ethnicity into discussions of mental health.   Grob
       shows how Jarvis's conception of the professional re-
       sponsibilities of physicians led him into social reform.

941.   Himelhoch,   Myra   Samuels   and   Arthur   H.   Shaffer.
       "Elizabeth Packard: Nineteenth-Century Crusader for the
       Rights   of   Mental   Patients."   <u>Journal   of   American</u>
       <u>Studies</u>, Vol. 13, No. 3 (December, 1979), 343-76.   This
       article   explores   an   aspect   of   the   late   nine-
       teenth-century asylum-reform movement--an attempt to
       secure   state   laws   protecting   the   rights   of   mental
       patients.   It focuses on Elizabeth Packard, a woman who
       charged that her husband had unjustly committed her to
       the Illinois State Hospital and who became an ardent
       spokesperson and publicist for the cause.

942.   Lasch, Christopher.   "Jane Addams: The College Woman
       and   the   Family   Claim."   In   <u>The   New   Radicalism   in</u>

<u>America, 1889-1963</u>. New York: Vintage, 1965, 3-37. Lasch argues that Addams' frustration with the life her stepmother expected her to live rather that the sudden awakening of social conscience impelled her toward social work. The settlementhouse served as an outlet for her strong moral sense and her intellectual talents.

943. Pumphrey, Ralph. "Michael Davis and the Transformation of the Boston Dispensary, 1910-1920." <u>Bulletin of the History of Medicine</u>, Vol. 49, No. 4 (Winter, 1975), 451-65. In 1910 the Boston Dispensary was an undistinguished locally known institution; by 1920 it was recognized nationally as one of the pioneering medical institutions of the twentieth century--a transformation attributable (by the author) largely to the efforts of Michael Davis, who had launched a half-century of leadership in the health care field. This article is an account of that remarkable achievement.

944. Sherrick, Rebecca Louise. "Private Visions, Public Lives: The Hull House Women in the Progressive Era." Unpublished Ph.D. Diss., Northwestern University, 1981. This dissertation examines the efforts of seven Hull House women to reconcile their ambitions for public service careers with prevailing definitions of women's role. Sherrick examines Hull House as a realization of these efforts.

945. Sicherman, Barbara. "The Paradox of Prudence: Mental Health in the Gilded Age." <u>Journal of American History</u>, Vol. 62, No. 4 (March, 1976), 890-912. In this essay, Sicherman analyzes the careers and views of George M. Beard and Mary Putnam Jacobi to illustrate how late-nineteenth-century physicians sought to prevent mental illness and promote mental health.

946. Tomes, Nancy Jane. "The Persuasive Institution: Thomas Story Kirkbride and the Art of Asylum Keeping, 1840-1883." Unpublished Ph.D. Diss., University of Pennsylvania, 1978. A study of the Pennsylvania Hospital and its first medical superintendent. Tomes examines the relationship between medical theory and institutional practice and the interaction between physicians and patients in the development of asylum treatment. She contends that Kirkbride's practice was successful especially when it is compared to state institutions.

947. Trattner, Walter I. "Homer Folks and the Public Health Movement." <u>Social Service Review</u>, Vol. 40, No. 4 (Dec., 1966), 410-28. An account of the many contributions to the public health movement by Homer Folks, child welfare worker, welfare administrator, and public health crusader (1867-1963), about whom Dr. Hermann Biggs, the

famed authority on the subject, said: "I don't think there is any man in this country--certainly no layman--who has contributed more to the promotion of health than Homer Folks."

948.   Vasilie, Russell G. James Jackson Putnam, From Neurology to Psychoanalysis: A Study of the Reception and Promulgation of Freudian Psychoanalytic Theory in America, 1895-1918. Oceanside, N.Y.: Dabor Science Publications, 1978. An intellectual biography. Vasilie's concern is to show how Putnam's development as a neurologist made him receptive to psychoanalytic theory and to understand his role in its diffusion.

949.   Winters, Eunice. "Adolf Meyer and Clifford Beers, 1907-1910." Bulletin of the History of Medicine, Vol. 43, No. 5 (Sept.-Oct., 1969), 414-43. Based largely on unpublished letters between Adolf Meyer, America's most influential psychiatrist, and Clifford Beers, the author of A Mind That Found Itself and the founder of the American mental health movement, this essay explores a three year relationship between the two men (1907-1909) that led to the creation of the National Committee for Mental Hygiene.

1.4.   DOCUMENTARIES

950.   Abbott, Grace. From Relief to Social Security: The Development of the New Public Welfare Services and their Administration. Chicago: University of Chicago Press, 1941. A chapter on "Mothers' Aid in the Modern Public Assistance Program" reviews the response to early mothers' aid laws, the provisions for dependent children under the Social Security Act, and the development of new programs to 1940.

954.   Action for Mental Health: Final Report of the Joint Commission on Mental Illness and Health. New York: Basic Books, 1961. Report and recommendations of a commission created by Congress in 1955. This volume provides a comprehensive review of mental health services--mental hospitals, outpatient clinics, and community services. It discusses public attitudes as an obstacle to quality care, and recommends more basic research and the expansion of mental health services as the solution to the inadequacy of mental health care.

952.   Baird, Edward G. "The Alcohol Problem and the Law: III. The Beginnings of Alcoholic Beverage Control Laws in America." Quarterly Journal of Studies on Alcohol, Vol. 6, No. 3 (Dec., 1945), 335-83. This article examines American legislation relating to alcoholic beverages from the perspective of legal theory. It provides

a useful chronology of laws.

953.   Brown, Josephine. <u>Public Relief, 1929-1939</u>. New York: Henry Holt, 1940. This is an important early attempt to describe and analyze New Deal relief and Social Security programs and place them in historical context. It remains a basic source of information on mothers' pensions.

953.   Cassedy, James H. "The Roots of American Sanitary Reform, 1843-47: Seven Letters from John R. Griscom to Lemuel Shattuck." <u>Journal of the History of Medicine and Allied Sciences</u>, Vol. 30, No. 2 (April, 1975), 136-47. Publication, for the first time, of some recently discovered letters which provide a lot of detail about the activities of these two important public health reformers during the 1840s, especially their successful efforts to help turn personal concerns and local reforms into a coherent national movement.

955.   Deutsch, Albert. <u>The Mentally Ill in America: A History of Their Care and Treatment from Colonial Times.</u> New York: Doubleday, 1946. A dated but still useful survey of institutions for the mentally ill. This volume lacks the sophisticated analysis of the ideology of institutional care which characterize more recent studies but is especially valuable for its discussions of the incarceration of the insane in poorhouses and the dilemma of caring for the chronically ill.

956.   Douglas, Paul H. <u>Social Security in the United States.</u> New York: McGraw Hill, 1936. This work by one of the architects of the Social Security system includes a brief discussion of mothers' pensions. Douglas explains the Social Security Act's provisions for dependent children and for maternal and child health care.

957.   Winslow, C. E. A. <u>The Conquest of Epidemic Disease.</u> Princeton, N.J.: Princeton University Press, 1943. This work is more than a compendium of data on and references to the subject. Rather, it is an extremely interesting and highly instructive story, from antiquity to the 1940s, rich in interpretation on the value of each stage of development regarding the spread of disease and its control.

1.5.   CLASSIC CASE STUDIES.

958.   Badenhausen, Carl W. "Self-Regulation in the Brewing Industry." <u>Law and Contemporary Problems</u>, Vol. 7, NO. 4 (Autumn, 1940), 689-95. The author, a brewing industry executive, traces the steps the industry took after repeal to assure the future of legal beer. He also reviews liquor control legislation.

959.   Insanity and Idiocy in Massachusetts: Report of the
        Commission on Lunacy, 1855 by Edward Jarvis (1855).   In-
        troduction by Gerald Grob.   Cambridge, Mass.:   Harvard
        University Press, 1971.   In his introduction to the
        famous Jarvis Report, Grob provides a lucid in-
        terpretation of Jarvis's significance in shaping ante-
        bellum public policy toward mental illness, which helped
        to corroborate conceptually the connection between
        lunacy and pauperism and to legitimize institutionally
        the function of state asylums as custodial warehouses.
        The volume might be read as a counterpoint to Rothman's
        Discovery of the Asylum.

960.   Jellinek, E. M.   "Recent Trends in Alcoholism and
        Alcohol Consumption."   Quarterly Journal of Studies,
        Vol. 8, No. 1 (June, 1947), 1-42.   Jellinkek a pioneer
        in post-World War II alcohol studies, views alcohol con-
        sumption and alcoholism in historical perspective.   His
        article contains statistics on alcohol consumption and
        on deaths from and mental hospitalization for chronic
        alcoholism.

961.   Kennedy, Albert J., et al.   Social Settlements in New
        York City: Their Activities, Policies, and
        Administration.   New York: Columbia University Press,
        1935.   A survey of the activities of 80 New York set-
        tlements during the 1930s.   The authors describe Girls
        and Boys' clubs, athletic activities for boys, the arts,
        instruction in English and citizenship, preschool edu-
        cation, and health work.

962.   Russell, William L.   The New York Hospital: A History
        of the Psychiatric Service, 1776-1936.   New York:
        Columbia University Press, 1945.   A largely chrono-
        logical and very detailed history.   Russell emphasizes
        medical thought and practice in this classic study.

963.   Winslow, C. E. A.   The Evolution and Significance of the
        Modern Public Health Campaign.   New Haven: Yale Univer-
        sity Press, 1935.   A detailed history of public health
        activities from the authority on the subject, one that
        goes from the dark ages of public health to the great
        sanitary awakening, to Pasteur and the scientific basis
        of preventive work, to the golden age of bacteriology,
        and finally to the "new public health."

1.6 TEXTBOOKS, READERS, BOOKS OF DOCUMENTS, BIBLIOGRAPHIES

2. PERIOD PIECES

2.1.   COLONIAL.

964.   Albertson, D. "Puritan Liquor in the Planting of New
England." New England Quarterly, Vol. 3, No. 4 (Dec.,
1950), 477-90. Albertson describes Puritan drinking
customs, alcohol manufacture, and legislation regulating
its sale and consumption. He argues that drinking
customs were transplanted from England. For Puritans,
the moral issue was sobriety rather than the use of
alcohol itself.

965.   Cott, Nancy. "Eighteenth-Century Family and Social Life
Revealed in Massachusetts Divorce Records." Journal of
Social History, Vol. 10, No. 1 (Fall, 1976), 20-43. In
this second article based on her study of Massachusetts
divorce proceedings Cott argues that the eighteenth century was transitional in the history of the American
family. The community's involvement in family life, and
attitudes toward sexuality, romantic love, and the economic roles of wives and minor children were characteristic of traditional societies. The reluctance of
parents to intervene in the lives of adult children, the
increasing number of petitions initiated by women, and
the expression of ideals of romantic love in a small
number of cases suggest modern concepts of family life
and relations between the sexes. However, readers may
remain skeptical about the degree to which divorce proceedings reflect typical marriages. (See also no. 991.)

966.   Lender, Mark. "Drunkenness as an Offense in Early New
England: A Study of 'Puritan' Attitudes." Quarterly
Journal of Studies on Alcohol, Vol. 34, No. 2 (June,
1973), 353-66. The author argues that Puritan attitudes
toward drunkenness were English in origin and were
shared by other colonists. He discusses the various
methods used to control the misuse of alcohol and the
frequent tolerance shown drunkards.

2.2.   REVOLUTIONARY AND EARLY NATIONAL

2.3.   ANTEBELLUM AND CIVIL WAR

967.   Rosenkrantz, Barbara and Maris A. Vinovskis.
"Sustaining 'the Flickering Flame of Life': Ac-
countability and Culpability for Death in Ante-Bellum
Massachusetts Asylums." In Susan Reverby and David
Rosner, eds., Health Care in America, Essays in Social
History. Philadelphia: Temple University Press, 1979,
155-82. Interesting examination of a little studied as-

pect of the history of the asylum based on published annual reports, journal articles, and records of the
McLean Asylum and the Worcester State Hospital.
Rosenkrantz and Vinovskis show how the medical superintendents' explanations for high mortality served to
deflect blame from the institution. Their quantitative
analysis suggests that the superintendents' understanding of the likelihood of death was basically correct. Their analysis is marred by the fact that their
sources did not provide data on the patients' physical
health and by their failure to examine more fully the
superintendents' claims as to the healthfulness of the
hospitals.

968.   Boase, Paul H. "In Case of Extreme Necessity: The
Methodists Take Action Against Tobacco Chewing and
Spitting in Church Along with the Excessive Use of
Alcohol." Bulletin of the Historical and Philosophical
Society of Ohio, Vol. 16 (1958), 191-205. This article
examines the efforts of antebellum Ohio's itinerant
Methodist preachers to deal with the problems of alcohol
abuse and tobacco use.

2.4. POSTBELLUM
969.   Fitzpatrick, Susan A. "Only the Poor in a Gilded Age:
Public Health Care for the Poor in St. Louis,
1890-1900." Unpublished Ph.D. Diss., St. Louis
University, 1979. An examination of the health services
provided by St. Louis to its poor from 1890-1900, which
concludes that the city maintained an adequate level of
services and care within the limitations of the system
as it was then established.

2.5. PROGRESSIVE
970.   Hamovitch, Maurice B. "History of the Movement for
Compulsory Health Insurance in the United States."
Social Service Review, Vol. 27, No. 3 (Sept., 1953),
281-99. The movement for compulsory health insurance is
not new; it dates back to 1912, when the American Association for Labor Legislation formed a Committee on
Social Insurance to consider the question. This article
traces the developments in that area from 1912 to 1946.

971.   Timberlake, James H. Prohibition and the Progressive
Movement, 1900-1910. Cambridge, Mass.: Harvard University, 1963. This study challenges interpretations of
Prohibition as a movement of evangelical, rural America
by demonstrating its central place in progressive reform.

2.6. THE 1920s AND THE GREAT CRASH

2.7. NEW DEAL AND WORLD WAR II
      972.   Lubove, Roy. "The New Deal and National Health."
              Current History, Vol. 45, No. 264 (Aug., 1964), 77-86,
              117. An excellent analysis of attempts to improve the
              nation's health in the decade from 1929-39 (from the
              final report of the Committee on the Costs of Medical
              Care to the introduction in Congress of Senator Robert
              F. Wagner's bill to establish a national health
              program)--and the medical profession's opposition to
              such efforts. Regarding the latter, Lubove concludes
              that, in the final analysis, the A.M.A.'s opposition to
              all efforts to create some sort of national health in-
              surance program was "based less on considerations of
              economic advantage or, for that matter, the concrete
              medical needs of the nation, than on intangible fears
              concerning the freedom and status of the physician."

2.8. POSTWAR

2.9. GREAT SOCIETY
      973.   Grant, Murray. "Poverty and Public Health." Public
              Welfare, Vol. 23, No. 2 (April, 1965), 111-115. A use-
              ful reminder of the relationship between poverty and
              poor health and the difficulties involved in treating
              the latter, both because it is often accepted as a way
              of life among the poor and because of certain medical
              practices, particularly the eligibility criteria of
              clinics and hospitals.

      974.   Hertz, Susan Handley. The Welfare Mothers' Movement: A
              Decade of Change for Poor Women? Washington, D.C.:
              University Press of America, 1981. This is an anthro-
              pological study based primarily on field research con-
              ducted in Minneapolis between 1969 and 1972. Hertz
              traces the history of a short-lived movement which de-
              veloped after 1965 to develop new options for welfare
              mothers, to change public attitudes toward welfare
              recipients, and to change local and national welfare
              systems.

      975.   Mechanic, David. Mental Health and Social Policy.
              Englewood Cliffs, N.J.: Prentice-Hall, 1969. Although
              the work is supposed to be a comprehensive survey of
              current issues regarding the relationship between mental
              health programs and the community at large, it is not

that; rather, it is a series of essays in which the author sets forth his own views on various aspects of current mental health concerns, with little attention paid
to newer approaches in the field.

976.   James, George. "Poverty and Public Health--New Outlooks, Poverty as an Obstacle to Health Progress in Our
Cities." American Journal of Public Health, Vol. 55,
No. 11 (Nov., 1965), 157-71. Poor people have more illness and disability, higher infant mortality rates,
more chronic disease, and more mental and nervous disorders that other people. Yet, because of the cost,
they secure less and poorer care, particularly dental
care, and have to surmount more difficulties to get it.

2.10. THE CONTEMPORARY PERIOD

3. SALIENT VARIATIONS

3.1. LOCAL, STATE, REGIONAL

977.   Galishoff, Stuart. Safeguarding the Public Health:
Newark, 1895-1918. Westport, Conn.: Greenwood Press,
1975. The subject of this solidly researched monograph
is Newark's successful attempt to create a healthy environment for its residents; between 1890 and 1915, it
made remarkable strides in "safeguarding the public's
health."

978.   Gish, Lowell. Reform at Osawatomie State Hospital:
Treatment of the Mentally Ill, 1866-1970. Lawrence:
University of Kansas Press, 1972. In this case study,
Gish traces the history of this early mental institution. By the end of the nineteenth century, the
facility had become so overcrowded that new programs had
to be established in the western part of the state.

979.   Gordon, Richard Lawrence. "The Development of
Louisiana's Public Mental Institutions, 1735-1940." Unpublished Ph.D. Diss., Louisiana State University,
1978. Gordon attributes Louisiana's consistent failure
to provide adequate care and treatment partly to the
South's distinctive development and experience and
partly to factors characteristic of asylums throughout
the U.S.

980.   Levstik, Frank R. "A History of the Education and
Treatment of the Mentally Retarded in Ohio, 1787-1920."
Unpublished Ph.D. Diss., Ohio State University, 1981.

This case study not only traces the development of special state institutions for the mentally ill but also describes changes in the experiences of the retarded in infirmaries, mental hospitals, children's homes, and public schools. Attitudes toward the mentally retarded shifted from extreme neglect in the early decades of the nineteenth century to a belief that self-sufficiency was possible to a late nineteenth-century stance that public institutions should serve custodial functions.

981.   Putnam, Edison Klein. "The Prohibition Movement in Idaho, 1863-1934." Unpublished Ph.D. Diss., Idaho University, 1979. Putnam examines the special characteristics of the Prohibition movement in Idaho—regional rivalries, rapid population growth, the presence of a significant Mormon population, and the state's extensive Indian population.

982.   Robison, Dale W. "Wisconsin and the Mentally Ill: A History of the 'Wisconsin Plan' of State and County Care, 1860-1915." Unpublished Ph.D. Diss., Marquette University, 1976. Robison traces the origins and development of Wisconsin's unique plan for removing the incurable or chronic insane from state mental hospitals and returning them to state-subsidized county asylums. Robison naively accepts the administrators' explanation of the benefits of this arrangement and minimizes the role of economic expediency in the adoption of the plan. He does not explore the relationship between county poorhouses and county asylums adequately.

983.   Smith, Thomas G. "The Treatment of the Mentally Ill in Alaska, 1884-1912." Pacific Northwest Quarterly, Vol. 65, No. 1 (Jan., 1974), 17-28. When Alaska was still a territory, the mentally ill were particularly vulnerable; most were sent to California or to the District of Columbia for care. In 1900, Congress began to provide for the mentally ill and contracted with states for their care. The territory's first mental hospital was constructed in 1913.

984.   Winkler, A. M. "Drinking on the American Frontier." Quarterly Journal of Studies on Alcohol, Vol. 29, No. 2 (June, 1968), 413-45. This study finds more drinking on the frontier than in the east and variations in drinking behavior according to occupation and patterns of daily activity. It includes an analysis of Indian drinking. According to Winkler, the temperance movement developed and was most successful in the West as frontier settlements reached maturity.

985.   Wisner, Elizabeth. Social Welfare in the South: From Colonial Times to World War I. Baton Rouge: Louisiana State University Press, 1970. This survey includes dis-

cussions of the care and treatment of the insane in the
colonial South. It traces the work of Dorothea Dix in
the South on behalf of the insane and reviews the history of southern insane asylums. The author's concern
in this book is to show how distinctive social and economic conditions shaped social welfare in the South.

3.2 RACIAL/ETHNIC

986. Diner, Steven J. "Chicago Social Workers and Blacks in
the Progressive Era." Social Service Review, Vol. 44,
No.4 (Dec., 1970), 393-410. This article includes an
analysis of Jane Addams's attitudes toward blacks and of
settlement projects to study and/or assist blacks. Social workers recognized that although blacks and immigrants had many problems in common, racial discrimination made the situation of blacks different.
Diner may overestimate the degree to which settlement
workers were concerned with blacks.

987. Kogut, Alvin. "The Settlements and Ethnicity:
1890-1914." Social Work, Vol. 17, No. 3 (May, 1972),
22-31. This study of Chicago, Boston, and New York settlements finds them to have been closer to immigrant
life than other progressive institutions. Their
policies and programs were tinged with racism and
nativism at times, however.

988. Savitt, Todd L. "Politics in Medicine: The Georgia
Freedmen's Bureau and the Organization of Health Care,
1865-1866." Civil War History, Vol. 28, No. 1 (March,
1982), 45-64. The function of the Freedmen's Bureau regarding medical care was to establish and staff hospitals, dispense drugs, and treat smallpox, cholera, and
maleria. Thanks both to internal and external prob-
lems--bureaucratic and financial ones within th agency
and "political" ones without--the Bureau, or its medical
department, did not function very well in Georgia. The
losers in all this were the sick freedmen, who, at
times, received poor medical care and inadequate assistance in developing medical independence. Indeed,
when the Bureau was gone, they had no system of health
care on which to rely--and they remained as dependent on
the largesse of whites as they had when they were slaves.

989. Torchia, Marion. "The Tuberculosis Movement and the
Race Question, 1890-1950." Bulletin of the History of
Medicine, Vol. 49, No. 2 (Summer, 1975), 152-68. The
author traces the development of social policy within
the anti-tuberculosis movement during its most active
years (1890-1950) and concludes that it was racist, as
is demonstrated by the persistent disparity in the
morbidity rate of the two races.

990.   White, George Cary. "Social Settlements and Immigrant Neighbors, 1886-1914." Social Service Review, Vol. 33, No. 1 (March, 1959), 55-66. White maintains that the settlementhouse movement was more appreciative of immigrant cultures and traditions than most of early twentieth-century America and developed a unique conception of their place in American society.

3.3. GENDER-SPECIFIC

991.   Cott, Nancy. "Divorce and the Changing Status of Women in Eighteenth-Century Massachusetts." William and Mary Quarterly Vol. 33, No. 14 (Oct., 1976), 586-614. This article examines 229 Massachusetts divorce petitions filed between 1692 and 1786 for information on the customs and ideals of eighteenth-century Puritan marriage as well as for evidence of marital behavior. Cott provides useful information on the grounds for divorce, the economic status of litigants, and the existence of a sexual double standard in divorce proceedings.

3.4. CLASS

992.   Monkkonen, Eric H. "A Disorderly People? UrbanOrder in the Nineteenth and Twentieth Centuries." Journal of American History, Vol. 68, No. 3 (Dec., 1981), 539-59. This investigation of drunk and disorderly arrest rates from 1860 to 1977 suggests a rise of urban order rather than increasing disorder. Monkkonen does not explore the ramificatons of drunkenness for social welfare.

993.   Faler, Paul. "Cultural Aspects of the Industrial Revolution: Lynn, Massachusetts Shoemakers and Industrial Morality, 1826-1860." Labor History, Vol. 15, NO. 3 (Summer, 1974), 367-94. Faler places temperance in the context of the drive for industrial morality. He discusses the impact of the movement on the administration of poor relief and on attitudes toward dependency, drink, and self-discipline.

4.   AGE-SPECIFIC AND LIFE-CYCLE STUDIES

4.1.   MENTAL HEALTH

994.   Brown, Philip M. "From Back Wards to Boarding Homes: U.S. Mental Health Policy Since World War II." Unpublished Ph.D. Diss., Brandeis University, 1979. This

study traces the growth of the National Institute of
Mental Health, its Community Mental Health Centers Program, deinstitutionalization, and the growth of boarding
and nursing home care. Brown argues that the failure of
mental health programs is due to the fact that fiscal
crisis is the driving force behind policy.

995.   Goldner, Nancy L. "The Medicalization of Insanity: A
Social History of the McLean Asylum for the Insane,
1811-1856." Unpublished Ph.D. Diss., Boston University,
1980. The theme of this sociology dissertation is the
"medicalization of social control"--the definition of
insanity as a medical problem and the development of
treatment. The author overestimates the role of medical
theory in forming the institution (often theory followed
practice) and slights the contribution of lay reformers.

996.   Pitts, John Albert. "The Association of Medical Superintendents of American Institutions for the Insane,
1842-1892." Unpublished Ph.D. Diss., University of
Pennsylvania, 1979. This study examines the role of the
AMSAII in the institutional care of the mentally ill and
in the making of public policy. It is also a case study
in the development of medical specialization.

997.   Stotland, Ezra and Arthur L. Kobler. Life and Death of
a Mental Hospital. Seattle: University of Washington
Press, 1965. History of a short-lived modern hospital
(1948-1960) by two psychologists, one a former staff
member. The authors emphasize social processes within
the hospital, the ideology of treatment, and the hospital's relationship with the community. This study reveals little about hospitals other than "the Crest
Foundation Hospital."

4.2. PUBLIC HEALTH/SANITARY REFORM
998.   Alewitz, Sam. "Sanitation and Public Health:
Philadelphia, 1870-1900." Unpublished Ph.D. Diss., Case
Western Reserve University, 1981. A history of sanitation and public health in Philadelphia between 1870
and 1900, an age when the city had impure water, filthy
and poorly paved streets, and unsanitary drainage and
sewage systems--conditions that went unchallenged by
municipal authorities, the medical profession, and city
residents, all of whom remained docile and contented;
they were more interested in low taxes and municipal
savings than in more sanitary living conditions.

999.   Kramer, Howard D. "The Beginnings of the Public Health
Movement in the United States." Bulletin of the History
of Medicine, Vol. 21, No. 3 (May-June, 1947), 352-76.
The first of three excellent articles on the subject by

the author which stresses 1) the need for public health reform if the city was to survive, and 2) the impetus given to such reform by the Civil War (which gave to the lay public a greater appreciation of the purposes of sanitation and the benefits to be derived from it).

1000.   Kramer, Howard D. "Early Municipal and State Boards of Health." Bulletin of the History of Medicine, Vol. 24, No. 6 (Nov.-Dec., 1950), 503-29. Organized efforts for public health reform in the United States began around the middle of the nineteenth century. Two major victories for American sanitarians, who had to battle public apathy, political opposition, and the medical profession's indifference, are here described--New York city's Metropolitan Health Bill, passed in February, 1866, and creation of the first real State Board of Health, in Massachusetts in 1869.

1001.   Kramer, Howard D. "The Germ Theory and the Early Public Health Program in the United States." Bulletin of the History of Medicine, Vol. 22, No. 3 (May-June, 1948), 233-47. An excellent analysis of the discovery of the germ theory of disease (in the 1870s-1880s) and its impact on the public health movement in the United States.

1002.   Temin, Peter. Taking Your Medicine: Drug Regulation in the United States. Cambridge, Mass.: Harvard University Press, 1980. This survey of the regulatory powers of the Federal Drug Administration in twentieth-century America has obvious pertinence to a study of modern social welfare history. More significantly, Temin offers an explicit model to bridge historical interpretations and public policy analysis. As such, it is the best model for "applied history" currently available.

1003.   Wasserman, Manfred. "The Quest for a National Health Department in the Progressive Era." Bulletin of the History of Medicine, Vol. 49, No. 3 (Fall, 1975), 353-80. An account of the unsuccessful attempt by physicians, philanthropists, social workers, and others to get Congress to create some sort of national board of health in the late nineteenth and early twentieth century--and why. Although that attempt failed, the efforts of reformers to improve the public health succeeded, as Wasserman points out.

4.3.   TEMPERANCE REFORM/ALCOHOL REHABILITATION

1004.   Blocker, Jack S., Jr. Retreat from Reform: The Prohibition Movement in the United States, 1890-1913. Westport, Conn.: Greenwood Press, 1976. This book studies the shift in the leadership of the temperance movement from the Prohibition Party to the Anti-Saloon

League. It provides a useful analysis of the geographic origins, occupations, and education of Prohibition Party leaders and of voting on the Prohibition issue. Blocker explains middle-class support of Prohibition as an attempt to establish a position between capitalists and militant labor. His decision to end his study at 1913, the date when the Anti-Saloon League decided to seek national prohibition limits its usefulness.

1005. Blumberg, Leonard U. "The Significance of Alcohol Prohibitionists for the Washingtonian Temperance Societies With Special Reference to Patterson and Newark, New Jersey." Journal of Studies on Alcohol, Vol. 41, No. 1 (Jan., 1980), 37-77. Blumberg views the Washingtonian movement as a therapeutic social movement emphasizing individual self-help. He attributes its decline to its loss of popularity and influence relative to the more outer-directed temperance movement with its increasing emphasis on legislative prohibition.

1006. Clark, Norman H. Deliver Us from Evil: An Interpretation of American Prohibition. New York: Norton, 1976. In this revision of the status-anxiety interpretation of temperance reform, Clark points to the enormity of American alcohol abuse as an explanation for the rise of temperance reform.

1007. Drescher, Nuala McGann. "Organized Labor and the Eighteenth Amendment." Labor History, Vol.8, No. 3 (Fall, 1967), 280-99. Drescher analyzes organized labor's opposition to the eighteenth amendment and finds that labor leaders made a distinction between temperance (which some unions had traditionally endorsed) and prohibition. She gives particular attention to unions in the brewing and distilling industries.

1008. Gusfield, Joseph R. Symbolic Crusade: Status Politics and the American Temperance Movement. Urbana: University of Illinois Press, 1963. Gusfield, a sociologist, characterizes the early phases of the antebellum temperance movement as the creation of conservative clergymen and laymen concerned with their declining status and authority and with the disorder of the lower classes. Control of the movement soon passed from their hands, however, and the movement became a vehicle for the common man's middle class aspirations.

1009. Kurtz, Ernest. Not God; A History of Alcoholics Anonymous. Center City, Minn.: Hazelden Educational Services, 1979. This study of an important modern temperance organization is flawed by the author's insistence in finding the religious meaning of A.A. and by his failure to explore the relationship between A.A. and psychiatry.

1010.   Kyvig, David E. <u>Repealing National Prohibition</u>. Chicago: University of Chicago Press, 1979. Kyvig uses important new sources for his study of organized efforts to secure repeal. These include the archives of wet pressure groups.

1011.   Weiner, Carol Licht. "The Politics of Alcoholism: Building an Arena Around a Social Problem." Unpublished Ph.D. Diss., University of California-San Francisco, 1978. This sociology dissertation is concerned with how alcohol use comes to be perceived as a social problem, Weiner's approach is partly historical. She examines the roots of the alcoholism treatment movement in the mental health field, the early isolation of alcohologists, and the failure of other professionals to respond to the movement. She explores the impact of New Deal welfare policies and the temperance movement on the definition of addiction.

4.4.   LEGAL ASPECTS OF DIVORCE

1012.   Blake, Nelson M. <u>The Road to Reno; A History of Divorce in the United States</u>. New York: Macmillan, 1962. This dated but useful work surveys the history of American divorce laws from colonial times. Blake is particularly interested in explaining New York state's conservative position on divorce and accounting for the rise of "divorce havens." He does little to place divorce in the context of changing definitions of marriage and the family or to explain the rising demand for divorce in the twentieth century.

1013.   Freed, Doris Jonas and Henry H. Foster. "Divorce American Style." <u>Annals of the American Academy of Political and Social Science</u>, Vol. 383 (May, 1969), 72-88. In this article the authors (who are lawyers) trace the legal history of divorce in nineteenth and twentieth-century America.

4.5.   MOTHERS' PENSIONS

1014.   Bell, Winifred. <u>Aid to Dependent Children</u>. New York: Columbia University Press, 1965. A thorough analysis of state and federal programs for dependent children. According to Bell, such programs have failed to realize their objectives of protecting dependent children, assuring the income levels of the poor, and enforcing community norms of parental behavior.

1015.   Bruno, Frank J. "Mothers' Pensions." In <u>Trends in Social Work, 1874-1956: A History Based on the</u>

Proceedings of the National Conference of Social Work. New York: Columbia University Press, 1957, 177-82. Bruno provides a useful chronology of the movement for mothers' pensions. He is at a loss to explain why the movement became a popular cause.

1016. Handler, Joel. F. "Theory and Development." In Reforming the Poor: Welfare Policy, Federalism, and Morality. New York: Basic Books, 1972, ch. 2. This chapter is part of a strong critique of the contemporary welfare system—especially AFDC programs. Handler argues that mothers' pensions, begun as a program for the deserving poor, failed to achieve their humanitarian goals because local authorities enjoyed vast discretionary powers in the administration of pension programs. The book includes a bibliography but lacks footnotes.

1017. Lubove, Roy. "Mothers Pensions and the Renaissance of Public Welfare." In The Search for Social Security, 1900-1935. Cambridge, Massachusetts: Harvard, 1968, 91-112. Lubove presents a history of the Progressive movement to provide state aid to mothers of dependent children. He shows how the adoption of mothers pensions redefined the division of responsibility for welfare between public and private agencies but failed to modernize the public welfare system. He gives little attention to the actual workings of pension programs.

1018. Piven, Frances Fox and Richard A. Cloward. Regulating the Poor: The Functions of Public Welfare. New York: Pantheon, 1971. This analysis of public welfare from the Depression through the 1960s includes an examination of Aid to Families with Dependent Children. The authors discuss the relationship between AFDC programs and the demands of the labor market. They explore the consequences of work maintenance rules and examine racial discrimination in the administration of AFDC. They place special emphasis on the role of welfare programs in maintaining social and political order.

1019. Rothman, David. "The State as Parent: Social Policy in the Progressive Era." In Willard Gaylin et al/. Doing Good: The Limits of Benevolence. New York: Pantheon, 1978, 66-95. Rothman uses the examples of mothers', or widows', pensions to demonstrate the paternalism of Progressive social welfare policies and programs. He argues that these policies and programs with their broad discretionary powers, greatly increased the power of the state to intervene in the lives of individuals. They often served the interests of the state more than the needs of clients.

1020. Steiner, Gilbert Y. The State of Welfare. Washington

D.C.: Brookings Institution, 1971. Chapters 2 and 3 of this study trace the fate of AFDC under the Kennedy, Johnson, and Nixon administrations. Chapter 8 deals with the Poor People's Campaign and the National Welfare Rights Organization.

1021. Tiffin, Susan. "Charity's Children: The Welfare of Dependent and Neglected Children in the United States, 1890-1920." Unpublished Ph.D. Diss., University of New South Wales, 1978. This study traces changes in legislation, institutions, and social work techniques and includes an analysis of mothers' pensions. Tiffin maintains that ambivalence undermined some programs for dependent children. In the case of mothers' pensions, for example, administrators frequently demanded conformity to native-born, white, middle-class norms as a condition of assistance.

4.6. SETTLEMENT HOUSES

1022. Chambers, Clarke and Andrea Hinding. "Charity Workers, the Settlements, and the Poor." Social Casework, Vol. 49, No. 2 (Feb., 1968), 96-101. The authors maintain that charity organization workers operated from an antiquated view of poverty as stemming from individual moral failings. Settlement workers, in contrast, used environmental explanations and spoke for the poor.

1023. Chambers, Clarke. "The Settlements in Service to Their Neighbors." In Seedtime of Reform; American Social Service and Social Action, 1918-1933. Minneapolis: University of Minnesota, 1963, 109-28. This chapter provides a useful description of settlements in the post-World War I era. Chambers chronicles the problems created by the Red Scare, the settlements' changed relationship with the labor movement, and the shifting demographic charactistics of settlement neighborhoods. He discusses the professionalization of social work and its impact on the settlement idea.

1024. Davis, Allen F. Spearheads For Reform: The Social Settlements and the Progressive Movement. New York: Oxford University Press, 1967. In this important study, Davis is more concerned with understanding the settlement movement in the context of Progressive reform than with providing an internal history of the movement. He demonstrates the role of settlement workers in initiating and popularizing reforms and explains how events involved settlement workers in local politics, and ultimately, in state and national politics as well. He refutes Hofstader's contention that settlement workers were motivated by status anxiety and shows that their motivation was complex. A concluding chapter

traces the dissolution of the settlement movement. One
limitation of Davis' study is his focus on settlements
in New York, Chicago, and Boston; these settlements led
the movement but may not have been entirely typical. A
second limitation is Davis' failure to explore the connection between the settlement movement and the woman
movement.

1025.   Kalberg, Stephen. "The Commitment to Career Reform:
The Settlement Movement Leaders." Social Service
Review, Vol. 49, No. 4 (Dec., 1975), 608-28. The author
uses biographies, autobiographies, and other published
writing to study 14 reformers (8 women, 6 men) who made
settlements their life work. He finds that family background was essential in shaping the initial commitment
and that subsequent experience reinforced that commitment. The author aims to understand the nature of
commitment to social movements (he makes comparisons
with the civil rights and student movements of the
1960s) rather than to illuminate our understanding of
the settlement movement. He gives insufficient attention to settlement workers who did not make the
life-time commitment.

1026.   Mohl, Raymond and Neil Betten. "Paternalism and
Pluralism: Immigrants and Social Welfare in Gary,
Indiana, 1906-1940." American Studies, Vol. 15, No. 1
(Spring, 1974), 5-30. In contrast to settlements in
other cities, the authors say, Gary's four settlements
were denominational in character and promoted assimilation rather than cultural pluralism. Their services were tinged with paternalism. Gary's International Institute was an exception to the general
pattern established by the settlements.

1027.   Rousmanier, John P. "Cultural Hybrid in the Slums: The
College Woman and the Settlement House, 1889-1894."
American Quarterly, Vol. 22, No. 1 (Spring, 1970),
45-66. This article studies the origins of the College
Settlement Association--the first successful settlement
organization. Rousmanier concludes that the women who
participated chose to do so because it was a socially
sanctioned service activity and because the settlement
house functioned both emotionally and ideologically as a
"home" for them. The settlement also stood in the
lower-class neighborhood as a symbol of middle-class
uniqueness and as an articulation of the college woman's
superiority.

5. THE AMERICAN EXPERIENCE IN COMPARATIVE PERSPECTIVE
    1028.   Armour, Philip Kenton. "The Cycles of Social Reform:
Community Mental Health Legislation in the United

States, England, and Sweden." Unpublished Ph.D. Diss., University of California-Berkeley, 1979. A comparative, historical study of the post-World War II period. The author attempts to place mental health policy in the larger context of health and welfare policy.

1029.   Cashman, Sean. Prohibition: The Lie of the Land. New York: Free Press, 1981. A British historian aims to explain why the United States adopted national prohibition and its consequences for American society.

Chapter Five

DEALING WITH THE ECONOMIC WOES OF ADULTHOOD

Michel Dahlin
University of Wisconsin-Milwaukee

Issues Covered: Migrant labor, tramps, manpower policy, organized labor, rural poverty, unemployment and Social Security.

1. SYNTHESES AND OVERVIEWS

1.1. THEMATIC

1030. Daniel, Cletus E. Bitter Harvest: A History of California Farmworkers, 1870-1941. Ithaca, New York: Cornell University Press, 1981. Daniel's thesis is the exploitation of farm workers. He discusses the powerlessness of the farmworkers, the failure of efforts at organizing the repressive policies of state and local officials, and the failure of New Deal measures to meet the needs of workers in the environment of large-scale agri-business in California.

1031. Garraty, John A. "Radicalism in the Great Depression." In L.H. Blair, ed., Essays on Radicalism in Contemporary America. Austin: University of Texas Press, 1972, 81-114. This is a brief overview of the Depression in the western world which sketches the response of radicals to the collapse of the capitalist world and tries to explain why radicals failed to bring about major changes and how the system was patched together.

1032. Garraty, John A. Unemployment in History: Economic Thought and Public Policy. New York: Harper and Row, 1978. This is an extremely valuable short history of economic thought on the problem of unemployment. Garraty provides a lucid explanation of the theories of classical and Keynesian economists with a brief discussion of the post-Keynesian era. This intellectual history covers a broad range of times and places in a graceful, even-handed manner. It is basic reading for any topic within the field of unemployment history.

1033. Gordon, David M., Richard Edwards, and Michael Reich. Segmented Work, Divided Workers: The Historical Transformation of Labor in the United States. Cambridge, England: Cambridge University Press, 1982. In this book, the economists who originally proposed the dual labor market theory and then refined it with the notion of a segmented labor market, attempt to sketch the his-

torical stages in the economy leading to the segmented
labor force. This study outlines but does not prove historical changes in the economy. While it says little directly about unemployment, it is nonetheless worth
reading as it provides a new theoretical exploration of
the labor market which students of unemployment will find
intriguing.

1034. Keyssar, Alex. Out of Work: A Social History of
Unemployment in Massachusetts. New York: Cambridge University Press, forthcoming 1983. Keyssar traces the history of unemployment from the early 19th century to the
New Deal. He investigates the extent of unemployment,
the identity of those out of work, how the unemployed
coped, and the impact on unemployment of a variety of social patterns and institutions. The book is particularly
valuable because, unlike most studies of unemployment, it
pays considerable attention to the unemployed themselves. It is also the first social history of unemployment.

1035. Nelson, Daniel. Unemployment Insurance: The American
Experience, 1915-1935. Madison: University of Wisconsin
Press, 1969. Nelson carefully delineates the efforts of
reformers and reform-minded businessmen to develop some
type of unemployment insurance. He pays close attention
to the New Emphasis reformers of the 1920s, details the
difference between preventive and welfare unemployment
insurance schemes and between voluntary and compulsory
plans. His thorough study of the Wisconsin school and
its critics is more sympathetic to the Wisconsin school
than is Lubove's book, The Struggle for Social Security.
High caliber research, organization, and writing make
this a valuable study of the unemployment insurance
movement.

1036. Piven, Frances Fox and Richard A. Cloward. Regulating
the Poor: The Functions of Public Welfare. New York:
Pantheon Books, 1971. The authors argue that welfare
services are provided not to eliminate poverty but to
control the poor, thereby keeping available a pool of in-
expensive and docile reserve labor for periods of economic expansion. This is an important argument which
other scholars consciously affirm or deny in their
writings.

1037. Sternsher, Bernard. "Victims of the Great Depression;
Self Blame/Non-Self Blame, Radicalism, and Pre-1929
Experiences." Social Science History, Vol. 1, No. 2
(Winter, 1977), 137-77. Sternsher reexamines the notion
that the unemployed during the Great Depression blamed
themselves for their plight. His footnotes serve as a
comprehensive bibliography of studies of the
social-psychological impact of unemployment on the un-

employed published during the 1930s.

1.2. TEMPORAL
    1038. Becker, Joseph M., ed. In Aid of the Unemployed.
           Baltimore: Johns Hopkins University Press, 1965. This
           volume of essays on unemployment covers such topics as
           the history of unemployment relief, who are the un-
           employed, the long-term unemployed, unemployment in-
           surance and its adequacy, private plans and public works,
           and public relief. It provides an overview of ideas
           about unemployment in the mid-1960s from the professional
           social worker's viewpoint.

    1039. Boleno, August C. "The Duration of Unemployment: Some
           Tentative Historical Comparisons." Quarterly Review of
           Economics and Business, Vol. 6, No. 2 (Summer, 1966),
           31-47. Using available studies of unemployment, Boleno
           argues that from 1890 to World War II, long-term un-
           employment rates were very high, and that these rates de-
           clined until 1953 when they began to climb again.

    1040. Coleman, Peter J. Debtors and Creditors in America:
           Insolvency, Imprisonment for Debt, and Bankruptcy,
           1607-1900. Madison: State Historical Society of
           Wisconsin, 1974. This legal history of the decline of
           the debtor's prison traces state and federal experiments
           with methods of discharging debt and with bankruptcy laws
           in the original thirteen states plus Vermont. The author
           details but does not explain the reasons for variation
           from state to state. This may prove a useful technical
           reference volume.

    1041. Elder, Glen H., Jr. Children of the Great Depression:
           Social Change in Life Experience. Chicago: University
           of Chicago Press, 1974. Elder's fine study of the
           long-term impact of deprivation on children during the
           Depression is based on the Oakland Growth Study of ado-
           lescents begun in 1931 and on the follow-up interviews
           with its subjects thirty years later. Attention is given
           to the psychological and social impact of unemployment on
           breadwinners and their families during the 30s and to the
           long-range effects of growing up in a household plagued
           by unemployment.

    1042. Lebergott, Stanley. "Annual Estimates of Unemployment in
           the United States, 1900-1954." In National Bureau of
           Economic Research, The Measurement and Behavior of
           Unemployment: A Conference of the Universities.
           Princeton, N.J.; Princeton University Press, 1957. This
           is a careful report on estimates of unemployment which
           considers the impact of the changing composition of the
           work force, decline of farm employment, social attitudes,

paid vacations, and other factors. This may prove useful to those interested in accurate measurements of unemployment in the past and how to get them.

1043. Lubove, Roy. The Struggle for Social Security, 1900-1935. Cambridge, Mass.: Harvard University Press, 1968. Unemployment is only one of several social welfare issues covered in Lubove's important study of the ideas, agencies and personalities involved in the lengthy fight for (and against) Social Security. His thesis is that the ideology of voluntarism retarded the development of social welfare in America. He carefully outlines the practical and ideological differences among reformers as to the best method of achieving security. (Lubove favors the Ohio plan over the Wisconsin plan.)

1044. Morris, Richard B. Government and Labor in Early America. New York: Octagon Books, 1965. This classic presents a clear picture of the nature of labor as it was understood in the mercantile empire. This is useful background reading for understanding the nature of unemployment in the colonial period and the way it was understood and treated.

1045. Rezneck, Samuel. Business Depressions and Financial Panics: Essays in American Business and Economic History. New York: Greenwood Publishing Corp., 1968. This is a collection of Rezneck's articles, all but one previously published from 1932 to 1956, analyzing the six depressions of the nineteenth century. Rezneck discusses the causes of these depressions, the way they affected people and how they changed the thinking of Americans about the workings of the economy, the nature of unemployment, appropriate relief measures and the relations of the classes. This book focuses more on intellectual trends in understanding poverty and unemployment than on the unemployed themselves. It is must reading for students of 19th century unemployment.

1046. Rodgers, Daniel T. The Work Ethic in Industrial America, 1850-1920. Chicago: University of Chicago Press, 1978. Rodgers argues that northern entrepreneurs, through hard work and a belief in progress, developed America into a powerful industrial nation. In the process, however, the old values and economic climate which generated the new industrial nation were destroyed. This is primarily a study of middle class cultural views. What Americans thought about work, however, affected how they responded to those out of work.

1047. Stein, Bruno. On Relief: The Economics of Poverty and Public Welfare. New York: Basic Books, 1971. Stein traces the history of welfare, current practices, and then explains various kinds of possible income transfer mechanisims. He sees poverty as inequality in the distribution of income and recommends reducing that inequality.

1048.   Tishler, Hace Sorel. Self-Reliance and Social Security, 1870-1917. Port Washington, New York: Kennikat Press, 1971. Tishler argues that American welfare was transformed-organized and professionalized-between 1870 and 1917 because Americans abandoned the ideas of total self-reliance. The depression of 1893 played an important role in accelerating this transformation of values. Tishler does not agree with Roy Lubove on the primary importance of the ideology of voluntarism in retarding public social welfare programs in America. He argues that private voluntary associations and charities actively opposed the drift toward compulsory social insurance.

1049.   Wallace, Phyllis A. "A Decade of Policy Developments in Equal Opportunities in Employment and Housing." In Robert H. Haveman, ed., A Decade of Federal Anti-Poverty Programs, Achievements, Failures, and Lessons. New York: Academic Press, 1977. Wallace describes the equal opportunity policies in employment and housing pursued by the federal government from the mid 60s to the mid-70s, including a review of relevant Supreme Court decisions. She finds too little evidence to assess the impact of such programs and policies on minority employment rates or income levels. She also discusses the impact of manpower training programs on the poor.

1050.   Yellowitz, Irwin. "The Origins of Unemployment Reform in the United States." Labor History, Vol. 9, No. 3 (Fall, 1968), 338-60. This article sketches the ideas of Progressive reformers on unemployment and credits them with developing the idea of unemployment insurance and keeping it before the public in the 1920s and 30s. Yellowitz and Daniel Nelson agree on the main points of the development of the idea of unemployment insurance in this period.

1.3   (AUTO)BIOGRAPHIES
1051.   Charles, Searle F. Minister of Relief: Harry Hopkins and the Depression. Syracuse, New York: Syracuse University Press, 1963. Charles describes the creation and operation of federal relief under the dynamic leadership of Hopkins. The author praises Hopkins for his humane vision and for introducing more modern social welfare procedures into his relief programs.

1052.   Fox, Daniel M. The Discovery of Abundance: Simon N. Patten and the Transformation of Social Theory. Ithaca, New York: Cornell University Press, 1967. The theme is the emergence of the concept of abundance-the idea that man could generate enough material wealth to supply the needs of everyone. The book is about the man who devoted his life to the study of the implications of abundance, Simon Patten. This provides a historical background for ideas in the modern battle against poverty.

1053. Hamilton, David E. "Herbert Hoover and the Great Drought of 1930." Journal of American History, Vol. 68, No. 4 (March, 1982), 850-75. Hamilton details Hoover's insistence on voluntary relief, through the Red Cross, to drought victims. This is a case study of Hoover's views and of the limitations of voluntary relief.

1.4.   DOCUMENTARIES

1054. Angell, Robert Cooley. The Family Encounters the Depression. New York: Charles Scribner's Sons, 1936. This is a study of 50 native-born, nuclear families (i.e. two parents and children) suffering an income loss of 25 percent or more for a long time. Angell reveals a bias toward middle class families which he considers "integrated" and "highly adaptable."

1055. Atkinson, Raymond, Louise C. Odencrantz, and Ben Deming. Public Employment Service in the United States. Chicago: Public Administration Service, 1938. This contains a brief history of the development of public employment service, via the Wagner-Peyser Act of 1933, and shows how national public employment office networks have been established. This volume deals with the technical aspects of employment office operation. It presents the state of the art in 1938.

1056. Bakke, E. Wight. Citizens Without Work: A Study of the Effects of unemployment upon the Workers' Social Relations and Practices. New Haven: Yale University Press, 1940. This book deals with the impact of unemployment on the community, on the family relationships of the unemployed, and their psychological adjustment to unemployment.

1057. Bakke, E. Wight. The Unemployed Worker: A Study of the Task of Making a Living without a Job. New Haven: Yale University Press, 1940. This book, part of a series for the Institute of Human Relations on the impact of unemployment on workers and their families, focuses on the world of work and what workers do to survive when they lose their jobs. It is based on a sample of New Haven's unemployed.

1058. Brown, Josephine C. Public Relief, 1929-1939. New York: Holt, 1940. The theme of this study by a charity worker who became an assistant to Harry Hopkins, is the shift from private to public responsibility for the unfortunate.

1059. Canan, Ruth S. and Katherine H. Ranck. The Family and the Depression: A Study of One Hundred Chicago Families. Chicago: University of Chicago Press, 1938. This study, combining psychology and sociology, shows how families dealt with the crisis of the Depression. Its bibliography focuses on the literature of the family and economic distress.

1060. Closson, Carlos C. "Notes on the History of 'Unemployment' and Relief Measures in the United States." Journal of Political Economy, Vol. 3 (September 1895), 461-69. Closson argues that unemployment is not a recent phenomenon of the 1890s. He cites earlier periods of distress in the nineteenth century and efforts of private relief agencies to help the unemployed. This is a pioneering investigation of the history of unemployment. It reveals some of the attitudes of the 1890s toward unemployment.

1061. Colcord, Joanna C., et al. Emergency Work Relief: As Carried Out in Twenty-six American Communities, 1930-1931, with Suggestions for Setting up a Program. New York: Russell Sage Foundation, 1932. This is a 1931 survey of 26 community work relief programs. Information is presented on each program's nature, origin, method of administration, expenses, and number of clients served.

1062. Hook, James W. Industry's Obligation to the Unemployed. New Haven: Tuttle, Morehouse and Taylor Co., 1938. In two addresses given in 1931, Hook argues for the need to provide charity to the unemployable, work relief to casual workers in times of unemployment crises, and employer reserves for stable employees. This is an example of progressive business opinion in the 1920s.

1063. Hopkins, Harry L. Spending to Save: The Complete Story of Relief. New York: W. W. Norton and Co., 1936. This is the personal account by FERA head Harry Hopkins of the Roosevelt Administration's relief efforts through 1935. Hopkins believed in the inevitability of unemployment and favored government responsibility for the unemployed through unemployment insurance and continued public works. This is an account full of facts, as well as personal opinions and judgments.

1064. Howard, Donald S. The WPA and Federal Relief Policy. New York: Russell Sage Foundation, 1943. Russell Sage Foundation administrator Howard has collected a large body of information on the origins and workings of the WPA. He brings into his study the general economic situation, earlier relief measures, currents of public

opinion shaping the program, conflicting goals of those
promoting or opposing WPA legislation, conflicting views
of WPA administrators and problems in the program. This
work will prove valuable to anyone interested in the
shaping of WPA, its workings, and the thirties debate
over issues related to relief and unemployment.

1065. Kester, Howard. Revolt Among the Sharecroppers. New
York: Arno Press, 1969.   Kester describes the
mal-administration of the AAA and the terrible conditions
of life for sharecroppers. He recounts the story of the
interracial Southern Tenant Farmers' Union in Arkansas in
1934. This is a very journalistic and sentimental contemporary account. For a more scholarly approach, also
from the 1930s, see The Collapse of Cotton Tenancy by
Charles S. Johnson, Edwin R. Embree and Will W.
Alexander, or Preface to Peasantry by Arthur Raper.

1066. King, Willford Ishbell. Employment HOurs and Earnings in
Prosperity and Depression: United States, 1920-1922.
New York: National Bureau of Economic Research, 1923.
This study, undertaken for the President's Conference on
Unemployment in 1921, measures employment, wages and
hours, and unemployment during the depression of 1921.

1067. Lubin, Isador. The Absorption of the Unemployed by
American Industry. Washington: Brookings Institution,
1942. Lubin's investigation of 750 cases of unemployment
in three large industrial cities in 1928 found that many
of those who lost their jobs went three or more months
before they were able to locate another job. Studies
like this served as ammunition for those demanding a
national unemployment insurance program. Another study
in this vein is Ewan Clague, Walter J. Cooper, and E.
Wight Bakke's After the Shutdown, New Haven: Institute
of Human Relations, Yale University, 1934.

1068. Lynd, Robert S. and Helen Merrell Lynd. Middletown in
Transition: A Study in Cultural Conflicts. New York:
Harcourt, Brace and Co., 1937. this sociological classic, the follow-up to Middletown, presents the town in
the grips of the Depression. It shows the impact of unemployment (and the lack of impact in some cases) on both
the employed and unemployed.

1069. Macmahan, Arthur W., John D. Millett, and Gladys Ogden,
The Administration of Federal Work Relief.   Chicago:
Public Administration Service, 1941. In 1935, the Committee on Public Administration of the Social Science Research Committee commissioned the authors to "capture and
record" the administrative evolution of federal work relief. This detailed administrative history discusses the
origins and management of these programs and their
relations with each other.

1070. Millis, Harry A. and Royal E. Montgomery. <u>The Economics</u>
       <u>of Labor</u>. 3 Vols. New York: McGraw-Hill, 1938. This
       three volume study includes an examination of the un-
       employment problem and the various solutions which had
       been suggested or tried up through the 1930s. For those
       interested in the contemporary reformist stance on labor
       and its problems, this volume is very valuable.

1071. National Industrial Conference Board. <u>Lay-Off and Its</u>
       <u>Prevention</u>. New York: National Industrial Conference
       Board, Inc., 1930. In response to the "minor business
       depression" of 1927-8, the National Industrial Conference
       Board collected information on industrial lay-off pro-
       cedures and produced this book of advice on how to avoid
       lay-offs and the best way to lay-off workers when
       necessary.

1072. <u>Rural Poor in the Great Depression: Three Studies</u>. New
       York: Arno Press, 1971. This volume reprints three
       studies of the deprived from the Depression: (1) <u>Rural</u>
       <u>Youth: Their Situation and Prospects</u>; (2) <u>Migrant</u>
       <u>Families</u>, and (3) <u>Rural Families on Relief</u>. All are WPA
       Research Monographs from 1938.

1073. Smith, Darrell Hevenor. <u>The United States Employment</u>
       <u>Service, Its History, Activities, and Organization</u>.
       Baltimore: Johns Hopkins Press, 1923. Smith provides a
       history of the service, begun in 1907, its development,
       its functions, and details its specific activities. His
       work is wholly descriptive, not analytical.

1074. Stewart, Bryce M. <u>Planning and Administration of</u>
       <u>Unemployment Compensation in the United States: A</u>
       <u>Sampling of Beginnings</u>. New York: Industrial Relations
       Counselors, 1938. This book explains the history and ad-
       ministration of the employment service begun under the
       Wagner-Peyser Act and unemployment compensation under
       Social Security. Field studies in several states provide
       the author with data on actual developments in the ad-
       ministration of these two programs, as of 1938.

1075. Sutherland, Edwin H. and Harvey J. Locke. <u>Twenty</u>
       <u>Thousand Homeless Men: A Study of Unemployed Men in the</u>
       <u>Chicago Shelters</u>. Philadelphia: J.B. Lippincott Co.,
       1936. This is an investigation of homeless men in public
       shelters focusing on their prior experiences and current
       attitudes. Since the investigators lived in the shelter,
       they collected their information via informal interviews
       with the inmates.

1076. Terkel, Studs. <u>Hard Times: An Oral History of the Great</u>
       <u>Depression</u>. New York: Pantheon Books, 1970. This col-
       lection of interviews contains several stories of the re-

membered personal hardships of unemployment during the
1930s.

1077. Two Unemployment Insurance Debates. New York: Barnes
and Noble, 1931. This book contains speeches in a debate
contest between the University of Wisconsin and University of Minnesota on the issue, "Resolved: that the
several states should enact legislation providing for
Compulsory Unemployment Insurance." This is a handy summary of contemporary arguments.

1078. U.S.   Department   of   Agriculture.   The   Yearbook   of
Agriculture: Farmers in a Changing World. Washington,
D.C.:   Government Printing Office, 1940. This is a good
source of information on the impact of the Depression on
agriculture.

1.5. CLASSIC CASE STUDIES
1079. Adams, Grace. Workers on Relief. New Haven: Yale University Press, 1939. Adams is critical of the WPA as
neither a relief nor a work program, but an unfortunate
mixture.   She interviewed many people about their experiences in the WPA and recorded their satisfactions and
gripes. Her book provides illustrations of the WPA's impact on individuals.

1080. Calkins, Clinch. Some Folks Won't Work. New York:
Harcourt, Brace and Co., 1930. This is an account of the
hardships of unemployment based on settlement house files
in the 1920s. Calkins calls for unemployment insurance
to relieve suffering and regularize production.

1081. Douglas, Paul H.   Real Wages in the United States,
1890-1926. Boston: Houghton Mifflin Co., 1930. Douglas
attempts to assess the changing standard of living of
American workers by using series of wage rates and
cost-of-living indices he developed. His study also includes several chapters on unemployment and attempts to
achieve accurate estimates of unemployment for the years
1890 to 1920. He finds unemployment constant over the
long run. This is a classic; its figures are still cited
today.

1082. Feder, Leah Hannah.   Unemployment Relief in Periods of
Depression: A Study of Measures Adopted in Certain
American Cities, 1857 through 1922. New York: Russell
Sage Foundation, 1936. This old, but still frequently
cited and valuable study of unemployment relief efforts
provides useful information on public and private welfare
efforts in every major depression for over six decades.
Feder focuses on the methods used by welfare agencies to
meet sudden demand and deplores their failure to learn

from previous depressions. She discusses trends in relief giving, public works, statistics of unemployment,
and reactions of communities. Her study is based on an
examination of relief agency reports, newspaper files,
oral interviews and published materials with special
focus on the efforts of several cities. This is a history from the viewpoint of professional social workers'
responses to depressions. The bibliography is quite
useful.

1083. Haber, William and Wilbur J. Cohen, eds. Social
Security: Programs, Problems, and Policies. Homewood,
Ill.: Richard D. Irwin, 1960. This text of selected
readings on Social Security presents some of the controversies and issues in Social Security policy. Chapter
4 deals with unemployment insurance and the employment
service and contains a brief useful bibliography.

1084. Kellor, Frances A. Out of Work: A Study of
Unemployment. New York: G.P. Putnam's Sons, 1914. In
this work, originally published in 1904, Kellor argues
that there is not enough work for all who wish it, and
she blames the disorganized state of the labor market.
She discusses current philanthropic experiments, such as
work relief, dovetailing, and missions, and favors unemployment insurance, employment bureaus, and public
works, as well as better data collection and cooperation
among welfare agencies.

1085. Klein, Philip. The Burden of Unemployment: A Study of
Unemployment Relief Measures in Fifteen American Cities,
1921-22. New York: Russell Sage Foundation, 1923.
Klein describes how workers coped with unemployment and
what provisions cities were making in terms of employment
bureaus and relief, and the difficulties of coordinating
voluntary agencies' efforts. His survey was designed to
serve as a blueprint for times of future unemployment by
pointing out the adequacies and inadequacies of relief
efforts in that year.

1086. Komarovsky, Mirra. The Unemployed Man and His Family -
The Effects of Unemployment upon the Status of the Man in
Fifty-Nine Families. New York: Dryden Press, 1940.
This is an important sociological study of the adverse
psychological effects of unemployment upon breadwinners
and their families. It is based on interviews taken in
the mid 1930s. This is a classic.

1087. McMurry, Donald L. Coxey's Army: A Study of the
Industrial Army Movement of 1894. Boston: Little, Brown
and Co., 1929. McMurry's dated study describes the
various armies of the unemployed which set off for the
Capitol in search of work relief. The author sees Coxey
and his movement as an outgrowth of Populist protest,

calling as it did for greater involvement by the government in insuring the welfare of its citizens and expanding natural rights.

1088. Smelser, D[avid] P. Unemployment and American Trade
Unions. Baltimore: Johns Hopkins University Press,
1919. Smelser's study surveys unemployment statistics,
union employment bureaus and unemployment insurance and
examines contemporary trade union theories on the causes
of unemployment.

1089. Stewart, Bryce M. Unemployment Benefits in the United
States. New York: Industrial Relations Counsellors,
Inc., 1930. Stewart provides extensive descriptions of
the various American voluntary unemployment insurance
plans before 1930.

1.6. TEXTBOOKS, READERS, BOOKS OF DOCUMENTS,BIBLIOGRAPHIES
1090. Ferman, Louis, et al. Negroes and Jobs: A Book of
Readings. Ann Arbor: University of Michigan Press,
1968. This volume contains several useful articles on
the economics of racial inequality in the present.

1091. Piore, Michael J., ed. Unemployment and Inflation:
Institutionalist and Structuralist Views. A Reader in
Labor Economics. White Plains, N.Y.: M. E. Sharpe,
Inc., 1979. This volume of readings discusses unemployment and inflation from the point of view that they
are two distinct and largely independent processes. It
adopts the dual labor market hypothesis and contrasts
that view with that of orthodox economics.

1092. Okun, Arthur M., ed. The Battle Against Unemployment.
Rev. ed. New York: W. W. Norton and Co., 1972. This
book contains a series of essays on unemployment and inflation by several economists debating the best policies
to solve this double-barreled modern problem.

1093. Recent Literature on Unemployment with Particular
Reference to Causes and Remedies. Compiled by L. A.
Thompson, Librarian, U.S. Dept. of Labor. Typed MS.,
circa 1920.

1094. Work Projects Administration (called Works Progress Administration from 1935-9). The research and statistical
publications of the WPA are invaluable to a study of unemployment during the Depression and are too numerous to
list here. The WPA did publish several bibliographies of
its publications. Readers are urged to consult the U.S.
Superintendent of Documents's Monthly Catalogue of United
States Public Documents. (Washington, D.C.: Government
Printing Office, annual volumes since 1895) for listings

of all WPA monographs on unemployment.

2. PERIOD PIECES

2.1. COLONIAL

1095. Jones, Douglas. "The Strolling Poor: Transiency in Eighteenth Century Massachusetts." Journal of Social History, Vol. 8, No. 3 (Spring 1975), 28-49. In response to increasing transiency, Jones claims, Massachusetts in the mid and late-eighteenth century abandoned the habit of warning away the poor and made towns take responsibility for all the poor, both residents and transients. His study of changing responses to poverty counters Rothman's more static view of eighteenth century society.

1096. Stiverson, Gregory A. Poverty in a Land of Plenty: Tenancy in Eighteenth Century Maryland. Baltimore: Johns Hopkins University Press, 1977. Stiverson's account of farm tenancy in colonial Maryland emphasizes the poverty of tenants and the unlikelihood of their advancement. The author describes in detail the daily life of these colonial workers.

2.2. REVOLUTIONARY AND EARLY NATIONAL

1097. Mohl, Raymond A. Poverty in New York, 1783-1825. New York: Oxford University Press, 1971. Mohl's thesis is that the orderly society of the eighteenth century broke down under the impact of urbanization, industrialization, and immigration. By 1820, the old ideas of community care for the ever-present poor as an expression of Christian charity had given way to a harsher and more moralistic view that poverty was the fault of character weakness in individual poor people. David Rothman shares this interpretation as well as the idea that welfare reform was designed for purposes of social control of the dangerous elements. Some scholars, like Gerald Grob, feel both Mohl and Rothman idealized the caring community of colonial America.

2.3. ANTEBELLUM AND CIVIL WAR

1098. Klebaner, Benjamin J. "Poor Relief and Public Works During the Depression of 1857." The Historian, Vol. 22, No. 3 (May, 1960), 264-79. While the idea of public works to aid the unemployed was not new, the author finds this method used much more extensively in the depression of 1857 than ever before. Traditional almsgiving, political conflicts, and fears of fiscal imprudence, however, did limit the implementation of such public works projects.

1099. Rezneck, Samuel. "The Influence of Depression upon American Opinion, 1857-1859." Journal of Economic History, Vol. 2, No. 1 (May, 1942), 1-23. This article surveys popular literature of the day on the question of the causes and consequences of the depression and its remedies. The plight of the unemployed and the debate over work relief or charity and the Tompkins Square riot are discussed briefly.

1100. Robbins, Roy Marvin. "Horace Greeley: Land Reform and Unemployment, 1837-1862." Agricultural History, Vol. 7, No. 1 (January, 1933), 18-41. Robbins traces Greeley's commitment to a homestead bill as a solution to the problem of poverty, unemployment and urban crowding from his famous pronouncement, "Go West, young man," during the Panic of 1837 to the eventual passage of the Homestead Act in 1862.

2.4. POSTBELLUM

1101. Bruce, Robert V. 1877: Year of Violence. Indianapolis: Bobbs-Merrill, 1959. Bruce's account of depression year 1877 ranges beyond the great railroad strike to investigate the problems of labor, including unemployment, in this era. This is relevant reading, providing a background on the economic plight of working men during the depression of the 1870s.

1102. Cox, LaWanda F. "Agricultural Wage Earners, 1865-1900: The Emergence of a Modern Labor Problem." Agricultural History, Vol. 22, No. 2 (April 1948), 95-114. Cox argues that between 1865 and 1900 farm laborers ceased to be the apprentice farmers that hired men traditionally had been and came instead to resemble industrial labor. In these years farm labor declined in status and pay, and farm laborers were in an increasingly disadvantaged position compared to other workers or to hired hands of earlier years. This old article is an excellent brief study of the roots of the modern migrant labor problem.

1103. Gutman, Herbert C. "The Failure of the Movement by the Unemployed for Public Works in 1873." Political Science Quarterly, Vol. 80, No. 2 (June, 1965), 254-76. Gutman discusses the efforts of the unemployed to force public officials to provide public works projects. He also discusses the hostile response of the public and the splits within the unemployed workers' movement. Gutman is one of a very few scholars examining unemployment from the viewpoint of the unemployed laborer.

1104. Gutman, Herbert C. "The Tompkins Square 'Riot' in New York City on January 13, 1874: A Re-examination of Its Causes and Its Aftermath." Labor History, Vol. 6, No. 1 (Winter 1975), 44-70. Gutman gives a detailed account of the Tompkins Square riot, a demonstration by the unemployed demanding public works and relief which was broken up by the police. The harsh reaction of press and public to the 'riot' reveals the unsympathetic attitude of the public toward those out of work.

1105. Hoffman, Charles. The Depression of the Nineties: An Economic History. Westport, Conn.: Greenwood Publishing Co., 1970. Hoffman provides a Keynesian analysis of the economic forces causing the depression of the 1890s. He traces the economic history of the U.S. from 1869 to 1913 and describes in detail the economic events of the depression. His appendix contains estimates of unemployment.

1106. McGuire, Robert A. "Economic Causes of Late-Nineteenth Century Agrarian Unrest: New Evidence." Journal of Economic History, Vol. 41, No. 4 (December, 1981), 835-52. McGuire, an economist, tests the hypothesis that economic instability in American agriculture was a major cause of agrarian discontent in the late nineteench century. He attempts to measure economic instability in agriculture and to locate and gauge the intensity of protest in 14 northern states from 1866 to 1909. His results, not surprisingly, suggest a very positive relation between unrest and economic instability.

1107. Rezneck, Samuel. "Patterns of Thought and Action in an American Depression, 1882-1886." American Historical Review, Vol. 61, No. 2 (January, 1956), 284-307. The depression of 1882-6 was unusual in that it began gradually without a panic. In this rambling article, Rezneck examines briefly ideas of the period about the nature of America's economic problems, unemployment, business responsibility, scientific charity, utopian novels, and fears of labor unrest and radicalism. He finds the public generally fearful and conservative and unwilling to embrace new ideas of social responsibility.

1108. Rezneck, Samuel. "Unemployment, Unrest and Relief in the United States during the Depression of 1893-97." Journal of Political Economy, Vol. 61, No. 4 (August, 1953), 324-97. This essay ranges over a variety of topics. Rezneck sees the depression precipitating a broad wave of unrest, such as Coxey's Army, the Pullman strike and the resurgence of Populism. He also traces the intellectual impact of the depression on figures like the Adams brothers and various social reformers.

1109. Steeples, Douglas W. "The Panic of 1893: Contemporary Reflections and Reactions." Mid-America, Vol. 47, No. 3 (July 1965), 155-75. Steeples outlines public responses to the depression and related events of the 1890s, such as unemployment protests, strikes and labor unrest, and describes contemporary theories of its cause. He argues that the experience of the depression altered attitudes toward poverty and made many people anxious for the government to play a larger role in the regulation of money, business and labor.

2.5. PROGRESSIVE

1110. Ewing, John B. Job Insurance. Norman, Okla.: University of Oklahoma Press, 1933. Ewing provides a history of early voluntary efforts at unemployment insurance and then discusses attempts at legislation of such programs. He gives a detailed account of the passage of Wisconsin's unemployment insurance plan. Ewing provides a compendium of facts, but readers are encouraged to read Daniel Nelson's more analytical account, Unemployment Insurance.

1112. Roberts, Dorothy. "Fort Amity, The Salvation Army Colony in Colorado." Colorado Magazine, Vol. 17, No. 5 (September, 1940), 168-74. Roberts tells the story of a Salvation Army effort to take unemployed workers from urban slums and make them independent rural farm owners. Because of poor soil, the Fort Amity experiment failed. This article is only descriptive, not analytical.

2.6. THE 1920s AND THE GREAT CRASH

1113. Bernstein, Irving. The Lean Years: A History of the American Worker, 1920-1933. Boston: Houghton, Mifflin, 1960. Bernstein studies the position of organized and unorganized labor in the 1920s and the first years of the Depression. His thesis is that workers were subject to manipulation by the business community because of the government's narrow interpretation of its regulatory powers. Labor lacked a counterveiling power to the economic, political and ideological strength of business. This provides an excellent background for any study of unemployment in this period.

1114. Daniels, Roger. The Bonus March: An Episode of the Great Depression. Westport, Conn.: Greenwood Publishing Corp., 1971. Daniels provides one of the few book-length studies of the bonus march of unemployed World War I veterans to Washington, D.C. demanding early payment of their pensions. The study, however, does not focus directly on unemployment. Donald Lisio's account is more even-handed and uses sources which were unavailable to

Daniels.

1115. Grin, Carolyn. "The Unemployment Conference of 1921: An Experiment in National Cooperative Planning." Mid-American, Vol. 55, No. 2 (April, 1973), 83-107. This excellent article carefully describes Commerce Secretary Hoover's unemployment conference and analyzes the thinking behind it. This effort at voluntary cooperation between business and government, which Hoover felt had succeeded in 1921, would be the model on which he would shape his response to the Great Depression.

1116. Romasco, Albert U. The Poverty of Abundance: Hoover, the Nation, the Depression. New York: Oxford University Press, 1965. Romasco investigates President Hoover's response to the problem of the "poverty of abundance" in the 1930s. This is a dispassionate examination of Hoover's ideas and efforts to coordinate voluntary cooperation in relieving and ending the misery of the Depression. Romasco feels Hoover was not entirely a do-nothing President; he did respond to the Depression, but his response was not adequate.

1117. Rosenzweig, Roy. "Organizing the Unemployed: The Early Years of the Great Depression, 1929-1933." Radical America, Vol. 10, No. 4 (July-August, 1976), 37-60. Rosenzweig traces the real but limited success of grass-roots organizations of the unemployed in the early 30s to meet their most pressing needs. He discusses the ideas and efforts of Communists, Socialists and Musteites to work with the unemployed.

1118. Leab, Daniel J. "Barter and Self-Help Groups 1932-33." Midcontinent American Studies Journal, Vol. 7, No. 1 (Spring 1966), 15-24. This is a brief, useful article on barter and self-help groups in the early years of the Depression before the One Hundred Days. The author feels these groups served to keep up the morale of those out of work but were never fully successful in sustaining their members. Some groups became protest organizations demanding food and work. The article has useful footnotes to sources on self-help and co-ops among the unemployed.

1119. Leab, Daniel J. "'United We Eat': The Creation and Organization of the Unemployed Councils in 1930." Labor History, Vol. 8, No. 3 (Fall 1967), 300-15. Leab recounts the unsuccessful efforts of the Communist Party to build an army of revolutionaries out of the Depression's unemployed by organizing unemployment councils. Leab argues that American workers were not drawn to the CP, but preferred less radical goals. He focuses narrowly on the CP.

1120. Lisio, Donald J. The President and Protest: Hoover, Conspiracy, and the Bonus Riot. Columbia, Mo.: University of Missouri Press, 1974. Using the then newly available sources at the Hoover Library, Lisio has written a revisionist interpretation of the Bonus March riot. He attempts to lay to rest the various conspiracy theories of the riot and its suppression. He includes the detailed story--presented in his earlier article, "A Blunder Becomes Catastrophe: Hoover, the Legion, and the Bonus Army," Wisconsin Magazine of History, Vol. 51, No. 1 (Autumn 1967), 37-50--that MacArthur, not Hoover, was responsible for routing the Bonus Army. Lisio sees the Bonus Marchers as a special interest group of the poor who were not representative of all the unemployed during the Depression. The book has a useful bibliographical essay.

2.7. NEW DEAL AND WORLD WAR II

1121. Bremer, William W. "Along the 'American Way': The New Deal's Work Relief Programs for the Unemployed." Journal of American History, Vol. 62, No. 3 (December, 1975), 636-52. Bremer argues that work programs were seen as superior to relief since they preserved the dignity of working men. But, despite the urgings of social workers and because such programs were always views as temporary, New Deal work programs were more charity than employment. Bremer stresses the concern of contemporaries for the morals of the poor. He includes an interesting examination of theories about work relief.

1122. Glick, Brian. "The Thirties: Organizing the Unemployed." Liberation, Vol. 12, No. 6-7 (September-October, 1967), 12-16. In this brief discussion of organizations of and actions by the unemployed during the Depression, Glick relates the efforts and often conflicting strategies of the Communists, Socialists and Musteites.

1123. Rosenzweig, Roy. "Radicals and the Jobless: The Musteites and the Unemployed Leagues, 1932-1936." Labor History, Vol. 16, No. 1 (Winter, 1975), 52-77. This article investigates the problem for American radicals of deciding whether to work for the day-to-day needs of the jobless or to build a revolutionary band to overthrow the system. A. J. Muste and his followers first attempted to organize the unemployed to demand assistance and later moved to push for revolution. They failed to turn the unemployed into revolutionaries but they did help unemployed workers by organizing strikes and protests against inadequate relief and the absence of government work programs.

1124.   Rosenzweig, Roy. "'Socialism in Our Time': The So-
        cialist Party and the Unemployed, 1929-1936." Labor
        History, Vol. 20, No. 4 (Fall, 1979), 485-509. This
        article discusses the Socialist Party efforts to organize
        the unemployed. Focused more on the SP than the un-
        employed, it examines disagreements within the party over
        this policy and examines the types of programs the party
        pursued and its success and failure in different
        locations.

1125.   Salmond, John A. The Civilian Conservation Corps,
        1933-1942: A New Deal Case Study. Durham, North
        Carolina: Duke University Press, 1967. This history of
        the CCC details its origins, development and method of
        operation. It sees the CCC as a successful effort to
        conserve human and natural resources, both pragmatic and
        humane, which avoided ideological swamps. This is an in-
        stitutional history, not a history of the CCC workers or
        of the impact of the agency on their lives.

1126.   Trolander, Judith Ann. Settlement Houses and the Great
        Depression. Detroit: Wayne State University Press,
        1975. Trolander traces the decline of te reform
        tradition embodied in the settlement house. She has two
        informative chapters on settlement house efforts to help
        the unemployed during the Depression. Her book supports
        the thesis of the inability of private enterprise and
        voluntarism to solve social problems.

1127.   Venkataramanie, M. S. "Norman Thomas, Arkansas Share-
        croppers, and the Roosevelt Agricultural Policies,
        1933-1937." Mississippi Valley Historical Review, Vol.
        47, No. 2 (September 1960), 225-62. The author shows how
        Socialist party leader Thomas worked to expose the harm
        which New Deal agricultural policies caused share-
        croppers. He examines the political and ideological is-
        sues involved and argues the Roosevelt administration
        could have done better and probably would have had share-
        croppers not been so powerless.

2.8. POSTWAR
      1128. Bailey, Stephen Kemp. Congress Makes a Law: The Story
             Behind the Employment Act of 1946. New York: Columbia
             University Press, 1950. Bailey uses the evolution of the
             Employment Act of 1946 as a test case of political re-
             sponsibility for public policy. He found the political
             process so tortuous that, in the end, the voters could
             not really hold any one political force or body or in-
             dividual responsible. This is a detailed study of the
             political process and public opinion and economic ideas
             involved in the creation of the "full employment" bill.

1129. Gilbert, Charles E. "Policy-Making in Public Welfare:
       The 1962 Amendments." Political Science Quarterly, Vol.
       81, No. 2 (June, 1966), 196-224. This article examines
       the relation among social workers, the welfare
       bureaucracy, and politics in the federal welfare amend-
       ments of 1962 which increased services to the poor.
       Gilbert discusses the social and political issues at
       stake in this policy shift.

1130. Gilman, Harry J. "Economic Discrimination and Un-
       employment." American Economic Review, Vol. 55, No. 5
       (December, 1965), 1077-96. Using an econometric model,
       Gilman attempts to discover the impact of racism on un-
       employment rates. He tries to separate discrimination in
       hiring and firing practices from differences in level of
       skill. His dates cover 1950 to 1963.

1131. Gilpatrick, Eleanor G. Structural Unemployment and
       Aggregate Demand: A Study of Employment and Unemployment
       in the United States, 1948-1964. Baltimore: Johns
       Hopkins University Press, 1966. Gilpatrick examines the
       debate of economists over the persistence of relatively
       high levels of unemployment in post-war America. She
       finds validity in both the structuralists' argument of
       structural barriers preventing employment and those who
       argue that inadequate aggregate demand is to be blamed.
       She bases her argument on an examination of unemployment
       data from 1948 to 1964. This is a good introduction to
       the modern eonomic debate over the causes of unemployment.

1132. Kerr, Clark, ed. Labor Markets and Wage Determination.
       Berkeley: University of California Press, 1977. This
       collection of essays contains Kerr's most famous "The
       Balkanization of Labor Markets" in which he first argued
       (1954) that there was not one labor market, but two—a
       secondary labor market which was unprotected and paid low
       wages, and a primary market of guild of craft workers and
       manorial or noncraft workers. Kerr's emphasis on the
       structural or institutional focus shaping the labor mar-
       ket is at odds with the neo-classical economists' em-
       phasis on market forces, known as aggregate demand. This
       collection is a useful source of background reading es-
       pecially for understanding the current debate on the
       causes and cures of unemployment.

1133. Thurow, Lester C. "The Changing Structure of Un-
       employment: An Econometric Study." Review of Economics
       and Statistics, Vol. 47, No. 2 (May 1965), 137-49.
       Thurow devises an econometric model to explain changes in
       unemployment by sex, race, age, occupation and industry
       from 1948 to 1963. The model predicts that changes in
       unemployment rates are tied to the growth rate of the GNP.

2.9. GREAT SOCIETY

1134. Anderson, James E. "Poverty, Unemployment and Economic Development: The Search for a National Antipoverty Policy." Journal of Politics, Vol. 29, No. 1 (February 1967), 70-93. Anderson discusses the evolution of the various antipoverty programs introduced in the 1960s and the reasons for the emergence of poverty as a political issue and the reasons why most antipoverty projects at first met only mild opposition. This is a good brief introduction to the War on Poverty.

1135. Brauer, Carl M. "Kennedy, Johnson, and the War on Poverty." Journal of American History, Vol. 69, No. 1 (June, 1982), 98-119. Brauer argues that Johnson undertook the War on Poverty not just because of Kennedy's interest in it, or because of pressure by social scientists or even to gain black votes; rather Johnson selected this as his program because it appealed to him.

1136. Dernberg, Thomas and Kenneth Stand. "Hidden Unemployment 1953-62: A Quantitative Analysis by Age and Sex." American Economic Review, Vol. 56, No. 1 (March 1966), 71-95. Using econometric models and current data, the authors attempt to identify and account for those workers who withdraw from the labor force in hard times and are not counted in unemployment figures.

1137. Jackson, Larry R. and William A. Johnson. Protest by the Poor: The Welfare Rights Movement in New York City. Lexington, Mass.: D.C. Heath and Co., 1974. This book analyzes in detail the origin, development, tactics and activities of welfare protest groups in NYS. The authors credit welfare rights group activities with increasing the welfare caseload in NYC.

1138. Levitan, Sar A. The Great Society's Poor Law: A New Approach to Poverty. Baltimore: Johns Hopkins University Press, 1969. This useful survey of antipoverty programs traces the development of the Economic Opportunity Act, describes its structure and evaluates its performance. Included are discussions of the Job Corps, aid to migrant laborers, and programs to aid the rural poor. Levitan has written many other books on various Great Society programs which, though overlapping and repetitive, may be of use to students of the Great Society.

2.10. THE CONTEMPORARY PERIOD

1139. Bluestone, Barry, William M. Murphy, and Mary Stevenson. Low Wages and the Working Poor. Ann Arbor: University of Michigan Press, 1973. This study attempts to define the age, gender, racial and occupational char-

acteristics of the working poor today and to account for
the persistence of low wage employment.

1140.   Corcoran, Mary and Martha S. Hill. "The Incidence and
Consequences of Short-And Long-Run Unemployment." In
Greg J. Duncan and James N. Morgan, eds. Five Thousand
American Families--Patterns of Economic Progress. Ann
Arbor: University of Michigan Press, 1979. The authors
analyze the economic burden of unemployment on heads of
household from 1967 to 1976, the relation between poverty
and unemployment, and the role of unemployment compensation in alleviating that burden.

1141.   Levitan, Sar A. Programs in Aid of the Poor for the
1970s. Baltimore: Johns Hopkins University Press,
1973. Levitan reviews and appraises existing programs to
aid the poor and explores other approaches for the
future. In general, he finds existing programs inadequate in scale and scope.

1142.   Rumberger, Russell W. and Martin Carnoy. "Segmentation
in the U.S. Labor Market: Its Effects on Mobility and
Earnings of Whites and Blacks." Cambridge Journal of
Economics, Vol. 4, No. 2 (June, 1980), 117-32. The authors test the theory of labor force segmentation; their
results neither totally confirm nor destroy it. They
found that increased education, for example, did blacks
little good (in terms of income) as long as they remained
in the secondary labor market. The earnings of blacks
and women in the primary market were similar to those of
white males in the secondary market. They found the
earnings of blacks and women rose if they moved from the
private to the public sector, while the reverse was true
for white males.

1143.   Wiegand, G. Carl, ed. Inflation and Unemployment:
Twelve American Economists Discuss the Unemployment
Problem. Old Greenwich, Conn.: Devin-Adair Publishing
Co., 1980. This book of essays on unemployment is critical of full employment policy as an inflationary practice
and tries to identify the best employment rate, i.e. the
rate with the least inflation. This reveals the changing
notion of what is an "acceptable" level of unemployment
in the present. The authors are anti-Keynesians.

3. SALIENT VARIATIONS

3.1. LOCAL, STATE, REGIONAL
1144.   Blumberg, Barbara. The New Deal and the Unemployed: The
View from New York City. Lewisburg, Pa.: Bucknell Uni-

versity Press, 1979. This is a well-researched study of
the operation of work relief in New York City. The author details the various efforts of the WPA, its political battles, and its relations with militant unemployment organizations. While arguing that work relief
policies were inconsistent and never met the needs of all
the unemployed, Blumberg feels the relief record of the
New Deal is fairly strong given the great opposition to
relief in Congress and the public. This is a very useful
local study.

1145. Fox, Bonnie R. "Unemployment Relief in Philadelphia,
1930-1932: A Study of the Depression's Impact on
Voluntarism." Pennsylvania Magazine of History and
Biography, Vol. 93, No. 1 (January 1969), 86-108. Fox
argues the failure of Philadelphia's voluntary local relief, one of the best coordinated efforts in an American
city, reveals the failure of Hoover's idea of local responsibility. Private resources were inadequate and so
voluntary efforts failed.

1146. Hillman, Arthur. The Unemployed Citizen's League of
Seattle. Seattle: University of Washington Press,
1934. This is a brief history of the Unemployed
Citizen's League of Seattle, a self-help and bartering
organization, from 1931 to 1933, which was destroyed, the
author argues, by internal dissension and external pressure. The author, a contemporary critic of the League,
provides useful facts on the movement, but his analysis
is rather dated.

1147. Huggins, Nathan Irvin. Protestants Against Poverty:
Boston's Charities, 1870-1900. Westport, Conn.:
Greenwood Publishing Corp., 1971. This fine study traces
the efforts of Bostonians to deal in a humanitarian
fashion with the new hoardes of poor generated by immigration and industrialization. It also covers the professionalization of social work. Huggins focuses
particularly on the Protestant charity reformers' mind
set and their assumptions, derived from their religious
beliefs, about the nature of poverty, its cures, and the
poor themselves. There is a chapter on relief during the
depressions of 1873 and 1893 showing how ordinary distinctions between public and private relief break down
during these crises.

1148. Koch, Raymond L. "Politics and Relief in Minneapolis
During the 1930s." Minnesota History, Vol. 41, No. 4
(Winter, 1968), 153-70. Koch explores the rapid expansion of public relief in Minneapolis in response to
the Depression, focusing on the political conflicts
generated. He argues that the chaotic conditions in public relief existed not only because of the Depression but
also because of pressures brought to bear upon it by the

Farmer-Labor Party, organizations of discontented relief clients, and the inadequate and inconsistent financing of the relief system

1149. Lambert, Roger. "Hoover and the Red Cross in the Arkansas Drought of 1930." Arkansas Historical Quarterly, Vol. 29, No. 1 (Spring 1970), 3-19. This article details the suffering and unemployment caused by the drought of 1930 and discusses the inadequacy of Red Cross relief and Hoover's refusal to move beyond private relief. The drought raised the issue of government responsibility to its distressed citizens.

1150. Leiby, James. "State Welfare Administration in California, 1930-1945." Southern California Quarterly, Vol. 55, No. 3 (Fall, 1973), 303-18. The federal government's subsidies for the poor and unemployed were administered through state government agencies. Leiby's study of the California welfare administration shows what happened in one state. In California, he argues, there was an increased acceptance of public responsibility for the needy and an expansion of public welfare bureaucracy to handle massive unemployment and destitution.

1151. Ortquist, Richard. "Unemployment and Relief: Michigan's Response to the Depression During the Hoover Years." Michigan History, Vol. 57, No. 3 (Fall, 1973), 209-36. This article describes the political response to the Depression in Michigan, focusing on the conflict between Detroit's Mayor Murphy and Governor Brucker.

1152. Schuyler, Michael W. "Federal Drought Relief Activities in Kansas, 1934." Kansas Historical Quarterly, Vol. 42, No. 4 (Winter, 1976), 403-24. The author claims, but does not prove, that the drought relief programs undermined the appeal of radical groups like the Farmers' Union and Farmers' Holiday Association. It provided relief and work and established experimental farm programs. These programs shaped the direction of New Deal policy. The author provides details of relief allocations and work programs.

1153. Winters, Donald L. Farmers Without Farms: Agricultural Tenancy in Nineteenth-Century Iowa. Westport, Conn.: Greenwood Press, 1978. Winters analyzes farm tenancy as an economic institution in Iowa from 1850 to 1900. He feels too many scholars approach the topic from the question, "What went wrong?". He does not see tenancy as an evil or as evidence of the malfunctioning of the economic system, but instead as a "natural outgrowth of a normally operating market system."

3.2. RACIAL/ETHNIC
 1154. Bodnar, John E. "The Impact of the 'New Immigration' on
        the Black Worker: Steelton, Pa., 1880-1920." Labor
        History, Vol. 17, No. 2 (Spring 1976), 214-29. Bodnar
        argues that the influx of Slavs into northern industrial
        towns had a devastating impact upon blacks. Slavs were
        hired to replace black semi-skilled workers and blacks
        were forced to move elsewhere in search of work.

 1155. Glassberg, Eudice. "Work, Wages, and the Cost of
        Living: Ethnic Differences and the Poverty Line,
        Philadelphia, 1880." Pennsylvania History, Vol. 46, No.
        1 (January, 1979), 17-58. The author tries to establish
        the poverty line for PHilhdelphia in 1880. She deter-
        mines what proportion of the black, Irish, German, and
        native white populations fell below this poverty line,
        she explores the strategies of survival of families whose
        wage earnings were inadequate.

 1156. Kruman, Marc W. "Quotas for Blacks: The Public Works
        Administration and the Black Construction Worker." Labor
        History, Vol. 16, No. 1 (Winter 1975), 33-52. Kruman's
        article is part of the debate on the New Deal's treatment
        of blacks. He finds that the WPA did attempt to ease
        discrimination against blacks in construction and was, in
        part, successful.

 1157. Mandle, Jay R. The Roots of Black Poverty: The Southern
        Plantation Economy After the Civil War. Durham, North
        Carolina: Duke University Press, 1978. Mandle argues
        that the sharecropping system which developed after the
        Civil War did not signal the end of the plantation
        system, but rather its continuation through the coercion
        of black labor. The poverty of blacks was not an ac-
        cident, but a necessary element in the perpetuation of an
        economic and social system. The book does not put black
        sharecropping in the context of the general economic woes
        of the agricultural South, however.

 1158. Salmond, John A. "The Civilian Conservation Corps and
        the Negro." Journal of American History, Vol. 52, No. 1
        (June, 1965), 75-88. Salmond investigates the policies
        of the CCC which prevented blacks from participating
        fully. For those who did get into a camp, the CCC pro-
        vided training and jobs which did represent real if
        limited success.

 1159. Wolters, Raymond. Negroes and the Great Depression: The
        Problem of Economic Recovery. Westport, Conn.:
        Greenwood Publishing Co., 1970. Wolter's thesis is that
        blacks were short-changed during the Depression by New
        Deal programs because the New Deal responded best to
        those who were organized and politically powerful, and
        blacks were not. He details the unsuccessful efforts of

the NAACP to promote the economic rights of blacks in the 1930s.

3.3.   GENDER-SPECIFIC

1160.   Cumbler, John T.   "The Politics of Charity: Gender and Class in Late 19th Century Charity Policy."   Journal of Social History, Vol. 14, No. 1 (Fall, 1980), 99–111. Comparing the charitable efforts of two towns' voluntary welfare agencies, Cumbler finds that female-dominated agencies were less interested in trapping welfare cheaters, more interested in helping their clients and more oriented toward women's issues than were male-dominated charity organizations.   Cumbler attributes these differences to differentials in the power of sex and class in 19th century America.

1161.   Ferber, Marianne A. and Helen M. Lowry.   "Women: The New Reserve Army of the Unemployed."   Signs, Vol. 1, No. 2, Pt. 2, Supplement (September, 1976), 213–32.   The authors argue that women's greater unemployment is due either directly or indirectly to discrimination in employment.

1162.   Humphries, Jane.   "Women: Scapegoats and Safety Valves in the Great Depression."   Review of Radical Political Economics, Vol. 8, No. 1 (Spring, 1976), 98–121. Humphries makes the familiar argument that the Depression strengthened traditional ideas about woman's place and weakened women's drive for liberation.   See Ruth Milkman's article for a different interpretation.

1163.   Mayo, Judith.   Work and Welfare: Employment and Employability of Women in the AFDC Program.   Chicago: University of Chicago Press, 1975.   This book examines the relationship between the welfare system and the labor market, and makes policy recommendations for mixing work and welfare through work incentives.

1164.   Milkman, Ruth.   "Women's Work and the Economic Crisis: Some Lessons of the Great Depression."   Review of Radical Political Economics, Vol. 8, No. 1 (Spring, 1976), 73–97.   Milkman questions the theory that women form a "reserve army" of labor who are integrated into the economy in times of expansion and sent home in times of slow down.   In the 1930s, Milkman found that sex-typing of occupations made the labor market inflexible and hence fewer women than expected were sent home.

1165.   Scharf, Lois.   To Work and to Wed: Female Employment, Feminism, and the Great Depression.   Westport, Conn.: Greenwood Press, 1980.   Scharf describes the devastating impact the Depression had on women's employment and on feminism.

1166. Tsuchigane, Robert and Norton Dodge. Economic
Discrimination against Women in the United States.
Lexington, Mass.: Lexington Books, 1974. This book provides useful data on discrimination against women in the
20th century labor force. The authors perceive a trend
of decreasing sexual discrimination.

1167. Weisskoff, Francine B. "Woman's 'Place' in the Labor
Market." American Economic Review, Vol. 62, No. 2 (May
1972), 161-66. Weisskoff argues that occupational segregation by sex causes women's inequality. She is concerned with the reasons for the poverty of employed women.

1168. Zellner, Harriet. "Discrimination Against Women, Occupational Segregation, and the Relative Wage." American
Economic Review, Vol. 62, No. 2 (May, 1972), 157-50.
Zellner argues that discrimination against women in
male-dominated occupations is a major reason for women's
occupational segregation and low relative wages.

3.4. CLASS
1169. Harrison, Bennett. "Welfare Payments and the Re-
production of Low-Wage Workers and Secondary Jobs."
Review of Radical Political Economics, Vol. 11, No. 2
(Summer, 1979), 1-16. On the basis of five annual interviews (in the late 1960s and early 1970s) of 27,000
households, the author concludes that AFDC seems to continue the secondary labor market by reinforcing low
paying, high turnover employment. He also argues that
welfare recipients are a permanently dependent class of
unable or unwilling workers because he found 92 percent
of households ever on welfare also contained adults who
worked at some time. His conclusions support the claims
of Piven and Cloward.

1170. Schlosman, Kay Lehman and Sidney Verba. Injury to
Insult: Unemployment, Class and Political Response.
Cambridge, Mass.: Harvard University Press, 1979. Two
political scientists, using a survey of 1370 respondents,
study contemporary unemployment. They focus on the
question of why the unemployed do not become politically
active in order to redress their perceived economic
grievances.

4. AGE-SPECIFIC AND LIFE-CYCLE STUDIES

4.1. MIGRANT LABOR

1171. Jones, Lamar B. "Labor and Management in California Agriculture, 1864-1964." Labor History, Vol. 11, No. 1 (Winter, 1970), 23-40. Jones outlines the early emergence of large-scale commercial agriculture in California and the violent history of the migrant labor force from the importation of the Chinese to the current use of Mexican labor.

1172. McWilliams, Carey. Ill Fares the Land: Migrants and Migratory Labor in the United States. New York: Barnes and Noble, 1967. The thesis iof this work, published originally in 1942, is that small and medium sized farmers have been squeezed out by large scale agri-business. This trend began considerably before World War I and has led to the impoverishment of farmers. McWilliams pays attention both to habitual migrants and to depression-generated migrants. The Great Depression is studied in detail. This is still a polemical classic in agricultural history.

1173. Schwartz, Harry. Seasonal Farm Labor in the United States With Special Reference to Hired Workers in Fruit and Vegetable and Sugar-Beet Production. New York: Columbia University Press, 1945. This is a historical account of the miserable position of migrant farm labor in the twentieth century. Schwartz describes the various ethnic and racial groups recruited to this kind of labor.

1174. Stein, Walter J. California and The Dust Bowl Migration. Westport, Conn.: Greenwood Publishing Corp., 1973. Stein argues that the dust storms of the 1930s did not cause the migration of Okies to California; it only accelerated a trend of the 20s, which he explains. Stein discusses the impact of the Okies on California, the failure of state and federal efforts to meet their needs, and the failure of unionization drives among the migrants. This is a valuable update to McWilliam's 1940s classic.

4.2. TRAMPS

1175. Ringenbach, Paul T. Tramps and Reformers, 1873-1916: The Discovery of Unemployment in New York. Westport, Conn : Greenwood Press, 1973. This well-researched study focuses on reformers and their ideas rather than on tramps themselves. Ringenbach finds significant change in the attitudes of reformers toward tramps (the mobile unemployed), from 1873 to 1916. Gradually the idea that anyone who wanted to work could do so yielded to a more sympathetic attitude in the Progressive era. Ringenbach traces the discovery of the tramp and the various relief and rehabilitative programs adopted. He supplies a helpful, partially annotated bibliography.

1176. Leonard, Frank. "'Helping' the Unemployed in the Nineteenth Century: The Case of the American Tramp." Social
Service Review, Vol. 40, No. 14 (December, 1966),
429-34. Leonard argues that nineteenth-century tramps
were harassed by local governments and citizens and given
"make work" as a punishment. He feels that people were
ambivalent toward work and may have envied tramps their
freedom while fearing them. Tramp was a term used to
cover all manner of social deviants. This is a very
brief suggestive article.

4.3 MANPOWER POLICY
1177. Bakke, E. Wight. The Mission of Manpower Policy.
Kalamazoo, Mich: W. E. Upjohn Institute for Employment
Research, 1969. Bakke criticizes the manpower policies
of the United States up through the Johnson Administration. He finds manpower policy overly concerned
with the most disadvantaged, impoverished worker to the
exclusion of others in the labor force. He also criticizes American policy as a series of uncoordinated programs with no comprehensive plan or clear goal for the
future.

1178. Davidson, Roger H. The Politics of Comprehensive
Manpower Legislation. Baltimore: Johns Hopkins University Press, 1972. While Davidson gives a brief history
of government manpower programs from 1946 to 1966, he
focuses on the years 1967-70 and in particular on the
political battles over manpower legislation waged in the
Nixon years. This very detailed study has a political
science approach and a narrow focus.

1179. Friedlander, Stanley L. et al. Unemployment in the Urban
Core: An Analysis of Thirty Cities with Policy
Recommendations. New York: Praeger Publishers, 1972.
Using data from a recession year, 1960, and a prosperous
year, 1966, the authors try to determine the principal
factors responsible for the differences in unemployment
in the nation's 30 largest cities. They see both structural and aggregate demand elements in the unemployment
rates and propose solutions geared to both these problems.

1180. Ginzberg, Eli, ed. Employing the Unemployed. New York:
Basic Books, 1980. This collection contains essays on
government employment training programs in the 1960s and
1970s. Ginzberg's own contribution summarizes federal
employment and training policies from 1962 to 1979

1181. Mangum, Garth L. The Emergence of Manpower Policy. New
York: Holt, Rinehart and Winston, 1969. Mangum here
presents the goals and background of federal manpower
policy, emphasizing the 1960s, and assesses its impact to

date. He sees the goal of manpower policy to be expanding the opportunities for employment of Americans
who, Mangum feels, prefer work to the dole. There is a
chapter on the history of manpower policy before the
1960s and a discussion of the various manpower policies
of the 60s with an evaluation of each. This is a useful
little book, summarizing manpower policies in the twentieth century and their rationales. It is written from a
liberal perspective and provides a good introduction to
the Great Society viewpoint.

1182. Mangum, Garth L. and John Walsh. A Decade of Manpower
Development and Training. Salt Lake City: Olympus Publishing Co., 1973. The authors, both economists, survey
various evaluations of MDTA and find it effective and
worthwhile overall. They present information on the
changing course of MDTA programs from 1962 to 1972.
Mangum has written several other books on federal manpower politics.

1183. Ostow, Miriam and Anna B. Dutka. Work and Welfare in New
York City. Baltimore: Johns Hopkins University Press,
1975. This is a study of the relationship between work
and welfare, based on public aid records in NYC in the
early 1970s. The authors found that most welfare
recipients had worked or were working.

1184. Perry, Charles R., et al. The Impact of Government
Manpower Programs, In General, and on Minorities and
Women. Philadelphia: University of Pennsylvania Press,
1975. Using 252 evaluations of manpower training programs, Perry concludes they have had limited positive impact on women and minorities. The second half of the
book is a detailed investigation of the major programs.
It contains an excellent bibliography of sources, published and unpublished, on manpower policy and specific
programs in the 1960s and early 70s. It will prove useful to those researching manpower policies in the 1960s.

1185. Schultz, George P. and Arnold R. Weber. Strategies for
the Displaced Worker: Confronting Economic Change. New
York: Harper & Row, 1966. The authors tell the story of
how Armour and Co., which was shutting one of its plants,
worked with the union to solve much of he problem of mass
labor displacement by relocating, retraining, reassigning
or retiring the affected workers.

1186. United States. President. Manpower Report of the
President, 13 vols. Washington, D.C.: U.S. Government
Printing Office, 1963-75. (continued since 1976 as
Employment and Training Report of the President). These
annual reports - -both inventories and in-house assessments of manpower training and its impact on unemployment - -may prove useful to scholars of un-

employment in the 1960s and 70s.

4.4. ORGANIZED LABOR

1187. Bernstein, Irving. The Turbulent Years: A History of the American Worker, 1933-1941. Boston: Houghton Mifflin Co. 1971. This is the volume in Bernstein's history of American labor dealing with trade unions from 1933 to 1941. It provides useful background on organized labor during the New Deal.

1188. Derber, Milton and Edwin Young, eds. Labor and the New Deal. Madison: University of Wisconsin Press, 1957. Two chapters are of particular interest. Chapter 3, "The Impact of the Political Left" by Bernard Karsh and Phillips L. Garman, gives a brief discussion of radicals and unions of the unemployed, the unemployed council and the National Unemployed League and the Workers Alliance of America. Chapter 7, "Organized Labor and Social Security," by Edwin E. Witte, explains how organized labor went from opposition to endorsement of Social Security and how organized labor came to have an increasing impact on changes in the program.

1189. Munts, Raymond and Mary Louise Munts. "Welfare History of the I.L.G.W.U." Labor History, Vol. 9, Special Supplement (Spring, 1968), 182-97. This article gives an account of the welfare activities of the I.L.G.W.U., emphasizing the powerful influence of David Dubinsky. Its discussion of the union's unemployment fund and its lobbying efforts on behalf of Social Security unfortunately is quite brief.

1190. Schwartz, Bonnie Fox. "New Deal Work Relief and Organized Labor: The CWA and the AFL Building Trades." Labor History, Vol. 17, No. 1 (Winter 1976), 38-57. Schwartz studies the relation between the CWA and the AFL and argues that the CWA not only helped those too proud to go on relief but also advanced the cause of organized labor.

1191. Shover, John L. Cornbelt Rebellion: The Farmers' Holiday Association. Urbana: University of Illinois Press, 1965. Shover describes the unsuccessful efforts of family farmers in the cornbelt to avoid annihilation by technological agriculture into the 1930s. His bibliography is useful.

4.5. RURAL POVERTY

1192. Baldwin, Sidney. Poverty and Politics: The Rise and Decline of the Farm Security Administration. Chapel

Hill: University of North Carolina Press, 1968. Baldwin tells the story of the FSA, the New Deal's major effort to help low income farmers, which was eliminated in the 1940s because it sought to enhance the economic and political power of tenants, sharecroppers, and migrant farm workers. Other established groups, like the American Farm Bureau Federation, felt threatened by th FSA and worked against it, Baldwin argues.

1193. Cantor, Louis. A Prologue to the Protest Movement: The Missouri Sharecropper Roadside Demonstration of 1939. Durham, North Carolina: Duke University Press, 1969. This book details the negative impact of the AAA on black sharecroppers. It makes a point of the political indifference of the New Deal to those on the lowest rungs of society and demonstrates the difficulties of developing programs which actually benefit the poor.

1194. Conrad, David Eugene. The Forgotten Farmers: The Story of Sharecroppers in the New Deal. Urbana, Ill.: University of Illinois Press, 1965. Conrad tells the tragic story of sharecroppers and the AAA from 1933 to 1936. The book is rather narrowly focused, e.g. it ignores blacks almost totally. Conrad is sympathetic to AAA administrators, stressing the political pressures and constraints acting upon them.

1195. Gilbert, Jess and Steve Brown. "Alternative Land Reform Proposals in the 1930s: The Nashville Agrarians and the Southern Tenant Farmers' Union." Agricultural History, Vol. 55, No. 4 (October, 1981), 351-69. The authors examine two never-implemented alternatives to New Deal farm policy, both critical of corporate capitalism and both advocating land reform.

1196. Grubbs, Donald H. Cry from the Cotton: The Southern Tenant Farmers' Union and the New Deal. Chapel Hill: University of North Carolina Press, 1971. Grubbs writes sympathetically about the STFU protest against AAA policies and tenant displacement. This scholarly account describes the misery of sharecroppers and the failure of their protest movement.

1197 Holley, Donald. Uncle Sam's Farmers: The New Deal Communities in the Lower Mississippi Valley. Urbana, Ill.: University of Illinois Press, 1975. Holley's book traces the development and operation of FERA resettlement projects in one region. This study of impoverished small farmers supplements Sidney Baldwin's study of the FSA, Poverty and Politics.

1198. Johnson, William R. "Rural Rehabilitation in the New Deal: The Ropesville Project." Southwestern Historical Quarterly, Vol. 79, No. 3 (January 1976), 279-95. This

is a study of one of the New Deal experiments—the establishment of self-sustaining farm families through resettlement. The Ropesville project was one on the more successful attempts at rural resettlement. Johnson gives a
detailed history of the establishment, management and
eventual sale of the project. He feels such efforts are
unable to solve the larger problems of rural relief and
farm tenancy.

1199. Worster, Donald. Dust Bowl: The Southern Plains in the
1930s. New York: Oxford University Press, 1979. This
Bancroft Prize winner studies the impact of technological
and economic change and federal policy innovations on
southern plains agriculture. Worster has little to say,
however, about rural workers themseves.

1200. Woofter, T[homas] J., Jr. and Ellen Winston. Seven Lean
Years. Chapel Hill: University of North Carolina Press,
1939. Using FERA and WPA files and interviews, the authors provide an account of rural misery. They describe
the inadequacy of drought and poverty relief measures in
various distressed rural regions and offer suggestions
for remedying this distress.

4.6. FEDERAL UNEMPLOYMENT AND SOCIAL SECURITY
1201. Adams, Leonard P. Public Attitudes Toward Unemployment
Insurance: A Historical Account With Special Reference
to Alleged Abuses. Kalamazoo, Mich; W. E. Upjohn Institute for Employment Research, 1971. This brief survey
of public attitudes toward unemployment insurance from
1935 to 1970 examines in turn the opinion of the general
public, employers and their associations, organized labor
leaders, and state administrators.

1202. Adams, Leonard P. The Public Employment Service in
Transition, 1933-1968: Evolution of a Placement Service
into a Manpower Agency. Ithaca, N.Y.: New York State
School of Industrial and Labor Relations, 1969. Adams
traces the evolution of the USES from the Depression to
1965. This volume, while rather dry, may prove useful to
those interested in the employment service.

1203. Altmeyer, Arthur J. The Formative Years of Social
Security. Madison: University of Wisconsin Press,
1968. Altmeyer, who helped devise Social Security legislation and served as commissioner of the Social Security
Board, gives an insider's view of the political considerations, negotiations, and personalities involved in
the implementation and operation of SS. He gives quite a
critical view of unemployment legislation, its amendments
and administration.

1204. Becker, Joseph M. Guaranteed Income for the Unemployed:
The Story of SUB. Baltimore: Johns Hopkins University
Press, 1968. Becker provides a history and analysis of
the workings of private supplemental unemployment benefits from their inception in 1955 to 1965. He sees SUB
as part of organized labor's postwar drive for a
guaranteed annual income.

1205. Booth, Philip. Social Security in America. Ann Arbor:
Institute of Labor and Industrial Relations, 1973. Booth
reviews, analyses and explains the main currents in Social Security program development frm 1935 to 1970. He
finds Social Security inadequate in both scope and
benefits.

1206. Burns, Eveline M. The American Social Security System.
Boston: Houghton Mifflin Co., 1949. Burns gives a description of the workings of the Social Security system,
including unemployment, detailing who gets covered, and
the nature and amount of benefits.

1207. Clague, Ewan and Leo Kramer. Manpower Policies and
Programs: A Review, 1935-75. Kalamazoo, Mich: W. E.
Upjohn Institute for Employment Research, 1976. This
brief book provides an outline of federal government
legislative programs established on behalf of the unemployed, with particular focus on the Johnson and Nixon
administrations.

1208. Douglas, Paul H. Social Security in the United States:
An Analysis and Appraisal of the Federal Social Security
Act. 2nd ed. New York: McGraw Hill Book Co., 1939.
Douglas explains the provisions of Social Security and
traces the steps whereby the system was created and outlines problems yet to be addressed. This is an early
evaluation of the system by a prominent social welfare
reformer.

1209. Gartner, Alan, Russell A. Nixon, and Frank Rossman, eds.
Public Service Employment: An Analysis of Its History,
Problems and Prospects. New York: Praeger, 1973. This
volume contains several valuable articles by radicals on
contemporary public works and their relationship to unemployment, the dual labor market, women, poverty, and
full employment. It focuses on the Emergency Employment
Act of 1971.

1210. Jerrett, Robert and Thomas A. Baracci. Public Works,
Government Spending and Job Creation. New York:
Praeger, 1979. This is an evaluation of the Job Opportunities Program of 1974. It is not an administrative
evaluation or an assessment of its direct impact on em-
ployment--studies which have been undertaken by the Economic Development Administration--but is a study of the

program's additional benefits to its participants and the community. The authors are interested in the counter-cyclical impact of government employment programs.

1211. Haber, William and Daniel H. Kruger. The Role of the United States Employment Service in a Changing Economy. Kalamazoo, Mich; W. E. Upjohn Institute for Employment Research, 1964. This monograph traces the development of the United States Employment Service and those ideas and pressures which have influenced its development. It contains a brief, lucid discussion of the historical development of the employment bureau from early labor exchanges to the USES.

1212. Haber, William and Merril G. Murray. Unemployment Insurance in the American Economy: An Historical Review and Analysis. Homewood, IL.: Richard D. Irwin, 1966. Haber and Murray describe the nature and operation of unemployment insurance in the economy and provide a historical summary of unemployment legislation efforts and achievements before the passage of Social Security. They also provide a discussion of amendments to the system in later years as well as the development of the public employment service and the problems of coverage and benefits, financial issues, and problems in federal-state relations and how these have been debated and resolved.

1213. Hallman, Howard W. Emergency Employment: A Study in Federalism. University, Ala.: University of Alabama Press, 1977. Hallman, a political scientist, uses the Emergency Employment Act of 1971 as a case study of the government when different parties control the legislative and executive branches. He explains the Act in detail.

1214. Walker, Forrest A. The Civil Works Administration: An Experiment in Federal Work Relief, 1933-1934. New York: Garland Publishing, Inc., 1979. This book, developed from the author's dissertation, argues that the CWA was an idealistic experiment; it was the first federal program to provide work instead of relief during the Depression. By providing meaningful work, the CWA gave its employees a sense of responsibility and dignity, Walter argues. The CWA was also a valuable precedent for later federal works projects. Walker's bibliography is worthwhile for those interested in the response to the CWA and the unemployment situation generally of the day.

1215. Wallis, John Joseph and Daniel K. Benjamin. "Public Relief and Private Employment in the Great Depression." Journal of Economic History. Vol. 41, No. 1 (March 1981), 97-102. The authors measured the impact of federal unemployment relief programs and found that those who took government work opportunities would otherwise have been on relief.

1216.   Witte, Edwin E. The Development of the Social Security
        Act. Madison: University of Wisconsin Press, 1962.
        This is Witte's personal account of the debates and ac-
        tions of the Committee on Economic Security which he
        chaired, the drafting of the Social Security Act, and its
        legislative history.

5. THE AMERICAN EXPERIENCE IN COMPARATIVE PERSPECTIVE

1217.   Industrial Relations Counsellors, Inc. An Historical
        Basis for Unemployment Insurance. Minneapolis: Univer-
        sity of Minnesota Press, 1934. This volume presents his-
        tories of state unemployment insurance programs in Great
        Britain, Germany, Sweden and Belgium, as well as giving
        an account of early voluntary programs in the United
        States.

1218.   Piore, Michael J. Birds of Passage: Migrant Labor and
        Industrial Society. New York: Cambridge University
        Press, 1979. This book traces the process of migratory
        labor in a global perspective. Piore argues that mi-
        grants are generally employed in the secondary labor mar-
        ket and that they hold lowest status though not neces-
        sarily the worst paid jobs. He compared occupational
        position of migrants in the U.S., Germany and France.

1219.   Rimlinger, Gaston V. "Welfare Policy and Economic De-
        velopment: A Comparative Historical Perspective."
        Journal of Economic History, Vol. 26, No. 4 (December
        1966), 556-71. Rimlinger puts forth the hypothesis that
        the historic shift from poor relief to a modern welfare
        system in America and Europe is at least partly "a re-
        sponse to the rising productivity and increasing scarcity
        of labor." When labor was cheap and unskilled, welfare
        was meager and designed to control the poor, but in
        highly developed modern economies, he argues, labor is
        scarce and worth the expense of greater welfare care.
        While this article is not directly about unemployment,
        its argument is relevant to an evaluation of changing
        responses to unemployment.

1220.   Rimlinger, Gaston V. Welfare Policy and
        Industrialization in Europe, America and Russia. New
        York: John Wiley and Sons, 1971. Rimlinger's com-
        parative approach to the development of social welfare
        places the movement in a broad perspective. He pays
        particular attention to the role of ideas about the
        nature of poverty in his analysis and hence emphasizes
        how the ideas of liberalism and individualism in the
        U.S., and to a lesser extent, in England and France, re-
        tarded the development of public social welfare
        institutions.

Chapter Six

COPING WITH THE DIFFICULTIES OF OLD AGE

W. Andrew Achenbaum
Carnegie-Mellon University

W. Andrew Achenbaum
Carnegie-Mellon University

Issues Covered: Old-age homes, retirement, widowhood,Social Security.

1. SYNTHESES AND OVERVIEWS

1.1. THEMATIC

1221.   Barron, Milton L. "Minority Characteristics of the Aged in American Society." Journal of Gerontology, Vol. 8 No. 3 (Fall, 1953), 477-82. This classic essay draws parallels between the aged's status in contemporary America and that of blacks and other disadvantaged groups.

1222.   Binstock, Robert H. and Ethel Shanas, eds. Handbook of Aging and the Social Sciences. New York: Van Nostrand Reinhold, 1976. The best "state of the art" volume of essays on the contemporary status of the aged, this volume reviews major social welfare responses in the United States and other advanced industrial societies. A revised edition will be published late in 1983.

1223.   Butler, Robert N. Why Survive?: Being Old in America. New York: Harper & Row, 1975. This Pulitzer Prize-winning volume offers a sobering assessment of the current plight of older people in America as well as practical recommendations for legislative action by a psychiatrist who became the first director of the National Institute on Aging.

1224.   Cowgill, Donald O. and Lowell Holmes. Aging and Modernization. New York: Appleton-Century-Crofts, 1972. A major critique of the relationship between at-titudes toward age and the processes of modernization, which is based largely on contemporary cross-cultural comparisons. The volume deals with the issue of old-age dependency.

1225.   Harris, Louis and Associates. The Myth and Reality of Aging in America. Washington, D.C.: National Council on the Aging, Inc., 1975. This important public opinion survey underscored a sharp divergence between what most people thought old age was like, and what the aged themselves reported their experiences to be. A follow-up survey, Aging in the Eighties, released just before the

1981 White House Conference on Aging, corroborated the persistence of this earlier trend. Social welfare issues are discussed.

1226. Maddox, George L. and James A. Wiley. "Scope, Concepts and Methods in the Study of Aging." In Binstock, Roberty H. and Ethel Shanas, eds. Handbook of Aging and the Social Sciences. New York: Van Nostrand Reinhold, 1976, 3-34. Although this article touches only briefly on social welfare issues, it merits careful attention because the authors provide a careful summary of theoretical difficulties in defining "age" in socio-historical analyses.

    1227.   Neugarten, Bernice L. "Age Groups in American Society and the Rise of the Young-Old." Annals of the American Academy of Political and Social Science, Vol. 320 (September, 1974), 187-98. In this seminal essay, Neugarten argues that there are two subsets of old people in post-World War II America. The young-old, those between the ages of 55 and 75, tend to be relatively healthy, financially self-sufficient and able to care for themselves. Those over seventy-five ("the old-old"), on the other hand, are prime targets for public and private welfare measures.

    1228.   Neugarten, Bernice L. and Robert J. Havighurst, eds. Social Ethics, Social Policy and the Aging Society. Washington, D.C.: Government Printing Office, 1977. This report summarizes an interdisciplinary roundtable on the ethical and economic foundations of federal income maintenance and health-care support for older people since the Great Depression. Though the participants made forecasts about events and developments in the proximate future, the volume is more useful for its assessments of current practices.

    1229.   Riley, Matilda W., et al. Aging and Society, 3 Vols. New York: Russell Sage Foundation, 1968-1972. This is a convenient compendium of theories and statistical data on the elderly. Volume 1 summarizes major demographic and socio-economic characteristics of the aged, emphasizing their household arrangements and sources of income. Volume 3 sets forth Riley's now-classic conceptual framework for analyzing changes over the life course in a broad interdisciplinary perspective.

1.2.   TEMPORAL
    1230.   Achenbaum, W. Andrew. "From Womb Through Bloom to

Tomb." <u>Reviews in American History</u>, Vol 6, No. 2 (June 1978), 178-84. This review of the strengths and weaknesses of David Hackett Fisher's <u>Growing Old in America</u> and Paula S. Fass's <u>The Damned and the Beautiful</u> sharpened the debate between Fischer and Achenbaum over their respective interpretations of the history of old age.

1231.   Achenbaum, W. Andrew. <u>Old Age in the New Land: The American Experience since 1790</u>. Baltimore: The Johns Hopkins University Press, 1978. This revised version of the author's Ph.D. diss. analyzes changes and continuities in the meanings and experiences of old age; it stresses that the intellectual history of old age does not always parallel the social history of being old. Issues in old-age dependency are treated at length. The book includes illustrations, technical appendices and a bibliographic commentary.

1232.   Achenbaum, W. Andrew. <u>Shades of Gray: Old Age, American Values and Federal Policies since 1920</u>. Boston: Little, Brown and Co., 1983. Employing a modernization model to reconstruct the history of older people during the last half-century, this extended essay deals at length with major social welfare developments during the New Deal and Great Society, and offers a preliminary assessment of the impact of Reaganomics on the well-being of the aged and the aging.

1233.   Achenbaum, W. Andrew. "Further Perspectives on Modernization and Aging". <u>Social Science History</u>, Vol. 6, No. 3 (Spring 1982), 347-68. This essay assesses the insights of humanists in general and social science historians in particular in explicating the impact of modernizatin on perceptions and conditions of older people in western civilization over time. Social welfare issues are discussed.

1234.   Achenbaum, W. Andrew and Peter N. Stearns. "Old Age and Modernization". <u>The Gerontologist</u>, Vol. 18, No. 3 (June, 1978), 307-13. This essay sought to correct major misunderstandings in the social gerontological literature about the "lessons of he past." The significance of retirement and social-security measures was treated at length.

1235.   Benedict, Robert C. "Trends in the Development of Services for the Aging under the Older Americans Act." In, Herzog, Barbara, R., ed., <u>Aging and Income</u> New York: Human Sciences Press, 1978. This essay by a leading state-level welfare administrator who shortly would become Commissioner of Aging in the Carter administration, assesses the progress since 1965 in enhancing the well-being of older Americans and in dealing with the challenges that lie ahead.

1236. Calhoun, Richard B. In Search of the New Old: Redefining Old Age in America, 1945-1970. New York: Elsevier, 1978. Although the author may overstate the extent to which "new" images of old age emerged shortly after World War II, this book offers a fine survey of the ways social scientists, advertisers, journalists, bureaucrats and the aged themselves manipulated the definitions of age to serve disparate agendas. Calhoun's analysis of old-age dependency is woven into his narrative.

1237. Campbell, John C. and John Strate. "Are Old People Conservative?" Gerontologist, Vol. 21, No. 6 (December 1981), 580-91. This essay reviews the literature on older Americans' political attitudes since World War II, and explains why the aged may not always support social welfare measures targetted for the old.

1238. Clem, Alan L. "Do Representatives Increase in Conservatism as They Increase in Seniority?" Journal of Politics. Vol. 39, No. 1 (February, 1977), 193-200. A roll-call analysis of members of the House of Representatives who served in 1953, 1963, and 1973 suggests that, while incumbents do grow more conservative in the use of federal power over time, they nonetheless were, on the whole, more liberal on welfare issues than their junior colleagues in each specific session.

1239. Cole, Thomas Richard. "Past Meridien: Aging and the Northern Middle Class, 1830-1930." Unpublished Ph.D. Diss., University of Rochester, 1980. This thesis traces evengelical Protestantism's contribution to the meaning of aging and the ambiguous legacy of the bourgeois preoccupation with health and longevity. Two paradigms--a neo-Calvinist view of the aged's responsibilities and a "civilized" view of the need to master old age--are explicated.

1240. Dahlin, Michel R. "From Poorhouse to Pension: The Changing View of Old Age in America, 1890-1929." Unpublished Ph.D. Diss., Stanford University, 1982. This dissertation focuses on the public disclosure of poverty among the old and the ensuing debate over old age pensions. Dahlin stresses the negative image of old age in the minds of liberal reformers.

1241. de Beauvoir, Simone. The Coming of Age. New York: G.P. Putnam's Sons, 1972. A felicitously written survey of major themes about old age culled from literature, history and the social sciences. The question of dependency in late life is treated throughout the book. The author's negative feelings about the process of senescence, however, casts some doubt about the objectivity of the study.

1242.   Detzner, Daniel F. "Growing Old Together: A Social History of Aging in America, 1930-1976." Unpublished Ph.D. Diss., University of Minnesota, 1977. This thesis emphasizes the negative impact of America's youth-oriented culture in exacerbating the problems of the aged. It develops this theme by exploring the treatment of older people's needs in media, public attitudes, and politics, and suggests how changes in the aged's household and economic patterns reinforced their disadvantageous position.

1243.   Estes, Carroll L. The Aging Enterprise. San Francisco: Jossey-Bass, 1979. This unabashedly polemical critique of the Older Americans Act's (1965) attempts to deal with older people's needs in the last two decades excoriates both federal bureaucrats and "the experts." Estes calls for a major overall of the ways we deliver social services and health care to the aged.

1244.   Fischer, David Hackett. Growing Old in America. New York: Oxford University Press, 1977. This is a path-breaking and controversial overview of the history of older people in America since colonial times. Before 1770, the aged grew steadily more powerful if not necessarily loved. Fischer contends that there was a "revolution in age relations" associated with the revolutionary upheavals in this country and in France. The elderly's position became more and more difficult as America became increasingly youth-oriented. Old age became a "national problem" after 1908, and there are signs that another shift in the pattern of change in generational relations is emerging.

1245.   Fischer, David Hackett. Growing Old in America. Expanded ed. New York: Oxford University Press, 1978. This edition refines the argument of the author's original overview. This book directly challenges the relationship between (old) age and modernization by reviewing the first wave of historical studies on the topic. Fischer also offers a proposal for a new method of providing income support for the elderly.

1246.   Gold, Byron, Elizabeth Kutza, and Theodore R. Marmor. "United States Social Policy on Old Age: Present Patterns and Predictions." In Neugarten, Bernice L. and Robert J. Havighurst, eds. Social Policy, Social Ethics and Aging Society. Washington, D.C.: Government Printing Office, 1977, 9-21. A concise overview of the evolution and impact of federal programs since the passage of Social Security in 1935 with sensible, centrist predictions about the shape of welfare reform in the next decade.

1247.   Haber, Carole. Beyond Sixty-Five: The Dilemma of Old
Age in America's Past. New York: Cambridge University
Press, 1983. Based on the author's Ph.D. dissertation,
this book focuses on the views of doctors, charity
workers and social planners in the United States. It
traces the process by which changing roles and perceptions of old age were incorporated into geriatric
medicine, old-age welfare schemes, and mandatory-
retirement plans.

1248.   Holtzman, Abraham. "An Analysis of Old Age Politics in
the United States." Journal of Gerontology, Vol. 9, No.
1 (January 1954), 56-66. This essay sets forth reasons
why the aged probably would be unwilling and unable to
mobilize their resources to press for categorical social
welfare programs that might drain resources from other
age groups.

1249.   Hudson, Robert B. "The 'Graying' of the Federal Budget
and Its Consequences for Old-Age Policy." The
Gerontologist, Vol. 18, No. 5 (October, 1978), 428-40.
This essay assesses the rising proportion of the federal
budget allocated to providing health care and income
support to the aged. It suggests that this development
portends unfortunate consequences for the aged unless
our views of aging, the economic situation, or the political climate change.

1250.   Institute of Gerontology. American Values and the
Elderly. Final Project Report, Ann Arbor: Institute of
Gerontology, 1979. This interdisciplinary survey of the
shifts since 1930 in the normative foundations of federal welfare programs for the elderly underscores both
the advantages and limitations of using public opinion
poll data to measure changes in public support for such
programs. Some shifts of attitude are quite sharply
delineated; others are more difficult to detect, because
of inherent problems with making longitudinal inferences
from cross-sectional data that do not uniformly address
the same issues over time.

1251.   Kastenbaum, Robert. "Exit and Existence: Society's Un-
written Script for Old Age and Death." In, Van Tassel,
David D., ed. Aging, Death, and the Completion of
Being. Philadelphia: University of Pennsylvania Press,
1979, 69-94. An eminent gerontologist summarizes the
conflicting attitudes toward age that have prevailed
since ancient times, and thus have affected the manner
in which people individually and collectively respond to
the physical needs and economic vicissitudes of late
life.

1252.   Lubove, Roy. <u>The Struggle for Social Security,</u>
        <u>1900-1935</u>. Cambridge, Mass.: Harvard University Press,
        <u>1968</u>. This important study of the origins of the Social
        Security Act emphasizes the clash between those who be-
        lieved that the federal government had a responsibility
        to the aged poor and those who preferred to rely on vol-
        untary institutions. Lubove carefully dissects dif-
        ferences of opinion among reformers, government of-
        ficials, and the public at large.

1253.   Martel, Martin U. "Age-Sex Roles in American Magazine
        Fiction (1890-1955)". In Neugarten, Bernice L., ed.
        <u>Middle Age and Aging</u>. Chicago: The University of
        Chicago Press, 1968, 47-57. This essay suggests that
        there was a shift in authors' minds in the "prime of
        life" from mature middle age to youth in this content
        analysis of stories in four different periodicals pub-
        lished in the 65-year period surveyed. At the same
        time, the aged were increasingly disengaged from contact
        with younger characters. Martel attributes this shift
        to a loss of parental authority, a decline in familial
        obligations to extended kin, and the rise of urban-
        industrial mores.

1254.   Oriol, William E. "Modern Age and Public Policy." <u>The</u>
        <u>Gerontologist</u>, Vol. 21, No. 1 (February, 1981), 35-46.
        This essay by the former staff director of U. S. Senate
        Special Committee on Aging assesses major trends in fed-
        eral policy toward the aged during the last half-century
        paying particular attention to developments since the
        passage of the Older Americans Act (1965). Despite the
        current political climate and economic morass, Oriol is
        fairly sanguine about the proximate future.

1255.   Pratt, Henry J. <u>The Gray Lobby</u>. Chicago: University
        of Chicago Press, 1976. This political history traces
        the origins of the so-called "gray lobby" from the
        old-age associations lobbying for pensions in the 1920s
        and 1930s to the emergence of a politically savvy
        cluster of special-interest groups based in Washington,
        which have formulated a well-defined set of grievances
        and proposals for political reform. The book builds on
        theoretical insights derived from Robert Binstock and
        Theodore Lowi's theses about interest-group liberalism.

1256.   Pratt, Henry J. "Symbolic Politics and White House Con-
        ferences on Aging." <u>Society</u>, Vol. 15, No. 5
        (July/August, 1978), 67-72. Elaborating on themes set
        forth in Murray Edelman's <u>The Symbolic Uses of Politics</u>
        (1967), Pratt argues that the White House Conferences in
        1951, 1961, and 1971 not only served as vehicles for
        arousing support for specific and tangible benefits for
        the elderly, but also provided a means for "cooling out"
        malcontents by appearing to deal with the problems and

proposals.

1257.   Simmons, Leo W.   The Role of the Aged in Primitive
Societies.   New Haven: Yale University Press, 1945.
This is a classic anthropological study based on
Murdock's Human Relations Area Files.   Simmons argued
that there was an inverse relationship between the stage
of societal development and the level of care for the
dependent aged in pre-industrial cultures.   Though his
thesis has been modified by subsequent investigation,
his data remain useful.

1258.   Smith, Daniel Scott.   "Old Age and the 'Great Transformation.'".   In Sprickler, Stuart F., Kathleen M.
Woodward and David D. Van Tassel, eds. Aging and the
Elderly.   Atlantic Highlands, N.J.:   Humanities Press,
1978, 285-302.   In this case study of Hingham,
Massachusetts, from the late seventeenth to late nineteenth centuries, Smith attempts to assess the impact of
"modernization" on the meanings and experiences of old
age.   Though he finds that material conditions did not
improve considerably until the nineteenth century, he
cautions against a "whig" interpretation of the history
of old age: values and structure diverge consistently,
thus confounding any sweeping, linear interpretation of
trends.

1259.   Spicker, Stuart F., Kathleen M. Woodward, and David D.
Van Tassel, eds.   Aging and the Elderly: Humanistic
Perspectives in Gerontology.   Atlantic Highlands:
Humanities Press, 1978.   This collection of essays was
underwritten by the "Human Values and Aging" project directed by David Van Tassel at Case Western Reserve University.   In addition to the essays by Gruman,
Rosenkrantz and Vinovskis, Daniel Scott Smith, Stephen
Smith, and Lance Tibbles (which are cited individually
in this chapter), students of social welfare history
might be interested in David E. Stannard's "Growing Up
and Growing Old: Dilemmas of Aging in Bureaucratic
America."

1260.   Stearns, Peter N.   "Toward Historical Gerontology."
Journal of Interdisciplinary History, Vol. 8, No. 4
(Spring, 1978), 737-46.   This review of David H.
Fischer's Growing Old in America sharply criticizes the
periodization and use of evidence presented in the
study, and stresses the importance of establishing valid
historical baselines if policy experts are to create
realistic and effective social programs for the aged
today.

1261.   Van Tassel, David D., ed.   Aging, Death, and the
Completion of Being.   Philadelphia: University of
Pennsylvania Press, 1979.   This collection of essays by

luminaries in the humanities and gerontology sets forth
a rationale for humanistic perspectives in gerontology.
Besides the essay by Kastenbaum cited in this chapter,
students of social welfare history should read the contribution on the economics of aging by Juanita Kreps and
the essay on "Wild Strawberries" by Erik Erikson, which
deals with the psychological crises of late life.

1262.   Vinyard, Dale. "White House Conferences and the Aged."
         Social Service Review, Vol. 53, No. 4 (December 1979),
         655-71. Vinyard, a political scientist, offers a judi-
         cious critique of the historical role that the decennial
         White House Conferences have played in mobilizing sup-
         port for extensions and reforms in prevailing aging
         policies at the federal level. This essay should be
         read in conjunction with Pratt's work.

1.3. (AUTO)BIOGRAPHIES
      1263.   Brinkley, Alan. Voices of Protest. New York: A. A.
               Knopf, 1982. This is a judicious biography of the roles
               played by Huey Long and Father Coughlin in the midst of
               the Great Depression, but it is much more than that. By
               contrasting the federalist assumptions underlying
               Roosevelt's social welfare proposals with the radical
               proposals set forth by these two figures, Brinkley is
               able to offer fascinating generalizations about the
               nature and direction of old-age programs in the New Deal.

      1264.   Schlabach, Theron F. E. Edwin E. Witte: Cautious
               Reformer. Madison: State Historical Society of
               Wisconsin, 1969. This balanced biography of the "Father
               of Social Security" traces the life and career of Edwin
               Witte. Based extensively on archival materials,
               Schlabach demonstrates how well Witte handled issues and
               personalities involved in drafting and enacting the
               Social Security bill in 1935.

1.4. DOCUMENTARIES, INCLUDING WHITE HOUSE CONFERENCES ON AGING
      1265.   Bauman, John F. and Thomas H. Coode. "'Old Bill': A
               New Deal Chronicle of Poverty and Isolation in
               Southwestern Pennsylvania." Western Pennsylvania
               Historical Magazine, Vol. 63, No. 3 (July, 1980),
               215-29. This is an edited copy of a 1934 report by
               Henry Francis to Federal Emergency Relief Administrator
               Harry Hopkins. A major focus of the report is a summary
               of "'Old Bill's'" mixed attitude about accepting relief
               as he enters late life.

      1266.   Dinkel, Robert M. "Attitudes of Children Toward Sup-
               porting Aged Parents". American Sociological Review,

Vol. 9, No. 3 (August, 1944), 375-89. This essay surveys the mixed, and oftimes ambivalent and conflicting,
feelings expressed by middle-aged children about their
responsibilities toward their parents.

Dinkel is not certain what effect, if any, Social
Security might have on changing traditional intergenerational relations.

1267.   Gaydowski, J. D. "Eight Letters to the Editor: The
Genesis of the Townsend National Recovery Plan."
Southern California Quarterly, Vol. 52, No. 4 (December,
1970), 365-81. After providing a biographical sketch of
Dr. Francis E. Townsend, this article reprints eight of
Townsend's letters, written between September 1933 and
February 1934, which show the genesis of his National
Recovery Plan.

1268.   Hart, Ethel J. "The Responsibility of Relatives Under
State Old Age Assistance Laws." Social Service Review,
Vol. 16, No. 1 (March, 1941), 16-24. This essay suggests that Social Security and other public old-age assistance measures would create a more felicitous dimension to intergenerational relations because younger
people would be freed from much of the responsibility of
caring for their elders, and the aged would not be left
stranded if their kin defaulted.

1269.   McKinley, Charles and Robert Frase. Launching Social
Security. Madison: University of Wisconsin Press,
1970. This volume gives a detailed, almost day-to-day
summary of the administrative decisions and problems
handled by the initial cadre of officials charged with
putting the Social Security System into place between
1935 and 1937. The diary is well annotated.

1270.   National Conference on the Aging. Man and His Years:
An Account of the First National Conference on Aging.
Raleigh, N.C.: Health Publications Institute, 1951.
The Federal Security Agency convened the first national
conference on aging in Washington, D. C. in 1950.
During the 1930s and 1940s, there had been
inter-disciplinary meetings underwritten by the Macy
Foundation and the Public Health Service, but this was
the first public conference sponsored at the federal
level. This report summarizes major findings and
recommendations.

1271.   Roosevelt, Franklin Delano. "Review of Legislative Accomplishments of the Administration and Congress." In
U. S. Congress, house, 73d Cong., 2d Sess. (1934) House
Document 397. In this paper, Roosevelt set forth the
broad parameters for a nationwide relief system that became translated into the original Social Security Act.

1272. U.S. Congress. Senate. Committee on Labor and Public
       Welfare. Background Studies, 14 Vols. Washington, D.C.
       Government Printing Office, 1960.

1273. U.S. National Advisory Committee for the White House
       Conference on Aging. Background Papers, 20 Vols.
       Washington, D.C.: Government Printing Office, 1960.

1274. White House Conference on Aging. The Nation and Its
       Older People. Washington, D. C.: U.S. Department of
       Health, Education and Welfare, Special Staff on Aging,
       1961. The first White House Conference on AGing was
       held in January, 1961, during the last month of the
       Eisenhower administration. Federal officials, state and
       local administrators, biological and social scien-
       tists, representatives of business and union groups, and
       private agency officials concerned with the aged
       participated. From the list of recommendations and
       findings emerged much of the intellectual scaffolding
       for the War on Poverty initiatives that benefited the
       aged, such as the creation of an Administration on Aging
       and the passage of more liberal benefits under Social
       Security and the enactment of Medicare.

1275. White House Conference on Aging. Background and Issues,
       14 Vols. Washington, D.C.: White House Conference on
       Aging, 1971. Of particular interest are the reports on
       planning (by Robert H. Binstock), income (by Yung-Ping
       Chen), retirement (by James H. Schulz), physical and
       mental health (by Sustin B. Chinn, et al.), facilities
       and social services (by Robert Morris and Ruth Lauder),
       and housing (by Ira S. Robbins).

1276. White House Conference on Aging. Toward a National
       Policy on Aging: Proceedings, 2 Vols.. Washington,
       D.C.: U. S. Government Printing Office, 1973. The 1971
       White House Conference on Aging reviewed the progress
       made during the Great Society and called for measures
       that shortly led to the creation of the National In-
       stitute on Aging and more entitlements under Social
       Security, such as the Supplemental Security Income (SSI)
       program.

1277. White House Conference on Aging, Post Conference Board.
       Towards a New Attitude on Aging: Final Report.
       Washington, D.C.: U.S. Government Printing Office,
       1973. Eight years after the publication of this report,
       there was another White House Conference on Aging. The
       1981 conference was highlighted by considerable partisan
       politics, as delegates wrestled with the ramifications
       of Reaganomics for the aged. Although final reports
       were not available when this chapter was written (in
       August 1982), they should be forthcoming.

1.5.   CLASSIC CASE STUDIES
        1278.   Armstrong, Barbara N. Insuring the Essentials: Minimum
                 Wage Plus Social Insurance--A Living Wage. New York:
                 Macmillan, 1932. This is a detailed summary of American
                 and European developments in the field of social
                 insurance by the Berkeley law professor who was in
                 charge of formulating the original old-age insurance
                 provisions of the 1935 Social Security Act.

        1279.   Burns, Eveline M. The American Social Security System.
                 Boston: Houghton Mifflin, 1949. This is a shrewd an-
                 alysis of the strengths and limitations of the program
                 by a Columbia University professor of social work.
                 Burns is more critical of the unemployment provisions
                 than she is of the old-age programs.

        1280.   Committee on Economic Security. Social Security in
                 America: The Factual Background of the Social Security
                 Act as Summarized from Staff Reports to the Committee on
                 Economic Security. Social Security Board, Publication
                 no. 20. Washington, D.C.: Government Printing Office,
                 1937. This is a summary of the various research reports
                 done by the staff dealing with unemployment com-
                 pensation, old-age security, and children's rights as
                 well as a justification for federal involvement in
                 social welfare.

        1281.   Conant, Luther, Jr. A Critical Analysis of Industrial
                 Pension Systems. New York: Macmillan Co, 1922. A
                 careful survey of the major retirement and welfare pro-
                 grams available to workers in large American corpor-
                 ations prior to the creation of a nationwide public
                 network.

        1282.   Douglas, Paul H. Social Security in the United States.
                 New York: McGraw-Hill, 1936. An account of the ration-
                 ale and conditions culminating in the passage of the
                 Social Security Act by an economist and future U.S.
                 Senator. Douglas's recommendations for changes in the
                 initial program set the tone for the debate over the
                 1939 amendments, which sought to liberalize the welfare
                 provisions of the old-age insurance program by extending
                 coverage to the wives and children of potential bene-
                 ficiaries.

        1283.   Epstein, Abraham. Insecurity, A Challenge to America:
                 A Study of Social Insurance in the United States and
                 Abroad. New York: Random House, 1938. This work elab-
                 orates themes in the author's Facing Old Age: A Study
                 of Old Age Dependency in the United States and Old Age
                 Pensions (1922 reprint) and extends the analysis to in-

clude an assessment of the 1935 Social Security Act.

1284.   Hall, G. Stanley, Senescence. New York: D. Appleton & Co., 1922. The last magnum opus by the psychologist who wrote Adolescence, this study surveys the evidence on old age in literature, history, economics, and other social sciences. Attention is paid to social welfare developments in the United States and western Europe in order to accentuate the author's thesis that older people can play a vital role in maintaining and advancing their individual and collective well-being.

1285.   Havighurst, Robert J. and Ruth Albrecht. Older People. New York: Longmans, Green and Co., 1953. This is probably the best sociological overview of old age in America written in the 1950s. Its analysis of social welfare programs for the aged is comprehensive and balanced.

1286.   Klein, Philip, et al. A Social Study of Pittsburgh. New York: Columbia University Press, 1938. This update of the original Pittsburgh Survey offers a fine case study of the blend of individual, familial, corporate, local, state and federal resources available to older people in the 1930s--and documents how vulnerable each of these resources were during the national economic crisis.

1287.   Meriam, Lewis. Relief and Social Security. Washington, D.C.: Brookings Institution, 1946. This is the most thorough study of relief and old-age and unemployment insurance published to that date. Meriam discusses the significance of the British Beveridge plan on American policymaking in social welfare.

1288.   Rubinow, I. M. Social Insurance. New York: Henry Holt, 1913. One of the earliest studies of social insurance published, this work traces European developments and makes a case for provisions in the United States.

1.6.   TEXTBOOKS, READERS, BOOKS OF DOCUMENTS, BIBLIOGRAPHIES
1289.   Atchley, Robert C. The Social Forces in Late Life, 3rd ed. Belmont, CA: Wadsworth Publishing Co., 1980. This introduction to social gerontology not only offers judicious assessments of the accomplishments and deficiencies in contemporary social-service programs for older Americans, but it also includes valuable references to the current literature.

1290.   Bortz, Abe. Social Security Sources in Federal Records, 1934-1950. Social Security Administration Research

Report No. 30. Washington, D. C.: Government Printing
Office, 1969. An invaluable guide to archival resources, including photographic materials, pertinent to
the system's evolution by the Administration's official
historian.

1291.   Edwards, Willie M. and Frances Flynn, eds.
Gerontology: A Core List of Significant Works. Ann
Arbor: Institute of Gerontology, 1978. This compilation of more than 1,000 basic references was prepared by experts in the field for librarians, information specialists and individuals interested in developing collections on aging. Besides highlighting
works in social gerontology, the bibliography includes
dissertation abstracts, indexes and journals.

1292.   Freeman, Joseph T. Aging: Its History and Literature.
New York: Human Sciences Press, 1979. Freeman, a prac-
ticing geriatrician and a "dean" of modern gerontology
offers here a useful, annotated bibliography of major
references to old age in the history and literature of
western civilization since ancient times.

1293.   Haber, William and Wilbur J. Cohen, eds. Readings in
Social Security. New York, Prentice Hall, 1948. This
book of readings and documents traces major policy issues in Social Security legislation, including unemployment insurance as well as the old-age provisions.
Most of the articles were written between 1938 and
1948. Reinhold Hohaus's essay on the relation between
"equity" and "adequacy" merits special attention. A revised edition of this collection was published by R. D.
Irwin in 1960 under the title Social Security:
Programs, Problems and Policies. Both volumes deal with
health care issues prior to the enactment of Medicare
and Medicaid.

1294.   Hendricks, Jon and C. Davis Hendricks. Aging in Mass
Society, 2nd ed. Cambridge: Mass.: Winthrop Publishing, 1981. This introduction to social gerontology
has become a respected source of citations and "current"
views on various issues, including those dealing with
ways to ensure the elderly's health care and income support. The authors include cross-national data wherever
possible.

1295.   LeFevre, Carol and Perry LeFevre, eds. Aging and the
Human Spirit. Chicago: Exploration Press, 1981. This
collection of essays on religion and aging includes
several articles that describe the theological bases for
helping the aged needy and the ways various groups practiced what they believed.

1296.   Schulz, James. The Economics of Aging, 2nd ed.

Belmont, CA: Wadsworth Publishing Co., 1980. This is
the best introduction to the economics of late life currently available. Schulz includes separate chapters on
private pensions, Social Security, and work patterns of
men and women over 60. His prognosis for future developments and recommendations for reforming existing
programs should be taken seriously.

1297.   Shock, Nathan. Trends in Gerontology, 2nd ed.
Stanford: Stanford University Press, 1957. This work
provides major citations in the gerontological literature from the 1940s through the mid-1950s. Though most
of these references deal with bio-medical matters the
economics and sociology of aging are also considered.

1298   Stevens, Robert B., ed. Statutory History of the United
States: Income Security. New York: Chelsea House,
1970. This invaluable collection of documents traces
the evolution of federal involvement in the area of income maintenance. Stevens offers splendid commentaries.

1299.   U.S. Department of Health and Human Services, Social
Security Administration, Office of Research and
Statistics. Basic Readings in Social Security.
Washington, D.C.: Government Printing Office, 1980.
This annotated bibliography of 1,593 different references is an indispensable research tool. It includes
chapters that critique primary and secondary sources
dealing with provisions of the Social Security Act, international issues, congressional hearings, and other
reference materials.

2. PERIOD PIECES

2.1. COLONIAL

1300.   Boyett, G. W. "Aging in 17th-century New England." New
England Historical and Genealogical Register, Vol. 134
(July, 1980), 181-93. This essay summarizes recent work
in American colonial history that deals with the problems and challenges of growing old.

1301.   Demos, John. "Old Age in Colonial New England." In,
Gordon, Michael, ed. The Family in Social-Historical
Perspective, 2nd ed. New York: St. Martin's Press,
1978, 220-57. This important essay suggests that being
old was socially advantageous but psychologically problematic in colonial provinces. The argument rests on
the author's distillation of court records, demographic
data, public laws and literary evidence.

1302.   Faragher, John. "Old Women and Old Men in Seventeenth-Century Wethersfield, Connecticut." Women's Studies, Vol. 4, No. 1 (Spring, 1976), 11-31. Using family reconstitution techniques on 180 nuclear households from 1640-1700, this essay sets forth the demographic incidence of remarriage and widowhood. Particularly insightful is Faragher's emphasis of gender-specific roles, liabilities, and options.

1303.   Waters, John J. "Patrimony, Succession and Social Stability in Guilford, Connecticut in the Eighteenth Century." Perspectives in American History, Vol. 10 (1976), 131-60. On the basis of Guilford's extensive tax records, Waters calculates the longevity, marital age and family size of two cohorts born between 1659-1702 and 1702-1719 respectively. The data indicate that older people constituted not only a significant percentage of the tax rolls, but also a sizable proportion of the community's needy.

2.2.   REVOLUTIONARY AND EARLY NATIONAL

1304.   Malone, Dumas. Jefferson and His Time: The Sage of Monticello. Boston: Little, Brown and Company, 1981. In the sixth and last volume of his biography of Thomas Jefferson, Malone deals at length with the family relatonships, the extraordinary range of retirement activities as well as the increasing physical incapacities and financial difficulties that characterized the third President's declining years. While it would be inappropriate to treat Jefferson as a "representative man," Malone nonetheless does indicate the sorts of problems the aged faced and the ways they dealt with the issue of dependency in the early national period.

2.3.   ANTEBELLUM AND CIVIL WAR

1305.   Zimmerman, Michael. "Old Age Poverty in Preindustrial New York City." In Hess, Beth B. ed. Growing Old in America. New Brunswick, N.J.: Transaction Press, 1976, 81-84. After describing the institutional arrangements established to deal with old-age dependency between 1736 and 1810, Zimmerman details the activities of philanthropic groups, immigrant aid societies, trade associations and savings banks. He contends that the aged poor were not well cared for by their kin--an assertion that diverges strikingly from other scholars' findings and, possibly, his own data that indicate that the aged constituted only 1.8 percent of the city's almshouse population in 1823.

2.4. POSTBELLUM
1306.   Achenbaum, W. Andrew. "The Obsolescence of Old Age in
America, 1865-1914." Journal of Social History, Vol. 8,
No. 1 (Fall 1974), 45-64. This essay traces major
changes in American society and culture that led to increasingly negative attitudes about the worth of the
last stage of life. Passing reference is made to new
ways of dealing with old-age dependency.

1307.   Gruman, Gerald J. "C. A. Stephens (1844-1931)--Popular
Author and Prophet of Gerontology." New England Journal
of Medicine. Vol. 254 (April 5, 1956), 658-60. This
brief piece summarizes the contributions of one of the
oft-ignored proponents of new ideas and remedies to deal
with the age-specific maladies of late life.

1308.   Smith, Daniel Scott. "A Community Based Sample of the
Older Population from the 1880 and 1900 United States
Manuscript Censuses. Historical Methods Newsletter,
Vol. 11, No. 2 (Summer 1978), 67-74. This essay is of
considerable methodological interest to those who con-
template doing survey analyses of old age based on federal census data. Particularly interesting is the manner in which Smith and his colleagues attempted to identify kin relations and sources of friendly assistance
available to the elderly in a given locale.

2.5. PROGRESSIVE
1309.   Hareven, Tamara K. "The Last Stage." Daedalus, Vol.
105, No. 3 (Fall 1976), 13-27. This essay traces the
individual and household (demographic) bases, socio-
economic structural patterns and cultural trends that
led early twentieth-century social reformers to view the
last stage of life as a "problem" of rising magnitude.

2.6. THE 1920s AND THE GREAT CRASH

2.7. NEW DEAL AND WORLD WAR II
1310.   Altmeyer, Arthur J. "The Wisconsin Idea and Social
Security. Wisconsin Magazine of History, Vol. 42, No. 1
(Autumn 1958), 19-25. An account by the former commissioner of Social Security of the actors, the philosophies, and the events that shaped the Social Security
Act. The significance of the Commons approach to social
insurance is underscored.

1311.   Davis, Karen J. "The Birth of Social Security."

American Heritage, Vol. 30, No. 3 (April/May 1979), 38-51. This essay assesses the strength of liberal and conservative forces and personalities on Roosevelt and the Committee on Economic Security as they drafted the original Social Security bill. While the analysis offers few revisionist points, the illustrations are compelling, for they underscore the virulence of opposition to this fundamental piece of social welfare legislation.

1312.   Leotta, Louis. "Abraham Epstein and the Movement for Old Age Security." Labor History, Vol. 16, No. 2 (Summer, 1975), 364-82. A judicious critique of the thoughts and activities of one of the reformers who lobbied for some sort of federal relief for aged poor. Epstein's disappointment with the original Social Security Act is explained.

1313.   Leuchtenburg, William E. Franklin D. Roosevelt and the New Deal. New York: Harper Torchbooks, 1963. This standard textbook on the Roosevelt years emphasizes the conservative nature and limited impact of the Social Security Act in addressing the problem of old-age poverty.

1314.   Zimmerman, Tom. "Ham and Eggs, Everybody." Southern California Quarterly. Vol. 62, No. 1 (Spring, 1980), 79-96. This essay traces the history of one of the Depression era's last pension panaceas, the California State Retirement Life Payments Act. This plan was rejected by voters in 1938 and 1939 because of suspicions about the "Ham and Eggs" leadership, constitutional questions, and perceptions of economic realities.

2.8.   POSTWAR

1315.   Cottrell, Fred. "Governmental Functions and the Politics of Age." In Tibbitts, Clark, ed. Handbook of Social Gerontology. Chicago: The University of Chicagp Press, 1960, 624-65. A judicious survey of the politics of aging and existing local, state, and federal-level welfare programs for the aged prior to the initiatives implemented as part of Johnson's Great Society.

1316.   Cumming, Elaine and William Henry. Growing Old New York: Basic Books, 1961. The thesis of this book--that the process of "disengagement" is a natural and proper feature of growing old--has been repudiated by social gerontologists. Nonetheless, the data cited in this book remain useful for historians who want to get a sense of attitudes toward age then espoused by the "experts" designing welfare programs for the elderly.

1317.   Gordon, Margaret S. "Aging and Income Security." In

Tibbitts, Clark, ed., <u>Handbook of Social Gerontology</u>. Chicago: The University of Chicago Press, 1960, 208-62. A concise overview of public and private means of dealing with old-age poverty in the United States in the first half of the twentieth century. Some attention is paid to European antecedents and parallels.

1318.   Morgan, James N. <u>et al</u>. <u>Income and Wealth in the United States</u>. New York: McGraw Hill, 1962. This socio-economic survey of income in America underscores th low relative economic status of individuals over sixty-five and families with aged heads prior to the federal government's efforts to wage a War on Poverty.

1319.   Steiner, Peter O. and Robert Dorfman. <u>The Economic Status of the Aged</u>. Berkeley: University of California Press, 1957. As its title suggests, this monograph analyzes labor force patterns and welfare programs available to older people through the mid-1950s. This is a standard reference that provides reliable analyses.

1320.   Tibbitts, Clark, ed. <u>Handbook of Social Gerontology</u>. Chicago: University of Chicago Press, 1960. This collection of essays summarizes the "state of the art" in social gerontology from the end of World War II through the 1950s. The contributors were the leading experts in the fields of political science, economics, sociology, social work, anthropology, and family studies. Their essays therefore are useful to readers of this work because they serve as an important source of historical data for recent times.

2.9. GREAT SOCIETY

1321.   Cohen, Wilbur J. and Robert M. Ball. "Social Security Amendments of 1967 and Legislative History." <u>Social Security Bulletin</u>, Vol. 31, No. 2 (February 1968), 3-19. This is an excellent summary of the legislative amendments to the Social Security System proposed and implemented as part of the Great Society legislation. This essay also offers two insiders' hopes for future developments.

1322.   Orshansky, Mollie. "Counting the Poor: Another Look at the Poverty Profile." <u>Social Security Bulletin</u>, Vol. 28, No. 1 (January 1965), 3-25. This article is probably one of the most frequently cited products of the War on Poverty years, because it provided data in terms consonant with the Johnson's administration's working definitions of poverty. The aged's absolute and relative poverty status was particularly distressing.

1323.   Reich, Charles A.   "Midnight Welfare Searches and the Social Security Act." Yale Law Journal, Vol. 72, No. 7 (June, 1963), 1347-60. A discussion of the legalities of midnight searches—made without warrants to check on recipients' eligibility for public assistance in programs supported by federal funds—by a vigorous opponent of the practice, who argues that it contravenes the fourteenth amendment, and undermines the Act's original guarantee to protect the independence and integrity of the home.

2.10. THE CONTEMPORARY PERIOD

1324.   Binstock, Robert H.   "Federal Policy Toward the Aging—Its Inadequacies and Its Politics." National Journal, November 11, 1978, 1838-44. This essay, intended to provoke policy-makers charged with planning the 1981 White House Conference on Aging, exposes serious deficiencies in Medicare, income maintenance and social service programs for the aged.

1325.   Binstock, Robert H. and Martin A. Levin. "The Political Dilemmas of Intervention Policies." In Binstock, Robert H. and Ethel Shanas, eds. Handbook of Aging and the Social Sciences. New York: Van Nostrand Reinhold, 1976, 511-36. This essay provides a theoretical overview of the tactical advantages and limitations to the politics of interest-group liberalism vis-a-vis the aged.

1326.   Green, Brent, Iris A. Parham, Ramsey Kleff, and Marc Pilisuch, eds. "Old Age: Environmental Complexity and Policy Interventions. Journal of Social Issues, Vol. 36, No. 2 (Summer, 1980), 1-165. This special edition treats such diverse topics as the construction of reality (as it shapes ageism and labelling of the elderly) and living arrangements (including variations in rural/urban settings and the needs of the handicapped old). It stresses ways in which the socio-situational context affects the experiences and behavior of old people, as well as reactions of others to them.

1327.   Samuelson, Robert J.   "Busting the Budget: The Graying of America." National Journal, February 18, 1978, 255-60. This article graphically illustrated the extent to which welfare entitlements at the federal level were earmarked for the elderly population. Gerontologists criticized the piece because it viewed the aged as "problems," who drained resources rather than adding to the commonweal.

1328.   Tibbitts, Clark. "Can We Invalidate Negative Stereotypes of Aging?" Gerontologist, Vol. 19, No. 1 (February, 1979), 10-20. Many of the sources of confusion over issues of old-age dependency arise from stereotypic thinking about the elderly. This essay illustrates several misconceptions concerning the meanings and experiences of being old in America today, and reviews efforts to extirpate stereotypes in public opinion, in policy circles, and in the media.

1329.   Tibbles, Lance. "Legal and Medical Aspects of Competence in Old Age." In Spicker, Stuart F., Kathleen M. Woodward, and David D. Van Tassel, eds. Aging and the Elderly: Humanistic Perspectives in Gerontology. Atlantic Heights: N.J.: Humanities Press, 1978, 127-51. This essay explores the "catch-22" elements characteristic of our current attempts to define the incompetence of aged clients and patients. The piece identifies key ethical issues involved in any definition of "competence".

1330.   U. S. Senate, Special Committee on Aging. 1982. Developments in Aging-1981, 2 parts. Washington, D.C.: Government Printing Office. This is the most recent volume in a series of publications that are produced by the senate committee charged with proposing legislation to promote the well-being of older Americans. Typically, these volumes review current legislative trends, highlight past programmatic successes and deficiencies, include special commissioned reports, and cite important works in the literature.

1331.   Work in America Institute Policy Study. The Future of Older Workers in America. Scarsdale, N.Y.: Work in America Institute, Inc., 1980. This report assesses the economic and social forces that will facilitate the reentry of older people into the labor market and enable those who are currently working to maintain their jobs. The volume also discusses the constraints and institutional barriers limiting the aged's employment prospects. Thus, while this volume does not deal with old-age dependency per se, it does offer an important vantagepoint from which to consider salient issues.

3.   SALIENT VARIATIONS

3.1.   LOCAL, STATE, REGIONAL

1332.   Linford, Alton A. Old Age Assistance in Massachusetts. Chicago: University of Chicago Press, 1949. This case study reviews the political obstacles delaying passage of an old-age assistance program in this heavily industrial state. Much of the book analyzes administrative matters, such as eligibility rules, standards of assistance, the responsibility of children for their parents, and financing.

1333.   Putnam, Jackson K. Old-Age Politics in California:
From Richardson To Reagan. Stanford: Stanford University Press, 1970. Although it covers developments
during the first two-thirds of the twentieth century,
this book concentrates on the pension politics between
1933 and 1942. Putnam's analyses of Upton Sinclair's
EPIC campaign, the Townsendite reform drive, and the Ham
and Eggs movement are excellent. His thesis underscores
a connection between the politics of old-age welfare and
governors' capacity to survive and lead effectively.

3.2.   RACIAL/ETHNIC

1334.   Bieder, Robert E. and Christopher Plant. "Annuity
Censuses as a Source of Historical Research: The 1858
and 1869 Tonawanda Seneca Annuity Censuses." American
Indian Culture and Research Journal, Vol. 5, No. 3
(Fall, 1981), 33-46. Because of mutual suspicions among
federal and state census recorders and Indian leaders,
there are potential problems in using such data to assess the place of older people in Indian tribes. An-
nuities offer another source of information. Though annuity censuses do not give precise ages for anyone or
specify the sexes of children, this particular source
indicates that the number of Seneca households in-
creased--particularly the number of female-headed
ones--while the size of the average household declined
in the middle of the nineteenth-century. Hence, unlike
the prevailing American culture, older Indian women may
have enjoyed a degree of independence that whites rarely
attained.

1335.   Gelfand, Donald E. Aging: The Ethnic Factor. Boston:
Little, Brown, 1982. This overview of the ethnic composition of America's current aged population documents
the extent to which race and ethnicity influence the
likelihood that an older person will take advantage of
or gain access to federal and private welfare programs.

1336.   Pollard, Leslie, J. "Aging and Slavery: A
Gerontological Perspective." The Journal of Negro
History, Vol. 66,. No. 3 (Fall 1981), 228-34. Relying
heavily on material found in the works by Genovese,
Gutman, and other historians of slavery, Pollard contends that the reverence for age transplanted by the
first blacks from Africa persisted in the slave community over time. Hence, care for the aged sick was
well integrated into the social structure.

1337.   Pollard, Leslie J. "The Stephen Smith Home for the
Aged: A Gerontological History of a Pioneer Venture in

Caring for the Black Aged, 1864-1953." Unpublished Ph.D. Diss., Syracuse University, 1977. This dissertation is a case study of an old-age home for women founded in Philadelphia by blacks and Quakers. Besides reviewing administrative features (particularly those changes instituted by Hobart Jackson) and resident activities, it also analyzes the geographic makeup and original reasons that brought 2,220 people to its doors.

1338.   Smith, Daniel Scott, Michel Dahlin and Mark Friedberger. "The Family Structure of the Older Black Population in the American South in 1880 and 1900." Sociology and Social Research, Vol. 63, No. 4, (April, 1979), 544-65. This essay, based on a sample of older households drawn at the Newberry Library, offers a succinct overview of black demographic, household and economic conditions a century ago. Differences in black-white trends are highlighted.

3.3. GENDER-SPECIFIC

1339.   Brody, Elaine. "Women's Changing Roles, the Aging Family and Long-Term Care for Old People." National Journal, October 17, 1978, 1828-33. This essay suggests that changing marital and career patterns for women in America, as well as the rise of four-generation families, pose serious limitations to the nation's ability to rely on existing methods of caring for older people.

1340.   Roebuck, Janet and Jane Slaughter. "Ladies and Pensioners: Stereotypes and Public Policy Affecting Old Women in England, 1880-1940." Journal of Social History, Vol. 13, No. 1 (Fall, 1979), 105-14. Stereotypes, not biological or social "facts", provide the conceptual underpinning for most pension policies affecting widows and housewives during the period. Women have been viewed as a special group who were (erroneously) thought to be "old" before men. Comparison is made to the situation in America.

1341.   Stearns, Peter N. "Old Women: Some Historical Perspectives." Journal of Family History, Vol. 4, No. 1 (Spring, 1980), 44-57. It has become increasingly clear to social gerontologists that many of the problems of old-age dependency are gender specific. The nature and dynamics of women's experiences as they grow old(er), however, has not been well developed in the literature. Stearns cites and synthesizes most of the historical data generated in the 1970s, and sets forth recommendations for future study.

3.4. WIDOWHOOD

1342.   Chevan, A. and J. H. Korson. "The Widowed Who Live Alone." <u>Social Forces</u>, Vol. 57, No. 1 (January, 1972), 45-53. Because women are more likely to be dependent in late life than men, this essay is instructive not only for the demographic data it offers but also for the analysis of the contemporary evidence it sets forth.

1343.   Keyssar, Alexander. "Widowhood in Eighteenth-Century Massachusetts: A Problem in the History of the Family." <u>Perspectives in American History</u>, Vol. 8 (1974), 83-119. Population patterns, economic conditions, laws, and customs all created variations in the effects of the death of a married man on his family and community. Limitations in widows' property rights made aged women especially vulnerable. The family was the primary source of care.

1344.   Lopata, Helena Znaniecki. <u>Widowhood in an American City</u>. Cambridge, Mass.: Schenckman, 1973. This cross-sectional case study of contemporary widowhood in Chicago is the best available theoretical model for research on this topic.

3.5. CLASS

4. AGE-SPECIFIC AND LIFE-CYCLE STUDIES

4.1. OLD-AGE HOMES AND ASYLUMS

1345.   Butners, Astreda I. "Institutionalized Altruism for the Aged: Charitable Provisions for the Aged in New York City, 1865-1930." Unpublished Ph.D. Diss., Columbia University, 1980. Asking what function charity performed during a period of rapid industrialization and urbanization, Butners concludes that it provided a basis for social integration and acted as a stabilizing influence. And insofar as officials and experts viewed old age as a stage of decline and decay, the mission of almshouses and private homes increasingly became supplying custodial care.

1346.   Cetina, Judith G. "A History of Veterans' Homes in the United States, 1811-1930." Unpublished Ph.D. Diss., Case Western Reserve University, 1977. This important thesis recounts the major developments in the transformation of veterans homes as institutions for disabled volunteer soldiers into homes for aged men. It highlights distinctions people made over time between the federal government's responsibility for caring for soldiers and sailors in late life, and its duties to other aged dependents. In so doing, it offers new insights into the nature of the almshouses as a refuge for the aged.

1347.   Gold, J. and S. Kaufman. "Development of Care of Elderly: Tracing the History of Institutional Facilities." The Gerontologist, Vol. 10, No. 4 (Winter, 1970), 262-274. This article highlights red-letter dates in the history of institutions for the aged, particularly in the United States. On the basis of their survey, Gold and Kaufman noted that there was no inevitable historical reason why an institutional environment had to be a permanent-stay facility for the aged.

1348.   Haber, Carole. "The Old Folks at Home: The Development of Institutionalized Care for the Aged in Nineteenth-Century Philadelphia." Pennsylvania Magazine of History and Biography, Vol. 101, No. 2 (April, 1977), 240-57. Because of new images of age coming into vogue during the late 19th century, most elderly adults, on the basis of their age alone, became possible candidates for extensive private care. In response to this shift in attitudes, as well as increasing concern for bureaucratic procedures and medical innovations, old-age homes expanded their appeal and their goals as they aspired to become "modern" medical establishments.

1349.   Koff, Theodore H. Long-Term Care: An Approach to Serving the Frail Elderly. Boston: Little, Brown and Company, 1982. This volume provides an historical overview and concise analysis of contemporary trends in long-term care for the aged. Special attention is placed on developments since the enactment of Medicare and Medicaid in 1965. The last chapter offers a series of recommendations for reforms.

1350.   Rosenkrantz, Barbara G. and Maris A. Vinovskis. "The Invisible Lunatics: Old Age and Insanity in Mid-Nineteenth-Century Massachusetts." In, Spicker, Stuart F., Kathleen M. Woodward, and David D. Van Tassell, eds., Aging and the Elderly: Humanistic Perspectives in Gerontology. Atlantic Highlands, N.J.: Humanities Press, 1978, 95-125. On the basis of institutional records, this essay suggests that 19th-century Americans not only ignored the extent of old people among the insane, but they also denied the aged insane equal access to treatment. Most of the people who were in asylums past the age of 60 had grown old there. By the latter part of the century, when custodial functions took precedence over therapeutic intervention in asylums, the proportion of old people admitted to institutions began to rise.

1351.   Townsend, Clare. Old Age: The Last Segregation. New York: Grossman Publishers, 1971. This is the trade edition of Ralph Nader's Study Group Report on Nursing Homes. It traces the legislative history of the insti- tution since the Progressive era, recounts present day abuses of the elderly, describes institutional alter- natives established in other countries, and makes pro- posals for reforms in the United States.

4.2.   RETIREMENT PROGRAMS--PUBLIC AND PRIVATE

1352.   Cohen, Wilbur, J. Retirement Policies under Social Security. Berkeley: University of California Press, 1957. This study by one of the junior staff members who drafted the original Social Security Act--and who ulti- mately became Secretary of Health, Education and Welfare under Lyndon Johnson--offers a concise and cogent ac- count of the deliberately vague retirement provisions operative during the first two decades of the federal program.

1353.   Damon, Allan L. "Veterans' Benefits." American Heritage, Vol. 27, No. 4 (June, 1976), 49-53. This article summarizes the major scope, provisions and costs of veterans benefits since 1775. It emphasizes that three-quarters of all men who served in the military were still alive in 1975, thus underscoring the extent to which the veterans programs' health-care provisions will be used to care for World War II veterans.

1354.   Donahue, Wilma, Harold L. Orbach, and Otto Pollack. "Retirement: The Emerging Social Pattern." In Tibbitts, Clark, ed. Handbook of Social Gerontology. Chicago: The University of Chicago Press, 1960, 330-406. This essay surveys major trends in retirement made pos- sible by the enactment of private and public income maintenance programs since the 1930s. Questions of old-age dependency are explicitly addressed here.

1355.   Drucker, Peter F. The Unseen Revolution. New York: Harper & Row, 1976. This extended essay sets forth the thesis that workers' stake in private-pension funds has had the unanticipated but undeniable effect of adding a "socialist" dimension to contemporary American capi- talism. In elucidating this idea, Drucker also offers a cogent analysis of recent trends in old-age welfare.

1356.   Fogelson, Robert M. "The Morass: An Essay on the Public Employee Pension Program." In Rothman, David J. and Stanton Wheeler, eds. Social History and Social Policy. New York: Academic Press, 1981, 145-73. After

reviewing the underlying philosophy and financing mechanisms of retirement programs provided for fire and
police in urban centers, Fogelson warns that most existing systems are grossly underfunded and could collapse
by the end of the decade.

1357. Graebner, William. A History of Retirement: The
Meanings and Function of an American Institution,
1885-1978. New Haven: Yale University Press, 1980. In
this first full-length treatment of the history of retirement, Graebner suggests that the policy of providing
older workers with a pension was not so much a humanitarian gesture as it was an instrument of social control
to ensure efficiency in a capitalist marketplace. The
case studies of private and public pension plans inaugurated between 1890 and 1920 are particularly
insightful.

1358. Haber, Carole. "Mandatory Retirement in 19th Century
America." Journal of Social History, Vol. 12, No. 1
(Fall, 1979), 77-97. Anticipating the thesis set forth
in Graebner's monograph, Haber delineates the social,
economic and cultural factors that led to the in-
aguration of mandatory-retirement programs in "progressive" industries in late-nineteenth century America.

1359. King, Gail Buchwalter and Peter N. Stearns. "The Retirement Experience as a Policy Factor: An Applied History Approach." Journal of Social History, Vol. 14, No.
4 (Summer, 1981), 589-625. This essay should be read in
conjunction with William Graebner's A History of
Retirement. Together, they offer the best overview of
the ways older people responded and adapted to new programs that affected their job security, employment
prospects and economic well-being in late life.

1360. Mowrer, Sherwyn W. "An Historical Analysis of the
Michigan Public School Employees' Retirement System,
1915-1975." Unpublished Ph.D. Diss., University of
Michigan, 1976. This is a detailed analysis of the administrative and legislative operations of the Michigan
system for retired school personnel. Its discussion of
the current funding shortfall is particularly
interesting.

1361. Schlabach, Theron F. Pensions for Professors. Madison,
Wis.: State Historical Society of Wisconsin, 1963. A
brief account of the stormy early years of the Carnegie
Foundation for the Advancement of Teaching, established
in 1905 with a $10 million endowment in order to attract
the ablest people to the teaching profession—a story of
institutional controversy, one which provides an inside
view of competing educational philosophies, the motives
and methods of the contenders, and a behind-the-scenes

glimpse of the shaping of the official policy of a leading American foundation.

1362.   Sheppard, Harold L. "Work and Retirement." In Binstock, Robert H. and Ethel Shanas, eds. Handbook of Aging and the Social Sciences. New York: Van Nostrand Reinhold, 1976, 286-309. This summarizes the major themes in The Graying of America, (Free Press, 1977), by Sheppard and Sarah Rix. In both works, the former Counsellor on Aging in the Carter administration synthesizes the literature on work patterns of the aged and assesses the relative likelihood that major changes in work patterns will take place during the next half-century.

4.3.   SOCIAL SECURITY

1363.   Achenbaum, W. Andrew. "Did Social Security Attempt to Regulate the Poor?" Research on Aging, Vol. 2, No. 4 (Winter, 1980), 270-88. After assessing the value of Piven and Cloward's interpretation of the rationale and initial impact of the Social Security Act in the United States, which was presented in Regulating the Poor (1971) this essay sets forth an alternative conceptual framework. Achenbaum argues that the origins of this measure can only be understood by reconstructing the operating assumptions and socio-historical constraints that policy-makers confronted at the time.

1364.   Altmeyer, Arthur J. The Formative Years of Social Security. Madison: Univ. of Wisconsin Press, 1966. Altmeyer served as a chief planner and administrator of the fledgling Social Security Sytem from 1934 to 1954. This volume recounts the author's impressions of the major personalities and issues of the era.

1365.   Bane, Frank. "The Social Security Expands." Social Service Review, Vol. 13, No. 6 (December, 1939), 608-609. This essay presents a judicious, centrist interpretation of the significance of the 1939 amendments to the Social Security Act, which extended old-age retirement benefits to employees' dependents.

1366.   Bortz, Abe. Social Security Sources in Federal Records, 1934-1950. Social Security Administration Research Report No. 30. Washington D.C.: U.S. Government Printing Office, 1969. This research guide to Social Security programs in the U.S. discusses the location and availability of federal records including the Committee on Economic Security and the files of the Social Security Board.

1367.   Brown, J. Douglas. An American Philosophy of Social

<u>Security</u>. Princeton: Princeton University Press, 1972. Written by one of the architects of the Social Security Act, this collection of essays merits attention. It presents cogent analyses of the implications of choosing between public and private means of helping the aged and of determining the proper mix between "adequacy" and "equity".

1368. Brown, J. Douglas. <u>Essays on Social Security</u>. Princeton: Princeton University Press, 1977. These essays amplify themes set forth in Brown's earlier work, and refer specifically to developments since the passage of the Supplemental Security Income program (1974), which affect the normative foundations of Social Security.

1369. Derthick, Martha. <u>Policy-making in Social Security</u>. Washington, D. C.: Brookings Institution, 1979. This distinguished monograph traces the evolution of the Social Security System during its first four decades by focussing on the explicit goals and hidden agendas of the elite group of academics and bureaucrats who ensured its well-being in the government maze. As such, it offers a cogent analysis of the politics of interest-group liberalism in its heyday.

1370. Hohaus, Richard. "Equity, Adequacy and Related Factors in Social Security." In Haber, William and Wilbur J. Cohen, eds. <u>Readings in Social Security</u>. Englewood Cliffs, N.J.: Prentice-Hall 1948. This article, written by a senior actuary at Metropolitan Life Insurance Company who frequently did consulting for the Social Security Board, set forth the major implications of philosophical tension between equity and adequacy in the federal government's old-age insurance program.

1371. Munnell, Alicia. <u>The Future of Social Security</u>. Washington, D.C.: Brookings Institution, 1977. The most important feature of this economic study are the distinctions Munnell draws among horizontal, vertical and intergenerational equity. Her point, quite simply, is that no federal old-age insurance program can satisfy all three definitions of equity simultaneously.

1372. Myers, Robert J. <u>Social Security</u>, 2nd ed. Homewood, Ill.: Richard D. Irwin, 1981. A fact-crammed but readable assessment of the actuarial and economic bases of the Social Security System and critique of various reform measures by a long-time Social Security actuary who subsequently was appointed by Reagan to serve as executive director of the National Commission on Social Security Reform.

1373. Pechman, Joseph, Henry J. Aaron, and Michael K.

Taussig. Social Security: Perspectives for Reform. Washington, D.C.: Brookings Institution, 1968. This often quoted work offers sets of recommendations encompassing immediate action, short-term options, and long-range goals for reforming the federal old-age insurance programs. Though most of these recommendations deal with the system as it operated prior to the enactment of the Supplemental Security Income program, the philosophical questions and economic issues raised here remain salient.

1374.   Phillips, Norma Kolko. "Social Work, Government and Social Welfare: The Social Security Act." Unpublished D.S.W. Diss., Yeshiva University, 1981. On the basis of the "Proceedings" of the American Association of Social Workers (1934-38) and articles in Social Work Today and Compass, Phillips traces the ideological and institutional tradeoffs that transpired between social workers and federal officials after the passage of Social Security.

1375.   Schiltz, Michael E. Public Attitudes toward the Social Security, 1935-1965. Social Security Administration Research Report No. 3. Washington, D.C.: Government Printing Office, 1970. This report summarizes public opinions about the need and legitimacy of Social Security during its first three decades. Schiltz documents that the program enjoyed overwhelming (90 percent and more) popularity from the start. Pressed on elementary facts about how the system worked, however, Americans expressed considerable ignorance about the program they so enthusiastically endorsed.

1376.   Schottland, Charles I. The Social Security Program in the United States. New York: Appleton-Century-Crofts, 1963. A brief but unanalytical summary of the major features of the system by a former Social Security commissioner. In his conclusion, Schottland proposes several ways to reform and expand entitlements.

1377.   Stearns, Peter N. "Political Perspective on Social Security Financing." In Skidmore, Felicity, ed. Social Security Financing. Cambridge, Mass.: MIT Press, 1981, 173-224. This essay treats current debate over the best way to finance income maintenance programs for the elderly in advanced industrial societies as an issue in historical political economy. The piece is especially effective in identifying points of convergence and divergence among various special-interest groups in labor, business, government, and the aged themselves.

1378.   Tufte, Edward R. Political Control of the Economy. Princeton: Princeton University Press, 1978. This monograph uses the rationale and timing behind various increases in benefits under the Social Security program to illustrate that amendments to social welfare programs do more than assist the aged. Very often, they are used to stimulate economic growth or reduce unemployment--and thereby consolidate the political advantages of incumbency.

1379. U.S. Department of Health, Education and Welfare. Social Security Bulletin, ser. (1937--). This monthly periodical summarizes statistical data on the scope and costs of the Social Security System. It also includes articles that evaluate existing strengths and weaknesses in the current program, assesses future options, and treats other timely topics.

1380. Witte, Edwin. The Development of the Social Security Act. Madison: The University of Wisconsin Press, 1962. This is another valuable memoir dealing with the formative years of the system by the chair of Committee on Economic Security, which drafted the initial enabling legislation. Witte quite candidly describes the considerable political infighting that transpired in 1934 and 1935.

4.4. MEDICARE AND OTHER HEALTH-CARE PROGRAMS

1381. Davis, Karen and Cathy Schoen. Health and the War on Poverty. Washington, D.C.: Brookings Institution, 1978. A judicious and insightful assessment of major developments in the planning and execution of health-care programs of older Americans since the enactment of Medicare and Medicaid in 1965. While supporting the notion that the federal government bears major responsibility in this area, the authors nonetheless suggest new ways to ensure a more equitable distribution of social services for minorities and low-income persons at the local level.

1382. Marmor, Theodore R. The Politics of Medicare. Chicago: Aldine-Atherton, 1973. This is the best history of the debate over establishing a federal health-care program for the aged currently available. Marmor is especially effective in elucidating the (mis)uses of images of age and data on the elderly's socio-economic conditions to advance the case for Medicare in 1965.

1383. Shanas, Ethel and George L. Maddox. "Aging, Health, and the Organization of Health Resources." In Binstock, Robert H. and Ethel Shanas, eds. Handbook of Aging and the Social Sciences. New York: Van Nostrand Reinhold, 1976, 592-618. Building on the framework set forth in Shanas's The Health of Older People. (Cambridge,

Mass.: Harvard Univ. Press, 1962), this article fairly summarizes major dimensions of health-care in this nation. By paying attention to ethnic and racial variations in access to services, and by making frequent comparisons to European systems, the authors are able to focus on major strengths and weaknesses in social programs that have evolved since the passage of Medicare and Medicaid.

1384.   Somers, Herman M. and Anne R. Somers. Medicare and the Hospitals. Washington, D.C.: Brookings Institution, 1967. This monograph assesses the initial impact of the federal health-care program on the financing and operation of private hospitals. Chapter one provides a useful historical overview. The gist of later chapters has become overtaken by events, and students would do well to read the monograph by Karen Davis and Cathy Schoen.

4.5.   FAMILY RELATIONS AND PUBLIC POLICY
1385.   Anderson, Michael. "The Impact on the Family Relationships of the Elderly of Changes since Victorian Times in Governmental Income-Maintenance Provision." In Shanas, Ethel and Marvin B. Sussman, eds. Family, Bureaucracy and the Elderly. Durham: Duke University Press, 1977, 36-59. This essay effectively demolishes the overly simplistic hypothesis that introducing public income maintenance provisions undermines family relationships. Indeed, as cash support functions diminish in importance, the reciprocal exchanges possible in generational relationships become less fraught with tension, thereby improving the "quality" of ties.

1386.   Chudacoff, Howard P. and Tamara K. Hareven. "From the Empty Nest to Family Dissolution: Life Course Transitions into Old Age." Journal of Family History, Vol. 4, No. 1 (Spring 1979), 69-83. This essay deals with the ways that men and women experienced transitions in the work lives, household arrangements and family organization as they entered old age. An analysis of census data from Providence, R.I. in 1865, 1880, and 1900 indicates that the aged at those times might have experienced less residential and functional isolation than obtains today.

1387.   Dahlin, Michel R. "Perspectives on the Family Life of the Elderly in 1900." The Gerontologist, Vol. 20, No. 1 (February 1980), 99-107. This essay offers a succinct summary of the aged's modal demographic and socio-economic conditions in the United States at the beginning of the century. Of particular importance is Dahlin's data on variations in family-network patterns by region, race, gender, and place of birth.

1388.   Foner, Anne. "Age Stratification and the Changing
Family." In Demos, John and Sarane Spence Boocock, eds.
Turning Points: Historical and Sociological Essays on
the Family. Chicago: The University of Chicago Press,
1978, 340-65. In the nineteenth and twentieth centuries, conflict across generations intermingles with
affection and cooperation. The forces of cohesion in-
teract with factors exacerbating conflict in a dialec-
tical manner: hence, while economic interdependence no
longer is an essential ingredient contributing to family
solidarity, the reduction in this area also removes a
source a tension between generations.

1389.   Hareven, Tamara K. "Historical Changes in the Life
Course and the Family: Policy Implications for the
Aged". Testimony in Joint Hearing before the Select
Committee on Population, U.S. House of Representatives
and the Select Committee on Aging, 95th Cong., Vol. 1,
No. 9. (Washington, D.C. Government Printing Office,
May 24, 1978). Reviewing major theoretical insights derived from her own research and other pioneers in the
field of family history, Hareven argued against the creation of a single, all encompassing family-policy program at the federal level. Such a stance, she claims,
could not embrace the variety of cultural assumptions,
economic factors and fluid demographic conditions that
have long affected the elderly's family networks.

1390.   Schorr, Alvin. "...Thy Father & Thy Mother": A Second
Look at Filial Responsibility & Family Policy.
Washington, D.C.: Social Security Administration,
1980. This is an elegant survey of the continuing importance and inherent conflicts in intergenerational
relations in the United States during the last
half-century. The "family" has not become forgotten;
people's attitudes toward their aged kin are not shaped
in direct response to the existence of federal social
programs. But perennial ambiguities and ethnic and
racial variations nonetheless persist.

1391.   Shanas, Ethel and Philip Hauser. "Zero Population
Growth and the Family Life of Old People." Journal of
Social Issues, Vol. 30, No. 4 (Winter, 1974), 79-92. If
zero population growth occurs in the United States by
2028, there will be an increase in the proportion of
aged people living alone, and the female:male imbalance
will widen. Under such circumstances, the federal
government will need to bear a greater share of the cost
of housing, recreation, health care and income maintenance.

1392.   Shanas, Ethel. "Family-Kin Networks and Aging in
Cross-Cultural Perspective." Journal of Marriage and

the Family, Vol. 35, No. 3 (August 1973), 505-11. On
the basis of cross-national data from Denmark, Britain,
Yugoslavia, Poland, Israel and the United States, this
essay documents that America's elderly, like those in
other countries, derive their primary support from their
family and kin networks.

1393.   Smith, Daniel Scott. "Life Course, Norms, and the
Family System of Older Americans in 1900." Journal of
Family History, Vol. 4, No. 3 (Fall 1979), 285-98. On
the basis of his subtle demographic analysis, Smith
demonstrates that the family was the chief welfare institution for older people in 1900. Demographic realities (such as comparatively high fertility rates and
relatively few men and women over 65) and prevailing
norms, however, also reduced the impact of the aged's
living patterns on the rest of the population.

1394.   Streib, Gordon F. and William E. Thompson. "The Older
Person in a Family Context." In, Tibbitts, Clark, ed.
Handbook of Social Gerontology. Chicago: The University of Chicago Press, 1960, 447-88. This is the best
synopsis   of   intergenerational   relations   and   the
elderly's household patterns in the United States during
the period between the original enactment of the Social
Security program and the late 1950s. As such, it serves
as an important resource for those attempting to analyze
continuities and changes in family relationships that
affect the handling of old-age dependency in "modern"
America.

5. THE AMERICAN EXPERIENCE IN COMPARATIVE PERSPECTIVE
1395.   Conrad, Christoph. "Altwerden und Altsein in his-
torischer   Perspektive   Zur   neueren   Literature."
Zeitschrift   Fur   Sozialisationsforschung   und
Erzeihungssoziologie, Vol. 2, No. 1 (January, 1982),
73-90. This article offers a critique of the recent
literature on the history of old age from the perspective of a German social historian who is familiar
with recent American historiography. What makes the essay particularly interesting is Conrad's review of work
in Austria, Switzerland, and West Germany, which few
British or American scholars have tapped.

1396.   Gruman, Gerald J. "Cultural Origins of Present-day
'Ageism': The Modernization of the Life Cycle." In
Spricker, Stuart F., Kathleen M. Woodward, and David D.
Van Tassel, eds. Aging and the Elderly. Atlantic Highlands, N.J.: Humanities Press, 1978, 359-87. Though
this essay deals only tangentially with social-welfare
issues, it nonetheless provides a compelling argument
for why late 19th century American and European ob-

servers viewed old age with dread, and considered the elderly's socio-economic status to be increasingly problematic.

1397.   Kohler, Peter A., Hans F. Zacher, and Martin Partington, eds. The Evolution of Social Insurance, 1881-1981. New York: St. Martin's Press, 1982. This collection of essays traces the development of social insurance programs in Austria, France, Germany, Great Britain, and Switzerland. Each essay blends the author's theoretical perspectives with a detailed recounting of the historical record. No effort has been made to synthesize the various case studies, though passing references are made to the American experience.

1398.   Laslett, Peter. "Societal Development and Aging." In Binstock, Robert H. and Ethel Shanas, eds. Handbook of Aging and the Social Sciences. New York: Van Nostrand Reinhold, 1976, 87-116. This article offers a demographic overview of the aged in western European society from the sixteenth to the twentieth centuries. Considerable attention is paid to British developments; passing references are made to conditions in the United States. Laslett's discussion of changes in the family's role in providing old-age assistance merits reading.

1399.   Laslett, Peter. "The History of Aging and the Aged". In idem. Family Life and Illicit Love in Earlier Generations, Cambridge: Cambridge University Press, 1977. This essay amplifies Laslett's data and hypotheses in his contribution to the Handbook on Aging and the Social Sciences. The ideal situation, in past and present times, is for the aged to have a place of their own, with access to their children, and within reach of support. This ideal, however, was difficult to obtain in traditional England; it was nearly impossible elsewhere.

1400.   Myles, John F. "Comparative Public Policies for the Elderly: Frameworks and Resources for Analysis." Unpublished paper prepared for the annual meetings of the Gerontological Society of America and the Canadian Association of Gerontology, in Toronto, November 1981. This paper set forth the main lines of the argument that Myles intends to elaborate in his contribution to the Little, Brown series on Gerontology, The Political Economy of Pensions. Relying on cross-national data and building a neo-Marxist conceptual framework, Myles assays to put public income maintenance programs into a broader context than do most social scientists.

1401.   Philibert, Michel. L'echelle des ages. Paris: Le Seuil, 1968. In describing continuities and changes in

images of aging in French culture and society since
medieval times, Philibert deals at length with the assumptions and practices of those charged with caring for
the poor. Sometimes the author underscores his points
by referring to similarities and differences in the
American situation.

1402.   Roebuck, Janet. "When Does Old Age Begin?: The
Evolution of the English Definition." Journal of Social
History, Vol. 12, No. 3 (Spring 1979), 416-28. Establishing an official, national definition of old age only
became an important question when people began to lobby
for state-sponsored old-age pension programs in the
1880s and 1890s. Heretofore, any age past 40 seemed
reasonable. By the end of the century, most commentators chose a figure between 60 and 75, but there
was yet no universal agreement. Roebuck notes the
relevance of this case study to the American experience.

1403.   Shanas, Ethel and Associates. Old People in Three
Industrial Societies. New York: Atherton Press, 1968.
This comparison of the health, income, and well-being of
men and women over sixty-five in Britain, Denmark and
the United States is a model of cross-national survey
research. The introductory chapter by Shanas and the
final summary section by Peter Townsend should be read
by all interested in social welfare issues affecting the
aged.

1404.   Stearns, Peter N. Old Age in European Society. New
York: Holmes and Meier, 1977. This first monograph on
the history of old age in Western Europe emphasizes the
developments in France. In a series of essays on medical perceptions of old age, as well as older people's
socio-economic status and dependency rates, Stearns contends that the process of modernization made the
elderly's already problematic status—ageism apparently
was more pervasive in France than in Britain and America
at the time—worse. After World War I, the elderly's
situation began to improve as new cultural and
structural forces took hold.

1405.   Stearns, Peter N. "The Modernization of Old Age in
France: Approaches Through History." International
Journal of Aging and Human Development, Vol. 13, No. 4
(Winter 1981), 297-315. This essay refines the argument
set forth in his Old Age in European Society in light of
subsequent research, including recent studies on the
history of age in the United States. Here, he
emphasizes the messiness of the historical process and
warns historians not to confuse precedents for
prevailing trends in discussing developments in the area
of social welfare.

1406.   Stone, Lawrence. "Walking over Grandma." New York
         Review, Vol. 24 (May 12, 1977), 26-29. In the course of
         a fairly negative assessment of the evidence and inter-
         pretation in David H. Fischer's Growing Old in America,
         Stone offers his interpretation of major developments in
         old-age dependency over time, based primarily on his re-
         search in family history and grasp of English history.

1407.   Thomas, Keith. "Age and Authority in Early Modern
         England." In Proceedings of the British Academy, Vol.
         62 (London, 1977), 205-248. This essay is primarily
         concerned with the status and prestige accorded older
         people in England prior to the Industrial Revolution.
         This essay was used by Fischer, among others, to suggest
         that the aged did enjoy prestige because of their pre-
         sumed understanding of the place of humans in the divine
         order. As such, it helps to put the American colonial
         experience into historical context.

1408.   von Kondratowitz, Hans-Joachin. "Zum Historischen
         Wandel   der   Altersposition   in   der   Deutschen
         Gessellschaft." Unpublished essay prepared for the 1982
         United Nation's World Conference on Aging, Vienna,
         August 1982. This essay offers an elaborate theoretical
         framework for understanding shifts in the status of the
         aged due to the impact of modernization on German so-
         ciety in particular and in advanced industrial societies
         (like the U.S.A.) in general. Careful attention is paid
         to the issue of old-age pauperism, especially the role
         that family members play in assisting the aged.

1409.   Wilensky, Harold L. The Welfare State and Equality:
         Structural   and   Ideological   Roots   of   Public
         Expenditures. Berkeley: University of California
         Press, 1975. This cross-cultural comparison of the wel-
         fare programs and costs in 64 countries uses Social
         Security as a test case to explore why various systems
         differ. Without discounting the interrelationships
         among economic systems, political patterns, and cultural
         values, Wilensky concludes that a country's demographic
         structure is the best predictor of the sort of welfare
         system it establishes.

1410.   Wilson, Richard Raymond. "The Corporatist Welfare
         State: Social Security and Development in Mexico." Un-
         published Ph.D. Diss., Yale University, 1981. This case
         study of the Mexican Social Security System, originally
         enacted in 1943, exposes flaws in theories that suggest
         that this program reflects a new stage of
         "modernization" or results from a desire to reduce
         worker conflict. Wilson compares the American and
         Mexican experiences.

Epilogue

AN AGENDA FOR FUTURE RESEARCH IN AMERICAN SOCIAL WELFARE HISTORY

W. Andrew Achenbaum
Carnegie-Mellon University

When the editors initially decided to prepare an annotated bibliography of American social welfare history, we anticipated that the final product would not exceed two hundred manuscript pages. Obviously, we underestimated the amount of significant work that has been undertaken during the past twenty years.[1] If the quality and quantity of the references cited here are a valid measure, it is evident that American social welfare historians already have generated a good deal of first-rate research. Indeed, the field shows every indication of growing even more important in the future.

The following agenda for future research in American social welfare history provides suggestions about topics and issues that await intensive and extensive examination. The comments and remarks are organized with the users of this volume in mind. On the basis of entries in Chapters One through Six, gaps that currently exist in the literature—periods and subjects that have not been sufficiently treated by professional historians—have been highlighted. Future researchers cannot limit themselves, however, to investigating areas or utilizing the methods that presently are in vogue. Practitioners of social welfare history should take cues from those engaged in other fields and subfields of history. The conceptual breakthroughs and methodological innovations advanced by the so-called new social, cultural, economic, political, public, and applied historians as well as by those who engage in comparative research deserve consideration. Accordingly, I have indicated areas in which the concerns of social welfare historians and other scholars converge and where appropriate, I have cited articles and books that might serve as catalysts, and possibly even models, for subsequent investigations.[2]

FILLING IN THE GAPS

Many historians suffer from "period bias." They think of their work—

and their contributions are often judged—in terms of the insights they offer about a specific time frame in American history. An appropriate way to begin this assessment of American social welfare historiography, therefore, is to note that scholars have not devoted the same amount of effort in reconstructing successive periods of American history. The literature on welfare ideas and provisions during the colonial period, for instance, is large. This certainly is not surprising, since much of the truly pathbreaking work in American history has been executed during the past two decades by specialists working with colonial data—county and provincial census returns, wills, court proceedings, church records and sermons, and other written testimonies. Similarly, scholars have concentrated on developments that reflected and resulted from ideals and practices set into motion during the Progressive era, the New Deal, and the Great Society. These moments in our twentieth-century national experience, of course, were characterized by great "reformist" impulses initiated by leaders wielding power in state and federal government as well as by crusaders and innovators operating in the private sector. Insofar as legislation and programs enacted during the early twentieth century, 1930s, and 1960s established crucial precedents for subsequent social welfare policies, historians' preoccupation with these periods is understandable.

That said, it quickly must be added that we know remarkably little about major developments in welfare history that took place during several other phases of the national experience. The years between 1776 and 1865 constitute the broadest (chronologically speaking), and possibly the most promising, arena for future research. This bibliography reveals that we desperately need case studies for the years between the Revolutionary and Civil wars that concentrate on regional variations in caring for children, youth, female heads of household, and the elderly. Three periods in twentieth-century American history, moreover, require greater attention than they have received to date. Developments during the 1920s have received surprisingly little attention: we must move beyond studies that describe overarching trends and focus on seminal welfare-reform figures, and begin to analyze age-specific welfare developments that extended Progressive methods and anticipated New Deal principles. Furthermore, future investigators would be well advised to elaborate themes enunciated in Edward Berkowitz and Kim McQuaid's *Creating the Welfare State* and James Patterson's *America's Struggle Against Poverty, 1900-1980*. They should assess the degree to which new theories set forth by academic researchers and welfare-capitalist initiatives inaugurated by the private sector between 1945 and

1960 set the stage for Lyndon Johnson's War on Poverty. Finally, historians should begin to join the debate over the historical significance of the 1970s. Do the welfare reforms proposed by Nixon, Ford, and Carter signal a reaction against the Great Society? How did they set the stage for Reaganomics? Or, did the reforms proposed after 1972 arise from broader fissures in the political economy, stemming from a growing lack of confidence in Washington's ability to govern amidst stagflation at home and crises abroad? Alternatively, do they constitute a transitional moment in which the politics of interest-group liberalism associated with the welfare state became firmly established in American society? Does the welfare bureaucracy now operate in accordance with its own systemic logic and dynamics—that is, independent of other macroeconomic priorities and international constraints?

The ebb and flow of activity in American social welfare activities during the twentieth century seems to demand the formulation of an ambitious interpretive model for studying developments throughout the entire "modern" period. A possible model already has been set forth by Albert O. Hirschman, who argues that marked alterations in collective behavior conform to a cyclical pattern of swinging from the pursuit of private ambitions to concerted public interests that has characterized Western nations for centuries.[3] The mainspring for this long-term trend, hypothesizes Hirschman, is the disappointments that motivate both consumers and citizens to change preferences and actions as they become disenchanted with the diminishing pleasure they derive from specific types of experience alternately in public and private spheres.

As we turn from an assessment of the chronological materials and period pieces listed in sections 1 and 2 in the different chapters to a review of the references cited under "Salient Variations" (section 3), a different set of research problems and approaches suggests itself. Specific case studies of New England, the Middle Atlantic states, and the South exist, but little has been written about developments west of the Mississippi during *any* period of our nation's history. Comparative studies of the American experience—not simply across national boundaries and cultures, but also within the United States—are necessary.[4] Why, for instance, did certain territories have more progressive welfare laws than states that had more resources and a longer tradition of commitment in this area? To what extent did innovations in one state or region affect developments elsewhere?

Furthermore, the recent interest in black studies and women's history has produced a spate of splendid articles on needy blacks and dependent women, but there are few studies dealing with Indians or the Spanish-speaking population. Though the historical record probably will produce a tale of neglect and deprivation, it is imperative that we determine the extent to which this is actually the case. Once we know more about the distinctive features of these and other subgroups in the population, then social welfare historians will have to engage in comparative studies that seek to account for marked racial, ethnic, and religious variations within the American experience.

Above all, it is clear that social welfare historians should pay more attention to possible class variations in welfare provisions. Few investigators have incorporated a Marxist framework to analyze historical trends in American welfare. Since poor people's needs and disadvantages often result from flaws in the evolution of American society itself, however, such a mode of analysis seems fruitful. Most mainline Marxists portray efforts to "regulate the poor" through welfare provisions as an inevitable result of the State's overriding need to protect, sustain, and advance capitalist economic structures.[5] Even those who eschew Marxist interpretations of the American past consider "class" a salient determinant of differences in popular attitudes and social patterns among the population at any given point in time. Both public and private responses in this country to those in need always have been colored by the existence of a ranking system in which it was possible to move up and down the social ladder. But so far, they have been unable to make a compelling case for the extent to which class factors outweigh—much less diverge from—the impact of age, gender, race, or ethnicity.[6]

SOCIAL WELFARE HISTORY AND SOCIAL HISTORY

Emphasizing the need for social welfare historians to put greater stress on the important socioeconomic and demographic variations that differentiate the poor from other members of society, I believe, makes the links between social welfare history and social history in general self-evident. Indeed, the editors hoped to make a case for viewing social welfare history as a legitimate subset of the social historian's province.[7] We organized our chapters so as to underscore the extent to which social reformers and welfare institutions over time have provided categorical assistance on the basis of age. Within this framework, three other areas should be mentioned in which the concerns of the respective specialties dovetail.

First, social welfare historians should increasingly join the ranks of those who engage in community studies and who identify themselves as urban historians. The monographs by Daniel J. Walkowitz (on Troy and

Cohoes, New York) and John T. Cumbler (on Lynn and Fall River, Massachusetts) serve as suitable models for work of this genre.[8] These case studies are pertinent to social welfare historians because they effectively elucidate working-class attitudes and describe the nature of formal and informal kinship and social networks during early stages of American industrialization. Tensions between class consciousness and ethnic identity among various immigrants are well treated. Though neither monograph exploits the welfare dimensions of its subject matter, other social-urban historians have underscored the social bases of responding to poor people's needs. Michael Katz's study of Hamilton, Ontario, for instance, offers important age-specific data on transiency and inequality in that Canadian city between 1850 and 1880.[9] By explicitly conjoining hypotheses about modernization and public welfare measures at the local level, Katz points the way to an immensely profitable way of conducting research.

Family history constitutes a second subfield of social history that has undeniable pertinence for scholars interested in welfare history. More than anyone else, Tamara K. Hareven has promoted this field of inquiry through her prolific research and editorship of the *Journal of Family History*.[10] Clearly, social welfare historians must recognize that fundamental changes have taken place in the demographic bases of family networks. Declining mortality rates in the twentieth century have affected family bonds, and inevitably, welfare patterns: the proportion of orphans has decreased; the number of potential aged dependents—especially widows who live alone—has soared.[11] Social welfare historians also must take account of the extent to which changes in the father's role as primary breadwinner and as head of the household affect other family members' employment status and potential need to rely on welfare.[12] Finally, social welfare historians would be well advised to view the family as a social welfare provider that interacts with other institutions in both the public and private spheres. In his provocative study of the relationships among government, social service institutions, and the family, Jacques Donzelot claims, for instance, that in the late nineteenth century the state intervened to create "companionate families" to solve the problems of poor people coping with dislocation in the new urban-industrial order.[13]

Because women historically have been the primary caregivers within the family network, social welfare historians will quickly find that their interest in family history leads them into the burgeoning literature on women's history.[14] Among the many questions that require investigation by social welfare historians, two stand out. On the one hand, scholars should determine the extent to which demographic changes in women's marital and employment status have changed the status and roles of women in the welfare arena. (Citations listed here in Chapters Four and Six deal with demographic questions.) The ramifications of a rising proportion of gainfully employed middle-class and working-class women, however, have not been well treated so far; social welfare historians must therefore explore the relationship in women's individual and collective biographies between attending to the needs of others and working to attain their personal goals.[15] On the other hand, scholars should begin to explore systematically the issue of gender in the "culture of professionalism." Monographs on the role of women in social work and education abound, of course, but few of these explicitly take up the question of how the entry of predominantly middle-class women has affected the professionalization process itself.[16]

SOCIAL WELFARE HISTORY AND CULTURAL HISTORY

Recommending that social welfare historians pay careful attention to the gender-specific features of the culture of professionalism moves the locus of this research agenda into that ill-defined frontier occupied by both social and cultural historians. Intellectual historians lately have stressed the need to delineate and explicate "the distinctness of communities of discourse."[17] This research tack can be utilized fruitfully in studying the mindset and sociopolitical environment in which welfare reformers (such as the architects of the Great Society) operated. Intellectual histories of the "big ideas" that have guided the ways that Americans have defined and provided social services—including the use of "planning" in shaping the welfare state—need to be written.[18] Furthermore, many intellectual biographies, especially of twentieth-century figures, remain to be written. The arguments of John Rawls, Robert Nozick, and Ronald Dworkin, and the debate about their views, for example, offer almost classic philosophical and jurisprudential cases for the importance of individual rights and concern for equality as they may have affected contemporary reformers' approaches to the problems of racial discrimination and poverty.[19]

Communities of discourse and philosophical statements, of course, are not conveyed exclusively through the printed word. Cultural historians in recent decades have demonstrated that material artifacts reveal much about social patterns and intellectual currents. Social welfare historians, accordingly, might seek to reconstruct the poor person's world by examining the physical record. Case studies of slums and skid rows, for instance, have amplified the connections among geographic space, economic activities, neighborhood vitality, and demographic change.[20] Many clues will be uncovered by viewing domestic architecture and examining the impact of public housing policies on poor people.[21] Social welfare historians also should follow in the tradition of Jacob Riis's *How the Other Half Lives* and Dorothea Lange's work for the Farm Security Agency during the 1930s, and use photographs to recover a vision of poor people in the past.[22]

By examining such cultural artifacts, social welfare historians will be in a better position to trace continuities and changes not only in the habitat but in "the mind of the poor" as well. America's needy were not merely passive objects, victims of circumstances and the actions of others. They exerted countermeasures of resistance and created instruments to maintain their dignity, values, beliefs, and, on occasion, even lifestyle. The case studies of Raymond Mohl and Michael Katz, for example, demonstrate that transients *used* the system—almshouses and police stations, etc.—to find shelter in cold weather.[23] In so doing the poor often took advantage of existing welfare institutions for their own benefit. Furthermore, the social and cultural functions of working-class institutions—such as saloons and public baths—offer insights into how the dominant welfare initiatives and social control objectives were both facilitated and frustrated in the neighborhood.[24] By studying the ways poor people adapted to harsh circumstances, we can begin to assess the instrumentalities by which they learned to cope with adversity and to achieve and retain a measure of control over their daily lives. Investigating the "group consciousness" of the poor, in short, must rank high on any social welfare research agenda.[25]

SOCIAL WELFARE HISTORY AND ECONOMIC HISTORY

In the preceding sections, ways to analyze the dimensions of poverty from "the bottom up" have been indicated. It was recommended that social welfare historians follow the lead of social historians and reconstruct the demographic basis of poor people's individual and family life cycles; they should use material artifacts and try to reconstruct the worldview of various subsets of the poor, as cultural historians have done, to comprehend the contours of everyday life. Students of social welfare history obviously should also attempt to determine long-term continuities and changes in needy Americans' economic status. Delving into the literature produced by labor historians is a promising way to begin. The monographs and articles written by E. P. Thompson, Herbert

Gutman, and David Montgomery clearly are pertinent here. Among other things, scholars should ascertain how various ethnic, racial, and structural factors have frustrated (or at least limited) the development of "class consciousness" among the poor and near-poor who struggle to make ends meet at the margins of the labor market.[26]

Social welfare historians also need to determine how cycles of boom and bust in the economy affected poor people over time. The ways in which periods of prosperity and depression have affected the welfare system and treatment of the poor must be better established. The data for such trend analyses are readily available in federal and state census data, published and unpublished reports issued by governmental bureaus of labor statistics and recent compendia such as *Social Indicators III*, published by the U.S. Department of Commerce (Washington, D.C.: Government Printing Office, December 1980). Case studies that amplify the socioeconomic ramifications of unemployment will enable scholars to test hypotheses proposed by John Garraty and Alexander Keyssar (see Chapter Four). Researchers also should extend the analysis (begun in James Patterson's work) concerning the economic assumptions used to establish official measures of a "poverty line." Historians have to construct an historically reliable, empirical baseline for comparing the means of economic support for workers and those who are not engaged in the marketplace.[27] And while much has been learned recently about the marginal status of black agricultural wage earners during Reconstruction, scholars have just begun to investigate the enduring plight of white tenants in the deep South and Southwest.[28]

Once social welfare historians have gathered and analyzed the data necessary to trace poor people's employment and income status throughout the American experience, they will be in a better position to assess the historical materials that support contemporary social and economic thinkers' interpretations of the relationship between long-term macroeconomic developments, prevailing welfare priorities, and responses to the needs of the poor. The writings of Karl Polanyi, Charles E. Lindblom, Daniel Bell, and John Kenneth Galbraith (to mention just the towering figures) offer classic theoretical perspectives on the consequences of alterations in price mechanisms, labor systems, and technostructures in determining the economic (mis)uses of existing welfare systems.[29] As critics already have noted, however, these seminal works rest on a shaky historical foundation. By offering a richer sense of the complexity of past socioeconomic systems and by illuminating contradictions inherent in earlier modes of providing relief to the poor, historians will be able to underscore the extent to which the current welfare mess represents only the latest accretion of past decisions and previous circumstances.

SOCIAL WELFARE HISTORY AND POLITICAL HISTORY

Rather than seizing upon the economic dimensions of welfare exclusively in light of budgetary costs or in terms of some other financial considerations, social welfare historians ought to view the welfare system as a fundamental feature of the political economy. Hence, they should determine how political forces led to the creation of social services and income-maintenance programs for less fortunate members of society. American historians, elaborating the views of Daniel Boorstin's *The Genius of American Politics* (Chicago: University of Chicago Press, 1953) and Richard Hofstadter's *The Age of Reform* (New York: Vintage Books, 1955), used to contend that government's increasing concern for the rights and needs of people at lower levels of the socioeconomic scale was the outcome of extending the franchise and increasing the political participation of those who were previously viewed as "outsiders." Refined formulations of this theme remain popular. To some, the civil rights movement and "war on poverty" initiatives were the logical extension of efforts to promote equality, which had been percolating up from the grassroots level as the balance of power shifted downward.[30] Another variation on this idea seeks to explain the rise of "interest group liberalism" as an ongoing struggle by increasingly more sophisticated coalitions to gain more entitlements and perquisites from governmental bodies. Thus underscoring the "pluralist" nature of present-day democracies, theorists explain the rise of the welfare state as the result of compromises designed to reconcile conflicting interest-group demands.[31]

Once established, welfare bureaucracies quickly develop a calculus and momentum of their own. Frances F. Piven and Richard A. Cloward, among others, have investigated the political imperatives that tend to perpetuate pressures for *maintaining* the welfare state in its current form. The vested interests of welfare clients and their representatives make changes in the status quo very difficult to institute.[32] Political sociologists have documented, moreover, that because there is such a surprisingly narrow range of options available to policymakers, principled choice typically gives way to political expediency. To expand the welfare system too far is to risk still greater inflation and unemployment; to attempt to "cap" entitlements in the face of adverse economic conditions is to risk defeat at the polls.[33] Thus it becomes imperative to understand not only how welfare bureaucracies originate but why they tend to evolve as they do.

One way for social welfare historians to contribute to this burgeoning literature is to take cues from the "ethnocultural" branch of the new political history. Voting patterns at the local, state, and regional levels should be investigated in order to determine whether (and how) changes in political party identification among various racial, ethnic, and special-interest groups signaled shifts in political behavior. Changes in women's voting behavior surely deserve careful analysis, as does the *embourgeoisement* of the working class.[34] Voting trends, of course, can be profitably examined at the upper strata of the political order, and not just analyzed from the bottom up. Jerome Clubb and his colleagues, for instance, recently presented a compelling case for believing that the leaders of political parties are primarily responsible for policy initiatives in the areas of social welfare and national defense.[35] Collective biographies of legislators and congressional roll call votes thus should be scrutinized with this interpretation as a guide; such data may provide crucial evidence concerning the direction of the national welfare agenda.

Historians already have devoted considerable attention to the origins and impact of various pieces of social welfare legislation. And if the citations in this bibliography are any indication, even more systematic emphasis will be given to the development of social policies during the last half-century. "Applied historians," among others, have set forth analogies and engaged in trend analysis and contextual analysis in their efforts to put the process of policymaking into historical perspective.[36] It is important to note, moreover, that pertinent models need not be taken solely from the field of social welfare. Monographs that deal with the policy issues involved in creating public works and tax codes and in dealing with the problems of prostitution and violence also offer untapped dividends for scholars.[37]

Ultimately, social welfare historians will want to put the American experience into comparative perspective. As mentioned in "A Note on the Principles Adopted in Compiling and Organizing the Bibliography," the literature on this subfield was not included in this bibliography unless specific mention was made of conditions in the United States. Needless to say, the number of books and articles on social welfare in Europe and other parts of the world is vast. Unfortunately, much of this material is uneven in quality; few American scholars, moreover, have engaged in cross-cultural research. Models, however, currently exist that do attempt to trace complex developments along international and historical lines.[38] Significantly, such models place as much emphasis on the ideological values embedded in social policies as they do on analyzing the political equation and economic calculus that gave rise to specific programs.

CODA

In sum, there is need for a great deal more research if scholars are to advance the field of social welfare history. The editors suspect that the historiographic landscape will look very different from the way it does now when, at a later date, this work is revised and expanded. It will be interesting to note the research paths that the next generation of scholars are pursuing. Some controversies—such as the debate between those who view social welfare institutions as humanitarian organizations and those who consider them instruments of social control—probably will not have been resolved, though, hopefully, the level of disagreement will have been elevated. A few prevailing verities may be invalidated and other well-known "facts" refined, in light of new evidence.

The editors hope that those who use this bibliography will find the citations and suggestions for future research useful in formulating more sophisticated conceptual frameworks. Social welfare history has come of age. The future of the field depends on how well its practitioners can continue to demonstrate the importance of their research and provoke interest among their colleagues and the general public. More than ever before, social welfare historians should derive insights from, and build conceptual bridges to, the issues that preoccupy social, cultural, economic, political, and comparative historians. For in order to see the "big picture," we will need to synthesize clues from all available research frameworks and techniques.

NOTES

1. And had we included all of the pertinent materials—(auto)biographies, classic case studies, statutes, documentaries, government reports, and national conference proceedings—this volume would surely have been much longer. It should also be noted again that we have not referred here to the various manuscript collections that are housed in the National Archives, universities, presidential libraries, or at the University of Minnesota's Social Welfare History Archives.

2. Because of the manner in which we defined "social welfare" for the purposes of this bibliography, many of the works that I cite here have not been included in earlier chapters. Some of the articles and books simply have nothing

to do with social welfare problems; others deal with the subject matter in a cursory or implicit fashion. Nevertheless, insofar as one of the purposes of this chapter is to make a case for conceptualizing and doing social welfare history in bolder—or at least different—ways than scholars are currently accustomed to, such works deserve mention: they provide important guideposts for the road ahead.

3. Albert O. Hirschman, *Shifting Involvements: Private Interest and Public Action* (Princeton: Princeton University Press, 1982). Hirschman's "cyclical" approach to studying American history, in my opinion, is more elegant than those previously adopted by political and economic historians. The schema should be tested for its pertinence for reconstructing the social welfare arena; Kirsten A. Grønbjerg's *Mass Society and the Extension of Welfare, 1960-1970* (Chicago: University of Chicago Press, 1976) might serve as a starting point.

4. Peter Kolchin, "Comparing American History," *Reviews in American History*, vol. 10, no. 4 (December 1982), pp. 65-81. See also, George M. Fredrickson, "Comparative History," in *The Past Before Us*, ed. Michael Kammen (Ithaca: Cornell University Press, 1980), pp. 457-73, and Raymond Grew, "The Case for Comparing Histories," *American Historical Review*, vol. 85, no. 4 (October 1980), pp. 763-78.

5. See, for instance, James O'Connor, *The Fiscal Crisis of the State* (New York: St. Martin's Press, 1973); Ronald Radosh and N. Rothbard, eds., *A New History of Leviathan* (New York: E. P. Dutton, 1972); and James Weinstein, *The Corporate Ideal in the Liberal State, 1900-1918* (Boston: Beacon Press, 1968). Marxists, of course, are not the only ones to interpret social welfare history in this manner. See the work of social-control theorists, such as *Regulating the Poor* by Frances F. Piven and Richard A. Cloward.

6. For an attempt to interpret recent American history along these lines, which is flawed precisely because it does not confront the changing interrelationships among class, race, and ethnicity, see Richard Polenberg, *One Nation Divisible* (New York: Penguin Books, 1980).

7. The label "social history" refers here not just to historical studies of social structure and societal processes, but also includes urban, family, and women's history. The overriding interests of these particular fields have diverged in the past decade as new journals and specialized networks have been created to facilitate communication among scholars. And yet, to the degree that urban, family, and women's historians are concerned with social welfare problems, they are sufficiently similar in their intellectual and methodological approaches to be discussed under the rubric of social history. Indeed, this might be an appropriate place to recommend that social welfare historians read journals such as *Social Science History* and *Historical Methods Newsletter* in order to keep abreast of preferred techniques in statistical analysis or the latest developments in computer technology.

8. Daniel J. Walkowitz, *Worker City, Company Town: Iron and Cotton-Worker Protest in Troy and Cohoes, New York, 1855-1884* (Urbana: University of Illinois Press, 1978); John T. Cumbler, *Working Class Community in Industrial America:*

Work, Leisure, and Struggle in Two Industrial Cities, 1880-1930 (Westport: Greenwood Press, 1979).

9. Michael B. Katz, *The People of Hamilton, Canada West: Family and Class in a Mid-Nineteenth-Century City* (Cambridge, Mass.: Harvard University Press, 1975). For related Canadian social welfare studies, see also, Terry Copp, *The Anatomy of Poverty: The Condition of the Working Class in Montreal, 1897-1929* (Toronto: McClelland & Stewart, 1974), and Rainer Baehre, "Pauper Emigration to Upper Canada in the 1830s," *Histoire Sociale—Social History*, vol. 14, no. 28 (November 1981), pp. 339-67.

10. Among other things, users of this bibliography should read Hareven's "The Family as Process: The Historical Study of the Family Cycle," *Journal of Social History*, vol. 7, no. 3 (Spring 1974), pp. 322-29, and her application of the family-cycle approach in *Family Time & Industrial Time* (New York: Cambridge University Press, 1982). See also, Glen H. Elder, Jr., *Children of the Great Depression* (Chicago: University of Chicago Press, 1974).

11. Two articles that concisely summarize major trends are Paul C. Glick, "Updating the Life Cycle of the Family," *The Journal of Marriage and the Family*, vol. 39, no. 1 (February 1977), pp. 5-13, and Peter Uhlenberg, "Death and the Family," *Journal of Family History*, vol. 5, no. 3 (Fall 1980), pp. 313-20.

12. See, for example, Mary P. Ryan, *Cradle of the Middle Class: The Family in Oneida County, New York 1790-1865* (New York: Cambridge University Press, 1981), and Steven John Dubnoff, "The Family and Absence from Work: Irish Workers in a Lowell, Massachusetts Cotton Mill, 1860," Unpub. Ph.D. diss., Brandeis University, 1976.

13. Jacques Donzelot, *The Policing of Families* (New York: Random House, 1979). In both his tone and themes, Donzelot parallels the interpretation set forth by Christopher Lasch in *Haven in a Heartless World* (New York: Basic Books, 1977). For alternative formulations, see Mary Jo Bane, *Here to Stay: American Families in the Twentieth Century* (New York: Basic Books, 1976), and Barbara Laslett, "The Family as a Public and Private Institution: An Historical Perspective," *The Journal of Marriage and the Family*, vol. 35, no. 3 (August 1973), pp. 480-92.

14. Perhaps the best introduction to women's history that argues that the "modern" family has been shaped in large measure by women's search for greater autonomy is Carl Degler's *At Odds: Women and the Family in America from the Revolution to the Present* (New York: Oxford University Press, 1980). Not surprisingly, many scholars challenge Degler's assumption that women's history is, or should be viewed, as a branch of family history. A different approach, and one which parallels the organization of this book, is to trace women's (self-)images and experiences in a life-cycle perspective. See, for instance, Howard P. Chudacoff, "The Life Course of Women: Age and Age Consciousness," *Journal of Family History*, vol. 5, no. 3 (Fall 1980), pp. 274-92; and William Chafe, *The American Woman: Her Changing Social, Economic, and Political Roles, 1920-1970* (New York: Oxford University Press, 1972).

15. For an introduction to this literature, see Nancy Seifer, *Absent from the*

Majority: Working Class Women in America (New York: National Project on Ethnic America, 1973); Leslie Woodcock Tentler, *Wage-Earning Women: Industrial Work and Family Life in the United States, 1900-1930* (New York: Oxford University Press, 1979); Lois Scharf, *To Work and To Wed* (Westport: Greenwood Press, 1980); Winifred D. Wandersee, *Women's Work and Family Values: 1920-1940* (Cambridge, Mass.: Harvard University Press, 1981); and Glen H. Elder, Jr., and Jeffrey K. Liker, "Hard Times in Women's Lives," *American Journal of Sociology,* vol. 88, no. 2 (June 1982), pp. 241-69.

16. This issue is developed quite well by Joan Jacobs Brumberg and Nancy Tomes in "Women in the Professions: A Research Agenda for American Historians," *Reviews in American History,* vol. 10, no. 2 (June 1982), pp. 275-96. The carefully prepared collection of biographies of 1,359 women in *Notable American Women, 1607-1950: A Biographical Dictionary,* 3 vols., ed. Edward T. James, Janet Wilson James, and Paul S. Boyer (Cambridge, Mass.: Harvard University Press, 1971) provides social welfare historians with an indispensable data base for future research.

17. David A. Hollinger, "Historians and the Discourse of Intellectuals," in *New Directions in American Intellectual History,* ed. John Higham and Paul K. Conkin (Baltimore: The Johns Hopkins University Press, 1979), p. 57. For an attempt by a social welfare historian to move in this direction, see James Lamb Gearity, "The First Brain Trust: Academic Reform and the Wisconsin Idea," Unpub. Ph.D. diss., University of Minnesota, 1979.

18. Intellectual spadework in this area has been done. See Otis L. Graham, Jr., *Toward a Planned Society: From Roosevelt to Nixon* (New York: Oxford University Press, 1976), and John F. McClymer, *Social Engineering in America, 1890-1925* (Westport: Greenwood Press, 1980). For an analysis of "planning" in Britain, see David A. Reisman, *Richard Titmuss: Welfare and Society* (London: William Heinemann, 1977).

19. John Rawls, *A Theory of Justice* (Cambridge, Mass.: Harvard University Press, 1971); Robert Nozick, *Anarchy, State and Utopia* (New York: Basic Books, 1974); Ronald Dworkin, *Taking Rights Seriously* (Cambridge, Mass.: Harvard University Press, 1977).

20. See Alvin Auerbach, "San Francisco's South of Market District, 1858-1958: The Emergence of a Skid Row," *California Historical Quarterly,* vol. 52, no. 3 (Fall 1973), pp. 196-223; Stephanie Greenberg, "Neighborhood Changes, Racial Transition, and Work Location: A Case Study in an Industrial City, Philadelphia, 1880-1930," *Journal of Urban History,* vol. 7, no. 2 (May 1981), pp. 267-314.

21. See, for instance, John F. Bauman, "Safe and Sanitary Without the Costly Frills," *The Pennsylvania Magazine of History and Biography,* vol. 101, no. 1 (January 1977), pp. 114-28; Anthony Downs, "The Impact of Housing Policies on Family Life in the United States since World War II," *Daedalus,* vol. 106, no. 2 (Spring 1977), pp. 163-80; and Eugenie Ladner Birch and Deborah S. Gardner, "The Seven-Percent Solution: A Review of Philanthropic Housing, 1870-1910," *Journal of Urban History,* vol. 7, no. 4 (August 1981), pp. 403-38.

22. Michael Lesy's *Bearing Witness: A Photographic Chronicle of American Life,*

1860-1945 (New York: Pantheon Books, 1983) is not only the latest in a series of works in this genre; it offers a helpful guide to archival materials.

23. Raymond A. Mohl, *Poverty in New York* (New York: Oxford University Press, 1971); Michael Katz, *The People of Hamilton, Canada West* (Cambridge, Mass.: Harvard University Press, 1975).

24. Jon M. Kingsdale, "The 'Poor Man's Club': Social Functions of the Urban Working-Class Saloon," *American Quarterly*, vol. 25, no. 4 (October 1973), pp. 472-89; Marilyn Thornton Williams, "Philanthropy in the Progressive Era: The Public Baths of Baltimore," *Maryland Historical Magazine*, vol. 72, no. 1 (Spring 1977), pp. 118-31.

25. Researchers interested in this topic might profit from reading Lawrence W. Levine's *Black Culture and Black Consciousness* (New York: Oxford University Press, 1977); Oscar Lewis, *La Vida* (New York: Vintage, 1966); and Gerald D. Suttles, *The Social Order of the Slum* (Chicago: The University of Chicago Press, 1968).

26. A possible model for research along these lines is Gilbert Wesley Moore's unpublished dissertation, "Poverty, Class Consciousness, and Racial Conflict: The Social Basis of Trade Union Politics in the UAW-CIO, 1937-1955," (Princeton University, 1978). Moore claims that tactical errors by Marxist organizers, the resistance of auto workers to Marxism, and the persistence of the racial and ethnic conflict over jobs, wages, and housing precluded the emergence of a class-conscious workers' movement within the UAW and CIO.

27. Fred Stricker's "The Wages of Inflation: Workers' Earnings in the World War One Era," *Mid-America*, vol. 63, no. 2 (April-July 1981), pp. 93-105, for instance, offers a lucid discussion of changes in real annual earnings for white-collar workers, public employees, and manufacturing workers. Stricker found that the least skilled and lowest paid among blue-collar workers received significant increases during wartime inflation, though their relative gains were temporary. Geoffrey Perrett makes a similar observation about the change in poor people's economic status during the World War II experience in *Days of Sadness, Years of Triumph* (New York: Penguin Books, 1973).

28. Social welfare historians might find useful Gregory A. Stiverson's *Poverty in a Land of Plenty: Tenancy in Eighteenth-Century Maryland* (Baltimore: Johns Hopkins University Press, 1977). Unfortunately, although Stiverson demonstrates the pervasiveness of tenancy and marginality of life in colonial Maryland, he is less helpful in elucidating how people at the time dealt with such poverty.

29. See, for instance, Karl Polanyi, *The Great Transformation* (Boston: Beacon Press, 1957); Charles E. Lindblom, *Politics and Markets* (New York: Basic Books, 1977); Daniel Bell, *The Coming of Post-Industrial Society* (New York: Basic Books, 1973); and John Kenneth Galbraith, *The New Industrial State*, rev. ed. (Boston: Houghton-Mifflin, 1980).

30. This interpretation received its fullest expression in G. Lenski, *Power and Privilege* (New York: McGraw-Hill, 1966), and Charles Hewitt, "The Effect of Political Democracy and Social Democracy in Industrial Societies," *American Sociological Review*, vol. 42, no. 2 (June 1977), pp. 450-64. Seymour Martin Lipset

anticipated this thesis in his *Political Man* (Garden City, N.Y.: Doubleday, 1960).

31. For classic statements of this position, see David B. Truman, *The Governmental Process* (New York: A. A. Knopf, 1951), and Theodore Lowi, *The End of Liberalism* (New York: W. W. Norton, 1968).

32. Frances Fox Piven and Richard A. Cloward, *The New Class War* (New York: Pantheon, 1981).

33. See, for instance, Aaron Wildavsky, *Speaking Truth to Power* (Boston: Little, Brown, 1979), and Claus Offe, "Advanced Capitalism and the Welfare State," *Politics and Society*, vol. 2, no. 4 (Summer 1972), pp. 479-88.

34. See Everett Carll Ladd, Jr., "Liberalism Upside Down," *Political Science Quarterly*, vol. 91, no. 4 (Winter 1976-1977), pp. 577-600, and Norman H. Nie, Sidney Verba, and John R. Petrocik, *The Changing American Voter* (Cambridge, Mass.: Harvard University Press, 1976). A model for a more traditional approach to political history is Richard L. McCormick's *From Realignment to Reform: Political Change in New York State, 1893-1910* (Ithaca: Cornell University Press, 1981).

35. Jerome M. Clubb, William H. Flanigan, and Nancy H. Zingale, *Partisan Realignment: Voters, Parties and Government in American History* (Beverly Hills: Sage, 1980).

36. For representative samples of this approach, see Peter N. Stearns, ed., "Special Issue on Applied History," *Journal of Social History*, vol. 14, no. 4 (Summer 1981), pp. 533-786; David J. Rothman and Stanton Wheeler, eds., *Social History and Social Policy* (New York: Academic Press, 1981), and Daniel A. Sipe, "A Moment of the State: The Enactment of the National Labor Relations Act, 1935," Unpub. Ph.D. diss., University of Pennsylvania, 1981.

37. See, for instance, Ellis L. Armstrong, Michael C. Robinson, and Suellen M. Hay, eds., *History of Public Works in the United States, 1776-1976* (Chicago: American Public Works Association, 1976); J. Mills Thornton III, "Fiscal Policy and the Failure of Radical Reconstruction in the Lower South," in *Region, Race and Reconstruction*, ed. J. Morgan Koussar and James M. McPherson (New York: Oxford University Press, 1982), pp. 349-94; James Lemuel Wunsch, "Prostitution and Public Policy: From Regulation to Suppression, 1858-1920," Unpub. Ph.D. diss., University of Chicago, 1976; and Hugh Davis Graham and Ted Robert Gurr, eds., *Violence in America*, rev. ed. (Beverly Hills: Sage, 1979).

38. Three volumes provide a suitable starting place. See Hugh Heclo, *Modern Social Politics in Britain and Sweden: From Relief to Income Maintenance* (New Haven: Yale University Press, 1974); Arnold J. Heidenheimer, ed., *Comparative Public Policy: Policies of Social Choice in Europe and America* (New York: St. Martin's Press, 1975), and Norman Furniss and Timothy Tilton, *The Case for the Welfare State: From Social Security to Social Equality* (Bloomington: Indiana University Press, 1979).

AUTHOR INDEX

SUBJECT INDEX

About the Editors

WALTER I. TRATTNER is Professor of History at the University of Wisconsin—Milwaukee. He has written extensively on social welfare history, including *Social Welfare or Social Control?, Homer Folks: Pioneer in Social Welfare, Crusade for the Children*, and *From Poor Law to Welfare State*. He has published articles on the subject in *Social Service Review, Child Welfare, Welfare in Review, Journal of American History, Journal of the History of Ideas*, and others.

W. ANDREW ACHENBAUM is Associate Professor of History at Carnegie-Mellon University, Pittsburgh. His previous publications include *Old Age in the New Land* and *Shades of Gray*, and "The Making of an Applied Historian" in *Public Historian* (Spring 1983).

DATE DUE

DEC 1 6 2016			
FEB 0 4 2017			